NATURE AND GRACE

THE LIBRARY OF CHRISTIAN CLASSICS

ICHTHUS EDITION

NATURE AND GRACE

SELECTIONS FROM THE SUMMA THEOLOGICA OF THOMAS AQUINAS

Translated and Edited by

A. M. FAIRWEATHER, M.A., S.T.M.

Lecturer in Philosophy
University of Edinburgh

Philadelphia

THE WESTMINSTER PRESS

Published simultaneously in Great Britain and the United States of America
by the S.C.M. Press, Ltd., London, and The Westminster Press, Philadelphia.

First published MCMLIV

Library of Congress Catalog Card No. 54-10259

9   8   7   6

Printed in the United States of America

GENERAL EDITORS' PREFACE

The Christian Church possesses in its literature an abundant and incomparable treasure. But it is an inheritance that must be reclaimed by each generation. THE LIBRARY OF CHRISTIAN CLASSICS is designed to present in the English language, and in twenty-six volumes of convenient size, a selection of the most indispensable Christian treatises written prior to the end of the sixteenth century.

The practice of giving circulation to writings selected for superior worth or special interest was adopted at the beginning of Christian history. The canonical Scriptures were themselves a selection from a much wider literature. In the Patristic era there began to appear a class of works of compilation (often designed for ready reference in controversy) of the opinions of well-reputed predecessors, and in the Middle Ages many such works were produced. These medieval anthologies actually preserve some noteworthy materials from works otherwise lost.

In modern times, with the increasing inability even of those trained in universities and theological colleges to read Latin and Greek texts with ease and familiarity, the translation of selected portions of earlier Christian literature into modern languages has become more necessary than ever; while the wide range of distinguished books written in vernaculars such as English makes selection there also needful. The efforts that have been made to meet this need are too numerous to be noted here, but none of these collections serves the purpose of the reader who desires a library of representative treatises spanning the Christian centuries as a whole. Most of them embrace only the age of the Church Fathers, and some of them have long been out of print. A fresh translation of a work already translated may shed much new light upon its meaning. This is true even of Bible translations despite the work of many experts through the centuries. In some instances old translations have been adopted in this series, but wherever necessary or desirable, new ones have been made. Notes have been supplied where these were needed to explain the author's meaning. The introductions provided for the several treatises and extracts will, we believe, furnish welcome guidance.

JOHN BAILLIE
JOHN T. MCNEILL
HENRY P. VAN DUSEN

CONTENTS

11

CONTENTS

OF SIN. PRIMA SECUNDAE, QUESTIONS 82, 85

TREATISE ON GRACE. PRIMA SECUNDAE, QUESTIONS 109–114

CONTENTS

14

CONTENTS

15

CONTENTS

TREATISE ON THE THEOLOGICAL VIRTUES

I. ON FAITH. SECUNDA SECUNDAE, QUESTIONS 1–7

CONTENTS

CONTENTS

CONTENTS

General Introduction

IN THIS VOLUME WE HAVE SOUGHT TO PRESENT THE view taken by Thomas Aquinas of the moral and spiritual world in which we live, and of the conditions of man's self-realization which are consequent upon it. The final end of man lies in God, through whom alone he is and lives, and by whose help alone he can attain his end. The teaching of Aquinas concerning the moral and spiritual order stands in sharp contrast to all views, ancient or modern, which cannot do justice to the difference between the divine and the creaturely without appearing to regard them as essentially antagonistic as well as discontinuous. For Aquinas, no such opposition obtains between God and the world which he has made. Any evil which disrupts the continuity of the context of human endeavour after self-realization in God is due to corruption, not to nature, and such corruption is never absolute.

The attitude of Thomas is best understood in its historical contrast to that of Augustine. Although Aquinas sought at every turn to harmonize his teaching as far as possible with Augustine's, to whose authority he refers more often than to any other, the difference between them was fundamental. His predecessor never seems to have freed himself entirely from the Manichaean conviction of cosmic evil. His mystical doctrine of the fall extended the effects of a cosmic evil will to nature itself, so that all nature is corrupt, not only human nature. Reason in man remains, but is helpless since it cannot operate apart from the will, which has lost its freedom through sin. There is consequently a sharp division between the realm of nature and the realm of grace, such as renders it impossible to explain how man can be regenerated through grace without apparently destroying the continuity of his own endeavour, and equally impossible to maintain that he can attain any knowledge of God or of divine things through knowledge of the created world. Since nature is corrupt, experience of created things, even if we could know them, could present nothing better than distorted images of what things ought to be. Anything learnt through sense would therefore be useless as a clue to the nature of the divine. The "inward way" is consequently the only way to true knowledge. The soul must develop within itself, and it can do so only through grace. True knowledge must be implanted in the mind by God, either gradually or all at once. Reliance on the ontological argument to divine existence automatically follows.

The teaching of Aquinas contrasts with that of Augustine on every point which we have mentioned, representing a kindlier view both of man and of nature. The will is free, and the natural desire for the good persists despite sin. Aquinas is more definite than Augustine that reason itself is impaired by sin. But he holds that it can be used, and that we must follow our reason as far as it will take us. Grace and revelation are aids which do not negate reason. Here as everywhere nature itself demands supernature for its completion, and the provision of divine grace meets the striving of human nature in its search for the ultimate good, this quest being itself due to the gracious moving of God. In so far as they are, created things are good, and in so far as they are and are good, they reflect the being of God who is their first cause. The natural knowledge of God is therefore possible through the knowledge of creatures. Not only so, but there is no human knowledge of God which does not depend on the knowledge of creatures. All knowledge begins from sense, even of things which transcend sense. For this reason alone Aquinas would have been bound to reject the ontological argument of Augustine, which depends on knowledge of ideal entities entirely unrelated to sense experience. The "five ways" of Pt. I, Q. 2, all involve the cosmological argument from the existence of created things as known through sense.

The task which Aquinas set himself to achieve was similar to that of Augustine. Augustine had sought to reconcile the principles of Christianity with the philosophy of Plato, without the pantheistic implications which had developed in the emanation theory of Plotinus. Aquinas sought to reconcile the philosophy of Aristotle with the principles of Christianity, avoiding the pantheism which it seemed to imply (cf. Pt. I,

Q. 3, Art. 8). Many of Aristotle's works had been introduced to the West during the eleventh and twelfth centuries from Arabian sources, particularly through Avicenna and Averroes, whose extensive commentaries interpreted the thought of Aristotle in a strongly pantheistic vein. Averroes had also maintained that the common basis of a universal natural religion, underlying the differences of any particular religion, was the highest of all, the "scientific" religion, of which Aristotle was the founder. The several "positive" religions he regarded as necessary for the masses, poorer versions of the same truth, whose trappings were better removed. Revelation, like anything else peculiar to any one religion, was merely a poorer way of stating what Aristotle had stated in a much better way as the content of the moral law. The whole presentation apparently led to such extravagances that for a time the writings of Aristotle were proscribed. But such a thinker was too valuable to be cast aside, and it was mainly due to the efforts of the Dominicans, Albertus Magnus and his pupil Aquinas, that Aristotle's philosophy came to be accepted by the Church as representing the highest to which unaided human reason could attain. Plato seems to be more in keeping with the Christian belief, since he regards the material universe as created, and the spiritual as above the natural. But the mystical elements of his thought encroached on the province of revelation, and had indeed been the source of heresies. The very limitations of Aristotle, on the other hand, served to emphasize that the truths of revelation were unknown to the Greeks because they were not discoverable by natural reason, but above reason.

Aquinas makes extensive use of Aristotle's psychology, which he applies throughout in order to define problems relating to faith and the operation of grace. There was indeed no other psychology available with any pretentions to systematic completeness. He also makes use of the Aristoteleian metaphysics wherever relevant. The treatment of all problems proceeds according to the conceptual distinctions by means of which Aristotle did his thinking. This unfortunately gives the impression that Aquinas was a rational conceptualist. Aquinas was no more of a conceptualist than Aristotle, who was certainly nothing of the kind. If Aristotle had been a conceptualist, he could never have written the *Prior Analytics*, which reveal the attitude of the biological scientist who insisted that all generic conceptions must be justified through induction from experienced particulars. Although the syllogistic method, which

Aquinas employs to the utmost, may put the original appeal to experience in the background, it should be realized that Aquinas uses conceptual thinking as a means to the knowledge of things, and declares that we formulate propositions only in order to know things by means of them, in faith no less than in science (22ae, Q. 1, Art. 2), and also that truth consists in conformity of the intellect with the thing known (cf. Pt. I, Q. 21, Art. 2). The charge of "a priorism" is justifiable only in so far as it can be brought against any view which maintains that knowledge transcends what is immediately experienced—not on the ground of conceptualism. According to Aquinas, divine reality is itself simple. But things known are in the knower according to his manner of knowing, and we cannot understand truth otherwise than by thinking, which proceeds by means of the combination and separation of ideas (22ae, Q. I, Art. 2, *ad* 5; cf. Q. 27, Art. 4), this being the way proper to the human intellect, which is confused by the things which are most manifest to nature, just as the eye of the bat is dazzled by the light of the sun (Pt. I, Q. 1, Art. 5). If the terminology is found puzzling, it should be borne in mind that it is intended as the way out of complexity, not as the way into it. Further, although Aquinas frequently appears to "prove by definition," what he really does is to answer a question by defining its elements as they must be defined according to the final view which he means to expound, clarifying the issue so that the question answers itself. It may be observed, also, that although objections dealt with sometimes contain plain logical fallacies, Aquinas never treats them as such, but invariably looks for a deeper reason behind them.

In Pt. I, Qq. 1–4 Aquinas defines sacred doctrine as the wisdom of all wisdoms. Its principal object is God, the first cause of all that is, in relation to whom alone are man and his place in the universe properly understood. Qq. 20–23 deal with God in relation to man, as determining the moral and spiritual world in which man must seek to attain the end which God ordains by means which God provides. In Prima Secundae, Qq. 82, 85 present Aquinas' view of original sin and its effects, and Qq. 109–114 his treatise on divine grace. In Secunda Secundae, Qq. 1–7; 17–21; 23, 27 treat of the three theological virtues, Faith, Hope, and Charity, by means of which man may attain to blessedness, the final end to which all his activities must be subordinate. We may now proceed to comment on each of these five sections in turn.

Questions 1–4

Sacred doctrine does not argue to prove its first principles, which are the articles of faith, since they cannot be proved to one who denies the revelation on which they are founded. Aquinas nevertheless maintains that human reason can demonstrate the existence, unity, and perfection of God. The "five ways" of arguing to divine existence could not be omitted from any representation of his thought, and call for some comment. The first article of Q. 2 rejects Anselm's version of the ontological argument, particularly on the ground of its question-begging form. Most commentators, however, are agreed that the criticism offered is not valid against Anselm. Anselm did not contend, as did Descartes, that the proposition "God exists" is self-evident from the nature of the concepts as anyone is bound to understand them. Nor did he argue in a purely *a priori* fashion from an idea existing in the mind to a corresponding existence in nature. To argue in this way would have been contrary to the whole spirit of the *Monologion*, with which the *Proslogion* was intended to harmonize. It would have been to give the primacy to reason, which in Anselm's view must never be given the primacy, since it depends on concepts built by imagination out of sense, which leads away from truth. Faith must precede reason, seeking to understand by means of reason what it already believes. There is indeed no "reason" why God should be, other than that he is (*De Veritate*, 10; cf. *Monologion* 18). The "necessity" involved is not imposed by thought upon itself, but imposed upon articulate utterance by inward experience of what is real, through the "eye of the soul." The line of Augustine's thought which he appears to follow most particularly is that of the *De Libero Arbitrio* II, ch. 6, 14: "If we could find something which we could not only not doubt to be, but which is prior to our reason, would we not call it God? That only should we call God, than which nothing is better." The distinction drawn in *Proslogion* IV between the two uses of the term "God," namely, *cum vox significans eam cogitatur*, and *cum res ipsa cogitatur*, seem to make it plain that the argument is fundamentally a short restatement of the claim of the *Monologion* in terms which fit the Realist-Nominalist controversy. If a nominalist uses the term, it is a mere *flatus vocis* (*De Fide Trinitatis* II, 1274), and proves nothing. But if a realist uses it, it indicates, as for Anselm, his own inward experience of divine reality which compels the utterance "God is." The self-evidence of the proposition is therefore derivative, since the reality is known. The very absence of any further explanation in Anselm's reply to Gaunilo's defence of the fool who said in his heart "there is no God," in which he merely repeats that the phrase he used has a definite meaning, and is not a meaningless sound, also supports the view that this is the argument of the realist against the nominalist. If he adopted realism only as a useful means of serving a greater end, his adoption of it shows that, for Anselm, everything depends on inward experimental awareness.[1]

Although Aquinas rejects the ontological argument, his argument from the existence of things to the reality of God as their first cause depends on its underlying import. For he maintain that although the first cause can be known to exist, its essence cannot be known; and as Aquinas himself quotes from Aristotle in 22ae, Q. 2, Art. 2, to know incomposites imperfectly is not to know them at all. The argument to a first cause cannot therefore be said to have proved anything, unless it is supplemented by the ontological argument, which depends on the mind's direct awareness. This is apparent from the manner in which each of the five ways concludes with the observation "and this we call God." But the five ways are not ultimately dependent on their outward form, any more than the argument of Anselm. If they were, they could readily be answered by anyone who has paid attention to Hume, since the mere fact that a thing exists does not imply that it requires a cause at all. No inference to a first cause is possible if a thing is initially apprehended merely as an existent. But things are not so apprehended according to Aquinas. The wording of Q. 2, Art. 3, suggests that his thought presupposes that of Aristotle's *Physics* III, ch. 3, 202a. There Aristotle maintains that the actuality of that which has the power of causing motion is identical with the actuality of that which can be moved. That is to say, when one thing is moved by another, this is a single, unified occurrence. The moving and the being moved are the same event, just as the interval between one and two is the same interval whichever way we read it, and just as a steep ascent and a steep

---

[1] This appears to be reconcilable with the insistence that Anselm regarded his argument as an argument or proof, not as the statement of an immediate intuition of God (cf. Prof. Copleston: *A History of Philosophy*, II, pp. 338 ff). It can be both without being merely the latter.

descent are the same thing, from whichever end we choose to describe it. Thus for Aquinas, anything which exists, or which is moved, is seen as continuous with its creation, or with its being moved, by God who is the first cause. This is the reason why he can affirm, as he does in *S. Contra Gentiles* II, ch. 1, that the divine act of creation is at once the act of God and a perfection of the thing made. Accordingly, when we contemplate any existing thing, the causal divine act of creation is actually present in the situation which we contemplate, and Aquinas would say that the fault is our own if we cannot perceive it. One may of course plead the inability to see. But one cannot refute the claim merely on the ground of its logical limitations, which are in fact parallel to those of Anselm's argument in so far as one may certainly contend that the conclusion has found its way into the premises. This, however, is invariably the case with any argument which makes any genuine advance, since in all progressive arguments the distinction between datum and conclusion is artificial. The evidence with which we start, to which we assign the logical status of a datum, is bound to transcend its original boundaries by the time we have finished, and to acquire a deeper significance as it is understood in the conclusion. When it is claimed that the evidence is properly what the conclusion shows it to be, we cannot refute the claim merely by pointing out that this is different from the original conception of it. That is all we do if we reply that a mere existence does not imply God as its cause, which is no answer to one who seeks to open our eyes to see that it does.

The reader may find the reasoning of Q. 3 rather intricate, and there are some who would say that it deals with a meaningless problem. To say so, however, would be to miss the point of it. Like all great thinkers, Aquinas was thoroughly aware of the extent to which the mechanism of thinking gets in the way of truth. Thought is like a prism which breaks up the light which it receives, creating false distinctions and relations which have no counterpart in the reality which it seeks to understand. The distinctions between form and matter, essence and underlying subject, essence and existence, substance and attribute, genus and difference, belong to thought only, not to the nature of God. There is consequently no possibility of proving divine existence by arguing from them. But although Aquinas applies this consideration to the appreciation of the divine, he does not apparently maintain, as do some later thinkers, that it falsifies our knowledge of created things, which he regards as genuinely composite in their own nature. Indeed, it is because our knowledge of God to a degree depends on the experience of composites that it is bound to remain inadequate. This question should be compared directly with 22ae, Q. 1, Art. 2.

As the first active principle and first efficient cause of all things, God is not only perfect in himself, but contains within himself the perfections of all things, in a more eminent way. It is this that makes possible the celebrated *analogia entis*, whereby the divine nature is known by analogy from existing things, and not only by analogy based on the memory, intellect, and will of man, as Augustine had maintained. It is a fundamental principle of Aquinas that every agent acts to the producing of its own likeness. Every creature must accordingly resemble God at least in the inadequate way in which an effect can resemble its cause. The analogy is especially an analogy of "being," which the mediaeval mind apparently conceived as in some way active, not merely passive. All created things resemble God in so far as they are, and are good. Goodness and beauty are really the same as "being," from which they differ only logically. Names which are derived from creatures may therefore be applied to God analogously, that is, proportionately, or we may say relatively, in the manner which the passages appended to Q. 3 should be sufficient to explain (cf. *S. Contra Gentiles* I, ch. 30). The application of them must, however, respect the principle of "negative knowledge," which is observed by most thinkers of the millennium following Plotinus when speaking of the transcendent. Plotinus had maintained that anything whatever could be truly denied of the divine being, and also that whatever we affirm, we must forthwith affirm the opposite (*Enneads* V). Aquinas maintains that we can know of God's essence only what it is not, not what it is, but that this is properly knowledge of God. Names may be applied in so far as they are intended to affirm what applies to him in a more eminent way than we can conceive, while they must at the same time be denied of him on account of their mode of signification. The principle is in keeping with the practice of the Old Testament, which repeatedly has recourse to negatives in reference to the divine.

Questions 20–23

In each of these four questions Aquinas begins by justifying the application to God of the terms employed, and then proceeds to show what we ought to mean by them. Love is the first movement of the divine will whereby God seeks the good of all things. He therefore loves all things that are. He loves better things the more in so far as he wills a greater good for them, and the universe would not be complete if it did not exhibit every grade of being. The justice and mercy of God are necessarily present in all God's works, since his justice consists in rendering to every creature what is its due according to its own nature as created by himself, while his mercy consists in remedying defects, which God owes it to himself to make good in accordance with his wisdom and goodness. Divine providence is the reason, pre-existing in the mind of God, why things are ordained to their end, the order of providence comprising all that God provides in his governance of all things through secondary causes, which may be either necessary or contingent. The providential order is thus the permanent condition of human life and of all existence, controlling the ultimate issue of secondary causes in such a way that the divine purpose shall inevitably be attained. Predestination is a part of providence. Here we find a reluctance to pronounce upon certain questions which Aquinas obviously believed were not for man to investigate. The reason why God predestines some and not others, for example, lies in God himself, and is not to be looked for in human merits or in anything of the kind. Aquinas insists, however, that the divine intention cannot be altered by the prayers of the devout, although it may be furthered by them as secondary causes, which, as part of providence, predestination permits.

PRIMA SECUNDAE

Questions 82, 85

The most serious aspect of sin is that it may deprive men of the effects of the providential order whereby they are directed to God as their final end. Original sin is the disordered disposition of nature which has resulted from the loss of original justice, and which in us has become almost second nature as a transmitted habit. Sin is thus regarded as unnatural, not as a natural opposition of man to God. Aquinas does justice to both sides of the effect of sin distinguished by Augustine as *vitium*, or moral damage, and *reatus*, or guilt, although he frequently prefers the milder term *culpa* in place of the latter. The distinctive contention of Aquinas is that the natural inclination to virtue is never entirely destroyed by sin. If it were, human nature would be destroyed at its very root. Man would then cease to be a rational being, since it is of the very nature of a rational being to seek the good, and would consequently be incapable even of sin. This does not mean, however, that sin cannot exclude from blessedness. Man cannot himself repair the damage of sin, nor remove the guilt of it, and mortal sin entails final rejection by God in accordance with his justice.

Questions 109–114

The treatise on grace raises several points worthy of special notice. Aquinas speaks of the "infusion of grace." Such a phrase befits a view of grace as something magical, if not physical, but is not intended as implying any positive description of the inward nature of grace. It may be regarded as no less incongruous with his whole teaching than is the lingering legal terminology of Paul, or simply as being Aquinas' way of acknowledging that grace is ultimately unanalysable and mystical, achieving its end outside the normal order of cause and effect— for Aquinas was certainly to some extent a mystic. It need not be understood as implying any self-circumscribed substitute for the regenerative and redemptive work of God himself, which is the damaging implication of any unspiritual view of grace. Any hypostatization of grace is ruled out by the very title of the first question, which makes it clear that grace is nothing less than the help of God, while the treatise itself expounds the manner in which divine grace is essential for every action of man, no less than for his redemption from sin and preparation for blessedness. It will be observed that sanctifying grace is distinguished from free grace, which denotes the divine gifts whereby one man may lead another to faith, but which do not sanctify ; and also that justification is taken in its literal etymological sense as meaning "to make just," not in the sense in which it is now normally understood to mean the acceptance of man by God despite the sin which God forbears to impute. As used by Aquinas, justification means the remission of sins ; but it is the creation of a just man that he has in mind, not the circumstance of a spiritual personal relationship. It is recognized that justification is by faith and not of works, and it is quite clear that Aquinas held no brief for the notion that salvation could be merited by good works. Merit itself is entirely the result of co-operative grace. When we say that a man merits anything, we ought to mean that what God has wrought in him merits further development and consummation, since God owes it to himself to perfect and complete the work which he has begun. The whole treatise causes one to wonder what would have happened at the time of the Reformation if Aquinas had been universally understood in the Catholic Church, and if all parties had used the same terms with the same meanings. The Reformation would still have been inevitable, but it might have taken a different course.

SECUNDA SECUNDAE

Questions 1–7; 17–21; 23, 27

The four cardinal virtues of Aristotle, wisdom, courage, temperance, and justice, were sufficient to make man perfect in his intellect, feeling, will, and social relationships. The three theological virtues, Faith, Hope, and Charity, are essential for the attainment of his final end which lies in God. They are called "theological" virtues because they have God for their object. Through them eternal life is begun in us.

In most contexts, faith means belief. While he accepted certain points made by Abelard (1079–1142) in defence of the free use of reason, Aquinas nevertheless takes a thoroughly authoritarian view of the relation of faith to reason. Abelard had maintained, especially in opposition to Anselm, that reason was of God, the ground of the *Imago Dei*, and consequently fitted to investigate divine things, the truth of which it could to some extent understand without their presence. He had also insisted that some understanding of what was believed was essential for faith, mere acceptance on authority being lifeless and without moral or spiritual value, since we are no longer in the position of Abraham, to whom the *Deus dixit* was immediately present, and who could therefore follow the way of blind trust with profit (*Introductio* 1050 D–1051). This meant that the things of faith were not to be believed merely because they were revealed by God, but because their own truth convinced the believer. He maintained further that only reason could bring men to faith (*Introd.* 1048: *Theologica Christiana* IV, 1284). Aquinas agrees with Abelard that reason can never contradict faith (Pt. I, Q. 1, Art. 10), and that reason must be convinced of the truth which it accepts, since to believe is "to think with assent" (22ae, Q. 1, Art. 1). But he insists that the unseen things of faith are entirely beyond the reach of reason,

31

and that faith is only of things unseen. He accordingly understands the conviction and assent of faith in a very different
way. Reason must be convinced not by the matter of faith
itself, but by the divine authority wherewith it is proposed
to us for belief. The inward moving of God enables one to
accept matters of faith on the strength of authority (22ae,
Q. 6, Art. 1), and such acceptance is meritorious (22ae, Q. 2,
Art. 9). Human reason can remove obstacles in the way of
faith (22ae, Q. 2, Art. 10), but can never do more than provide
a preamble to faith itself, though it may discover reasons for
what is already believed through faith. Aquinas will go no
further than to say that those whose office it is to teach others
must have a fuller knowledge of what ought to be believed, and
must believe it more explicitly, than those whom they instruct.

The principal object of faith is the "first truth" declared
in sacred Scripture, according to the teaching of the Church,
which understands it perfectly since the universal Church
cannot err. The promise given to Peter in Luke 22:32 is interpreted as a guarantee of present infallibility, while John 16:13
is rendered "he will teach you all truth." Thus although
Aquinas maintains that an increase of grace is granted not immediately, but in its own time, i.e., when a man is sufficiently
well disposed to receive it (12ae, Q. 114, Art. 8), he does
not regard any such principle as applicable to the appreciation
of scriptural revelation on the part of the Church. His explanation that the words of the Creed "I believe in the holy catholic
Church" properly mean "in the Holy Spirit which sanctifies
the Church" (22ae, Q. 1, Art. 9) consequently loses something of
its value. The articles of faith are held to be permanent and infallible in substance, and Aquinas can conceive of no other
reason for rejecting them than the defective opinion of one's
own will (22ae, Q. 5, Art. 3). The soteriological significance of
belief lies in the circumstance that one must believe in the final
end as possible of attainment, before one can either hope for it
or strive for it. The absence of any further explanation of the
saving dynamic of faith is inevitable in so far as belief is treated
in abstraction by itself, without reference to the element of
fiducia, or personal trust. It is merely observed that faith must
be referred to the end of charity (22ae, Q. 3, Art. 2).

Hope is the virtue whereby man unites himself to God as his
final end in a manner which is immediately practical. Despair
is the deadliest of sins, a contention which provides an interest-
ing contrast to later views which regard it as an essential

preliminary to any spiritual attainment. Fear is the converse of hope, and in its essential substance is equally a gift of God which helps to keep us within the providential order which leads to blessedness. Charity is the supreme virtue which brings faith to its true form, uniting us directly to God, and directing all other virtues to this final end. Charity is, as it were, friendship with God, and herein Aquinas preserves the element which one may have missed in the treatise on faith. For charity is itself of the very essence of God. When present in us, it likens us to God, and likens us to him further in those works of mercy in which the whole Christian religion outwardly consists.

Part I. Questions *1–4; 20–23*

WHAT SACRED DOCTRINE IS, AND WHAT IT CONCERNS

IN ORDER TO CONFINE OUR PURPOSE WITHIN DEFINITE limits, we must first inquire into sacred doctrine itself, what it is and what it concerns. Ten questions are asked 1. Whether sacred doctrine is necessary. 2. Whether it is a science. 3. Whether it is one science, or several. 4. Whether it is speculative or practical. 5. How it is related to other sciences. 6. Whether it is wisdom. 7. What is its subject-matter. 8. Whether it proceeds by argument. 9. Whether it ought to make use of metaphors or figures of speech. 10. Whether the sacred Scriptures of this doctrine should be expounded in several ways.

Article One

WHETHER ANOTHER DOCTRINE IS NECESSARY, BESIDES THE PHILOSOPHICAL SCIENCES

We proceed to the first article thus:

1. It seems that there is no need for any other doctrine besides the philosophical sciences. Man should not strive to know what is above reason, since it is said in Ecclesiasticus 3:22: "seek not to know what is higher than thyself." Now what is within the reach of reason is adequately dealt with in the philosophical sciences. It seems superfluous, therefore, that there should be another doctrine besides the philosophical sciences.

2. Again, a doctrine can be concerned only with "what is," since only what is true can be known, and whatever is true, is. Now all things which "are" are dealt with in the philosophical sciences, which treat even of God, wherefore one part of philosophy is called theology, or the science of divine things, as the

35

philosopher [1] says in 6 *Metaph.* (Commentary II). There was therefore no need for another doctrine, besides the philosophical sciences.

On the other hand: it is said in II Tim. 3:16: "All scripture is given by inspiration of God, and is profitable for doctrine, for reproof, for correction, for instruction in righteousness. . . ." [2] Now the divinely inspired Scriptures are quite distinct from the philosophical sciences, which are devised by human reason. It is therefore expedient that there should be another science which is divinely inspired, besides the philosophical sciences.

I answer: it was necessary for man's salvation that there should be a doctrine founded on revelation, as well as the philosophical sciences discovered by human reason. It was necessary, in the first place, because man is ordained to God as his end, who surpasses the comprehension of reason, according to Isa. 64:4: "neither hath the eye seen, O God, besides thee, what he hath prepared for him that waiteth for him." Men must have some foreknowledge of the end to which they ought to direct their intentions and actions. It was therefore necessary that some things which transcend human reason should be made known through divine revelation. It was necessary also that man should be instructed by divine revelation even in such things concerning God as human reason could discover. For such truth about God as could be discovered by reason would be known only by the few, and that after a long time, and mixed with many errors. Now the whole salvation of man, which lies in God, depends on the knowledge of this truth. It was therefore necessary that men should be instructed in divine things through divine revelation, in order that their salvation might come to pass the more fittingly and certainly. It was necessary, therefore, that there should be a sacred doctrine given through revelation, as well as the philosophical sciences discovered by reason.

On the first point: although things which are beyond human knowledge are not to be sought by man through reason, such things are revealed by God, and are to be accepted by faith. Hence Ecclesiasticus adds in the same passage: "many things beyond human understanding have been revealed unto thee" (3:25).

---

[1] I.e., Aristotle. Bekker's pages are quoted in the index for all references to Aristotle's works except the *Ethics*, to which references in the text should be sufficiently clear.

[2] Scriptural passages are quoted from the Authorized Version, any significant divergences in the text being indicated by footnotes.

On the second point: sciences are distinguished by their different ways of knowing. The astronomer and the naturalist prove the same thing, for example, that the world is round. But the astronomer proves it by mathematics, without reference to matter, whereas the naturalist proves it by examining the physical. There is no reason, then, why the same things, which the philosophical sciences teach as they can be known by the light of natural reason, should not also be taught by another science as they are known through divine revelation. The theology which depends on sacred Scripture is thus generically different from the theology which is a part of philosophy.

Article Two

WHETHER SACRED DOCTRINE IS A SCIENCE

We proceed to the second article thus:

1. It seems that sacred doctrine is not a science. For every science depends on principles which are self-evident, whereas sacred doctrine depends on articles of faith which are not self-evident, since they are not conceded by everybody. As is said in II Thess. 3:2: "all men have not faith." Hence sacred doctrine is not a science.

2. Again, there is no science of particulars.[1] But sacred doctrine is concerned with particulars, such as the deeds of Abraham, Isaac, Jacob, and others. It is not therefore a science.

On the other hand: Augustine says (14 *De Trin.* 1): "by this science only is faith begun, nourished, defended, and strengthened." Now this is true of no science except sacred doctrine. Sacred doctrine is therefore a science.

I answer: sacred doctrine is a science. But we must realize that there are two kinds of sciences. Some of them, such as arithmetic, geometry, and the like, depend on principles known by the natural light of reason. Others depend on principles known through a higher science. Thus the science of perspective depends on principles known through geometry, and music on principles known through arithmetic. Sacred doctrine is a science of the latter kind, depending on principles known through a higher science, namely the science of God and the

---

[1] Aristotle held that the sheer individuality of a particular, its "primary substance," could never be an object of science because it could never be a predicate. Only the "secondary substance," or essence, comprising the universals which must apply to a particular of a certain kind, could be known scientifically. Cf. *Categories V.*

blessed. Just as music accepts the principles given to it by arithmetic, so does sacred doctrine accept the principles revealed to it by God.

On the first point: the principles of any science are either self-evident, or derived from what is known through a higher science. The principles of sacred doctrine are so derived, as we have said.

On the second point: sacred doctrine does not narrate particular things because it is principally concerned with them. It introduces them as examples to follow, as do the moral sciences ; and also as proofs of the authority of those through whom the divine revelation, on which sacred Scripture and sacred doctrine are founded, reaches us.

Article Three

WHETHER SACRED DOCTRINE IS A SINGLE SCIENCE

We proceed to the third article thus:

1. It seems that sacred doctrine is not a single science. As the philosopher says: "one science treats of one kind of subject only" (I *Post. An.*, Text 43). Now sacred doctrine treats of the Creator and also of creatures, and these do not belong to one kind of subject. Hence it is not a single science.

2. Again, sacred doctrine treats of angels, of creatures with bodies, and of the customs of men. These belong to different philosophical sciences. Hence sacred doctrine is not a single science.

On the other hand: sacred Scripture speaks of these things as of a single science, for it is said in Wisdom 10:10: "She hath given him the science of holy things."

I answer: sacred doctrine is a single science. The unity of a power or habit [1] is indeed to be judged by its object, but by the formal nature of its object, not by the material nature of it. For example, man, ass, and stone agree in possessing the formal nature of "the coloured," which is the object of sight. Now since sacred doctrine treats of things as divinely revealed, as we said in the previous article, all things which are divinely revealed agree in the one formal nature which is the object of this science. They are therefore comprehended under sacred doctrine as a single science.

On the first point: sacred doctrine is not concerned with God and with creatures equally. It is concerned with God funda-

[1] See note to 12ae, Q. 82, Art. 1.

mentally, and with creatures in so far as they relate to God as their beginning or end. Thus the unity of the science is not destroyed.

On the second point: there is nothing to prevent lower powers or habits being differentiated in their relation to matters which yet go together for a higher power or habit, because a higher power or habit comprehends its object under a more universal aspect. Thus the object of the common sense is "the sensible," which includes both the "visible" and the "audible." Common sense is a single power which comprehends all objects of the five senses. Similarly, sacred doctrine remains a single science while it treats under one aspect, in so far as they are all revealed by God, matters which are dealt with by separate philosophical sciences. Sacred doctrine is thus like an imprint of God's knowledge, which is one and undivided, yet is knowledge of all things.

Article Four

WHETHER SACRED DOCTRINE IS A PRACTICAL SCIENCE

We proceed to the fourth article thus:

1. It seems that sacred doctrine is a practical science. For "the end of practical knowledge is action," according to the philosopher (2 *Metaph.*, Text 3), and sacred doctrine is concerned with action, according to James 1:22: "Be ye doers of the word, and not hearers only." Sacred doctrine is therefore a practical science.

2. Again, sacred doctrine is divided into the Old and the New Law, and the Law has to do with the science of morals, which is practical. Sacred doctrine is therefore a practical science.

On the other hand: every practical science is concerned with the works of men. Ethics is concerned with their actions, and architecture with their buildings. But sacred doctrine is concerned principally with God, whose works men are. Hence it is not a practical science. Rather is it speculative.

I answer: as was said in the preceding article, sacred doctrine embraces matters dealt with by separate philosophical sciences while it itself remains one, because the formal nature to which it attends in diverse things is their being made known by the divine light. Hence even though some matters in the philosophical sciences are speculative and some practical, sacred doctrine includes them all within itself, just as God knows both himself and his works by the same knowledge. But sacred doctrine is more speculative than practical, since it is concerned with divine things more fundamentally than with the actions of men, in which it is interested in so far as through them men are brought to the perfect knowledge of God in which their eternal happiness consists. The answer to the objections is then obvious.

Article Five

WHETHER SACRED DOCTRINE IS NOBLER THAN OTHER SCIENCES

We proceed to the fifth article thus:

1. It seems that sacred doctrine is not nobler than other sciences. For the dignity of a science is indicated by its certainty, and other sciences whose principles cannot be doubted appear to be more certain than sacred doctrine, whose principles, i.e., the articles of faith, are the subject of debate. Thus it seems that other sciences are nobler.

2. Again, a lower science depends on a higher, as music depends on arithmetic. Now sacred doctrine derives something from the philosophical sciences. Hieronymus, indeed, says that "the ancient teachers filled their books with so many philosophical doctrines and opinions that one does not know which to admire the more, their secular learning or their knowledge of the scriptures" (*Epist.* 84 to Magnus the Roman orator). Sacred doctrine is therefore lower than other sciences.

On the other hand: other sciences are said to be subsidiary to this doctrine in Prov. 9:3: "She hath sent forth her maidens: she crieth upon the highest places of the city."

I answer: since sacred doctrine is speculative in some things and practical in others, it transcends all other sciences, whether speculative or practical. One speculative science is said to be nobler than another either because it is more certain, or because it treats of a nobler subject. Sacred doctrine surpasses other speculative sciences in both respects. It is more certain, since the certainty of other sciences depends on the natural light of human reason, which is liable to err, whereas its own certainty is founded on the light of divine knowledge, which cannot be deceived. Its subject is also nobler, since it is concerned principally with things above reason, whereas other sciences deal with things within the reach of reason. Finally, one practical science is nobler than another if it serves a more ultimate end. Politics is nobler than military science, because the good of an army is subsidiary to the good of the state. Now in so far as sacred doctrine is practical, its end is eternal happiness, and all other ends of the practical sciences are subsidiary to this as their ultimate end. It is plain, then, that it is nobler than the others in every way.

On the first point: there is nothing to prevent what is in itself the more certain from appearing to us to be the less certain, owing to the weakness of the intellect, "which is to the things most manifest to nature like the eyes of a bat to the light of the sun," as is said in *Metaph.* 2. The doubt felt by some in respect of the articles of faith is not due to any uncertainty in the thing itself. It is due to the weakness of human understanding. Nevertheless, the least knowledge which one can have of higher things is worth more than the most certain knowledge of lesser things, as is said in the *De Partibus Animalium* (bk. 1, ch. 5).

On the second point: this science can make use of the philosophical sciences in order to make what it teaches more obvious, not because it stands in need of them. It does not take its principles from other sciences, but receives them directly from God through revelation. It thus derives nothing from other sciences as from superiors, but uses them as ancillary inferiors, as the master sciences use subsidiary sciences, or as politics uses military science. Its use of them is not due to any defect or inadequacy in itself. It is due to the limitation of our understanding. We are more easily led from what is known by natural reason, on which other sciences depend, to the things above reason which this science teaches us.

Article Six

WHETHER SACRED DOCTRINE IS WISDOM

We proceed to the sixth article thus:

1. It seems that sacred doctrine is not wisdom. No doctrine which derives its principles from elsewhere is worthy of the name of wisdom. As it is said in *Metaph.* 1, cap. 2: "the wise man must order, and not be ordered." Now the preceding article makes it plain that sacred doctrine derives its principles from outside itself. It follows that it is not wisdom.

2. Again, wisdom proves the principles of other sciences, and is accordingly called the head of the sciences in 6 *Ethics* 7. But sacred doctrine does not prove the principles of other sciences. It follows that it is not wisdom.

3. Again, sacred doctrine is acquired through study. But

wisdom is infused, and is accordingly numbered among the seven gifts of the Holy Spirit in Isa. 11. It follows that sacred doctrine is not wisdom.

On the other hand: it is said at the beginning of the law, "this is your wisdom and your understanding in the sight of the nations" (Deut. 4:6).

I answer: this doctrine is the wisdom of all wisdoms, absolutely so, and not only in respect of one kind of wisdom. The wise man orders and judges, and we may say that a man is wise in respect of a certain genus of things when he takes account of the highest cause of that genus, since we judge inferior things by means of a higher cause. An architect who plans the form of a house is said to be wise in regard to buildings, and is called a master-builder in distinction from the subsidiaries who hew the wood and prepare the stones. Thus it is said in I Cor. 3:10: "as a wise master-builder, I have laid the foundation." Again, a prudent man is said to be wise in what matters for the whole of human life, since he directs his human actions to their proper end. Thus it is said in Prov. 10:23: "a man of understanding hath wisdom." Hence he who attends to the absolute and highest cause of the whole universe, which is God, is called wise above all. That is the reason why wisdom is also defined as the knowledge of divine things, as Augustine explains (12 *De Trin. c.* 14). Now it is the quintessence of sacred doctrine that it treats of God as the highest principle, as he is known only to himself, and to others by revelation, not merely as he is known through creatures in the philosophical way spoken of in Rom. 1:19: "Because that which may be known of God is manifest in them." Hence sacred doctrine is especially said to be wisdom.

On the first point: sacred doctrine does not derive its principles from another human science, but from divine knowledge, whereby all our knowledge is ruled as by the highest wisdom.

On the second point: the principles of other sciences are either self-evident and indemonstrable,[1] or proved by natural reason in some other science. But the special principles of this science are founded on revelation, not on natural reason. It is not therefore for sacred doctrine to prove the principles of other sciences, but only to judge them. It repudiates anything in the other sciences which is inconsistent with its truth, as wholly false. Thus it is said in II Cor. 10:5: "Casting down imagina-

[1] Cf. 1 *Post. An.,* ch. 3.

tions, and every high thing that exalteth itself against the knowledge of God."

On the third point: since wisdom judges, and since there are two ways of judging, there are two kinds of wisdom. One may judge as the result of inclination, as does a man who has the habit of virtue, who judges rightly of the things which virtue requires him to do because he is inclined to do them. Thus it is said in 10 *Ethics* 5 and in 3 *Ethics* 4: "the virtuous man is the measure and rule of human actions." One may also judge as the result of knowledge, as one who is versed in the science of morals can judge of virtuous actions even though he is not virtuous. The wisdom which is defined as a gift of the Holy Spirit judges of divine things in the first way, according to I Cor. 2:15: "he that is spiritual judges all things," and as Dionysius relates (2 *Div. Nom.*, lect. 4): "Hierotheus was taught not only by learning, but by the experience of divine things." This doctrine, on the other hand, judges in the second way, since it is acquired through study, even though its principles are received through revelation.

Article Seven

WHETHER GOD IS THE SUBJECT OF THIS SCIENCE

We proceed to the seventh article thus:

1. It seems that God is not the subject of this science. The philosopher says that the subject of any science must be presupposed (1 *Post. An.*). But sacred doctrine does not presuppose what God is. Indeed, as the Damascene says, "it is impossible to say what is in God" (3 *De Fid. Orth.* 24). It follows that God is not the subject of this science.

2. Again, the conclusions of any science are all contained in its subject. But in sacred Scripture conclusions are reached about many things other than God, for example, about creatures, and the customs of men. It follows that God is not the subject of this science.

On the other hand: it is its main theme that is the subject of a science, and the main theme of this science is God. It is indeed called theology because its theme is God. It follows that God is the subject of this science.

I answer: God is the subject of this science. Its subject is related to a science as is its object to a power or habit. Now that under the aspect of which all things are referred to any power or habit is rightly named as the object of that power or habit.

Thus a man and a stone are referred to sight because they are coloured, and hence colour is the proper object of sight. Likewise all things are viewed by sacred doctrine under the aspect of God, either because they are God himself, or because they have God for their beginning or end. It follows that God is truly the subject of this science. This is indeed obvious from its principles, the articles of faith, which are about God. The subject of the principles and the subject of the whole science are the same, since the whole science is virtually contained in its principles. Anyone who attends to the matters with which it deals without attending to the aspect under which it views them may indeed attribute a different subject to this science, such as things, signs, the work of salvation, or Christ in his fullness as both Head and members. Sacred doctrine deals with all of these things, but deals with them in their relation to God.

On the first point: although we cannot know what God is, in this doctrine we can use the effects of God, whether of nature or of grace, in place of a definition of the divine things of which the doctrine treats. We similarly use an effect in place of a definition of a cause in certain philosophical sciences, when we demonstrate something about a cause by means of its effect.

On the second point: all other things about which sacred Scripture reaches conclusions are comprehended in God, not indeed as parts or species or accidents, but as related to God in some way.

Article Eight

WHETHER SACRED DOCTRINE PROCEEDS BY ARGUMENT

We proceed to the eighth article thus:

1. It seems that sacred doctrine does not proceed by argument. For Ambrose says: "where faith is sought, eschew arguments" (*De Fid. Cath.*), and it is especially faith that is sought in this doctrine. As it is said in John 20:31: "these are written, that ye might believe." It follows that sacred doctrine does not proceed by argument.

2. Again, if sacred doctrine proceeded by argument, it would argue either on the ground of authority or on the ground of reason. But to argue from authority would be beneath its dignity, since "authority is the weakest kind of proof," as Boethius says (*Topica* 6), and to argue by reason would be unworthy of its end, since "faith has no merit when human reason

proves it by test," as Gregory says (*Hom. in Evang.* 26). It follows that sacred doctrine does not proceed by argument.

On the other hand: Titus 1:9 says of a bishop, "holding fast the faithful word as he hath been taught, that he may be able by sound doctrine both to exhort and to convince the gainsayers."

I answer: just as other sciences do not argue to prove their own principles, but argue from their principles to prove other things which the sciences include, so neither does this doctrine argue to prove its principles, which are the articles of faith, but argues from these to prove other things. Thus in 1 Cor. 15 the apostle argues from the resurrection of Christ to prove the general resurrection. We must remember, however, that the inferior philosophical sciences do not prove their own principles, nor defend them against one who denies them. They leave this to a higher science. The highest of them, metaphysics, does argue in defence of its principles, provided that he who denies them concedes anything at all. But it cannot argue with him if he concedes nothing, although it can refute his reasoning. Now sacred doctrine, which has no superior, likewise argues at times with one who denies its principles, provided that its adversary concedes something of what is received through revelation. Thus we argue from the authority of sacred doctrine against heretics, and from the authority of one article of faith against those who deny another. But when an adversary believes nothing at all of what has been revealed, there is no way of proving the articles of faith by argument, except by disproving any grounds which he may bring against the faith. For since faith takes its stand on infallible truth, the contrary of which cannot possibly be demonstrated, it is obvious that proofs cited against the faith are not demonstrative, but answerable.

On the first point: although arguments of human reason cannot suffice to prove matters of faith, sacred doctrine argues from the articles of faith to other things, as said above.

On the second point: proof by authority is especially characteristic of this science, because its principles are obtained through revelation. The authority of those who received revelation has to be believed. But this does not detract from the dignity of the science. Appeal to an authority which depends on human reason is the weakest kind of proof. Appeal to an authority founded on divine revelation is the most telling. Yet sacred doctrine does make use of human reason, not indeed to prove the faith (which would take away its merit), but to clarify certain points of doctrine. Since grace does not supplant nature, but perfects it, reason ought to be the servant of faith in the same way as the natural inclination of the will is the servant of charity—"bringing into captivity every thought to the obedience of Christ," as the apostle says in II Cor. 10:5. Sacred doctrine uses even the authority of philosophers in this way, wherever they have been able to know the truth through natural reason. In Acts 17:28, for example, Paul quotes the words of Aratus: "as certain also of your poets have said, For we also are his offspring." Sacred doctrine uses such authorities, however, as supporting and probable arguments. It uses the canonical Scriptures as the proper authority from which it is bound to argue, and uses other teachers of the Church as authorities from which one may indeed argue with propriety, yet only with probability.

Article Nine

Whether Sacred Doctrine should Use Metaphors

We proceed to the ninth article thus:

1. It seems that sacred doctrine should not use metaphors. What is fitting for lesser doctrines would appear to be inappropriate to this doctrine, which holds the supreme place among the sciences, as was said in the preceding article. Now to proceed by various similies and figures is fitting for poetry, the least of all doctrines. Hence this doctrine should not use metaphors.

2. Again, the purpose of this doctrine is, apparently, to explain the truth, since a reward is promised to those who explain it. "They who explain me shall have eternal life" (Ecclesiasticus 24:21). Now truth is obscured by metaphors. This doctrine should not, therefore, record divine things under the form of corporeal things.

3. Again, the more sublime are creatures, the greater their likeness to God. Hence if any of them are to be used in the manifestation of God, it ought to be the more sublime creatures especially—not the lowest, as is often the case in Scripture.

On the other hand: it is said in Hos. 12:10: "I have multiplied visions, and used similitudes, by the ministry of the prophets." Now to declare something by a similitude is to use a metaphor. The use of metaphors therefore befits sacred doctrine.

I answer: it is fitting that sacred Scripture should declare divine and spiritual things by means of material similies. God provides for all things according to the capacity of their nature, and it is natural for man to reach intelligible things through sensible things, since all his knowledge begins from sense. Hence spiritual things are appropriately given to us by Scripture in material metaphors. This is what Dionysius is saying in 2 *Coel. Hier.*: "It is impossible for the divine ray to lighten us unless it is shaded by a variety of sacred veils." It is also appropriate that the sacred Scriptures which are given for all alike ("I am debtor . . . both to the wise and to the unwise," Rom. 1:14), should expound spiritual things by means of material similitudes, so that simple people who cannot understand intelligible things as they are should at least be able to understand them in this way.

On the first point: poetry uses metaphors to depict, since men naturally find pictures pleasing. But sacred doctrine uses them because they are necessary and useful.

On the second point: as Dionysius says, the ray of divine revelation is not destroyed by the sensible images which veil it (2 *Coel Hier.*). It remains in its truth, not allowing the minds of men to rest in the images, but raising them to know intelligible things.[1] It instructs others also in intelligible things, through those to whom the revelation is made. Thus what is veiled by metaphor in one passage of Scripture is declared more explicitly in others. This veiling in metaphors is useful for stimulating the thoughtful, and useful also against unbelievers, of whom it is said in Matt. 7:6: "Give not that which is holy unto the dogs."

On the third point: as Dionysius says, it is more fitting that Scripture should declare divine things in simple than in higher corporeal forms (2 *Coel. Hier.*). There are three reasons for this. First, the human mind is the more saved from error when it is abundantly plain that these forms are not a proper signification of divine things. This might be doubtful if divine things were described in terms of higher corporeal forms, especially with those who cannot think beyond higher corporeal things. Secondly, it is better suited to the knowledge of God which we have in this life. We know what God is not, better than we know what he is. Likenesses of things farther removed from him lead us to appreciate the more truly that God transcends

---

[1] According to the *De Adhaerendo Deo*, of Albertus Magnus, the mind should strive to pass entirely beyond the images of sensible things in its contemplation of God. It seems to have been acknowledged, however, that the human mind cannot dispense with such images altogether.

whatever we say or think about him. Thirdly, divine things are the better hidden from the unworthy.

Article Ten

WHETHER ONE PASSAGE OF SACRED SCRIPTURE MAY HAVE SEVERAL INTERPRETATIONS

We proceed to the tenth article thus:

1. It seems that one passage of sacred Scripture cannot have several interpretations, such as the historical or literal, the allegorical, the tropological or moral, and the anagogical. For many meanings in one passage make for confusion and deception, and destroy the cogency of argument. We cannot argue from ambiguous propositions, which are blamed for certain fallacies, whereas Scripture must be capable of showing the truth without any fallacy. There cannot, therefore, be several meanings intended by the same passage.

2. Again, Augustine says (*De Utilitate Credendi*): "The Scriptures which we call the Old Testament bear a fourfold record —the historical, the aetiological, the analogical, and the allegorical." Now these appear to be quite different from the four interpretations mentioned. It seems wrong, therefore, that the same words of sacred Scripture should be expounded according to the latter.

3. Again, besides these four interpretations, there is the parabolical, which has been omitted.

On the other hand: Gregory says (20 *Moral.* 1): "The sacred Scriptures surpass all sciences by their manner of speaking. In one and the same word they record an event and proclaim a mystery."

I answer: God is the author of sacred Scripture, and he is able not only to adapt words (which even a man can do), but also to adapt things to signify something. While words mean something in every science, it is characteristic of this science that the things which the words indicate themselves signify something. The signification by which words signify things belongs to the first interpretation of Scripture, namely the historical or literal. The interpretation wherein things signified by words stand for other things is called the spiritual interpretation, which is based on the literal, and presupposes it. The spiritual interpretation is threefold. As the apostle says in Heb. 7, the Old Law is the figure of the New Law, and as Dionysius says (5 *Eccles. Hier.*, cap. 1): "the New Law is itself the figure of future glory." In the New Law, things done by the Head are signs of what we ourselves ought to do. Thus in so far as the contents of the Old Law indicate the contents of the New, the sense is allegorical. In so far as the deeds of Christ or the things which signify Christ are signs of what we ought to do, the sense is moral, and in so far as they signify what belongs to eternal glory, the sense is anagogical. Finally, since it is the literal sense which the author intends, and since the author is God, who comprehends all things in his mind together, "it is not unfitting that there should literally be several interpretations contained in one scriptural word" (12 *Confessions* 18–20; 24; 31).

On the first point: this manifold interpretation does not make for equivocation, or for any other kind of multiplicity. As we have said, its manifold nature does not mean that one word indicates different things, but that things indicated by words can be signs of different things. Thus no confusion results, since all interpretations are based on one, that is on the literal, from which alone we can argue. As Augustine says (*Contra Vincent. Donatist.* 48), we cannot argue from the allegorical meaning. Yet sacred Scripture loses nothing thereby, since nothing essential to the faith is contained in the spiritual sense of one passage which is not clearly expressed in the literal sense of another.

On the second point: the historical, the aetiological, and the anagogical are all three interpretations of the one literal interpretation. As Augustine explains in the same passage, it is history when something is merely narrated; aetiology when a reason is given for what is narrated, as when our Lord gave the reasons why Moses permitted the dismissal of wives, namely, for the hardness of their hearts (Matt. 19:8); analogy when the truth of one passage of Scripture is shown to be compatible with that of another. Of the four, allegory itself stands for the three spiritual interpretations. Thus Hugo St. Victor includes the anagogical under the allegorical, naming only the historical, the allegorical, and the tropological (Sentences 3. Prologue to 1 *De Sacrament.* 4).

On the third point: the parabolical meaning is contained in the literal, since the words indicate something directly, and also something figuratively. The literal sense is not the figure itself, but the thing which is figured. For when Scripture speaks of the arm of the Lord, the literal sense is not that God has such a bodily member, but that he has what such a bodily member indicates, namely active power. It is thus clear that the literal interpretation of Scripture cannot contain what is false.

Question Two

THE EXISTENCE OF GOD

Three questions are asked concerning the existence of God.
1. Whether it is self-evident that God exists. 2. Whether the existence of God can be demonstrated. 3. Whether God exists.

Article One

WHETHER IT IS SELF-EVIDENT THAT GOD EXISTS

We proceed to the first article thus:

1. It seems to be self-evident that God exists. Things are said to be self-evident when the knowledge of them is naturally in us, as is obviously the case with first principles. Now the Damascene says that "the knowledge that God exists is naturally inborn in all men" (1 *De Fid. Orth.* 1, 3). It is therefore self-evident that God exists.

2. Again, as the philosopher says of the first principles of demonstration, whatever is known as soon as the terms are known is self-evident (1 *Post. An.*, ch. 2). Thus we know that any whole is greater than its part as soon as we know what a whole is, and what a part is. Now when it is understood what the term "God" signifies, it is at once understood that God exists. For the term "God" means that than which nothing greater can be signified, and that which exists in reality is greater than that which exists only in the intellect. Hence since "God" exists in the intellect as soon as the term is understood, it follows that God exists also in reality. It is therefore self-evident that God exists.

3. Again, it is self-evident that truth exists. For truth exists if anything at all is true, and if anyone denies that truth exists, he concedes that it is true that it does not exist, since if truth does not exist it is then true that it does not exist. Now God is truth itself, according to John 14:6: "I am the way, and the truth, and the life." It is therefore self-evident that God exists.

On the other hand: no one can conceive the opposite of what is self-evident, as the philosopher explains in dealing with the first principles of demonstration (4 *Metaph.*, text 9; 1 *Post. An.*, texts 5 and *ult.*). Now the opposite of "God exists" can be conceived, according to Ps. 53:1: "The fool hath said in his heart, There is no God." It follows that it is not self-evident that God exists.

50

I answer: there are two ways in which a thing may be self-evident. It may be self-evident in itself, but not self-evident to us. It may also be self-evident both in itself and to us. A proposition is self-evident when its predicate is contained in the meaning of its subject. For example, the proposition "man is an animal" is self-evident, because "animal" is contained in the meaning of "man." Hence if the predicate and the subject are known to everyone, the proposition will be self-evident to everyone. This is obviously the case with regard to the first principles of demonstration, whose terms are universals known to everyone, such as being and not-being, whole, part, and the like. But when there are some to whom the predicate and the subject are unknown, the proposition will not be self-evident to them, however self-evident it may be in itself. Thus Boethius says (*Lib. de Hebd.*—Whether all Existence is Good): "it happens that some universal concepts of mind are self-evident only to the wise, e.g., that the incorporeal is not in space." I say, then, that this proposition "God exists" is self-evident in itself, since its predicate is the same with its subject. For God is his existence, as we shall show in Q. 3, Art. 4. But since we do not know what God is, it is not self-evident to us, but must be proved by means of what is better known to us though less well known to nature,[1] i.e., by means of the effects of God.

On the first point: the knowledge that God exists is inborn in us in a general and somewhat confused manner. For God is the final beatitude of man, and a man desires beatitude naturally, and is also naturally aware of what he desires. But this is not absolute knowledge that God exists, any more than to know that someone is coming is to know that Peter is coming, even though it should actually be Peter who comes. Many indeed think that riches are man's perfect good, and constitute his beatitude. Others think that pleasures are his perfect good, and others again something else.

On the second point: he who hears the term "God" may not understand it to mean that than which nothing greater can be conceived, since some have believed that God is a body. But given that one understands the term to mean this, it does not

---

[1] According to 1 *Post. An.*, chs. 2, 3, the ultimate grounds of scientific proof must be self-evident principles which are "better known to nature," i.e., first in the order of nature, and thus naturally prior to the conclusions drawn from them. The order of our knowing is then the same as the order of being, so that we understand things through their causes. This is obviously impossible in the present instance. Cf. Art. 2.

follow that he understands that that which the term signifies exists in the nature of things, but only that it exists in the intellect. Neither can it be argued that God exists in reality, unless it is granted that that than which nothing greater can be conceived exists in reality, which is not granted by those who suppose that God does not exist.

On the third point: it is self-evident that truth in general exists. But it is not self-evident to us that the first truth exists.

Article Two

WHETHER GOD'S EXISTENCE CAN BE DEMONSTRATED

We proceed to the second article thus:

1. It seems that God's existence cannot be demonstrated. God's existence is an article of faith. But matters of faith cannot be demonstrated, since demonstration makes a thing to be known, whereas the apostle makes it clear that faith is of things not seen (Heb., ch. 11). It follows that God's existence cannot be demonstrated.

2. Again, the medium of demonstration is the essence. But as the Damascene says (1 *De. Fid. Orth.* 4), we cannot know what God is, but only what he is not. It follows that we cannot demonstrate that God exists.

3. Again, God's existence could be demonstrated only from his effects. But his effects are not proportionate to God himself, since God is infinite while they are finite, and the finite is not proportionate to the infinite. Now a cause cannot be demonstrated from an effect which is not proportionate to itself. It follows that God's existence cannot be demonstrated.

On the other hand: the apostle says in Rom. 1:20: "the invisible things of him . . . are clearly seen, being understood by the things that are made." Now this is possible only if God's existence can be demonstrated from the things that are made. For the first thing that is understood about anything is its existence.

I answer: there are two kinds of demonstration. There is demonstration through the cause, or, as we say, "from grounds," which argues from what comes first in nature. There is also demonstration by means of effects, or "proof by means of appearances," which argues from what comes first for ourselves. Now when an effect is more apparent to us than its cause, we reach a knowledge of the cause through its effect. Even though the effect should be better known to us, we can demonstrate from any effect that its cause exists, because effects always depend on some cause, and a cause must exist if its effect exists. We can demonstrate God's existence in this way, from his effects which are known to us, even though we do not know his essence.

On the first point: the existence of God, and similar things which can be known by natural reason as Rom., ch. 1, affirms, are not articles of faith, but preambles to the articles. Faith presupposes natural knowledge as grace presupposes nature, and as perfection presupposes what can be perfected. There is no reason, however, why what is in itself demonstrable and knowable should not be accepted in faith by one who cannot understand the demonstration of it.

On the second point: when a cause is demonstrated by means of its effect, we are bound to use the effect in place of a definition of the cause in proving the existence of the cause. This is especially the case with regard to God. For in proving that something exists, we are bound to accept the meaning of the name as the medium of demonstration, instead of the essence, since the question of what a thing is must follow the question of its existence. Since the names applied to God are derived from his effects, as we shall show in Q. 13, Art. 1,[1] we may use the name "God" as the medium in demonstrating God's existence from his effect.

On the third point: effects which are not proportionate to their cause do not give us perfect knowledge of their cause. Nevertheless, it can be clearly demonstrated from any effect whatever that its cause exists, as we have said. In this way we can prove God's existence from his effects, even though we cannot know his essence perfectly by means of them.

Article Three

WHETHER GOD EXISTS

We proceed to the third article thus:

1. It seems that God does not exist. If one of two contraries were to be infinite, the other would be wholly excluded. Now the name "God" means that he is infinite good. There would therefore be no evil if God were to exist. But there is evil in the world. It follows that God does not exist.

2. Again, what can be explained by comparatively few principles is not the consequence of a greater number of

[1] See appendix to Q. 4, Art. 3.

principles. Now if we suppose that God does not exist, it appears that we can still account for all that we see in the world by other principles, attributing all natural things to nature as their principle, and all that is purposive to human reason or will. There is therefore no need to suppose that God exists.

On the other hand: in Ex. 3:14 God says in person: "I AM THAT I AM."

I answer: God's existence can be proved in five ways. The first and clearest proof is the argument from motion.[1] It is certain, and in accordance with sense experience, that some things in this world are moved. Now everything that is moved is moved by something else, since nothing is moved unless it is potentially that to which it is moved, whereas that which moves is actual. To move is nothing other than to bring something from potentiality to actuality, and a thing can be brought from potentiality to actuality only by something which is actual. Thus a fire, which is actually hot, makes wood, which is potentially hot, to be actually hot, so moving and altering it. Now it is impossible for the same thing to be both actual and potential in the same respect, although it may be so in different respects. What is actually hot cannot at the same time be potentially hot, although it is potentially cold. It is therefore impossible that, in the same respect and in the same way, anything should be both mover and moved, or that it should move itself. Whatever is moved must therefore be moved by something else. If, then, that by which it is moved is itself moved, this also must be moved by something else, and this in turn by something else again. But this cannot go on for ever, since there would then be no first mover, and consequently no other mover, because secondary movers cannot move unless moved by a first mover, as a staff cannot move unless it is moved by the hand. We are therefore bound to arrive at a first mover which is not moved by anything, and all men understand that this is God.

The second way is from the nature of an efficient cause. We find that there is a sequence of efficient causes in sensible things. But we do not find that anything is the efficient cause of itself. Nor is this possible, for the thing would then be prior to itself, which is impossible. But neither can the sequence of efficient causes be infinite, for in every sequence the first efficient cause

[1] This paragraph may be compared with Aristotle's *Physics*, bk. 7, ch. 1, 242a; bk. 8, ch. 4, 254b, ch. 5, 256a. Cf. also *S. Contra Gentiles* I, ch. 13, which contains all except the third way. The third way is contained with slight variations in *ibid.* I, ch. 15, II, ch. 15.

is the cause of an intermediate cause, and an intermediate cause is the cause of the ultimate cause, whether the intermediate causes be many, or only one. Now if a cause is removed, its effect is removed. Hence if there were no first efficient cause, there would be no ultimate cause, and no intermediate cause. But if the regress of efficient causes were infinite, there would be no first efficient cause. There would consequently be no ultimate effect, and no intermediate causes. But this is plainly false. We are therefore bound to suppose that there is a first efficient cause. And all men call this God.

The third way is from the nature of possibility and necessity. There are some things which may either exist or not exist, since some things come to be and pass away, and may therefore be or not be. Now it is impossible that all of these should exist at all times, because there is at least some time when that which may possibly not exist does not exist. Hence if all things were such that they might not exist, at some time or other there would be nothing. But if this were true there would be nothing existing now, since what does not exist cannot begin to exist, unless through something which does exist. If there had been nothing existing, it would have been impossible for anything to begin to exist, and there would now be nothing at all. But this is plainly false, and hence not all existence is merely possible. Something in things must be necessary. Now everything which is necessary either derives its necessity from elsewhere, or does not. But we cannot go on to infinity with necessary things which have a cause of their necessity, any more than with efficient causes, as we proved. We are therefore bound to suppose something necessary in itself, which does not owe its necessity to anything else, but which is the cause of the necessity of other things. And all men call this God.

The fourth way is from the degrees that occur in things, which are found to be more and less good, true, noble, and so on. Things are said to be more and less because they approximate in different degrees to that which is greatest. A thing is the more hot the more it approximates to that which is hottest. There is therefore something which is the truest, the best, and the noblest, and which is consequently the greatest in being, since that which has the greatest truth is also greatest in being, as is said in 2 *Metaph.*, text 4. Now that which most thoroughly possesses the nature of any genus is the cause of all that the genus contains. Thus fire, which is most perfectly hot, is the cause of all hot things, as is said in the same passage.

There is therefore something which is the cause of the being of all things that are, as well as of their goodness and their every perfection. This we call God.

The fifth way is from the governance of things. We see how some things, like natural bodies, work for an end even though they have no knowledge. The fact that they nearly always operate in the same way, and so as to achieve the maximum good, makes this obvious, and shows that they attain their end by design, not by chance. Now things which have no knowledge tend towards an end only through the agency of something which knows and also understands, as an arrow through an archer. There is therefore an intelligent being by whom all natural things are directed to their end. This we call God.

On the first point: as Augustine says (*Enchirid.* 11): "since God is supremely good, he would not allow any evil thing to exist in his works, were he not able by his omnipotence and goodness to bring good out of evil." God's infinite goodness is such that he permits evil things to exist, and brings good out of them.

On the second point: everything that can be attributed to nature must depend on God as its first cause, since nature works for a predetermined end through the direction of a higher agent. Similarly, whatever is due to purpose must depend on a cause higher than the reason or will of man, since these are subject to change and defect. Anything which is changeable and subject to defect must depend on some first principle which is immovable and necessary in itself, as we have shown.

Question Three

OF THE SIMPLE NATURE OF GOD

When we know that something exists, it still remains to inquire into the manner of its existence, in order to know what it is. But we cannot inquire into the manner in which God exists. We can inquire only into the manner in which he does not exist, since we cannot know of God what he is, but only what he is not. We must therefore consider how God does not exist, how we know him, and how we name him. The manner in which God does not exist can be shown by excluding what is incompatible with God, such as composition, movement, and the like. We shall therefore inquire into the simple nature of God which repels composition. We shall also inquire into the divine perfection, since the simple natures of corporeal things are imperfect, having parts.

Eight questions are asked concerning the simple nature of God. 1. Whether God is a body. 2. Whether there is composition of form and matter in God. 3. Whether there is composition of the quiddity, essence, or nature of God, and God as subject. 4. Whether there is composition of essence and existence in God. 5. Or of genus and difference. 6. Or of substance and attribute. 7. Whether God is composite in any way, or altogether simple. 8. Whether God enters into composition with other things.

Article One

WHETHER GOD IS A BODY

We proceed to the first article thus:

1. It seems that God is a body. For what has three dimensions is a body, and sacred Scripture attributes three dimensions to God, as in Job 11:8–9: "It is as high as heaven; what canst thou do? deeper than hell; what canst thou know? The measure thereof is longer than the earth, and broader than the sea." God is therefore a body.

2. Again, everything that has figure is a body, since figure is a mode of quantity. Now it seems that God has figure, since it is said in Gen. 1:26: "Let us make man in our image, after our likeness," and image means figure, according to Heb. 1:3: "Who being the brightness of his glory, and the express image [1] of his person. . . ." God is therefore a body.

3. Again, every thing that has bodily parts is a body, and Scripture attributes bodily parts to God, as in Job 40:9: "Hast thou an arm like God?" and in Ps. 34:15: "The eyes of the Lord are upon the righteous," and in Ps. 118:16: "The right hand of the Lord doeth valiantly." God is therefore a body.

4. Again, there cannot be position without a body, and scriptural sayings about God imply position. It is said in Isa. 6:1: "I saw also the Lord sitting upon a throne," and in Isa. 3:13: "The Lord standeth to judge the people." God is therefore a body.

5. Again, only a body or something which has a body can be a local *terminus a quo* or *ad quem*, and Scripture speaks of God as

---

[1] Migne: ". . . and the figure of his substance."

a *terminus ad quem* in Ps. 34:5: "They looked unto him, and were lightened," and as a *terminus a quo* in Jer. 17:13: "they that depart from me shall be written in the earth." God is therefore a body.

On the other hand: it is said in John 4:24: "God is a spirit."

I answer: God is certainly not a body. This can be proved in three ways. First, particular examples make it plain that no body moves unless it is moved. But it was shown in Q. 2, Art. 3, that God is the unmoved first mover. This proves that God is not a body. Secondly, the first being must be actual, and in no sense potential. Potentiality precedes actuality within any one thing which passes from potentiality to actuality, but actuality is prior to potentiality absolutely, since the potential can become actual only through something which is actual. Now it was shown in Q. 2, Art. 3, that God is the first being. It is therefore impossible that there should be anything potential in him. But every body is potential, since it is continuous, and consequently infinitely divisible. It is therefore impossible that God should be a body. Thirdly, it is clear from Q. 2, Art. 3, that God is the noblest being. Now a body cannot possibly be the noblest being, since it can be either alive or lifeless. A live body is obviously nobler than a lifeless one. But a live body is not alive because it is a body, otherwise all bodies would be alive. It therefore owes its life to something else, as our own bodies owe their life to the soul, and that which gives life to the body is nobler than the body. It is therefore impossible that God should be a body.

On the first point: as was said in Q. 1, Art. 9, sacred Scripture records spiritual and divine things for us in the similitude of corporeal things. The ascription of three dimensions to God denotes the extent of his power, by the simile of physical quantity. His power to know hidden things is denoted by depth, the surpassing excellence of his power by height, his everlasting being by length, and the love which he bears to all things by breadth. Or as Dionysius says: "The depth of God means his incomprehensible essence, the length the power which permeates all things, the breadth the extension of God over all things, in the sense that all things are under his protection" (9 *Div. Nom.*, lect. 3).

On the second point: it is not in respect of the body that man is said to be the image of God, but because he excels the other animals. Thus after saying: "let us make man in our image, after our likeness," Gen. 1:26 adds: "and let them have dominion over the fish of the sea." For man excels all animals in reason and understanding, and is made in the image of God in respect of them. But these are incorporeal.

On the third point: Scripture attributes bodily parts to God metaphorically, in respect of his actions. The function of the eye being to see, the mention of the eye of God denotes his power to see intellectually, not sensibly. Similarly with the other parts mentioned.

On the fourth point: anything attributed to God which implies position is purely metaphorical. Sitting denotes his unchangeableness and his authority. Standing denotes his power to overcome whatever opposes him.

On the fifth point: since God is everywhere, we do not approach him by physical steps, but by the feelings of the mind. We also depart from him in this way. Approach and departure denote spiritual feelings by the metaphor of movement in space.

Article Two

WHETHER THERE IS COMPOSITION OF FORM AND MATTER IN GOD

We proceed to the second article thus:

1. It appears that there is composition of form and matter in God. Anything which has a soul is composed of matter and form, since soul is the form of body. Scripture attributes a soul to God, saying in the person of God: "Now the just shall live by faith: but if any man draw back, my soul shall have no pleasure in him" (Heb. 10:38). Hence God is composed of matter and form.

2. Again, according to 1 *De Anima*, texts 12, 14, 15, anger, joy, and the like are passions of the composite. Scripture ascribes such passions to God in Ps. 106:40: "Therefore was the wrath of God kindled against his people." Hence God is composed of matter and form.

3. Again, matter is the principle of individuation. Now God must be an individual, since he is not predicated of many. Hence God is composed of matter and form.

On the other hand: anything composed of matter and form is a body, since the primary quality of matter is quantitative extention. But it was shown in the preceding article that God is not a body. It follows that God is not composed of matter and form.

I answer: there cannot possibly be matter in God. In the first

place, matter is characterized by potentiality, and it has been
shown that God is pure act, without any potentiality (Q. 2,
Art. 3). It is therefore impossible that God should be composed
of matter and form. Secondly, anything composed of matter
and form owes its goodness to its form. It must therefore be
good through participation, its matter participating in its
form. But the first and best good, which is God, is not good
by participation, since good which belongs essentially is better
than good which is participated. It is therefore impossible that
God should be composed of matter and form. Thirdly, every
agent acts by means of its form, and the manner in which a
thing is an agent depends on how it is related to its form.
Therefore that which is first, and an agent in its own right, must
be a form primarily and by means of itself. Now God is the first
agent, since he is the first efficient cause, as was shown in Q. 2,
Art. 3. God is therefore his own form through his essence, and
not a composition of form and matter.

On the first point: a soul is attributed to God metaphorically,
in order to denote action, since it is by the soul that we will.
What is pleasing to God's will is thus said to be pleasing to his
soul.

On the second point: such things as anger are attributed to
God metaphorically, in order to denote his effects, since an
angry man punishes. Anger metaphorically signifies divine
punishment.

On the third point: forms which can be received by matter
are made individual by the matter of a primary underlying subject, which cannot be in another subject, although the form itself may be in many subjects unless some obstacle intervenes.
But a form which cannot be received by matter, and which
subsists by itself, is individual for the very reason that it cannot
be received by anything else. God is such a form. It does not
then follow that there is matter in God.

Article Three

WHETHER GOD IS THE SAME AS HIS ESSENCE, OR NATURE

We proceed to the third article thus:

1. It seems that God is not the same as his essence, or nature.
Nothing can be in itself. But the essence or nature of God,
which is his divinity, is said to be in God. God cannot then be
the same as his essence or nature.

2. Again, an effect is similar to its cause, since every agent

acts to produce its own likeness. Now with creatures, a subject is not the same as its essence. A man, for example, is not the same as his humanity. Neither then is God the same as his Divinity.

On the other hand: in John 14:6 it is clearly said that God is not merely living, but life: "I am the way, and the truth, and the life." Thus Divinity is to God as is life to one who lives. God is therefore Divinity itself.

I answer: God is the same as his essence, or nature. In order to understand this, we must realize that the essence or nature is bound to be different from the underlying subject where things are composed of matter and form, because their essence or nature comprises only what is included in their definition.[1] Thus humanity comprises what is included in the definition of man, or that by which a man is a man, and means that by which a man is a man. But the particular matter of the subject, and all the accidents which it possesses as an individual, are not included in the definition of the species. This flesh, these bones, whether the subject be white or black, and such things, are not included in the definition of man. Hence this flesh, these bones, and the accidents which distinguish this matter as individual are not included in the humanity, even though they are included in the man. The subject which is a man, therefore, included something which humanity does not include, so that a man is not precisely the same as his humanity. Humanity denotes the formal part of a man, since the defining principles are related to the individuating matter as its form. But where things are not composed of matter and form, and where individuation is not due to individual matter, that is, to this particular matter, but where forms individualize themselves, the forms are bound to be identical with the subsisting subjects, so that there is no difference between a subject and its nature. Now it was shown in the preceding article that God is not composed of matter and form. It follows that God must be his Divinity, and whatever else is predicated of him.

On the first point: we cannot speak of simple things except in terms of the composites by means of which we know anything. When we speak of God, therefore, we use concrete names to denote his substance, because only composite things subsist around us, and use abstract names to denote his simple nature. Hence when we say that Divinity, or life, or anything of this

[1] Cf. Aristotle's distinction between "primary substance" and "secondary" substance," in *Categories* V, §2, a$^{1-5}$.

kind is in God, the compositeness belongs to the way in which our intellect understands, and not at all to that of which we speak.

On the second point: God's effects do not resemble him perfectly, but only in so far as they are able. Their likeness to God is deficient in that they can reflect what is simple and single only by what is many. They have the compositeness which necessitates the difference between a subject and its nature.

Article Four

WHETHER ESSENCE AND EXISTENCE ARE THE SAME IN GOD

We proceed to the fourth article thus:

1. It seems that essence and existence are not the same in God. If they were the same, nothing would be added to God's existence. Now the existence to which nothing is added is the universal existence which is predicable of all things. Hence God would be the universal existence which is predicable of all things. But this is false, according to Wisdom 4:21: "they gave the incommunicable name to stones and wood." It follows that God's essence is not his existence.

2. Again, it was said in Q. 2, Arts. 2 and 3, that we can know that God exists. But we cannot know what God is. Hence God's existence is not the same as what he is, or his quiddity, or nature.

On the other hand: Hilary says: "Existence is not an accident in God, but subsisting truth" (*De Trin.* 7).

I answer: God not only is his essence, as was shown in Art. 3, but also is his existence. This can be shown in many ways. First, whatever a thing possesses in addition to its essence must either be caused by the principles of its essence, as is a property which is consequential to a species, such as laughing, which is consequential to "man" and caused by the essential principles of his species; or it must be caused by something external, as heat in water is caused by a fire. Hence when a thing's existence is different from its essence, its existence must either be caused by the principles of its essence, or be caused by something external. Now a thing's existence cannot possibly be caused by the principles of its own essence alone, since nothing can be the sufficient cause of its own existence, if its existence is caused. Hence anything whose existence is different from its essence must be caused by something other than itself. But we cannot say this of God, who is defined as the first efficient cause. It is therefore impossible that God's existence should be different from his essence.

Secondly, existence is the actuality of every form, or nature. That is, we do not say that goodness or humanity, for example, are actual, unless we mean that they exist. Hence where essence and existence are different, existence must be related to essence as the actual to the potential. But it was shown in Q.2, Art. 3, that there is nothing potential in God. It follows that essence and existence are not different in God. God's essence, therefore, is his existence.

Thirdly, anything which has existence without being existence exists through participation, just as anything which is alight but is not itself fire is alight through participation. Now we proved in Art. 3 that God is his essence. It follows that, if God were not his own existence, he would exist not through his essence but through participation. But God would not then be the first being, which is an absurd thing to say. God is therefore his own existence, as well as his own essence.

On the first point: "that to which nothing is added" may mean two things. It may mean that a thing's nature precludes the addition of something. The nature of an irrational animal, for example, excludes reason. But it may also mean that a nature does not necessitate the addition of something. Thus the common nature of animal does not have reason added to it, because it does not necessitate the addition of reason, though neither does it exclude reason. It is in the first sense that nothing is added to God's existence, and in the second sense that nothing is added to universal existence.

On the second point: "is" may signify two things. It may signify the act of existing, or it may signify the synthesis by which the mind joins a subject to a predicate in a proposition. Now we cannot know the divine act of existing, any more than we can know the divine essence. But we do know that God "is" in the second sense, for we know that the proposition which we put together when we say "God exists" is true. We know this from his effects, as we said in Q. 2, Art. 2.

Article Five

WHETHER GOD BELONGS TO A GENUS

We proceed to the fifth article thus:

1. It seems that God does belong to a genus. For "substance" means self-subsistent being, and this is pre-eminently

applicable to God. God therefore belongs to the genus "substance."

2. Again, each thing is measured by what belongs to its own genus. Thus lengths are measured by length, and numbers by number. Now the commentator on 10 *Metaph.* says that God is the measure of all substances. God therefore belongs to the genus "substance."

On the other hand: we think of a genus as prior to what it contains. But there is nothing prior to God, whether in reality or in the understanding. Therefore God does not belong to any genus.

I answer: a thing may belong to a genus in two ways. It may belong to it absolutely and properly, as does a species which the genus contains. Or it may be reducible to a genus, as are principles and privations. Point and unity, for example, are reducible to the genus "quantity" as principles of it, while blindness, and all privation, are reducible to the genus of their habits. But God does not belong to a genus in either of these ways.

There are three proofs that God cannot be a species of any genus. First, a species is made up of a genus and a difference. Now that from which the difference which constitutes a species is derived is always related to that from which the genus is derived as the actual to the potential. Thus "animal" is concretely derived from "sensitive nature," a thing being called animal because it has a sensitive nature, while "the rational" is derived from "intellectual nature," since the rational is that which has an intellectual nature. The intellectual is then related to the sensitive as the actual to the potential. This is likewise clear in other things. It is therefore impossible that God should belong to a genus as a species of it, since in God there is no adjunction of the potential with the actual.

Secondly, it was proved in the preceding article that God's existence is his essence. Hence if God belonged to any genus, this genus would have to be "being," since a genus indicates the essence of a thing, and is predicated because of what the thing is. But the philosopher proves that "being" cannot be the genus of anything (3 *Metaph.*, text 10), since every genus includes differences which are external to its essence, and there are no differences external to being, since "not-being" cannot be a difference. It follows from this that God cannot belong to a genus.

Thirdly, all things which belong to one genus agree in their "what," or the essence of their genus, which is predicated of them because of what they are. But they differ in point of existence, since the existence of a man is not the same as that of a horse, nor the existence of one man the same as that of another. Existence and essence are thus bound to be different in anything which belongs to a genus. But they are not different in God, as we proved in the preceding article. This makes it plain that God does not belong to a genus as a species.

It is clear from the foregoing that God has neither genus nor differences, and that there is no definition of God, nor any way of demonstrating him except through his effects. For definition is by means of genus and difference, and definition is the means of demonstration.

That God does not belong to a genus as a principle reducible to it is obvious from the fact that a principle which is reducible to a genus does not extend beyond that genus. The point, for example, is the principle of continuous quantity only, and the unit of discrete quantity only. But God is the ground of all existence, as we shall prove in Q. 44, Art. 1. Consequently, he is not contained in any genus as a principle.

On the first point: the term "substance" signifies more than self-subsistent being, for we have shown above that "being" cannot by itself be a genus. It signifies an essence which has the ability to exist, i.e., which can exist through itself, but whose existence is not identical with its essence. This makes it plain that God does not belong to the genus "substance."

On the second point: this objection argues from the measure of proportion. God is not in this way the measure of anything. He is said to be the measure of all things because all things have existence in so far as they are like him.

Article Six

WHETHER THERE IS ANY ACCIDENT IN GOD

We proceed to the sixth article thus:

1. It appears that there are some accidents in God. It is said in 1 *Physics*, texts 27, 30, that a substance can never be an accident. This means that what occurs as accident in one thing cannot be the substance of another, and is used to prove that heat is not the formal substance of fire, since heat occurs as an accident of other things. Now wisdom, virtue, and the like occur as accidents in ourselves, and are also ascribed to God. They must therefore be in God as accidents.

2. Again, in every genus there is something which is first, and there are many genera of accidents. Hence if the principles of these genera are not in God, there will be many things which are first, and which are not in God. But this is impossible.

On the other hand: every accident is in a subject. But God cannot be a subject, since "an absolute form cannot be a subject," as Boethius says (*De Trin.*). There cannot then be any accident in God.

I answer: what we have already said makes it quite clear that there cannot be any accident in God. In the first place, a subject is related to its accident as the potential to the actual, and is actualized through its accident in a particular way. But potentiality is altogether alien to God, as we explained in Q. 2, Art. 3. In the second place, God is his existence. But as Boethius says (*Lib. de Hebd.*), existence itself cannot be augmented by the addition of anything else, although that which is something may have something else added to it. A thing which is hot may have something other than heat added to it, such as whiteness, but heat itself cannot contain anything other than heat. In the third place, what exists through itself is prior to what exists accidentally. But God is altogether primary being, and therefore nothing in him can exist accidentally. Nor can there be in God any inherent accident, such as the accident of laughing in man. Accidents of this kind are caused by the principles of the subject, whereas nothing in God is caused, since God is the first cause. There is therefore no accident in God.

On the first point: virtue and wisdom are not predicated of God and of ourselves univocally, as will be shown (Q. 13, Art. 5). It does not then follow that they are accidents in God as they are in us.

On the second point: principles of accidents are reducible to prior principles of substance because substances are prior to their accidents. God is not the primary content of the genus "substance." He is nevertheless first in relation to all being, and outside every genus.

Article Seven

WHETHER GOD IS ALTOGETHER SIMPLE

We proceed to the seventh article thus:

1. It seems that God is not altogether simple. God's creatures resemble him. Thus all things have being from God the first being, and all things are good since he is the first good.

Now nothing that God creates is altogether simple. Therefore God is not altogether simple.

2. Again, whatever is better must be ascribed to God. Now in things around us, what is composite is better than what is simple. Composite bodies, for example, are better than their elements, and animals are better than their parts. Hence we should not say that God is altogether simple.

On the other hand, Augustine says: "God is absolutely and altogether simple" (4 *De Trin.* 6, 7).

I answer: it can be shown in many ways that God is altogether simple. In the first place, this can be proved from what we have already said. There is no combination of quantitative parts in God, since he is not a body. Neither is there in God any composition of form and matter. Neither is there any difference between God's nature and God as subject, nor between his essence and his existence. Neither is there in God any composition of genus and difference. It is thus clear that God is in no way composite, but altogether simple. Secondly, everything that is composite is consequential to its elements, and dependent on them. But God is the first being, as we proved in Q. 2, Art. 3. Thirdly, everything that is composite has a cause, since elements which are naturally separate cannot be combined into one unless some cause unites them. But we proved in the same article that God has no cause, since he is the first efficient cause. Fourthly, everything that is composite must contain both potentiality and actuality. Either one part is the actuality of another, or at least all parts are as it were the potentiality of the whole. But this is not true of God. Fifthly, everything that is composite is more than any of its parts. This is obvious when the parts are dissimilar. No part of a man is a man, and no part of a foot is a foot. But even when the parts are similar, although something can be affirmed equally of the whole and of every part of it, since a part of air is air, and a part of water is water, we can still say something about the whole which cannot be said of any part. For if the whole water measures two cubits, no part of it does so. In this way, there is something other than itself in everything that is composite. We may also say that there is something other than itself in everything that has a form. A thing that is white, for example, may contain something that is not white. But a form itself cannot contain anything other than itself. Now God is pure form, or rather, pure being. He cannot then be composite in any way. Hilary argues in somewhat the same fashion when he says: "God, who is power, is not compounded from what is weak, nor is he who is light composed of things of darkness" (*De Trin.* 7).

On the first point: God's creatures resemble him as effects resemble their first cause. But an effect is naturally composite in some way, since its existence is at least different from its essence, as we shall show in Q. 4, Art. 3.

On the second point: composite things around us are better than simple things because the perfection of creaturely good is to be found not in one simple thing, but in many. The perfection of divine goodness, on the other hand, is to be found in what is single and simple, as we shall prove in Q. 4, Art. 1, and in Q. 6, Art. 2.

Article Eight

WHETHER GOD ENTERS INTO THE COMPOSITION OF
OTHER THINGS

We proceed to the eighth article thus:

1. It seems that God enters into the composition of other things. For Dionysius says (4 *Coel. Hier.*): "the being of all things, which transcends existence, is Divinity." The being of all things enters into the composition of all things. Hence God enters into the composition of other things.

2. Again, God is a form. For Augustine says: "The word of God, which is God, is a form not formed" (*De Verb. Dom.*, *Sermo* 33). Now a form is part of a composite. Therefore God is part of a composite.

3. Again, all things which exist, and which are in no wise different, are identical. Now God and primary matter exist, and are in no wise different. They are therefore fundamentally identical. But primary matter enters into the composition of things. Hence God also enters into their composition. The minor premise is proved as follows. Whatever things differ, differ by reason of certain differences, and must accordingly be composite. But God and primary matter are not composite in any way. Hence they do not differ in any way.

On the other hand: Dionysius says: "there is neither contact nor communion with God in the intermingling of parts" (2 *Div. Nom.*, lect. 3). It is also said in the Book on Causes [1] (*Inter-*

---

[1] A translation from Proclus, containing references to the Neoplatonic distinction between the Aristoteleian categories which the Neoplatonists regarded as derivative, and the more universal concepts "ens," "unum,"

pretation of Aristotle, prop. 6): "the first cause rules all things without mingling with them."

I answer: there have been three errors on this question. Augustine writes of some who said that God is a world-soul (7 *De Civ. Dei.* 6), and it is due to this that others have thought God to be the soul of the first heaven. Others again have thought that God is the formal principle of all things, as the Almaricians are said to have believed. The third error was that of David of Dinant, who very foolishly supposed that God was primary matter. But it is obvious that all these notions are false, and that God cannot possibly enter into the composition of other things in any way, either as their formal or as their material principle. In the first place, God is the first efficient cause, as we proved in Q. 2, Art. 3. Now an efficient cause is not numerically one with the thing made, but one with it in kind only. One man begets another man. The matter is neither numerically one with the efficient cause nor similar to it in kind, since it is potential, while the efficient cause is actual. Secondly, God is the first efficient cause, and therefore acts primarily and through himself. Now that which enters into the composition of something does not act primarily and through itself. Rather does the thing composed do so. Thus it is not the hand that acts, but the man who acts by means of it, and it is the fire that heats by means of heat. It follows that God cannot be a part of any composite thing. Thirdly, no part of any composite thing can be the first of all beings, not even its matter or its form, which are the fundamental parts of composite things. Matter is potential, and what is potential is subsequent to what is absolute and actual, as we explained in the first article. The form which is part of a composite thing is a participated form, and this is no less subsequent to what exists through its essence than is the thing which participates. Fire in that which is ignited, for example, is subsequent to what exists through its essence. Now we have proved in Q. 2, Art. 3 that God is the absolute first being.

On the first point: Divinity is said to be the being of all things as their efficient cause and example, not as their essence.

"verum," and "bonum." Aquinas gives a theological application to the latter, "ens" pertaining to essence, and the others to the Persons of the Father, Son, and Holy Spirit respectively. Prof. A. E. Taylor considered that Prantl was in error in describing the work as of Arabian origin, in *Geschichte der Logic im Abendlande* III, pp. 114, 244–245 (quoted from N. Kemp Smith, *Commentary on Kant's Critique of Pure Reason,* p. 73).

On the second point: the word of God is the exemplary form of a composite thing, not the form which is a part of it.[1]

On the third point: simple things do not differ from each other by reason of differences, which is the way in which composite things differ. A man and a horse, for example, differ by reason of the difference between the rational and the irrational. But these differences do not themselves differ by reason of further differences. Properly speaking, we ought to say that differences are contrary, rather than different. As the philosopher says (10 *Metaph.*, texts 24–25): "Contrariety is predicated absolutely, whereas things which differ differ in some way." Properly speaking, then, God and primary matter do not differ. But they are contrary to each other. It does not then follow that they are identical.

Question Four

THE PERFECTION OF GOD

After considering the simple nature of God, we must now consider the perfection of God, concerning which there are three questions. 1. Whether God is perfect. 2. Whether God is perfect universally, comprehending within himself the perfections of all things. 3. Whether creatures can be said to be like God.

Article One

WHETHER GOD IS PERFECT

We proceed to the first article thus:

1. It seems that perfection is not applicable to God. To be perfect means to be made complete, and we cannot say that God is made. Neither then can we say that God is perfect.

2. Again, God is the first beginning of things. Now the beginnings of things appear to be imperfect. The beginning of an animal, or of a plant, for example, is but a seed. It follows that God is imperfect.

---

[1] On Augustine's view, known as "Exemplarism," forms are ideas in the mind of God—perfect representations of what things ought to be. They are neither constitutive of what things actually are, nor operative in supporting their existence.

3. Again, it was proved in Q. 3, Art. 4, that God's essence is the same as his existence. But God's existence appears to be very imperfect. It is entirely universal, and therefore receives all things as additional to itself. Hence God is imperfect.

On the other hand: it is said in Matt. 5:48: "Be ye therefore perfect, even as your Father which is in heaven is perfect."

I answer: Aristotle tells us that of the ancient philosophers, the Pythagoreans and Leucippus did not ascribe what is best and most perfect to their first principle (12 *Metaph.*, text 40). This was because they believed the first principle to be purely material. A material first principle is very imperfect. Matter, as matter, is potential, and a material first principle is bound to be supremely potential, and therefore exceedingly imperfect. Now God is the first principle, but he is not material. He is defined as efficient cause, and must accordingly be supremely perfect. Just as matter as such is potential, so an agent as such is actual. The first active principle is therefore bound to be superlatively actual, and consequently superlatively perfect. For we say that a thing is perfect in so far as it is actual, and we call a thing perfect when it lacks nothing of its perfection.

On the first point: Gregory says (5 *Moral.* 26, 29): "Let us declare the glory of God by lisping as we can. We cannot rightly say that he is perfect, since he is not made." But since a thing which "becomes" is said to be perfect when it has passed from potentiality to actuality, we borrow the word "perfect" to signify anything which is not lacking in actuality, whether this is achieved through its being made perfect, or otherwise.

On the second point: the material beginning of things around us is imperfect. But it cannot be first absolutely, because it must be derived from something else which is perfect. Even though the seed be the beginning of the animal which develops from it, there is bound to be a previous animal, or plant, from which it came. Something actual must precede the potential, since only what is actual can enable the potential to become actual.

On the third point: existence itself is the most perfect of all things, since it is the actuality of all things. Nothing is actual save in so far as it exists. Existence itself is therefore the actuality of everything, even of forms. It is not a recipient which receives other things. Rather is it that which other things receive. When I speak of the existence of a man, or of a horse, or of anything else, I think of existence as something formal which is received, not as something which can receive existence.

Article Two

WHETHER THE PERFECTIONS OF ALL THINGS ARE IN GOD

We proceed to the second article thus:

1. It seems that the perfections of all things are not in God. For it was proved in Q. 3, Art. 7, that God is simple, whereas the perfections of things are many and diverse. The perfections of all things cannot then be in God.

2. Again, contraries cannot occur in the same thing. Now the perfections of things are contrary to one another. Each thing is made perfect by the difference which belongs to its own species, and the differences which divide a genus and constitute its species are contrary to one another. But if contraries cannot be in the same thing, it seems that the perfections of all things cannot be in God.

3. Again, one who lives is more perfect than one who exists, and one who is wise is more perfect than one who lives. Thus to live is more perfect than to exist, and to be wise is more perfect than to live. Now God's essence is his existence. His essence cannot then contain within itself the perfection of life, or of wisdom, or any similar perfection.

On the other hand: Dionysius says: "God precontains all existence in one" (5 *Div. Nom.*, lect. 3).

I answer: the perfections of all things are in God. God is said to be perfect in every way because he lacks no excellence discoverable in any genus, as the commentator on 5 *Metaph.*, text 21, remarks. We may see this in two ways. First, any perfection which occurs in an effect must occur in its efficient cause, either in the same mode if the agent be univocal, as in the case of a man who begets a man, or in a more eminent way if the agent be equivocal, as in the case of the sun which contains the likenesses of the things generated by its power. For it is plain that an effect virtually pre-exists in its active cause. But whereas a thing pre-exists in a less perfect way in the potentiality of its material cause, since matter as such is imperfect, it pre-exists in its active cause in a more perfect way, not in a less perfect way, since an agent, as such, is perfect. Now God is the first efficient cause of all things. The perfections of all things must therefore pre-exist in God in a more eminent way. Dionysius argues in similar fashion when he says: "God is not one thing without being another, but is all things, as their cause" (5 *Div. Nom.*, lect. 2). Secondly, it was shown in Q. 3,

Art. 4, that God is existence which subsists through itself. This proves that he must contain within himself the whole perfection of existence. For it is clear that if a thing which is hot does not possess the whole perfection of heat, this is because it does not participate in heat which is perfect in nature. If the heat were such as to subsist through itself, the thing which is hot would not lack any of the power of heat. Now God is existence which subsists through itself. He cannot then lack any perfection of existence. Dionysius argues in similar fashion when he says: "God exists not in a certain way, but absolutely, comprehensively precontaining the whole in unity within Himself" (5 *Div. Nom.*, lect. 5), to which he adds: "He is the existence of things which subsist."

On the first point: as Dionysius says (5 *Div. Nom.*, lect. 2): "Just as the sun illumines things in a single way, and thereby contains in a single form within itself the substances of sensible things, and many different qualities, so and all the more must all things pre-exist as a natural unity in the cause of all things." In this way, things which are in themselves diverse and contrary pre-exist as one in God, without destroying the unity of God. The reply to the second point is then obvious.

On the third point: as the same Dionysius says in the same passage, existence itself is more perfect than life, and life more perfect than wisdom, if we consider them as distinct ideas. But one who lives is nevertheless more perfect than one who merely exists, since one who lives also exists, while one who is wise both lives and exists. Accordingly, although to exist does not include to live and to be wise, since one who participates in existence need not participate in every mode of existence, God's existence includes life and wisdom, since he who is self-subsistent existence itself cannot lack any perfection of existence.

Article Three

WHETHER ANY CREATURE CAN BE LIKE GOD

We proceed to the third article thus:

1. It seems that no creature can be like God. It is said in Ps. 86:8: "Among the gods there is none like unto thee, O Lord." Now it is the most excellent of all the creatures that are said to be gods by participation. Still less, then, can other creatures be said to be like God.

2. Again, likeness implies that things can be compared. But there is no comparing things which belong to different genera,

and consequently no likeness between them. We do not say, for example, that sweetness is like whiteness. Now no creature belongs to the same genus with God, since God does not belong to any genus, as was proved in Q. 3, Art. 5. It follows that no creature can be like God.

3. Again, we say that things are alike when they have the same form. But nothing has the same form as God, since nothing has an essence identical with its existence, save God alone. It follows that no creature can be like God.

4. Again, the likeness between similar things is reciprocal, since like is like to like. Hence if any creature were like God, God would also be like a creature. But this is contrary to the words of Isa. 40:18: "To whom then will ye liken God?"

On the other hand: it is said in Gen. 1:26: "Let us make man in our image, after our likeness," and in I John 3:2: "when he shall appear, we shall be like him."

I answer: there are many kinds of likeness, since likeness depends on agreement or similarity of form, and there are many kinds of similarity of form. Some things are said to be like because they agree in possessing a form which is similar both in nature and in measure. They are then said to be not only like, but equal in their likeness. Thus two things which are equally white are said to be alike in whiteness. This is perfect likeness. Again, some things are said to be alike because they agree in possessing a form of the same nature, but not in the same measure, being more and less. Thus we say that one white thing is like another which is whiter. This is imperfect likeness. Thirdly, some things are said to be alike because they agree in possessing the same form, but not according to the same nature. This is apparent in the case of agents which are not univocal. Every agent, as such, acts to produce what is like itself. It makes each thing after its own form, and hence the likeness of its form is bound to be in its effect. Consequently, if the agent belongs to the same species as its effect, that which makes and that which is made will have the same specific nature. Thus it is when a man begets a man. But if the agent does not belong to the same species, there will be a likeness, but not a likeness of specific nature. For example, things generated by the power of the sun have a certain likeness to the sun, although it is the likeness of genus, not of specific form. Now if there be an agent which does not belong to any genus, its effect will reflect its likeness all the more remotely. It will not reflect the likeness of the form of the agent by possessing the same specific nature, nor by having the same genus, but by some kind of analogy, since existence itself is common to all things. The things which God has made are like him in this way. In so far as they are beings, they are like the first and universal principle of all being.

On the first point: according to Dionysius, sacred Scripture does not deny that there is likeness when it says that something is not like God. For "the same things are like God and unlike him. They are like him, since they imitate him who cannot be imitated perfectly, so far as he can be imitated; they are unlike him, since they fall short of their cause" (9 *Div. Nom.*, lect. 3). They fall short not only qualitatively and quantitatively, as one white thing falls short of another which is whiter, but because they have no community either of specific nature or of genus.

On the second point: God is not related to creatures as things of different genera are related. He is related to them as that which is outside every genus, and the principle of every genus.

On the third point: when we say that a creature is like God, we do not mean that it has the same form according to genus and species. We speak by analogy, since God exists through his essence, whereas other things exist through participation.

On the fourth point: when we affirm that a creature is like God, we are not in any way compelled to say that God is like a creature. As Dionysius says (9 *Div. Nom.*, lect. 3), and as we shall ourselves affirm in Q. 42, Art. 1, there may be mutual likeness between two things of the same order, but not between a cause and its effect. Hence we say that an effigy is like a man, but not that a man is like his effigy. Similarly, we can in a sense say that a creature is like God, but not that God is like a creature.

APPENDIX TO Q. 4, ART. 3

Q. 12, Art. 12. (Whether, in this life, God can be known through natural reason.)

Our natural knowledge begins from sense. It can therefore extend so far as it can be led by sensible things. But our intellect cannot in this way attain insight into the divine essence. Sensible things are indeed effects of God, but they are not proportionate to the power of their cause, and for this reason the whole power of God cannot be known from them. Neither, consequently, can his essence be seen. But since effects depend on their cause, sensible things can lead us to know that God exists, and to know what is bound to be attributable to him as the first cause of all things, and as transcending all his effects. In

this way we know that God is related to creatures as the cause of them all; that he differs from creatures, since he is none of the things caused by him; and that creatures are separated from God because God transcends them, not because of any defect in God.
Q. 13, Art. 1. (Whether any name is applicable to God.)

According to the philosopher (1 *De Interpretatione,* cap. 1), words are the signs of concepts, and concepts are copies of things. It is thus plain that words refer to things through the medium of concepts. We can therefore name things in so far as we can understand them. Now it was proved in Q. 12, Art. 2, that in this life we cannot see God in his essence. But we do know God through creatures, as their principle, in terms of the excelling and the remote. We can accordingly apply to God names which are derived from creatures. Such a name, however, does not express what the divine essence is in itself, as "man" by its own meaning expresses the very essence of a man. The name "man" signifies the definition which explains the essence of a man, since it stands for the definition.

Q. 13, Art. 5. (Whether the things which are affirmed of God and also of creatures are affirmed of them univocally.)

It is impossible for anything to be predicated of God and of creatures univocally, because an effect which is not proportionate to the power of its active cause resembles its cause in an inadequate way. It does not have the same nature. What is separated and multiple in the effects is simple in the cause, in which it exists in a single mode. The sun, for example, produces many and various forms in inferior things, yet its power by which it does so is one. Similarly, the many perfections which exist separately in created things all pre-exist as a simple unity in God. Thus any name given to a perfection of a creature indicates a perfection which is distinct from its other perfections. When we call a man wise, for example, we name a perfection which is distinct from his essence as a man, and distinct from his power and from his existence. But when we apply this same name to God, we do not mean to signify anything distinct from his essence, power, or existence. Accordingly, when the name "wise" is applied to a man, it circumscribes and comprehends what it signifies. But when it is applied to God, it leaves what it signifies uncomprehended, and beyond its power to denote. It is thus plain that the name "wise" is not applied to God and to a man with the same meaning. This is true of other names also. No name is applied univocally to God and to creatures.

Yet neither are such names ascribed merely equivocally, as some have said. If they were, nothing could be known or proved of God at all. We should always fall into the fallacy of equivocation. But this is contrary to what the philosopher says in 8 *Physics* and in 12 *Metaph.*, where he demonstrates many things about God. It is contrary also to Rom. 1:20: "the invisible things of him are clearly seen, being understood by the things that are made." We must therefore say that it is by way of analogy, that is, according to a relation of proportion, that such names are ascribed to God as well as to creatures. There are two ways of applying a name analogously. First, when many things are related to one thing. Thus "healthy" is applied both to medicine and to urine, because these both relate to the health of an animal, one being the sign of it and the other the cause of it. Secondly, when the one thing is related to the other. Thus "healthy" is applied both to medicine and to an animal, because medicine is the cause of health in an animal. Now it is in this second analogous way that some names are ascribed both to God and to creatures, and such names are neither purely equivocal nor purely univocal. As we said in Art. 1., it is only from what we know of creatures that we can ascribe names to God. But when we ascribe any one name to God as well as to creatures, we do so in accordance with the relation in which creatures stand to God as their principle and cause, in whom the perfection of all things pre-exist in an eminent way. This common ascription is midway between merely equivocal and purely univocal ascription. There is no one nature common to what is ascribed, as there is when things are ascribed univocally. Yet neither are the things ascribed entirely different, as they are when ascribed equivocally. A name ascribed in different senses by analogy signifies different relations to one and the same thing, as "healthy" signifies the sign of an animal's health when ascribed to urine, and the cause of its health when ascribed to medicine.

Question Twenty

THE LOVE OF GOD

There are four questions concerning the love of God. 1. Whether there is love in God. 2. Whether God loves all things. 3. Whether he loves one thing more than another. 4. Whether God loves better things the more.

Article One

WHETHER THERE IS LOVE IN GOD

We proceed to the first article thus:

1. It seems that love is not in God. For there is no passion in God, and love is a passion. It follows that love is not in God.

2. Again, love, anger, sadness, and the like are condivided.[1] But sadness and anger are not attributed to God otherwise than metaphorically. Neither, therefore, is love.

3. Again, Dionysius says (4 *Div. Nom*, lect. 12): "Love is a power which unites and binds." But there is no place for this in God, since God is simple. It follows that love is not in God.

On the other hand: it is said in I John 4:16: "God is love."

I answer: we are bound to say that there is love in God, because the first movement of the will, and indeed of any appetitive power, is love. An act of will or of any appetitive power seeks both good and evil as its proper object, but good is the object of will or appetite more fundamentally and essentially. Evil is its object secondarily and derivatively, that is, in so far as it is opposed to good. Hence actions of will or appetite which refer to good are bound to be naturally prior to those which refer to evil, as joy is prior to sadness, and love prior to hate. Again, that which is more universal is naturally prior. Thus the intellect is related to universal truth before it is related to any particular truths. Now some actions of will and appetite refer to the good under some special circumstance. Joy and delight, for example, refer to good which is present and possessed, while desire and hope refer to good which is not yet possessed. Love, on the other hand, refers to the good universally, whether it be possessed or not possessed, and is therefore naturally the first action of the will and of the appetite. Hence all other appetitive movements presuppose love, as their first root. No one desires anything except as a good which is loved. Neither does anyone rejoice except in a good which is loved. Neither is there hatred, except of that which is opposed to what is loved. It is likewise obvious that sadness and other such feelings depend on love as their first principle. There must therefore be love in whomsoever there is will, or appetite, since if that which is first is removed, the rest is

[1] Distinguished as separate species of one genus.

removed. Now it was proved in Q. 19, Art. 1, that there is
will in God. We are therefore bound to say that there is love
in God.

On the first point: the cognitive power moves only through
the medium of the appetitive power. Thus the notion of the
universal moves us through the notion of the particular, as is
said in 3 *De Anima*, texts 57–58. So also the intellectual appetite,
which we call the will, moves in us through the medium of the
sensitive appetite, whose action is always accompanied by some
sensible change, especially in the heart, which according to the
philosopher is the first principle of movement in animals (*De
Part. Animalium* 2, ch. 1; 3, ch. 4). It is indeed because they are
accompanied by bodily change that actions of the sensitive
appetite are called passions, and not actions of will. Accordingly, in so far as love, joy, and delight signify actions of the
sensitive appetite, they are passions. But in so far as they
signify actions of the intellectual appetite, they are not passions.
Now they signify the latter when referred to God. That is why
the philosopher says: "God rejoices by one, simple operation"
(7 *Ethics*, text *ult.*). God also loves in the same manner, without
passion.

On the second point: we must pay attention to the material
element in the passions of the sensitive appetite, namely to the
bodily change, and also to the formal aspect of an appetite. The
material element in anger is the increase of blood around the
heart, or something of the kind, while formally it is the desire
for revenge. Further, the formal aspect of some passions involves a certain imperfection. Desire, for example, involves an
unattained good. Sadness involves an evil which is endured,
as does anger also, since it presupposes sadness. Other passions,
however, such as love and joy, involve no imperfection. Now
none of these can be attributed to God in respect of their
material element, as we argued above. Nor can we attribute to
God any passion which even formally involves imperfection,
except in the metaphorical manner permissible in view of
the likeness borne by an effect. (Q. 3, Art. 2; Q. 19, Art. 2.)
But those which do not involve imperfection, such as love and
joy, are rightly attributed to God, yet as without passion, as we
have said.

On the third point: an act of love is always directed to two
things. It is directed to the good which one wills for someone,
and also to the person for whom one wills it. To love someone is
in fact to will good for him. Hence when anyone loves himself

he wills good for himself, and seeks to acquire it so far as he can. This is the reason why love is called a "uniting" power, even in God. Yet love is not composite in God, because the good which God wills for himself is not other than himself, since God is good by his own essence, as we proved in Q. 4, Arts. 1 and 3. Again, when anyone loves another and wills good for him, he substitutes this other for himself, and counts good for him as good for himself. For this reason love is called a "binding" power. It joins another to oneself, and relates oneself to him as if to oneself. In so far as God wills good to others, the love which is in God is an incomposite binding power.

Article Two

Whether God Loves all Things

We proceed to the second article thus:

1. It seems that God does not love all things. Dionysius says: "love carries the lover outside himself, in a sense transferring him to the loved one" (4 *Div. Nom.*, lect. 10). But we cannot possibly say that God is carried outside himself and transferred to other things. Neither, then, can we say that he loves what is other than himself.

2. Again, God's love is eternal. Now other things are eternal only as they exist in God. It is consequently only as they exist in himself that God loves them. But what is in God is not other than God. Hence God does not love what is other than himself.

3. Again, there are two kinds of love, namely the love of desire and the love of friendship. But God does not love irrational creatures with the love of desire, since he needs nothing besides himself. Neither does he love them with the love of friendship, since there cannot be friendship with irrational things, as the philosopher says in 8 *Ethics* 2. Hence God does not love all things.

4. Again, it is said in Ps. 5:5: "thou hatest all workers of iniquity." But hate has nothing in common with love. Hence God does not love all things.

On the other hand: it is said in Wisdom 11:25: "Thou lovest all things that are, and hatest nothing that thou hast made."

I answer: God loves all things that exist. For all things that exist are good, in so far as they are. The very existence of anything whatsoever is a good, and so is any perfection of it. Now we proved in Q. 19, Art. 4, that God is the cause of all things.

A thing must therefore be, and be good, to the extent which God wills. It follows that God wills some good to each thing that is. Now to love is just to will good for something. Clearly, then, God loves all things that are. But God does not love as we love. Our will is not the cause of the goodness in things, but is moved by their goodness as its object. Consequently, the love by which we will good for anyone is not the cause of his goodness. On the contrary, it is his goodness, whether real or imagined, that inspires the love whereby we will both the preservation of the good which he has and the provision of the good which he lacks, and whereby we also work to this end. God's love, on the other hand, creates and infuses the goodness in things.

On the first point: the lover is carried beyond himself and transferred to the loved one in the sense that he wills good for him, and works to provide it as if for himself. Thus Dionysius says in the same passage: "in the interest of truth we must say that even God, who in his abundant loving-kindness causes all things, is carried beyond himself by his care for all that exists."

On the second point: it is only in God that creatures have existed from eternity. Yet, since they have existed in himself from eternity, God has known their proper natures from eternity, and for the same reason has also loved them from eternity. Our own knowledge of things as they are in themselves is similar. We know them through their likenesses which exist in us.

On the third point: friendship is possible only with rational creatures who can return it, and who can share in the work of life, and fare well in fortune and happiness. Benevolence, also, is properly towards rational creatures. Irrational creatures can neither love God nor share his intellectual life of happiness. Properly speaking, therefore, God does not love them with the love of friendship. But he does love them with the love of desire. For he has ordained them for rational creatures, indeed for himself—not as if he needed them, but for the sake of his loving-kindness, in as much as they are useful to us. We can desire something for others no less than for ourselves.

On the fourth point: there is nothing to prevent the same thing being loved in one respect and hated in another respect. God loves sinners in so far as they are natures, because they are, and have their being from himself. But in so far as they are sinners they fail to be, and are not. This deficiency is not from God, and they are hateful to God in respect of it.

Article Three

WHETHER GOD LOVES ALL THINGS EQUALLY

We proceed to the third article thus:

1. It seems that God loves all things equally. Wisdom 6:8 says: "He cares for all things equally." Now God's providential care for all things is due to his love for them. He therefore loves all things equally.

2. Again, God's love is his essence. But his essence does not admit of more and less. Neither, consequently, does his love. He does not, therefore, love some things more than others.

3. Again, God's knowledge and will extend to all things, in the same manner as his love. But we cannot say that God knows, or wills, some things more than others. Neither then does he love some things more than others.

On the other hand: Augustine says (*Tract. 110 in Joan.*): "God loves all that he has made. He loves rational creatures more; members of his only begotten still more; his only begotten much more."

I answer: since to love is to will good for something, there are two ways in which one thing may be loved more or less than another. First, the act of the will may be more or less intense. God does not love some things more than others in this sense, because he loves all things by the same simple act of will, which is always of the same degree. Secondly, the good which is willed for something may be more or less. We are said to love one thing more than another when we will a greater good for it, even if the will is not more intense. Now we are bound to say that God loves some things more than others in this latter sense. For we said in the preceding article that his love is the cause of the goodness in things, and hence one thing would not be better than another, if God did not love one thing more than another.

On the first point: God is said to care for all things equally because he administers all things with equal care and wisdom, not because he provides an equal good for each thing.

On the second point: this reasoning argues from the intensity of the act of will which love involves. This does belong to the divine essence. But the good which God wills for a creature does not belong to the divine essence, and there is nothing to prevent it being more or less.

On the third point: knowledge and will signify the divine

act only. Their meaning does not include any of the objects, whose diversity permits us to say that God knows and wills more and less, just as we said above concerning his love.

Article Four

WHETHER GOD ALWAYS LOVES BETTER THINGS THE MORE

We proceed to the fourth article thus:

1. It seems that God does not always love better things the more. It is obvious that Christ is better than the entire human race. Yet according to Rom. 8:32 God loved the human race more than he loved Christ. "He that spared not his only Son, but delivered him up for us all . . ." Thus God does not always love better things the more.

2. Again, an angel is better than a man, according to Ps. 8:5: "Thou hast made him a little lower than the angels." Yet God loved a man more than an angel, according to what is said in Heb. 2:16: "For verily he took not on him the nature of angels; but he took on him the seed of Abraham." Thus God does not always love better things the more.

3. Again, Peter was better than John, since he had a greater love for Christ. Christ knew this when he asked of Peter, "Simon, son of Jonas, lovest thou me more than these?" Nevertheless, Christ loved John more than Peter. In his commentary on John 20:2, ". . . the disciple whom Jesus loved," Augustine says: "John is distinguished from the other disciples by this very sign, not that Christ loved him alone, but that he loved him more than the rest." Thus God's love is not always greater towards the better.

4. Again, an innocent is better than a penitent. For in his commentary on Isa. 3:9, "they declare their sin as Sodom," Hieronymus says that penitence is like a shipwreck. But God loves a penitent more than an innocent man, since he rejoices in him the more. For it is said in Luke 15:7: "I say unto you, that likewise joy shall be in heaven over one sinner that repenteth, more than over ninety and nine just persons, which need no repentence." Thus God does not always love more that which is better.

5. Again, a just man foreknown is better than a sinner who is predestined. Now God has a greater love for the sinner who is predestined, since he wills a greater good for him, namely, eternal life. Hence God does not always love more that which is better.

On the other hand: "everything loves what is like itself," as is clear from Ecclesiasticus 13:19: "every beast loves what is like itself." Now the better anything is, the more is it like God. God therefore loves better things the more.

I answer: what we have already said compels us to say that God loves better things the more. We said in Arts. 2 and 3 that for God to love something more just means that he wills a greater good for it, and also that God's will is the cause of the goodness in things. It is therefore because God wills a greater good for them that some things are better. It follows that God has a greater love for things which are better.

On the first point: God loves Christ not only more than the entire human race, but more than the whole universe of creatures. For he willed a greater good for Christ, and gave him the name that is above every name, as true God. Nor did it in any way diminish his excellence, that God should deliver him up to die for the salvation of the human race. On the contrary, he thereby became a glorious conqueror, in keeping with Isa. 9:6: "the government shall be upon his shoulder."

On the second point: It accords with what we have said on the first point, that God should love the human nature assumed by his Word in the person of Christ more than all the angels. For this nature is better than the angels, in consequence of this union. But if we are speaking of common human nature, and comparing it in grace and glory with that of an angel, we find that they are equal. For according to Rev. 21:17 the measure of a man and the measure of an angel are the same, although some angels may be better in respect of it than some men, and some men better than some angels. Yet the natural condition of an angel is better than that of a man. Hence it was not because he loved man more that God assumed the nature of a man, but because man needed him more. A good master of a house gives something costly to a sick servant which he does not give to a healthy son.

On the third point: this puzzle about Peter and John may be solved in several ways. Augustine, in his commentary, regards this passage as mystical, and explains that the active life signified by Peter is greater in love to God than the contemplative life signified by John, since it is more alive to the sufferings of this present life, and desires more fervently to be set free and to draw near to God; but that God loves the contemplative life the more, since he preserves it longer, for it does not end with the life of the body, as does the life of action.

Others say that Peter had a greater love for Christ in his members, and that he was consequently the more loved of Christ, who for this reason commended the Church to his care; or that John had a greater love for Christ in himself, and that he was consequently the more loved of Christ, who for this reason commended his mother to his care. Others again say that it is doubtful which of them loved Christ the more with the love of charity, and doubtful which of them was destined by God's love to the greater glory of eternal life. But it is said that Peter loved the more spontaneously and with the greater fervour, and that John was the more loved, on the evidence of the signs of familiarity which Christ accorded to him and not to others, on account of his youth and purity. Others again say that Christ loved Peter the more for his more excellent gift of charity, and John the more for his greater gift of intellect. If so, Peter was the better, and was the more loved, in an absolute sense, while John was the more loved conditionally. But it seems presumptuous to judge of this matter, since it is said in Prov. 16:2: "the Lord weigheth the spirits," and none other than the Lord.

On the fourth point: penitents are related to innocents as the exceeding to the exceeded. For those who have the more grace are better, and are loved the more, whether they be innocents or penitents. But innocence is more worthy than penitence, other things being equal. The reason why God is said to rejoice in a penitent more than in an innocent man is that penitents often arise more cautious, more humble, and more fervent. Thus Gregory says, in his comments on this passage, "the leader in a battle rejoices more in one who turns from flight to press hard upon the enemy than in one who has neither fled nor fought bravely at any time." We may also say that a gift of grace is greater when bestowed on a penitent who deserves punishment than when bestowed on an innocent man who does not. A hundred marks is a greater gift when given to a pauper than when given to a king.

On the fifth point: since God is the cause of the goodness in things, we must take into account the time at which God in his benevolence intends to bestow good on one whom he loves. At the time when God in his benevolence will bestow upon him the greater good of eternal life, the predestined penitent is better than the other. But at any other time he is worse. There is also a time when he is neither good nor bad.

Question Twenty-One

THE JUSTICE AND MERCY OF GOD

After considering the Love of God, we must now consider his Justice and Mercy, concerning which there are four questions. 1. Whether there is justice in God. 2. Whether God's justice is truth. 3. Whether God is merciful. 4. Whether God's justice and mercy are present in all his works.

Article One

Whether there is Justice in God

We proceed to the first article thus:

1. It seems that justice is not in God. Justice is condivided with temperance, and temperance is not in God. Neither, therefore, is justice in God.

2. Again, he who does whatsoever pleases his will does not act from justice. Now the apostle says that God "worketh all things after the counsel of his own will" (Eph. 1:11). Justice ought not then to be attributed to him also.

3. Again, a just act consists in giving to someone his due. But God owes nothing to any man. It follows that justice is not applicable to God.

4. Again, whatever is in God belongs to his essence. But justice cannot belong to his essence, since "good pertains to an essence, and justice to an act," as Boethius says (*Lib. de Hebd.*). It follows that justice is not applicable to God.

On the other hand: it is said in Ps. 11:7: "the righteous Lord loveth righteousness."

I answer: there are two kinds of justice. One kind has to do with giving and receiving in return, with buying and selling, for example, and other kinds of transaction and exchange. The philosopher calls this commutative justice, or the justice which regulates transactions and exchanges (5 *Ethics* 4). This justice does not apply to God, for "who hath first given to him, and it shall be recompensed unto him again?" as the apostle says in Rom. 11:35. The other kind of justice has to do with distribution. It gives to each according to his worth, like a manager or steward, and is consequently called distributive justice. Now the just rule of a family, or of a nation, reveals that there is justice of this kind in its governor. So also the order of the universe, which appears in natural things as well as in matters of the will, reveals the justice which is in God. Thus Dionysius says: "we ought to see that God is truly just, in that he gives to each thing that exists whatever is due to its worth, and preserves it in its proper order and virtue" (8 *Div. Nom.*, lect. 4).

On the first point: some moral virtues are concerned with the passions. Temperance is concerned with desire, fortitude with fear and daring, meekness with anger. We cannot attribute such virtues to God, since God has no passions, as we said in Q. 19, Art. 2, and Q. 20, Art. 1. Neither has he any sensitive appetite, which these virtues would require as their subject, according to what the philosopher says in 3 *Ethics* 2. There are, however, certain moral virtues concerned with actions like giving and spending, such as justice, liberality, and magnificence. These belong to the will, not to the sensitive part of the soul. There is therefore no reason why we should not attribute them to God. But we must attribute them as they apply to the actions of God, not as they apply to the actions of a citizen. It would indeed be ridiculous to praise God for the virtues of citizenship.

On the second point: since the object of the will is some good which the intellect appreciates, God can will only what accords with his wisdom. His wisdom is like a law of justice. It ensures that his will is right and just, and that he does justly whatever he does by his will, in the same way as we do legitimately whatever we do according to the law. But while we obey the law of one who is above us, God is a law unto himself.

On the third point: to each is due what is its own. But its own is that which is ordained for it. Thus a servant belongs to his master, and this relationship cannot be reversed, since the free is the cause of itself. The word "due," therefore, denotes the relation of exigence or necessity which obtains between a thing and that for which it is ordained. Now there is a twofold order in things. There is the order whereby one created thing exists for the sake of another. Parts exist for the sake of a whole, accidents for the sake of substances, and each thing for the sake of its end. There is also the order whereby all things are ordained to God. We may accordingly discern two ways in which God acts with justice—in respect of what is due to himself, and in respect of what is due to a creature. In either way, God renders what is due. It is due to God that created things should fulfil whatever his wisdom and his will ordains, and that they should manifest his goodness. God's justice upholds his right in this respect, rendering to himself what is due to himself. It is also due to each creature that it should have what is ordained for it. It is due to a man that he should have a hand, and that other animals should serve him. Herein also God acts with justice, giving to each thing what is due according to its nature and condition, although this is due only because each thing is entitled to what God's wisdom has ordained for it in the first place. But although God renders to each thing what is its due in this way, he is not thereby a debtor, since he is not ordained to serve anything. Rather is everything ordained to serve God. God's justice, then, sometimes means the condescension of his goodness. At other times it means that he gives merit its due. Anselm speaks of it in both senses in *Proslogion* 10, "it is just when thou punishest the wicked, since they deserve it. It is just when thou sparest the wicked, for this is the condescension of thy goodness."

On the fourth point: justice can belong to God's essence even though it relates to an act, since what belongs to an essence may also be a principle of action. In any case, good does not always relate to an act. We say that a thing is good not only because of what it does, but also because it is perfect in its essence. For this reason, the passage quoted affirms that good is related to the just as the general to the special.

Article Two

Whether God's Justice is Truth

We proceed to the second article thus:

1. It seems that God's justice is not truth. Justice is in the will. It is in fact uprightness of will, as Anselm says (*De Verit.* 13). But the philosopher says that truth is in the intellect (6 *Metaph.* 8; 6 *Ethics* 2, 6). Hence justice has no relation to truth.

2. Again, according to the philosopher, truth is a virtue distinct from justice. Hence truth is not included in the idea of justice.

On the other hand: it is said in Ps. 85:10: "Mercy and truth are met together," and truth here means justice.

I answer: truth consists in conformity between an intellect and a thing (Q. 16, Art. 1). But an intellect which causes a thing is the rule and the measure of it, whereas the thing itself is the rule and the measure of a mind which apprehends it. When things are the rule and measure of the intellect, truth consists in conformity of the intellect to the thing. So it is with ourselves. What we think and say is true or false according to what the thing is or is not. But when the intellect is the cause and rule of things, truth consists in conformity of the thing to the intellect. The work of an artist, for example, is said to be true when it conforms to his art. Now just works bear the same relation to the law which they obey as do works of art to the art itself. God's justice is therefore rightly called truth, because it determines the order of things in conformity with his wisdom, which is its law. We ourselves speak of the truth of justice, in this same sense.

On the first point: the justice which obeys a regulative law is in the reason, or intellect. But the justice which obeys a command which regulates an action according to a law is in the will.

On the second point: the truth of which the philosopher is speaking is that virtue by which a man plainly shows what manner of man he is through his words or his deeds. This consists in the conformity of a sign to what it signifies. It does not consist in the conformity of an effect to its cause and rule, as we have said of the truth of justice.

Article Three

WHETHER THERE IS MERCY IN GOD

We proceed to the third article thus:

1. It seems that mercy cannot be attributed to God. For mercy is a kind of misery, as the Damascene says (2 *De Fid. Orth.* 14), and there is no misery in God. Neither, then, is there mercy in God.

2. Again, mercy is the mitigation of justice. But God cannot rescind what his justice requires, for it is said in II Tim. 2:13: "If we believe not, yet he abideth faithful: for he cannot deny himself," and God would deny himself if he were to deny his own words, as the gloss says. We cannot therefore attribute mercy to him.

On the other hand: it is said in Ps. 111:4: "the Lord is gracious, and full of compassion."

I answer: mercy is pre-eminently attributable to God, albeit as an effect, not as the affection of a passion. In evidence of this we may reflect that one is said to be merciful[1] when one has misery in one's heart, grieving for the misery of another as if it were one's own, and consequently striving to dispel it as if it were one's own. This is the effect of mercy. God does not grieve

---

[1] The Latin word is *misericors*.

over the misery of another, but he pre-eminently does dispel the misery of another, whatever be the defect for which this word may stand. Now defects are remedied only by the perfection of some goodness, and the first origin of goodness is God, as we said in Q. 6, Art. 4. But we must bear in mind that God bestows perfections on things not only through his goodness, but in a different sense also through his justice, generosity, and mercy. Considered absolutely, it is through his goodness that God bestows a perfection (Art. 2). Yet in so far as God bestows perfections on things in accordance with their status, he bestows them through justice. In so far as he bestows them purely by his goodness, and not because things are useful to him, he bestows them through liberality. In so far as the perfections which God bestows dispel every defect, he bestows them in mercy.

On the first point: this objection argues from the manner in which mercy affects a passion.

On the second point: when God acts mercifully he does not do what is contrary to his justice, but does more than his justice requires, as it were like one who gives two hundred *denarii* to a person to whom he owes one hundred. Such a one acts with liberality or with mercy, without denying justice. So also does one who forgives an offence against himself. He who forgives something in a sense gives it. Thus the apostle calls forgiveness a gift in Eph. 4:32: "forgiving one another, even as God for Christ's sake hath forgiven you."[1] It is plain from this that mercy does not destroy justice, but is a fulfilment of it. As James says: "mercy rejoiceth against judgment."[2]

Article Four

WHETHER JUSTICE AND MERCY ARE PRESENT IN ALL GOD'S WORKS

We proceed to the fourth article thus:

1. Justice and mercy do not appear to be present in every work of God. For some of God's works are attributed to his mercy, as for example the justification of the ungodly, while other works are attributed to his justice, as for example the condemnation of the ungodly. Thus it is said in James 2:13: "he shall have judgment without mercy that hath showed no mercy." Hence justice and mercy are not present in every work of God.

[1] Migne: "Give without stint, as Christ hath given to you."
[2] Migne: "mercy riseth above judgment."

2. Again, in Rom., ch. 15, the apostle attributes the conversion of the Jews to justice and to truth, but the conversion of the Gentiles he attributes to mercy. Hence justice and mercy are not present in every work of God.

3. Again, many just men are afflicted in this life. But this is an injustice. Hence justice and mercy are not present in every work of God.

4. Again, justice is payment of a debt, and mercy is delivery from a misery. Thus justice, no less than mercy, presupposes something as the condition of its operation. But the work of creation does not presuppose anything. There is therefore neither justice nor mercy in the work of creation.

On the other hand: it is said in Ps. 25:10: "All the paths of the Lord are mercy and truth."

I answer: mercy and truth are bound to be present in every work of God, if mercy means delivery from any defect whatsoever—though we cannot properly call every defect a misery, but only the defects of a rational nature which is capable of happiness, the opposite of misery. The reason why they are bound to be present is that divine justice renders either what is owed to God, or what is owed to a creature.

No work of God can lack justice in either of these senses. For God cannot do anything which is not in accordance with his wisdom and goodness, and this accordance is what we mean when we say that it is owed to God. Similarly, God cannot create anything in the realm of things which is not in accordance with order and proportion, which is what we mean by justice to creatures. Justice is therefore bound to be present in every work of God.

Further, a work of divine justice invariably presupposes a work of divine mercy as its foundation. For a creature has a right to something only on the ground of what it already possesses, or on the ground of what is already intended for it, and if this in turn is owed to the creature, it can be owed only on the ground of what is previous to it again. But this regress cannot be infinite. There must therefore be something which the creature possesses only by the goodness of God's will, which is the final end. For example, we say that a man has the right to possess hands because he has a rational soul. But his right to a rational soul depends in turn on his being a man, and he is a man only by the goodness of God. Thus mercy is present from the very beginning of every work of God. Moreover, its power persists throughout all that follows, and is the more effective

since a primary cause has a greater influence than a secondary
cause. Thus it is that God in his abundant goodness bestows
what is owing to a creature more liberally than its relative
status deserves. The order of justice would indeed be maintained by less than is bestowed by the divine goodness, which
exceeds the deserts of every creature.

On the first point: the reason why some works are attributed
to justice and others to mercy is that justice is more thoroughly
apparent in some of them, and mercy in others. Yet we can
see that there is mercy even in the condemnation of sinners,
reducing their punishment to less than they deserve, though
not altogether remitting it. Justice is likewise present in the
justification of the ungodly, since God remits their guilt for the
sake of their love, even though he himself bestowed this love in
mercy. Thus Luke 7:47 says of Magdelene: "Her sins, which
are many, are forgiven; for she loved much."

On the second point: the justice and mercy of God are apparent in both conversions. Yet in one respect justice is present
in the conversion of the Jews and not in that of the Gentiles,
since the Jews were saved for the sake of the promise given to
their fathers.

On the third point: justice and mercy can be seen even in the
punishment of the just in this world. Their afflictions purge
them of trivial faults, and they are the more drawn to God
through deliverance from worldly affections. As Gregory says
in 26 *Moral.* 9: "The evils which oppress us in this world compel
us to draw near to God."

On the fourth point: even though the work of creation presupposes nothing in the nature of things, it does presuppose
something in the divine knowledge. It maintains the character
of justice in that it brings things into being in accordance with
divine wisdom and goodness. It also in a sense maintains the
character of mercy, in that it transforms things from not-being
to being.

Question Twenty-Two

OF DIVINE PROVIDENCE

Four questions are asked concerning divine providence.
1. Whether providence is appropriately ascribed to God.
2. Whether all things are under divine providence. 3. Whether

divine providence affects all things directly. 4. Whether divine providence imposes a necessity on all that it provides.

Article One

Whether Providence is Appropriately Ascribed to God

We proceed to the first article thus:

1. It seems that providence is not appropriately ascribed to God. For Tullius says that "providence is part of prudence" (2 *De Invent.*), and prudence cannot be ascribed to God. Prudence, according to the philosopher (6 *Ethics* 5, 8, 18), gives good counsel, whereas God is not subject to any doubt which could require good counsel. Hence providence is not appropriately ascribed to God.

2. Again, whatever is in God is eternal. But providence is not eternal, since it is concerned with existing things, which are not eternal, as the Damascene says (1 *De Fid. Orth.* 3). Hence providence is not in God.

3. Again, there is nothing composite in God. But providence seems to be composite, since it involves both intellect and will. Hence providence is not in God.

On the other hand: it is said in Wisdom 14:3: "Thou, O Father, rulest all things by providence."

I answer: we are bound to say that there is providence in God, since God has created every good that exists in things, as we said in Q. 6, Art. 4. Now there is good not only in the substance of things, but also in their ordination to an end, especially to the ultimate end, which is a divine good, as we said in Q. 21, Art. 4. God is therefore the source of the good which exists in the order which relates created things to their end. Further, since God is the cause of things through his intellect, the reason for every one of his effects must pre-exist in his intellect, as we explained in Q. 21, Art. 4, also. Hence the reason why things are ordained to their end must pre-exist in the mind of God. But the reason why things are ordained to their end is, properly speaking, providence, because it is the principal part of prudence. The other two parts of prudence, memory of the past and understanding of the present, are subordinate to it, helping us to decide how to provide for the future. As the philosopher says in 6 *Ethics* 12, prudence directs other capacities to an end, whether it be for one's own sake or for the sake of one's dependents in a family, state, or kingdom. Thus we say that a man is prudent when he directs his actions well in view of the end of life, and Matt. 24:45 speaks of "a faithful and wise servant, whom his lord hath made ruler over his household." Prudence or providence of this kind is appropriately ascribed to God. There is indeed nothing in God which needs to be directed to its end, since God is himself the ultimate end. But what we mean by "providence" in God is the reason for the ordination of things to their end. Thus Boethius says (4 *De Consol.* 6): "Providence is the divine reason which resides in the highest principle of all things, and which disposes all things." We may add that this disposition is the reason for the ordination of things to their end, as well as for the ordering of parts in a whole.

On the first point: as the philosopher says in 6 *Ethics* 9 and 10, "prudence properly directs us in what good deliberation rightly advises, and in what sound judgment rightly judges." God does not indeed take counsel, for this means to inquire into what is doubtful. But he does decree the ordering of things to their end, since the true idea of things lies in him. As Ps. 148:6 says: "he hath made a decree which shall not pass." Prudence and providence in this sense are appropriately ascribed to God. The reason for doing things may be called "counsel" in God, not because it involves inquiry, but because of the certainty of the knowledge of it, to which those who take counsel can attain only by means of inquiry. Thus it is said in Eph. 1:11: ". . . who worketh all things after the counsel of his own will."

On the second point: there are two aspects of providential care. There is the reason for the order in things, which is called providence, and there is the disposition and execution of this order. The former is eternal, the latter temporal.

On the third point: providence does belong to the intellect, and also presupposes an end which is willed, since no one determines the means to an end unless he wills the end. Prudence likewise presupposes the moral virtues through which desires are related to the good, as is said in 6 *Ethics* 12. But even though providence should relate both to the will and to the intellect of God, this would not destroy the simple nature of God, since in God will and intellect are the same, as we said in Q. 19, Arts. 2 and 4.

Article Two
WHETHER ALL THINGS ARE UNDER DIVINE PROVIDENCE

We proceed to the second article thus:

1. It seems that not all things are under divine providence.

For nothing that is ordained happens contingently, and if all things were provided by God, nothing would happen contingently. There would then be no such thing as chance or fortune. But this is contrary to common opinion.

2. Again, every wise provider, so far as he is able, preserves those in his care from defect and from evil. But we see many evils in things. Hence either God cannot prevent evil, and is not omnipotent, or not all things are under his care.

3. Again, that which happens by necessity does not require providence, or prudence. As the philosopher says (6 *Ethics* 4, 9, 11): "prudence is right reason applied to contingencies, which demand deliberation and choice." Now many things happen by necessity. Not all things, therefore, are ruled by providence.

4. Again, he who is left to himself is not under the providence of any governor. Now God leaves men to themselves, according to Ecclesiasticus 15:14: "God made man from the beginning, and left him in the hands of his own counsel," especially so the wicked, according to Ps. 81:12: "So I gave them up unto their own hearts' lust." Not all things, therefore, are under divine providence.

5. Again, the apostle says in 1 Cor. 9:9: "Doth God take care for oxen?"—or, we may say, for any irrational creature. Not all things, therefore, are under divine providence.

On the other hand: Wisdom 8:1 says of the wisdom of God: "It extends from end to end with power, and disposes all things sweetly."

I answer: Democritus and the Epicureans, and others also, denied any such thing as providence, maintaining that the world was made by chance. Others again have held that incorruptible things are under the care of providence, but that only the incorruptible species of corruptible things are so, not the corruptible individuals. The voice in Job 22:14 speaks their views: "Thick clouds are a covering to him, that he seeth not; and he walketh in the circuit of heaven." Rabbi Moses, also, excluded men from the class of corruptible things on account of their surpassing intelligence, but followed the opinion of the others concerning things which pass away.

But we are bound to say that all things are under divine providence, individually as well as collectively. We prove this as follows. Every agent acts for the sake of an end. The effects of a first agent will therefore serve his end to the extent to which his causality extends. This means that the works of an agent may contain something which results from some cause other than his own intention, and which does not serve his end. But God's causality extends to all being, since God is the first of all agents. It extends to the principles of individuals as well as of species, and to the principles of corruptibles as well as of incorruptibles. Everything which has any kind of being is therefore bound to be ordained by God to some end. As the apostle says in Rom. 13:1: "the powers that be are ordained of God." [1] Now we said in the previous article that God's providence is nothing other than the reason why things are ordained to an end. It follows that all things which have any kind of being must be under the rule of divine providence. We also said that God knows all things, whether universal or particular, and that his knowledge is related to things as the knowledge of an art to the things which it makes (Q. 14, Arts. 6, 11). It follows from this that all things are under the ordinance of God, just as the creations of an art are under the ordinance of the art.

On the first point: there is a difference between a universal cause and a particular cause. A thing may avoid being determined by a particular cause, but it cannot avoid being determined by a universal cause. It can avoid determination by one particular cause only through the intervention of another, as wood is prevented from burning by the action of water. It is therefore impossible for any effect to escape determination by the universal cause to which all particular causes are subordinate. Now in so far as an effect escapes determination by one particular cause, it is said to occur by chance, or to be contingent so far as that particular cause is concerned. But it is still said to be provided by the universal cause whose ordinance it cannot escape. For example, the meeting of two slaves may be due to chance so far as they are concerned, but it has nevertheless been arranged by the master who wittingly sent them to the same place, without either of them knowing about the other.

On the second point: there is a difference between a universal provider and one who cares for a particular thing. One who is entrusted with the care of a particular thing guards it from defect so far as he can. But a universal provider allows some defect to occur in some things, lest the good of the whole should be impaired. Corruptions and defects in natural things are said to be contrary to their particular natures, but to be nevertheless in harmony with universal nature, in as much as

[1] Migne: "The things which are of God are ordained."

the defect of one issues in the good of another, even of the whole universe. The passing away of one individual is the generation of another, and the species is preserved by means of it. Now God is the universal provider of all that is. It is therefore fitting that his providence should permit certain defects in particular things, lest the perfect good of the universe should be impaired. The universe would lack many good things, if all evils were excluded. There would not be the life of a lion, if there were no slaying of animals. There would not be the endurance of martyrs, if there were no persecution by tyrants. Thus Augustine says: "God omnipotent would not allow any evil thing to exist in his works, were he not able by his omnipotence and goodness to bring good out of evil" (*Enchirid.* 2). Those who have believed that corruptible things subject to chance and to evil are outside the care of divine providence seem to have been influenced by these two objections which we have answered.

On the third point: man uses nature when he practises the arts and the virtues. But he did not make nature, and for this reason man's providence does not extend to what nature determines by necessity. But God's providence does so extend, since God is the author of nature. It was, apparently, this objection that induced Democritus and other ancient naturalists to think that the course of natural things was outside the scope of divine providence, and due to a material necessity.

On the fourth point: the saying that man is left to himself does not mean that he is altogether cut off from God's providence. It means that the power which works determinately towards a single end is not extended to him as it is even to natural things, which act for an end only through the direction of something else, and do not direct themselves to it like rational creatures, who deliberate and choose by free will. The words "in the hands of his own counsel" are therefore significant. Yet the activity of man's free will still derives from God as its cause, so that whatever he does by means of it is still under the rule of God's providence. Even man's own providence remains under God's providence, as a particular cause under a universal cause. Nevertheless, God's providence cares for the just in a more excellent way than it cares for the ungodly, since he allows nothing to happen to the just which might finally prevent their salvation. As Rom. 8:28 says: "all things work together for good to them that love God." When it is said that God leaves the ungodly to themselves, this means that he does not restrain them from the evil of guilt, not that they are altogether excluded from his providence. They would indeed fall away into nothing, if his providence did not preserve them in being. When Tullius said that the matters concerning which men take counsel were outside the scope of divine providence, he seems to have been influenced by this objection.

On the fifth point: as we said in Q. 19, Art. 10, a rational creature is master of its own actions, since it possesses a free-will. But it is under divine providence in a special way as the recipient of blame or praise, and of punishment or reward. It is this aspect of God's care which the apostle denies to oxen. He does not say that God's providence has no regard for irrational creatures, as Rabbi Moses thought.

Article Three

WHETHER GOD PROVIDES FOR ALL THINGS DIRECTLY

We proceed to the third article thus:

1. It seems that God does not provide for all things directly. We must ascribe to God whatever dignity requires, and the dignity of a king requires that he provide for his subjects through the medium of ministers. Much more, then, does God provide for all things through some medium.

2. Again, providence ordains things to their end. Now the end of anything is its perfection and good, and every cause directs its effect to its good. Hence every active cause achieves the aim of providence. Secondary causes would therefore be done away, if God provided for all things directly.

3. Again, Augustine says (*Enchirid.* 17): "it is better not to know some things than to know them," e.g., trivial things. The philosopher says this also in 12 *Metaph.*, text 51. Now whatever is better must be attributed to God. Hence God does not have direct foresight of anything trivial or evil.

On the other hand: it is said in Job 34:13: "Who hath given him a charge over the earth? or who hath disposed the whole world?" [1] And on this Gregory comments (24 *Moral.* 26): "God himself rules the world which he himself has made."

I answer: providence includes two things, namely, the reason for the order in things ordained to an end, and the execution of this order, which is called government. Now God provides the first of these directly for all things, since the reason for all things, even for the most trivial, lies in the divine intellect.

[1] Migne: "What other hath he set over the earth, or whom hath he put in charge of the world which he hath made?"

Moreover, to whatever causes God provides for any effects, he gives the power to produce them. The order of these effects must therefore have been in God's mind beforehand. But divine providence uses certain media in carrying out this order, since it directs lower things by means of higher things. This is not due to any defect in God's power. It is due to his abundant goodness, whereby he confers the dignity of causality even upon creatures. These considerations rule out the view of Plato, quoted by Gregory of Nyssa (8 *De Providentia*, 3), which supposed three kinds of providence. 1. The providence of the highest deity, which provides first and principally for spiritual things, and through them provides genera, species, and universal causes for the whole world. 2. The providence which provides for such individuals as come to be and pass away, which he attributes to the gods who encircle the heavens, i.e., to the separate substances which move the heavenly bodies in a circle. 3. The providence which watches over human affairs. This he attributes to demons, which the Platonists place betwixt ourselves and the gods, as Augustine tells us (*De Civ. Dei.* 9, ch. 1–2; 8, ch. 14).

On the first point: the dignity of a king requires that his dispensations be carried out by ministers. But his ignorance of how they do it is a defect, since a practical science is the more perfect the more it takes account of the details of what it achieves.

On the second point: the directness with which God provides for all things does not do away with secondary causes, which are the means by which his ordinances are carried out, as we said in Q. 19, Arts. 5, 8.

On the third point: it is better for us not to know evil or trivial things, because they hinder us from contemplating better things. But it is not so with God. God sees all things in one intuition, and his will cannot be turned to evil.

Article Four

WHETHER PROVIDENCE IMPOSES A NECESSITY ON WHAT IT PROVIDES

We proceed to the fourth article thus:

1. It seems that divine providence does impose a necessity on what it provides. An effect happens by necessity if it follows inevitably from a cause which exists or pre-exists through itself. The philosopher proves this in 6 *Metaph.*, text 7. Now

divine providence pre-exists, since it is eternal. Its effects also follow inevitably, since it cannot be frustrated. Divine providence therefore imposes a necessity on what it provides.

2. Again, every provider makes as certain as possible that his work shall not fail. Now God is all powerful. He therefore ensures what he provides by means of the certainty of necessity.

3. Again, Boethius says (4 *De Consol.* 6): "the destiny which is unalterably decreed by providence confines the actions and fortunes of men by the indissoluble connections of causes." This implies that providence imposes a necessity on what it provides.

On the other hand: Dionysius says (4 *Div. Nom.*, lect. 23): "the corruption of nature is not due to divine providence." Some things, indeed, are contingent by nature. Divine providence does not therefore impose necessity on things to the exclusion of contingency.

I answer: divine providence imposes necessity on some things, but not, as some have believed, on all things. Providence ordains things for an end, and except for the divine goodness which is an end separated from them, the principal good in things themselves is the perfection of the universe. Now the universe would not be perfect if things did not exhibit every grade of being. Divine providence therefore produces every grade of being. It has accordingly prepared necessary causes for some effects, so that they may occur through necessity, and contingent causes for other effects, that they may occur contingently, each according to the condition of its proximate cause.

On the first point: the effect of divine providence is not merely that a thing should happen in some way. Its effect is either that it should happen contingently, or that it should happen through necessity. Whatever divine providence decrees shall happen inevitably and through necessity, happens inevitably and through necessity. Whatever it intends to happen contingently, happens contingently.

On the second point: the order of divine providence is immovable and certain in this, that everything that God provides happens in the manner in which God provides it, whether through necessity or contingently.

On the third point: the indissolubility and unalterability of which Boethius speaks refer to the certainty of providence itself, which fails neither to provide its effect nor to provide it in the manner which it decrees. They do not characterize the effects as occurring through necessity. We must bear in mind that necessity and contingency properly depend on the manner in which a thing exists. Its mode of contingency or necessity, therefore, really depends on the manner in which God provides it, since God is the universal provider of all that exists. It does not depend on the manner in which any particular provider provides it.

Question Twenty-Three

OF PREDESTINATION

After divine providence, we must consider predestination. There are eight questions on predestination. 1. Whether God predestines. 2. What predestination is, and whether it implies anything in one who is predestined. 3. Whether God rejects some men. 4. How predestination relates to election, or, whether the predestined are chosen. 5. Whether merits are the ground or cause of predestination or reprobation, or of election. 6. Of the certainty of predestination, or, whether the predestined are bound to be saved. 7. Whether the number of the predestined is certain. 8. Whether predestination can be furthered by the prayers of the saints.

Article One

Whether Men are Predestined by God

We proceed to the first article thus:

1. It seems that men are not predestined by God. For the Damascene says: "We ought to know that God foreknows all things, but does not predetermine all things. He has foreknowledge of all that is in us, but does not predetermine it" (2 *De Fid. Orth.* 30). Now human merits and demerits are in us, since free will makes us master of our actions. It follows that whatever has to do with merit or demerit is not predestined by God. But this makes the predestination of men impossible.

2. Again, it was said in Q. 22, Arts. 1 and 2 that all creatures are directed to their end by divine providence. Yet other creatures are not said to be predestined by God. Neither, then, are men.

3. Again, angels are capable of blessedness no less than men.

But predestination does not apply to angels, apparently because they have never known misery and because predestination is the decision to have mercy, as Augustine says (*De Praed. Sanct.* 17). Neither, therefore, does it apply to men.

4. Again, the benefits which God bestows on men are revealed to the saints by the Holy Spirit, according to I Cor. 2:12: "Now we have received, not the spirit of the world, but the spirit which is of God; that we might know the things that are freely given to us of God." Hence if men were predestined by God, their predestination would be known to those who were predestined, since predestination is a benefit which God bestows. But this is obviously untrue.

On the other hand: it is said in Rom. 8:30: "whom he did predestinate, them he also called."

I answer: it is rightly said that God predestines men. We have shown that all things are ruled by divine providence (Q. 22, Art. 4), and that providence ordains things to their end (Q. 22, Arts. 1 and 2). Now the end to which God ordains creatures is twofold. There is, first, the end which exceeds the proportion and the capacity of created nature. This is eternal life, which consists in the vision of the divine essence, which is beyond the nature of any creature, as we said in Q. 12, Art. 4. There is, secondly, the end which is proportionate to created nature, which a created thing may attain by means of its own natural power. Now when a thing cannot attain something by its own natural power, it must be directed to it by another, as an arrow is directed to its mark by an archer. Properly speaking, then, although a rational creature is capable of eternal life, he is brought to this life by God. The reason why he is brought to eternal life must therefore pre-exist in God, since the reason why anything is ordained to its end lies in God, and we have said that this is providence. The reason which exists in the mind of an agent is, as it were, a pre-existence in him of the the thing which he intends to do. We give the name of "predestination" to the reason why a rational creature is brought to eternal life, because to destine means to bring. It is plain, then, that predestination is a part of providence, if we consider it in relation to its objects.

On the first point: by predetermination the Damascene means the imposition of a necessity such as occurs in natural things predetermined to a single end. His next words make this clear—"God does not will malice, nor compel virtue." This does not make predestination impossible.

On the second point: irrational creatures are not capable of the end which exceeds the capacity of human nature. Hence they are not properly said to be predestined, although we do speak loosely of predestination in relation to other ends.

On the third point: predestination applies to angels as well as to men, even though they have never known misery. A movement is defined by its *terminus ad quem*, not by its *terminus a quo*. To be made white means the same thing whether one who is made white was formerly black, pale, or red. Predestination also means the same thing whether or not one is predestined to eternal life from a state of misery.

On the fourth point: their predestination is revealed to some by special privilege. But to reveal it in every case would be improvident. Those who are not predestined would despair, and security would engender negligence in those who are.

Article Two

WHETHER PREDESTINATION IMPLIES ANYTHING IN THE PREDESTINED

We proceed to the second article thus:

1. It seems that predestination does imply something in the predestined. Every action produces a passion in something external. Hence if predestination is an action in God, it is bound to be a passion in those who are predestined.

2. Again, commenting on the passage in Rom., ch. 1, "He who was predestined . . .," Origen says: "Predestination is of one who is not yet, and destination of one who now is." But Augustine asks: "What is predestination, if it is not the destination of one who exists?" (*De Praed. Sanct.*). Hence predestination is only of one who exists. It thus implies something about the predestined.

3. Again, preparation implies something in the thing prepared, and predestination is "the preparation of God's benefits," as Augustine says (*De Dono Persev.* 14). Predestination is therefore something in the predestined.

4. Again, nothing temporal is included in the definition of the eternal. Yet grace, which is temporal, is included in the definition of predestination, which is defined as preparation for present grace and future glory. It follows that predestination is not anything eternal. It cannot then be in God, since everything in God is eternal. It must therefore be in the predestined.

On the other hand: in the same passage Augustine says that

predestination is "the foreknowledge of God's benefits." But foreknowledge is in one who foreknows, not in what is foreknown. Predestination is therefore in him who predestines, not in the predestined.

I answer: predestination is not anything in the predestined. It is solely in him who predestines. We have already said that predestination is a part of providence, and providence is an intention in the mind of the provider, as we said in Q. 22, Art. 1, not something in what is provided.

The carrying out of providence, however, which we call government, is passively in the governed while it is actively in him who governs. It is clear, then, that predestination is the reason which exists in the divine mind for the ordination of some to eternal life, and that the carrying out of this ordinance is passively in the predestined while it is actively in God. According to the apostle, predestination is put into effect as calling and glorification—"whom he did predestinate, them he also called: and whom he called . . . them he also glorified" (Rom. 8:30).

On the first point: actions which pass out to an external object do issue in some passion, as do heating and cutting, for example. But actions which remain within the agent, such as understanding and willing, do not. (Q. 14, Art. 4; Q. 18, Art. 3.) Predestination is an action of this latter kind, and therefore does not imply anything in the predestined. The carrying out of predestination, however, does pass out to its objects, and so implies something about them.

On the second point: destination sometimes means the actual directing of something to an end. It then refers only to the existent. But it also means the mental conception of so doing. For example, we are said to destine something if we firmly intend it in our minds. This is what it means in II Maccabees 6:20: "Eleazar determined to do nothing unlawful through love of life." Destination may, then, refer to what does not exist. But whatever the destination of it may mean, predestination can refer to something which does not exist, because predestination contains the notion of antecedence.

On the third point: there are two kinds of preparation. There is the preparation of a passive agent to undergo passion. This is in the thing prepared. But there is also an agent's preparation for action. This is in the active agent. Predestination is a preparation in this second sense, in which an agent is said to prepare himself mentally for action when he preconceives the idea of doing something. In this sense of the word, God has prepared himself from all eternity by predestination, preconceiving the idea of ordaining some to eternal life.

On the fourth point: grace is not included in the definition of predestination as part of its essence. It is included as the effect which predestination implies as a cause, and as the object of its action. It does not then follow that predestination is temporal.

Article Three

WHETHER GOD REJECTS ANY MAN

We proceed to the third article thus:

1. God, it seems, rejects no man. Nobody rejects one whom he loves, and God loves every man, according to Wisdom 11:24: "Thou lovest all things that are, and hatest nothing that thou hast made." It follows that God rejects no man.

2. Again, if God does reject anyone, rejection must be related to the rejected as predestination is related to the predestined. Rejection must then be the cause of the perdition of the rejected, as predestination is the cause of the salvation of the predestined. But this is not true, since it is said in Hos. 13:9: "O Israel, thou hast destroyed thyself; but in me is thine help." It follows that God does not reject anyone.

3. Again, no one can be held responsible for what he cannot avoid. But no one could avoid destruction if God were to reject him. As Ecclesiastes says (7:13): "Consider the work of God: for who can make that straight which he hath made crooked." [1] Men would not then be responsible for their own destruction. But this is false. It follows that God does not reject any man.

On the other hand: it is said in Mal. 1:2–3: "I loved Jacob. And I hated Esau."

I answer: God does reject some men. We have said that predestination is a part of providence (Art. 1), and that providence permits a measure of defect in the things over which it rules (Q. 22, Art. 2). Now although providence ordains men to eternal life, it permits some of them to fail to attain this end. This is what is called rejection. Rejection is the part of providence which relates to those who fail to attain eternal life, just as predestination is the part of providence which relates to those who are ordained to it. Rejection therefore means more than foreknowledge, just as we agreed with Augustine (1 *Ad Simplician* 3) that providence means more than this (Q. 22,

[1] Migne: "whom he hath despised."

Art. 1). While predestination includes the will to bestow grace and glory, rejection includes the will to allow some to incur guilt, and to impose the penalty of damnation on account of guilt.

On the first point: God loves every man, and every creature also, in that he wills some good for every one of them. But he does not will every good for every one, and is said to hate some in so far as he does not will for them the good of eternal life.

On the second point: predestination is the cause of the glory which the predestined expect to receive in the life to come, and also of the grace which they receive in this present life. Rejection is the cause of desertion by God, but not of present guilt. It is the cause of eternal punishment to come, but guilt is due to the free will of him who is rejected and deserted by grace. What the prophet says is therefore true—"O Israel, thou hast destroyed thyself."

On the third point: rejection by God does not deprive the rejected one of any power. When it is said that a rejected man cannot receive grace, this does not mean that it is absolutely impossible for him to do so. It means that this is conditionally impossible. The salvation of a predestined man is ensured by a necessity which is likewise conditional, in that it permits freedom of choice. Thus even though one who is rejected by God cannot receive grace, it lies with his free will whether he falls into one sin or another, and his sin is deservedly imputed to him as guilt.

Article Four

WHETHER THE PREDESTINED ARE CHOSEN BY GOD

We proceed to the fourth article thus:

1. It seems that the predestined are not chosen by God. For Dionysius says: "just as the corporeal sun sheds its light upon all bodies without discrimination, so does God bestow his goodness' (4 *Div. Nom.*, lect. 1). Now it is especially God's goodness that we receive when we share in grace and glory. It follows that God bestows grace and goodness without discrimination, and this belongs to predestination.

2. Again, election is of those who exist. But predestination is also of those who do not exist, since predestination is from eternity. There must therefore be some who are predestined without being elected.

3. Again, election implies discrimination. But it is said in

1 Tim. 2:4: "Who will have all men to be saved." Thus pre-destination preordains all men to salvation. It is therefore without election.

On the other hand: it is said in Eph. 1:4: "according as he hath chosen us in him before the foundation of the world."

I answer: predestination presupposes election by its very nature, and election presupposes love. The reason for this is that predestination is part of providence, as we observed in Art. 1. We also said that providence, like prudence, is the reason preconceived in the mind for the ordination of things to an end (Q. 22, Art. 2). Now the ordination of something to an end cannot be preconceived unless the end is already willed. The predestination of some to eternal salvation therefore means that God has already willed their salvation. This involves both election and love. It involves love, because God wills the good of eternal salvation for them, to love being the same as to will good for someone (Q. 20, Arts. 2, 3). It involves election, because he wills this good for some in preference to others, some being rejected, as we said in Art. 3. But election and love are not the same in God as they are in ourselves. Our will is not the cause of the good in what we love. We are induced to love by good which exists already. We thus choose someone whom we shall love, and our choice precedes our love. With God, it is the reverse. When God wills some good to one whom he loves, his will is the cause of this good being in him, rather than in any other. It is plain, then, that the very meaning of election pre-supposes love, and that predestination presupposes election. All who are predestined are therefore elected, and loved also.

On the first point: we said in Q. 6, Art. 4, that there is nothing which does not share something of God's goodness. There is therefore no election in the universal bestowal of God's goodness, if this is what we have in mind. But if we are thinking of the bestowal of one particular good or another, this is not without election, since God gives certain good things to some which he does not give to others. Election is likewise involved in the bestowal of grace and glory.

On the second point: election is bound to be concerned with the existent when the will of the chooser is decided by a good which already exists in something. So it is with our own will. But it is otherwise with God, as we said in Q. 20, Art. 2. In Augustine's words, "they who do not exist are elect of God, and his choice does not err" (De Verb. Apost., Sermo 11).

On the third point: antecedently, God wills that all men

should be saved (Q. 19, Art. 6). But this is to will conditionally, not absolutely. God does not will this consequentially, which would be to will it absolutely.

Article Five

WHETHER THE FOREKNOWLEDGE OF MERITS IS THE CAUSE OF PREDESTINATION

We proceed to the fifth article thus:

1. It seems that the foreknowledge of merits is the cause of predestination. For the apostle says: "whom he did foreknow, he also did predestinate" (Rom. 8:29), and the gloss of Ambrose on the words "I will have mercy on whom I will have mercy" (Rom. 9:15) says: "I will have mercy on whom I foreknow will return to me with his whole heart." It thus appears that the foreknowledge of merits is the cause of predestination.

2. Again, divine predestination includes the divine will. Now the divine will cannot be irrational, since Augustine says that predestination is "the decision to have mercy" (2 *De Praed. Sanct.* 17). But there is no rational ground for predestination except foreknowledge of merits. Foreknowledge of merits is therefore the cause, or rational ground, of predestination.

3. Again, it is said in Rom. 9:14: "Is there unrighteousness[1] with God? God forbid." Now it would be unrighteous to give unequal things to those who are equal, and all men are equal in nature, and also in original sin. It is in the merits and demerits of their actions that they differ. It is therefore only because he foreknows their unequal merits that God prepares for men such unequal things as predestination and rejection.

On the other hand: the apostle says (Titus 3:5): "Not by works of righteousness which we have done, but according to his mercy he saved us." Now God predestines us to salvation in the same way as he saves us. It follows that the foreknowledge of merits is not the cause or ground of predestination.

I answer: we said in the preceding article that predestination involves will. We must therefore look for the reason for predestination in the same way as we looked for a reason for the divine will. Now we said in Q. 19, Art. 5, that we cannot assign any cause for the divine act of will, although it is possible to find a reason why things are willed, in so far as God wills one thing for the sake of another. No one has been so foolish as to say that merits are the cause of the divine act by which God

---

[1] Migne: "non est iniquitas apud Deum."

predestines. The question is as to whether there is a reason for the effects of predestination, that is, whether God has pre-ordained that he will give the effects of predestination to anyone on account of merits.

Some have said that the effect of predestination is ordained for us beforehand, on account of merits already earned in a previous life. This was the view of Origen. He thought that the souls of men were created first, and that according to their works they were assigned different states on becoming united with bodies in this world. But the apostle rules out such a view by what he says in Rom. 9:11–12: "For the children being not yet born, neither having done any good or evil . . . not of works, but of him that calleth. It was said unto her, The elder shall serve the younger."

Others have said that merits already earned in this life are the ground and cause of the effects of predestination. The Pelagians, for example, held that the beginning of well-doing lies with ourselves, although its consummation lies with God; and that this explains why the effect of predestination is given to one and not to another, since one has made a beginning by preparing himself, while another has not. But this is contrary to what the apostle says in II Cor. 3:5: "Not that we are sufficient of ourselves to think anything as of ourselves." For we cannot point to any beginning which is previous to thinking, and consequently cannot say that there is anything within us which could be the reason for the effect of predestination.

Others again have said that the reason for predestination is to be found in the merits which result from the effects of it. By this they mean that God bestows grace on someone, and also preordains that he will bestow it, because he foreknows that such a one will make good use of it, just as a king gives a horse to a soldier because he knows that he will use it well. But they appear to have drawn a distinction between the results of grace and the results of free will, as if the same thing could not be the result of both. It is obvious, however, that anything which is due to grace is also the effect of predestination, and cannot be the reason for predestination, since it is included in it. And if anything else about ourselves is to be the reason for pre-destination, it must not be part of the effect of it. But again, anything which is due to free will is no more distinct from the effect of predestination than the result of a secondary cause is distinct from the result of a primary cause. Providence produces its effects through the operation of secondary causes, as we said

in Q. 19, Art. 5, and even what is due to free will is the effect
of predestination.

We must observe that the effect of predestination may be
considered in two ways. If we are thinking of its particular
effects, there is no reason why one effect of predestination
should not be the ground and cause of another, nor any reason
why a later effect should not be the final cause of an earlier
effect. Nor is there any reason why an earlier effect of predestination should not be the cause of a later effect through its
merit, which properly means its material disposition. We should
then say that God has preordained that he will bestow glory on
account of merits, and that he will give grace in order that
glory may be merited. But if we are thinking of the effect of
predestination as a whole, it is impossible that its entire, universal effect should have any cause which lies within ourselves,
because anything within a man which ordains him to salvation
is wholly included in the effect of predestination. Even his very
preparation for grace is included in the effect of predestination,
since even this is impossible without divine help, according to
Lam. 5:21: "Turn thou us unto thee, O Lord, and we shall be
turned." The reason for the effect of predestination is therefore
the divine goodness. The whole effect of predestination is
ordained for the sake of the divine goodness as its end, and
proceeds from the divine goodness as its prime mover.

On the first point: as we have said above, it is only as a final
cause that foreknowledge of the use which will be made of grace
is the ground of its bestowal.

On the second point: the rational ground for the whole
effect of predestination is the divine goodness itself. But one particular effect may still be the cause of another, as we have
said.

On the third point: the reason why some are predestined and
others rejected is to be found in the goodness of God. God is
said to do all things for the sake of his goodness, in order that
his goodness may be reflected in things. Now the divine goodness itself is single and simple. But created things cannot attain
to the simple nature of the divine, and must therefore reflect
the divine goodness by means of many forms. The universe thus
requires diverse grades of things for the sake of its completeness,
some things holding an exalted place in it and others a lowly
place. In order to preserve this variety of grades, moreover,
God permits some evils to arise, lest many good things should
be prevented. We explained this in Q. 22, Art. 2, and Augus-

tine agrees with it (1 *Ad Simplician* 11; 2 *De Bono Persev.*).[1]
Now we may consider the whole race of men in the same light
as the whole universe of things. God has willed to show forth
his goodness in men by mercifully sparing some of them, whom
he predestines, and by justly punishing others, whom he rejects.
This is the reason why he chooses some and rejects others, and
it is the reason given by the apostle in Rom. 9:22: "What if
God, willing to show his wrath [that is, to vindicate his justice],
and to make his power known, endured [that is, permitted]
with much longsuffering the vessels of wrath fitted to destruction: and that he might make known the riches of his glory on
the vessels of mercy, which he hath afore prepared unto glory,"
and also in II Tim. 2:20: "But in a great house there are not
only vessels of gold and of silver, but also of wood and of earth;
and some to honour, and some to dishonour." There is indeed
no reason why some are elected to glory while others are
rejected, except the will of God. Augustine says accordingly
(*Tract. 26 in Joan.*): "If thou wouldst not err, seek not to judge
why God draws one man and not another." In the realm of
nature, also, we can see a reason why one part of primary
matter should be made originally in the form of fire, and
another part of it in the form of earth. This was necessary for
the diversity of species in natural things, since primary matter
in itself is wholly uniform. But why one particular part of
primary matter should be under one form, and another particular part of it under another form, depends entirely on the will of
God; just as it depends entirely on the will of a builder whether
one individual stone shall be in one part of a wall and another
in another part of it, even though his art supplies the reason
why some stones should be in the one part and some in the
other. But there is no injustice in God's preparation of unequal
things for those who are not unequal. There would indeed be
injustice if the effects of predestination were rendered as a debt
which is due, and not given by grace. But when something is
given gratuitously, one may give more or less of it to whomsoever
it may please one's will, without injustice, provided that one
does not withhold what is due. This is what the master of the
house is saying in Matt. 20:14–15: "Take that thine is, and go
thy way. . . . Is it not lawful for me to do what I will with
mine own?"

[1] Cf. *De Corrept. et Grat.*, 8, §17.

Article Six

WHETHER PREDESTINATION IS CERTAIN

We proceed to the sixth article thus:

1. It seems that predestination is not certain. For on Rev. 3:11, "hold that fast which thou hast, that no man take thy crown," Augustine says: "no other will take it if one does not lose it." The crown to which one is predestined may therefore be lost as well as won. Hence predestination is not certain.

2. Again, if something is possible, none of its consequences are impossible. Now it is possible for a predestined man, like Peter, to sin and to fall. But if he should, the effect of predestination would be frustrated in consequence. The frustration of the effect of predestination is therefore not impossible. Hence predestination is not certain.

3. Again, what God could have done, that he can do. But God could have omitted to predestine one whom he has predestined, and therefore may not predestine him now. Hence predestination is not certain.

On the other hand: in a gloss on Rom. 8:29, "whom he did foreknow, he also did predestinate," Augustine says: "predestination is the foreknowledge and preparation of God's blessings, by which[1] whosoever will be set free will most certainly be set free" (*De Dono Persev.* 14).

I answer: predestination achieves its effect most certainly and infallibly. But it does not impose necessity of such a kind that its effect is realized through necessity. We said in Art. 1 that predestination is part of providence. But the things over which providence rules do not all come about through necessity. Some of them are realized through contingency, in accordance with the condition of the immediate causes which providence has provided for them. The ordinance of providence is nevertheless infallible, in spite of this. Now the ordinance of predestination is infallible in the same way. It does not exclude the freedom of the will, but realizes its effects contingently by means of it. What we said concerning the knowledge and will of God (Q. 14, Art. 13; Q. 19, Art. 4) must be understood in this light. They do not preclude contingency in things, even though they are certain and infallible.

On the first point: when we say that a crown belongs to someone, we may mean either of two things. We may mean that

---

[1] Migne *"qua."* Augustine *"quibus'."*

he is predestined to it. If we mean this, no one loses his crown. But we may also mean that a crown is due on account of merit acquired through grace, since what we deserve in a sense belongs to us. If we mean this, then anyone may lose his crown through subsequent mortal sin. Another then receives the crown which he has lost, being substituted in his stead, since God does not allow any to fall without putting others in their place. As it is said in Job 34:24: "He shall break in pieces mighty men without number, and set others in their stead." Men are thus set in the place of fallen angels, and Gentiles in the place of Jews. One who is substituted in the state of grace also receives the crown of the fallen in the sense that he rejoices in eternal life in the good which the other has done. For in eternal life everyone will rejoice in the good which has been done, whether by oneself or by another.

On the second point: considered in itself, that he should die in mortal sin is a possibility for one who is predestined. But if it is determined that he actually is predestined, this is not a possibility.

On the third point: as we said in Art. 4, predestination involves the divine will. Now the divine will is immutable. That God should will what he has created is therefore necessary, given that he has created it, though it is not necessary absolutely. We are bound to say the same of predestination. If all factors are taken into consideration, we must not say that God might not have predestined one whom he has predestined. We could say, speaking absolutely, that God either might or might not have predestined him. But this does not affect the certainty of predestination.

Article Seven

WHETHER THE NUMBER OF THE PREDESTINED IS CERTAIN

We proceed to the seventh article thus:

1. The number of the predestined does not seem to be certain. For a number which may be increased is not certain, and it appears from Deut. 1:11 that the number of the predestined may be increased. "The Lord God of your fathers make you a thousand times so many as ye are." The gloss says that the number is "definite with God, who knows them that are his." Hence the number of the predestined is not certain.

2. Again, no reason can be given why God should preordain any one number to salvation rather than any other. Now God

determines nothing without a reason. Hence the number of those preordained to salvation is not certain.

3. Again, the works of God are more perfect than those of nature. Now the works of nature reveal good in the many, and defect and evil in the few. It follows that if God were to determine the number of the saved, the saved would outnumber the damned. But Matt. 7:13 declares the very opposite: "Wide is the gate, and broad is the way, that leadeth to destruction, and many there be which go in thereat: Because strait is the gate, and narrow is the way, which leadeth unto life, and few there be that find it." The number of those who will be saved cannot then be determined by God.

On the other hand: Augustine says "the number of the predestined is certain, and cannot be increased or diminished" (*De Corrept. et Grat.* 13).

I answer: the number of the predestined is certain. Some have said that their number is formally certain, but not materially certain. This would mean that we could say with certainty that a hundred, for example, or a thousand, would be saved, but not that any particular persons would be saved. This view, however, destroys the certainty of predestination, of which we spoke in the preceding article. We must therefore affirm that the number of the predestined is known to God with material certainty, not only with formal certainty. We must declare that the number of the predestined is certain with God not only because he is aware of it, knowing how many will be saved—indeed he knows the number of the drops of rain and of the sands of the sea with equal certainty—but also because he chooses and determines each one.

To make this clear, we must understand that every agent intends to make something finite, as we explained when speaking of the infinite (Q. 7, Arts. 2, 3).[1] When anyone intends a determinate measure in what he makes, he thinks out the number of its essential parts, which are necessary for the perfection of the whole. But he does not select any definite number for such elements as are required only for the sake of other elements, and not as principal parts. He accepts whatever number of them may be required for the sake of the others. Thus a builder thinks out the determinate measurement of a house, the determinate number of rooms which he wishes,

---

[1] Even the infinite power of God can make only what is made, and what is made is bound to be finite, since its essential form is rendered determinate when received by its material element.

and the determinate numerical measurements of its walls and roof. But he does not select any definite number of stones. He accepts whatever number of stones may be required to complete the measurements of its walls. Now we must think in this way when we think of God in relation to the whole universe which he has made. He has preordained the measure in which it ought to exist, and the appropriate number of its essential parts, whose order is in a manner perpetual. He has preordained the number of worlds, the number of the stars, of the elements, and of the species of things. But individuals which pass away are not ordained for the good of the universe as principals. They are ordained secondarily, in order to preserve the good of their species. Hence although God knows the number of all individuals, he has not preordained the number of oxen, midges, and the like. His providence produces whatever number of them may be required in order to preserve their species. Now rational creatures, to a greater extent than all other creatures, are ordained for the good of the universe as principals. For in so far as they are rational, they are incorruptible—especially those who seek to attain blessedness, since they are more immediately in touch with the final end. The number of the predestined is therefore known to God with certainty, not only because he knows it, but because he has predetermined their number as a principal.

It is not quite the same, however, with the number of the rejected. They seem to have been preordained by God for the sake of the elect, for whom "all things work together for good" (Rom. 8:28). As to what the total number of the predestined may be, some say that as many men will be saved as angels have fallen. Others say that as many will be saved as angels remain. Others again say that the number of the saved will be equal to the number of fallen angels added to the whole number of angels created. But it is better said that "the number of the elect for whom there is a place in supernal happiness is known only to God."

On the first point: this quotation from Deuteronomy refers to those whose righteousness in this life was foreknown of God. The number of these both increases and diminishes, but not the number of the predestined.

On the second point: the reason for the measure of any part is to be found in its proportion to the whole. The reason why God has made so many stars, or so many species of things, and the reason why he has predestined so many, is to be found in the proportion of its principal parts to the good of the universe.

On the third point: such good as is proportionate to the normal state of nature is found in the many, and is lacking in the few. But good which exceeds the normal state of nature is found in the few, and is lacking in the many. It is obvious, for example, that the majority of men have sufficient knowledge to regulate their lives, and that those who have not are few, and are called morons or idiots, while those who attain to a profound knowledge of intelligible things are very few. Now the eternal blessedness which consists in the vision of God exceeds the normal state of nature, especially since the normal state is bereft of grace through the corruption of original sin. It is therefore the few who will be saved. Yet the mercy of God is abundantly apparent, in that very many of those whom he chooses for salvation fall short of it according to the course and inclination of nature.

Article Eight

WHETHER PREDESTINATION CAN BE FURTHERED BY THE PRAYERS OF THE DEVOUT

We proceed to the eighth article thus:

1. It seems that predestination cannot be furthered by the prayers of the devout. Nothing that is eternal can be preceded by anything that is temporal. Consequently nothing that is temporal can help to bring about anything that is eternal. Now predestination is eternal. The prayers of the devout cannot then help anyone to be predestined, since they are temporal. Hence predestination cannot be furthered by the prayers of the devout.

2. Again, counsel is needed only if knowledge is lacking, and help is needed only if strength is lacking. But God predestines without either counsel or help. As it is said in Rom. 11:34: "For who hath known [1] the mind of the Lord? or who hath been his counsellor?" Hence predestination is not furthered by the prayers of the devout.

3. Again, anything which can be furthered can also be hindered. But predestination cannot be hindered by anyone. Neither therefore can it be furthered by anyone.

On the other hand: it is said in Gen. 25:21: "And Isaac entreated the Lord for his wife, because she was barren: . . . Rebekah his wife conceived." Thus was born Jacob, and he

[1] Migne: "Who hath helped the Spirit of the Lord?"

was predestined. But he would not have been predestined had he not been born. Thus predestination is furthered by the prayers of the devout.

I answer: there have been various errors concerning this question. Some, having in mind the certainty of predestination, have said that prayers are superfluous, and that anything else which we may do to ensure eternal salvation is equally so, because the predestined will attain eternal salvation and the rejected will not, whether such things are done or not. But all the warnings of sacred Scripture which exhort us to prayer and to other good works are against this opinion. Others have said that divine predestination is altered by prayers. Such is said to have been the belief of the Egyptians, who thought that the divine dispensation could be thwarted by means of prayers and sacrifices, and called it Fate. But the authority of sacred Scripture is against this also. It is said in I Sam. 15:29: "the Strength of Israel will not lie nor repent," and in Rom. 11:29: "the gifts and calling of God are without repentance."

In contrast, we must say that there are two things to be considered in predestination. We must distinguish the divine preordination from its effect. The divine preordination cannot in any wise be furthered by the prayers of the devout, since their prayers cannot cause anyone to be predestined. But the effect of predestination may be furthered by their prayers, and by other good works also. The reason for this is that predestination is part of providence. Providence does not suppress secondary causes, but achieves its effects through subordinating their operation to itself. God provides effects in nature by ordaining natural causes to produce them, without which they would not be produced. He predestines the salvation of a man in the same way, subordinating to the ordinance of predestination everything which can help him towards salvation, whether it be his own prayers, or the prayers of another, or good works of any other kind, while his salvation would not be attained without them. Those who are predestined must therefore be diligent in good works and in prayer, since the effect of predestination is thereby fulfilled with certainty. For this reason it is said in II Peter 1:10: "Give diligence to make your calling and election sure."

On the first point: this reasoning proves only that the preordination of predestination is not furthered by the prayers of the devout.

On the second point: there are two ways in which one may

be helped by another. One may receive strength from another, as do the weak when they are helped. God does not receive strength from anyone, this being the meaning of the words "who hath known the mind of the Lord?" But one is also said to be helped by another when one achieves one's purpose by means of another, as does a master by means of his servant. God is helped in this way by ourselves, when we carry out what he has ordained. As it is said in I Cor. 3:9: "ye are God's husbandry." But this is not due to any lack of power in God. It is due to his use of secondary causes for the sake of preserving the beauty of the order of things, and for the sake of conferring the dignity of causality even upon creatures.

On the third point: as we said in Q. 19, Art. 6, secondary causes cannot evade the ordinance of the first and universal cause. They implement it. Predestination can therefore be furthered by creatures, but cannot be hindered by them.

Of Sin. Prima Secundae, Questions 82, 85

THE ESSENCE OF ORIGINAL SIN

WE MUST NOW CONSIDER THE ESSENCE OF ORIGINAL sin. There are four questions asked concerning it. 1. Whether original sin is a habit. 2. Whether original sin is one only, in any one man. 3. Whether original sin is desire. 4. Whether original sin is equally in all men.

Article One

WHETHER ORIGINAL SIN IS A HABIT

We proceed to the first article thus:

1. It seems that original sin is not a habit. As Anselm says (*De Conceptu Virginali* 2, 3, 26), original sin is the lack of original justice. It is therefore a kind of privation. But a privation is opposed to a habit. Hence original sin is not a habit.

2. Again, the character of guilt attaches to actual sin more than to original sin, since actual sin has more of the nature of the voluntary. But there is no guilt in the habit of actual sin. If there were, a man would sin guiltily while he slept. There cannot then be any guilt in a habit which is original.

3. Again, an act of sin always precedes the habit of it, because sinful habits are always acquired, never infused. But there is no act which precedes original sin. Hence original sin is not a habit.

On the other hand: Augustine says (*De Baptismo Puer; De Peccat. Mer. et Remis.* I, ch. 39; *De Tempt., Sermo* 45): "because of original sin infants have a tendency to desire, even though they do not actually desire." Now we speak of a tendency where there is a habit. Original sin is therefore a habit.

I answer: as we said in Q. 50, Art. 1, there are two kinds of habit.[1] There is the habit which inclines a power to act, of the kind which enables us to say that sciences and virtues are habits. Original sin is not a habit of this kind. But we also give the name of habit to the disposition by which a composite nature is well or ill disposed in a certain way, especially when such a disposition has become almost second nature, as in the case of sickness or of health. Original sin is such a habit. It is the disordered disposition which has resulted from the dissolution of the harmony which was once the essence of original justice, just as bodily sickness is the disordered disposition of a body which has lost the equilibrium which is the essence of health. Original sin is accordingly called the languor of nature.

On the first point: just as sickness of the body involves positive disorder in the disposition of the humours, as well as privation of the equilibrium of health, so original sin involves disorder in the disposition of the parts of the soul, as well as the privation of original justice. It is more than mere privation. It is a corrupt habit.

On the second point: actual sin is the disorder of an act. But original sin is the disordered disposition of nature itself, since it is the sin of nature. Now this disordered disposition has the character of guilt in so far as it is inherited from our first parent, as we said in Q. 81, Art. 1. It also has the character of a habit, which the disordered disposition of an act has not. Original sin can therefore be a habit, though actual sin cannot be a habit.

On the third point: this objection argues about the kind of habit which inclines a power to act. Original sin is not a habit of this kind, although it does result in an inclination to disordered actions. It results in such inclination not directly but indirectly, through depriving us of the original justice which would have prevented disorderly actions, and once did prevent them. The inclination to disordered bodily functions results from sickness in this same indirect way. But we should not say that original sin is an infused habit, nor that it is acquired through action (unless the action of our first parent, but not that of any present person). It is inborn by reason of our corrupt origin.

[1] A habit is defined as "a disposition of a subject which is in a state of potentiality either in respect of form or in respect of operation," but is distinguished from a "disposition" as being difficult to change. See "The Role of Habitus in the Thomistic Metaphysics of Potency and Act" in *Essays in Thomism*, Ed. R. E. Brennan.

Article Two

WHETHER THERE ARE MANY ORIGINAL SINS IN ONE MAN

We proceed to the second article thus:

1. It seems that there are many original sins in one man. For it is said in Ps. 51:5: "Behold, I was shapen in iniquity; and in sin[1] did my mother conceive me." The sin in which one is conceived is original sin. There are therefore several original sins in one man.

2. Again, one and the same habit does not cause us to tend towards opposite things. For a habit inclines us through a modification of nature, which tends in one direction. But original sin, even in one man, inclines him to different and opposite sins. It is therefore not one habit, but several.

3. Again, original sin infects all parts of the soul. But the several parts of the soul are separate subjects of sin, as was explained in Q. 74, and the same sin cannot be in separate subjects. It seems, then, that original sin is not one, but many.

On the other hand: it is said in John 1:29: "Behold the Lamb of God, which taketh away the sin of the world." As the gloss explains, the singular is used because "the sin of the world," which is original sin, is one.

I answer: there is only one original sin in any one man. We may see the reason for this in two ways. We may see it from the cause of original sin. It is only the first sin of our first parent that is transmitted to posterity, as we said in Q. 81, Art. 2. The original sin that is in any one man is therefore numerically one, while it is also proportionately one in all men, that is, one in respect of its first beginning. We may see the reason also if we consider the essence of original sin itself. Any disordered disposition is considered to be one if its cause is of one kind, and to be numerically one if it occurs in a single subject. This is obvious in the case of bodily sickness. There may indeed be many kinds of sickness arising from different causes, such as excessive heat or cold, or lesion of the lungs or of the liver. But a sickness of any one kind in one man is numerically one. Now there is only one cause of the corrupt disposition which we call original sin. Its cause is the privation of original justice, which took away from man the subjection of his mind to God. Original sin is therefore of one kind, and can only be numerically one in any one man. It is, however, numerically different in different men, though one in kind and in proportion.

[1] Migne: *in peccatis* (plural).

On the first point: the plural "in sins" is here used in the customary manner of divine Scripture, which frequently uses the plural instead of the singular, as for example in Matt. 2:20: "they are dead which sought the young child's life." It is used either because all natural sins virtually pre-exist in original sin as their principle, so that original sin is virtually many; or because the sin transmitted to us through generation from our first parent includes many deformities, such as pride, disobedience, gluttony, and the like; or because many parts of the soul are infected by original sin.

On the second point: the same habit cannot incline us to opposite things directly and of itself, by means of its own form. But it can do so indirectly and accidentally, by taking away a preventative. The elements of a composite body tend in different directions when its harmony is destroyed. The several powers of the soul also tend in different directions when the harmony of original justice is taken away.

On the third point: original sin infects the different powers of the soul as parts of a single whole, just as original justice once held all parts of the soul together as a single whole. There is therefore only one original sin, just as there is only one fever in one man, though different parts of his body may be aggravated by it.

Article Three

Whether Original Sin is Desire

We proceed to the third article thus:

1. It seems that original sin is not desire. For every sin is contrary to nature, as the Damascene says (2 *De Fid. Orth.* 4, 30). But desire is in accordance with nature, since it is the proper act of the power of concupiscence, which is a natural power. It follows that desire is not original sin.

2. Again, the apostle says that original sin is responsible for the "passions of sin" that are in us (Rom. 7:5). But there are many passions besides desire, as was said in Q. 23, Art. 4. Hence original sin is not desire rather than any other passion.

3. Again, it was said in Art. 2 that all parts of the soul are deranged by original sin. Now the chief part of the soul is the intellect, as the philosopher explains in 10 *Ethics* 7. Original sin is therefore ignorance, rather than desire.

On the other hand: Augustine says (1 *Retract.* 15): "Desire is the guilt of original sin."

I answer: the species of each thing depends on its formal

122

nature. Now we said in the preceding article that the species of
original sin is determined by its cause. The formal nature of
original sin is therefore determined by the cause of original
sin. We must understand the cause of original sin, however, in
contrast to the cause of the original justice which is its opposite,
the causes of opposites being themselves opposites. The
whole order of original justice consisted in the subjection of
man's will to God. Man was subject to God first and foremost
through his will, which directs all other parts of his soul to their
end, as we said in Q. 9, Art. 1. Disorder in any other part of his
soul is therefore the consequence of his will turning away from
God. Privation of original justice, by which the will of man
was subject to God, is therefore the formal element in original
sin. Every other disorder of the powers of the soul is related to
original sin as the material which it affects. Now the disorder
of these other powers consists especially in this, that they are
wrongly directed to changeable good. Such disorder may be
called by the common name of "desire." Materially, then,
original sin is desire. Formally, it is the lack of original justice.

On the first point: in man, the power of desire is naturally
ruled by reason. Desire is therefore natural to man in so far as
it is subject to reason.[1] But desire which exceeds the bounds of
reason exists in him as something contrary to nature. Such is
the desire of original sin.

On the second point: we said in Q. 25, Art. 1, that the
passions of anger are reducible to the passions of desire, which
are more fundamental, and in Q. 25, Art. 2, that desire itself
moves us more vehemently than any other of these latter
passions, and is felt more. Original sin is accordingly ascribed
to desire, since it is more fundamental than other passions, and
virtually includes all of them.

On the third point: intellect and reason have the primacy
where good in concerned. But, conversely, the lower part of the
soul comes first where evil is concerned. For it darkens reason
and drags it down, as we said in Q. 80, Art. 1. Original sin is
therefore said to be desire rather than ignorance, although
ignorance is one of its material defects.

[1] The "rational" desire which is peculiar to man is elsewhere referred to
as "non-natural" (12ae, Q. 30, Art. 3). This does not imply that it is unnatural, but that it is distinct from the "irrational" desire common to man
and the animals. Rational desire is natural and proper to man. Being
infinite, it is never satisfied in this life, and in its highest form is the desire
for blessedness. The inordinate desire for changeable good is thus a corruption of a capacity which ought to lead towards final good if subject to reason.

Article Four

WHETHER ORIGINAL SIN IS IN ALL MEN EQUALLY

We proceed to the fourth article thus:

1. It seems that original sin is not in all men equally. It was said in the preceding article that original sin is inordinate desire. But all men are not equally subject to desire. It follows that original sin is not in all men equally.

2. Again, original sin is the disordered disposition of the soul, as sickness is the disordered disposition of the body. Now sickness admits of more or less. Therefore original sin also admits of more and less.

3. Again, Augustine says: "lust transmits original sin to posterity." (1 *De Nup. et Concup.* 23–24.) But the lust in generation may be greater in one than in another. Original sin may therefore be greater in one than in another.

On the other hand: it was said in the preceding article that original sin is the sin of nature. But nature is in all men equally. Original sin is therefore also in all men equally.

I answer: there are two things in original sin. One is the lack of original justice. The other is the relation of this lack to the sin of our first parent, from whom it is inherited through our corrupt origin. Now original sin cannot be greater or less in respect of the lack of original justice, since the whole gift of original justice has been taken away. Privations do not admit of more and less when they deprive us of something altogether, as we said of death and darkness in Q. 73, Art. 2. Nor can original sin be greater or less in respect of its relation to its origin. Everyone bears the same relation to the first beginning of the corrupt origin from which sin derives its guilt, and relations do not admit of greater and less. It is plain, then, that original sin cannot be greater in one man than in another.

On the first point: since man has lost the control of original justice which once kept all the powers of his soul in order, each power tends to follow its own natural movement, and to follow it more vehemently the stronger it is. Now some powers of the soul may be stronger in one man than in another, because bodily characteristics vary. That one man should be more subject to desire than another is not therefore the consequence of original sin, since all are equally deprived of the control of original justice, and the lower parts of the soul are equally left to themselves in all men. It is due to the different dispositions of their powers, as we have said.

On the second point: sickness of the body does not have an equal cause in all cases, even if it is of the same kind. For example, fever which results from putrefaction of the bile may be due to a greater or lesser putrefaction, or to one which is more or less removed from a vital principle. But the cause of original sin is equal in respect of everyone. There is therefore no comparison.

On the third point: it is not actual lust that transmits original sin to posterity, for one would still transmit original sin even if it were divinely granted that one should feel no lust in generation. We must understand it to be habitual lust, on account of which the sensitive appetite is not subject to reason, now that the control of original justice is lost. Lust of this kind is equally in all.

Question Eighty-Five

THE EFFECTS OF SIN

We must now consider the effects of sin. We must consider the corruption of natural good, concerning which there are six questions. 1. Whether natural good is diminished by sin. 2. Whether it is entirely destroyed by sin. 3. Of the four wounds which Bede names as the wounds inflicted on human nature as the result of sin. 4. Whether privation of mode, species, and order is the effect of sin. 5. Whether death and other bodily defects are the effects of sin. 6. Whether these are in some way natural to man.

Article One

WHETHER SIN DIMINISHES NATURAL GOOD

We proceed to the first article thus:

1. It seems that sin does not diminish natural good. For the sin of a man is no worse than the sin of a devil, and Dionysius says that what is naturally good in devils remains intact after they sin (4 *Div. Nom.*, lect. 19). It follows that sin does not destroy the natural good in man.

2. Again, that which is prior is not changed by an alteration in that which is consequential to it. Thus a substance remains

the same when its attributes are altered. Now nature is prior to voluntary action. It follows that nature is not changed, nor the good of nature thereby diminished, by any derangement of voluntary action which results from sin.

3. Again, sin is an action, and diminution a passion. Now an agent cannot possibly be affected by its own action, although it may act on one thing and be affected by another. It follows that one who sins cannot diminish the good of his own nature by his own sin.

4. Again, no accident acts upon the subject to which it belongs, since what is acted upon is potentially something, whereas the subject of an accident is already the actuality of which its accident is an accident. Now sin occurs in the good of nature as an accident in its subject. It follows that sin does not diminish the good of nature, since to diminish anything is in a sense to act upon it.

On the other hand: according to a gloss by another, Bede expounds Luke 10:30 thus—"a certain man going down from Jerusalem to Jericho (that is, incurring the defect of sin) was stripped of his raiment and wounded in his natural powers." It follows that sin diminishes the good of nature.

I answer: by natural good we may mean three things. We may mean the constitutive principles of nature itself, together with the properties consequential to them, such as the powers of the soul, and the like. Secondly, we may mean the inclination to virtue. This is a good of nature, since a man possesses it naturally, as we said in Q. 63, Art. 1. Thirdly, we may mean the gift of original justice, which was bestowed on the whole of human nature when it was bestowed on the first man. The constitution of human nature is neither destroyed nor diminished by sin. The gift of original justice was totally lost through the sin of our first parent. The natural inclination to virtue, finally, is diminished by sin. Actions generate an inclination to similar actions, as we said in Q. 51, Art. 2, and the inclination to one of two contraries is bound to be diminished by an inclination to the other. Now sin is the contrary of virtue. The good of nature which consists in the inclination to virtue is therefore bound to be diminished by the very fact that a man sins.

On the first point: anyone who reads his words can see that Dionysius is speaking of the primary good of nature, which consists of being, living, and understanding.

On the second point: although it is prior to voluntary action, nature includes the inclination to voluntary action of some kind. Hence although nature itself is not changed by any alteration in its voluntary action, its inclination is changed in respect of its direction to an end.

On the third point: voluntary action is the outcome of diverse powers, of which some are active and others passive. Hence it may either cause something in him who acts voluntarily, or take something away from him, as we said when discussing the formation of a habit (Q. 51, Art. 2).

On the fourth point: an accident does not act upon its subject in the sense of producing an effect in it. But it does act on it formally, in the sense in which whiteness makes things white. There is therefore nothing to prevent sin diminishing the good of nature by being itself the diminution of it, as a derangement of action. It must be said, however, that the derangement of the soul is due to the circumstance that there is both activity and passivity in its actions. The sensitive appetite is moved by a sensible object, and also inclines the reason and the will, as we said in Q. 77, Art. 1, and Q. 80, Art. 2. Disorder arises through an object acting on one power which acts on another power and deranges it, not through an accident acting upon its own subject.

Article Two

WHETHER THE WHOLE GOOD OF HUMAN NATURE CAN BE DESTROYED BY SIN

We proceed to the second article thus:

1. It seems that the whole good of human nature can be taken away by sin. The good of human nature is finite, since human nature itself is finite. Now a finite thing is removed altogether if it is continually reduced, and the good of human nature may be continually reduced by sin. It seems that it may finally be taken away altogether.

2. Again, what is simple in nature is the same in its wholeness as it is in its parts. This is obvious in the case of air, water, flesh, or any body whose parts are similar. Now the good of nature is altogether uniform. Hence since part of it may be taken away by sin, it seems that the whole of it may be taken away by sin.

3. Again, the natural good which is diminished by sin is the capacity for virtue. Sin destroys this capacity altogether in some persons. It obviously does so in the damned, who can no

more recover virtue than a blind man can recover his sight. Thus sin may entirely destroy natural good.

On the other hand: Augustine says (*Enchirid.* 13, 14): "evil exists only in what is good." But the evil of guilt can be neither in the good of virtue nor in the good of grace, since these are contrary to it. It must therefore be in the good of nature. It cannot then totally destroy the good of nature.

I answer: we said in the preceding article that the natural good which sin diminishes is the natural inclination to virtue. Now the reason why man inclines to virtue is that he is rational. It is because he is rational that he acts in accordance with reason, and this is to act virtuously. But a man would not be able to sin without his rational nature. Sin cannot then deprive him of it altogether. It follows that his inclination to virtue cannot be entirely destroyed.

Since this natural good is found to be continually diminished by sin, some have sought to illustrate the diminution of it by the continuous reduction of a finite thing which is yet never entirely removed. As the philosopher says in 1 *Physics*, text 37, any finite magnitude will at length be exhausted if the same quantity is repeatedly taken from it—if I were to subtract a handbreadth from a finite quantity, for instance. But subtraction can go on indefinitely if the same proportion is subtracted instead of the same quantity. For example, if a quantity is divided in two, and the half taken from the half of it, subtraction can go on indefinitely, so long as each subsequent reduction is less than the preceding. This illustration, however, is irrelevant, because a subsequent sin diminishes the good of nature not less than a previous sin, but much more, if it be more serious.

We must say instead that the natural inclination to virtue is to be understood as a medium between two things. It depends on rational nature as its root, and inclines to the good of virtue as its term and end. The diminution of it may accordingly be understood either as referring to its root, or as referring to its term. Its root is not diminished by sin, because sin does not diminish nature itself, as we said in the preceding article. But it is diminished in respect of its term, in so far as an obstacle is put in the way of its attaining its end. If the natural inclination to virtue were diminished in respect of its root, it would be bound to be wholly destroyed in the end, along with the complete destruction of a man's rational nature. But since it is diminished by way of an obstacle preventing the attainment of its end, it is manifest that it can be diminished indefinitely.

Obstacles can be interposed indefinitely. A man can add sin to sin without end. But it cannot be entirely destroyed, since the root of inclination always remains. The same sort of thing is apparent in the case of a diaphanous body, which has the inclination to take in light because it is diaphanous, and whose inclination or capacity to do so is diminished by intervening clouds, yet always remains rooted in its nature.

On the first point: this objection argues from diminution by subtraction. But the good of nature is diminished by way of an obstacle which is interposed, and which neither destroys nor diminishes the root of inclination, as we have said.

On the second point: natural inclination is indeed wholly uniform. But it is related both to its principle and to its end, and is diminished in one way and not in another because of this diversity of relation.

On the third point: the natural inclination to virtue remains even in the damned, who would not otherwise feel the remorse of conscience. The reason why it does not issue in act is that grace is withheld in accordance with divine justice. The capacity to see similarly remains in a blind man, at the root of his nature, in so far as he is an animal naturally possessed of sight, but fails to become actual because the cause which would enable it to do so, by forming the organ which sight requires, is lacking.

Article Three

WHETHER WEAKNESS, IGNORANCE, MALICE, AND DESIRE ARE RIGHTLY NAMED AS THE WOUNDS OF NATURE DUE TO SIN

We proceed to the third article thus:

1. Weakness, ignorance, malice, and desire do not seem to be rightly named as the wounds of nature due to sin. For they are clearly named as causes of sin in Q. 76, Art. 1, Q. 77, Arts. 3, 5, and Q. 78, and the same thing is not both cause and effect of the same thing. They should not therefore be named as effects of sin.

2. Again, malice is called a sin. It should not therefore be named as one of the effects of sin.

3. Again, desire is natural, since it is the act of the power of concupiscence. But what is natural should not be named as a wound of nature. Therefore desire should not be named as a wound of nature.

4. Again, it was said in Q. 77 that to sin from weakness is the same thing as to sin from passion. Now desire is a passion. It should not then be distinguished from weakness.

5. Again, Augustine says that the sinner's soul suffers two penalties, namely "ignorance" and "difficulty," and that "error" and "vexation" arise out of them (*De Nat. et Grat.* 67; 1 *Retract.* 9). But these do not coincide with the four wounds named. Either the one list or the other is therefore inadequate.

On the other hand: this is said by Bede. (Reference unknown.)

I answer: there was a time when original justice enabled reason to have complete control over the powers of the soul, and when reason itself was subject to God and made perfect by him. But original justice was lost through the sin of our first parent, as we said in Q. 81, Art. 2. In consequence, all powers of the soul have been left to some extent destitute of their proper order, by which they are naturally inclined to virtue. It is this destitution that we call "a wound of nature." Now there are four powers of the soul which can be the subject of virtue. There is reason, the virtue of which is prudence; will, the virtue of which is justice; the irascible power, the virtue of which is fortitude; and desire, the virtue of which is temperance. In so far as reason has lost the way to truth, there is the wound of ignorance. In so far as the will has lost its inclination to good, there is the wound of malice. In so far as the irascible power has lost its aggressiveness towards the difficult, there is the wound of weakness. Finally, in so far as desire is no longer directed to the delectable under the restraint of reason, there is the wound of desire.

These four, then, are the wounds inflicted on the whole of human nature by the sin of our first parent. But all four are also caused by other sins, since actual sin diminishes the inclination to virtue in every one of us, as we said in Arts. 1 and 2. Reason is darkened by sin, especially in practical matters. The will is hardened against the good. To act well becomes more difficult. Desire becomes more impulsive.

On the first point: there is no reason why the effect of one sin should not be the cause of another. Indeed, the derangement caused by a previous sin inclines the soul to sin more readily.

On the second point: "malice" does not here mean the sin. It means that proneness of the will to evil which is mentioned in Gen. 8:21: "the imagination of man's heart is evil from his youth."

On the third point: as we said in Q. 82, Art. 3, desire is

130

natural to man in so far as it is subject to reason, but is contrary to his nature if it exceeds the bounds of reason.

On the fourth point: every passion may be called a weakness in a general sense, since it saps the soul's strength and hinders reason. Bede, however, means weakness in the strict sense in which it is opposed to fortitude, which is a character of the irascible power.

On the fifth point: the "difficulty" of which Augustine speaks includes the three wounds which affect the appetitive power, namely malice, weakness, and desire. One does not readily tend to good if these are present. Error and vexation are consequential wounds. A man grieves because he lacks the strength for what he desires.

Article Four

Whether Privation of Mode, Species, and Order is the Effect of Sin

We proceed to the fourth article thus:

1. It seems that privation of mode, species, and order is not the effect of sin. Augustine says (*De Nat. Boni* 3): "where these are great, good is great; where these are small, good is small; where these are absent, good is absent." But sin does not take away natural good altogether. Therefore it does not deprive us of mode, species, and order.

2. Again, nothing is the cause of itself. But sin is the privation of mode, species, and order, as Augustine says (*De Nat. Boni* 4, 36, 37). Such privation is not then the effect of sin.

3. Again, different sins have different effects. Now mode, species, and order are different. The privations of them are therefore different also. The privations of them are therefore the effects of different sins, not the effect of each sin.

On the other hand: sin is in the soul as sickness is in the body, according to Ps. 6:2: "Have mercy upon me, O Lord; for I am weak." Now weakness deprives the soul of mode, species, and order. Therefore sin deprives the soul of mode, species, and order.

I answer: as we said in Pt. I, Q. 5, Art. 5, every created good possesses mode, species, and order because it is a created good, and because it exists. Every being and every good is conceived according to some form, and its form determines its species. Now the form of any thing of any kind, whether of a substance or of an accident, has a certain measure. For this reason it is said in 8 *Metaph.*, text 10, that "the forms of things are like numbers." Each thing has thus a certain mode, according to its measure. The form of each thing, finally, determines its order in relation to other things. Thus the degree of the mode, species, and order of things varies according to the degree of the good which is in them.

There is a certain good, with its mode, species, and order, which belongs to the very nature of man. This is neither taken away by sin, nor diminished by it. There is also good in the natural inclination to virtue, with its mode, species, and order. This is diminished by sin, but not entirely taken away. There is also the good of virtue and of grace, with its mode, species, and order. This is entirely taken away by mortal sin. There is, further, the good of orderly action, with its mode, species, and order. The privation of this last is essentially sin itself. The way in which sin is privation of mode, species, and order, and the way in which it deprives us of them or diminishes them, is thus made clear.

The answers to the first and second objections are obvious.

On the third point: what we have said above makes it clear that mode, species, and order follow one upon the other. They are therefore taken away, or diminished, together.

Article Five

WHETHER DEATH AND OTHER DEFECTS OF THE BODY ARE THE EFFECTS OF SIN

We proceed to the fifth article thus:

1. It seems that death and other defects of the body are not the effects of sin. If a cause is equal, its effect will be equal. But these defects are not equal in everyone. They are greater in some than in others, whereas original sin, to which they seem principally due, is in all men equally, as was said in Q. 82, Art. 4. It follows that death and defects of this kind are not the effects of sin.

2. Again, when a cause is removed, its effect is removed. But when every sin is removed by baptism or by penitence, these defects are not removed. It follows that they are not the effects of sin.

3. Again, actual sin has more of the nature of guilt than original sin, and actual sin does not cause any defect in the body. Much less, then, does original sin. It follows that death and other defects of the body are not the effect of sin.

On the other hand: the apostle says in Rom. 5:12: "by one man sin entered into the world, and death by sin."

I answer: one thing may be the cause of another in either of two ways—either through itself, or accidentally. It is the cause of another through itself if it produces its effect by its own natural power, or by the power of its form. The effect is then essentially intended by the cause. It is obvious, then, that sin is not through itself the cause of death or of similar evils, because the sinner does not intend them. But one thing may also be the cause of another accidentally, by removing something which prevents it. It is said in 8 *Physics*, text 32, that one who dislodges a pillar is accidentally the mover of the stone which it supports. The sin of our first parent is, thus accidentally, the cause of death and of all similar defects of human nature. For it took away original justice, which not only kept the lower powers of the soul in subjection to reason, without any disorder, but also kept the whole body in subjection to the soul, without any defect (as was said in Pt. I, Q. 97, Art. 1). When original justice was taken away by this sin, human nature was so wounded by the derangement of the powers of the soul (as we said in Art. 4, and Q. 83, Art. 3), that it was rendered corruptible by the derangement of the body. Now the loss of original justice has the character of a punishment, comparable with the withholding of grace. Death and all attendant defects of the body are therefore the punishments of original sin. They are in accordance with the punitive justice of God, even though they are not intended by the sinner.

On the first point: an equal cause produces an equal effect, and an effect is increased or diminished along with its cause, provided that the cause produces its effect through itself. But equality of cause does not imply inequality of effect when the cause operates by removing a preventative. If someone applies equal force to two columns, it does not follow that the stones which rest on them will be disturbed equally. The heavier stone will fall the more quickly, because it is left to its own natural heaviness when the column which supports it is taken away. Now the nature of the human body was similarly left to itself when original justice was taken away. Some bodies are consequently subject to more defects and others to fewer defects, according to their different natural conditions, even though original sin is equal in all of them.

On the second point: according to what the apostle says in Rom. 8:11, the same power which takes away the guilt of original sin and of actual sin will take away these defects also: ". . . he shall also quicken your mortal bodies by his Spirit that dwelleth in you." But all things are done in their due time, as God's wisdom ordains. We must first be made to conform with Christ's passion, before we attain to the immortal and undying glory which was begun in Christ and obtained by him for us. His passion must remain in our bodies for a time, before we share, like him, in undying glory.

On the third point: there are two things in actual sin which we may have in mind, namely, the act itself, and the guilt of it. The act of sin can cause a defect in the body. Some people take ill and die through over-eating. But the guilt of it deprives a man of grace for rectifying the actions of the soul, not of grace for preventing defects of the body. Original justice did prevent defects of the body. Hence actual sin is not the cause of such defects in the same way as original sin is the cause of them.

Article Six

Whether Death and Other Defects are Natural to Man

We proceed to the sixth article thus:

1. Death and similar defects seem to be natural to man. It is said in 10 *Metaph.*, text 26, that corruptibles and incorruptibles belong to different genera. But man belongs to the same genus as other animals, and they are naturally corruptible. Hence man is naturally corruptible.

2. Again, anything composed of contraries is naturally corruptible, since it contains the cause of its corruption within itself. The human body is composed of contraries. It is therefore naturally corruptible.

3. Again, the natural action of heat is to dispel humidity. Now the life of man is maintained by heat and humidity together. Since it is by the natural action of heat that his vital functions are sustained (as is said in 2 *De Anima*, text 50), it appears that death and similar defects are natural to man.

On the other hand: 1. God has made everything in man that is natural to him. But Wisdom 1:13 says that "God did not make death." It follows that death is not natural to man.

2. What is natural cannot be called a punishment or an evil, since what is natural is congenial. But we said in Art. 5 that death and similar defects are the punishments of original sin. They cannot then be natural to man.

3. Matter is adapted to its form, and each thing is adapted to its end. Now the end of man is eternal blessedness, as we said in Q. 3, Art. 8, and the form of his body is his rational soul, which is incorruptible, as we said in Pt. I, Q. 75, Art. 6. His body is therefore naturally incorruptible.

I answer: we can speak of any corruptible thing in two ways—according to its universal nature and according to its particular nature. The particular nature of each thing is an active and conserving power of its own, which intends both its existence and its conservation. According to this particular nature, therefore, every corruption and every defect is contrary to nature, as is said in 2 *De Coelo*, text 37.

The universal nature of a thing, on the other hand, is the active power of some universal principle of nature, such as one of the heavenly bodies, or some higher substance. This is the reason why God has been called *Natura Naturans* by some persons. Now a power of this kind intends the good and conservation of the universe, for which alternate generation and corruption in things is indispensable. According to their universal nature, therefore, the corruptions and defects of things are natural. They are not natural according to the inclination of the form of a thing, since its form is the principle of its existence and perfection. But they are natural according to the inclination of the matter which the active universal agent proportionately distributes to a form of such a kind. Each form strives to be as permanent as it can be, but no form of any corruptible thing can secure permanence for itself, with the exception of the rational soul. The rational soul is not entirely dependent on corporeal matter, as are other forms. It at least has an activity of its own which is not material, as we said in Pt. I, Q. 75, Art. 2, and Q. 76, Art. 1. Incorruption of form is therefore more natural to man than to other corruptible things. But his form is nevertheless a form whose matter is composed of contraries, and his being as a whole is consequently rendered corruptible by the inclination of its matter. According to what the nature of his material element is in itself, therefore, man is naturally corruptible. But according to the nature of his form, he is not naturally corruptible.

The first three contentions argue from the material element in man. The three which follow argue from his form. To answer them, we must observe two things. The first is that the form of man, which is his rational soul, is adapted in point of incorruptibility to his end, which is eternal blessedness. The second is that his naturally corruptible body is adapted to its form in one way, but not in another. This is because there are two kinds of condition which may be discerned in any material. There is a condition which an agent chooses, and a condition which he does not choose, but which is just the natural condition of the material itself. Thus a smith who wishes to make a knife chooses a hard and workable material, such as can be sharpened and made useful for cutting. Iron, in these respects, is a material adapted to a knife. But that it is breakable, and liable to rust, is the natural disposition of iron which the ironworker does not choose, but which he would exclude if he could. It is thus a condition adapted neither to the intention of the artisan nor to the purpose of his art. Now the human body is the material similarly chosen by nature for the sake of its moderately varied constitution, which makes it the most convenient organ of touch, and of the other sensitive and motive powers. But its corruptibility is due to the condition of matter, and nature did not choose it. Nature would rather have chosen an incorruptible material, if it could have done so. But God, to whom all nature is subject, made good this defect of nature when he created man. He bestowed a certain incorruptibility on the body by his gift of original justice, as we said in Pt. I, Q. 97, Art. 1. This is the reason why it is said that "God did not make death," and that death is the punishment of sin.

The answers to the objections are now obvious.

Treatise on Grace. Prima Secundae Questions 109–114

Question One Hundred and Nine

CONCERNING THE EXTERNAL PRINCIPLE OF HUMAN ACTIONS, THAT IS, THE GRACE OF GOD

WE MUST NOW CONSIDER THE EXTERNAL PRINCIPLE of human actions, that is, God, in so far as we are helped by him to act rightly through grace. We shall consider first the grace of God, secondly its cause, and thirdly its effects. The first of these inquiries will be threefold, since we shall inquire first into the necessity of grace, second into the essence of grace itself, and third into the divisions of it.

There are ten questions concerning the necessity of grace.
1. Whether without grace a man can know any truth.
2. Whether without grace a man can do or will any good.
3. Whether without grace a man can love God above all things.
4. Whether without grace a man can keep the commandments of the law, by his own natural powers. 5. Whether without grace he can merit eternal life. 6. Whether without grace a man can prepare himself for grace. 7. Whether without grace he can rise from sin. 8. Whether without grace he can avoid sin. 9. Whether, having received grace, a man can do good and avoid sin without further divine help. 10. Whether he can persevere in good by himself.

Article One

WHETHER A MAN CAN KNOW ANY TRUTH WITHOUT GRACE

We proceed to the first article thus:
1. It seems that a man cannot know any truth without grace. The gloss by Ambrose on I Cor. 12:3, "no man can say that Jesus is the Lord, but by the Holy Ghost," says that "every truth, by whomsoever uttered, is by the Holy Ghost." Now the

Holy Ghost dwells in us by grace. Hence we cannot know truth without grace.

2. Again, Augustine says (1 *Soliloq.* 6): "the most certain sciences are like things lit up by the sun so that they may be seen. But it is God who gives the light. Reason is in our minds as sight is in our eyes, and the eyes of the mind are the senses of the soul." Now however pure it be, bodily sense cannot see any visible thing without the light of the sun. Hence however perfect be the human mind, it cannot by reasoning know any truth without the light of God, which belongs to the aid of grace.

3. Again, the human mind cannot understand truth except by thinking, as Augustine explains (14 *De Trin.* 7). Now in II Cor. 3:5 the apostle says: "Not that we are sufficient of ourselves to think anything as of ourselves." Hence a man cannot know truth by himself, without the help of grace.

On the other hand: Augustine says (1 *Retract.* 4): "I do not now approve of having said in a prayer 'O God, who dost will that only the pure shall know truth.' For it may be replied that many who are impure know many truths." Now a man is made pure by grace, according to Ps. 51:10: "Create in me a clean heart, O God, and renew a right spirit within me." It follows that a man can know truth by himself, without the help of grace.

I answer: to know truth is a use or action of the intellectual light, since the apostle says that "whatever doth make manifest is light" [1] (Eph. 5:13), and every use involves movement, in the broad sense in which understanding and will are said to be movements, as the philosopher explains in 3 *De Anima*, text 28. In corporeal things, we see that any movement not only requires a formal principle of the movement or action itself, but also requires a motion of the first mover. Since the first mover in the order of material things is the heavenly body, fire could not cause change otherwise than through the motion of the heavenly body, even though it should possess perfect heat. It is plain, then, that just as every corporeal movement derives from the movement of the heavenly body as the first corporeal mover, so all movements, whether corporeal or spiritual, derive from the absolute prime mover, which is God. Hence no matter how perfect any corporeal or spiritual nature is supposed to be, it cannot issue in its act unless it is moved by God, whose moving is according to the plan of his providence, not neces-

[1] Migne: "All that is made manifest is light."

sitated by nature like the moving of the heavenly body. Now not only is every motion derived from God as first mover, but every formal perfection is likewise derived from God, as from the first act. It follows that an action of the intellect, or of any created thing, depends on God in two ways: first, in that it has from him the perfection or the form by means of which it acts, and second, in that it is moved to its act by him. Every power bestowed by God upon created things has the power to achieve some definite action by means of its own properties. But it cannot achieve anything further, unless through a form which is added to it. Water, for example, cannot heat unless it is itself heated by fire. So also the human intellect possesses the form of intellectual light, which by itself is sufficient for the knowledge of such intelligible things as we can learn through sense. But it cannot know intelligible things of a higher order unless it is perfected by a stronger light, such as the light of faith or prophecy, which is called "the light of glory" since it is added to nature.

We must therefore say that, if a man is to know any truth whatsoever, he needs divine help in order that his intellect may be moved to its act by God. But he does not need a new light added to his natural light in order to know the truth in all things, but only in such things as transcend his natural knowledge. Yet God sometimes instructs men miraculously by grace in matters which can be known through natural reasons, just as he sometimes achieves by miracle things which nature can do.

On the first point: "every truth, by whomsoever uttered, is by the Holy Ghost"—but as bestowing the natural light and as moving us to understand and to speak the truth, not as dwelling in us through sanctifying grace, or as bestowing any permanent gift superadded to nature. This is the case only with certain truths which must be known and spoken—especially with truths of faith, of which the apostle is speaking.

On the second point: the corporeal sun illumines externally, God internally. The natural light bestowed on the mind is God's light, by which we are enlightened to know such things as belong to natural knowledge. Other light is not required for this, but only for such things as transcend natural knowledge.

On the third point: we always need divine help for any thinking, in so far as God moves the intellect to act. For to think is to understand something actively, as Augustine explains (14 *De Trin.* 7).

Article Two

WHETHER A MAN CAN WILL OR DO GOOD WITHOUT GRACE

We proceed to the second article thus:

1. It seems that a man can will and do good without grace. For that of which he is master is within a man's power, and it was said previously that a man is master of his actions, especially of his willing. (Q. 1, Art. 1; Q. 13, Art. 6.) It follows that a man can will and do good by himself, without the help of grace.

2. Again, a man is master of what conforms with his nature more than of what is contrary to it. Now to sin is contrary to nature, as the Damascene says (2 *De Fid. Orth.* 30), whereas the practice of virtue conforms with nature, as was said in Q. 71, Art. 1. It seems, therefore, that since a man can sin by himself, he can much more will and do good by himself.

3. Again, "truth is the good of the intellect," as the philosopher says in 6 *Ethics* 2. Now the intellect can know truth by itself, just as any other thing can perform its natural action by itself. Much more, then, can a man will and do good by himself.

On the other hand: the apostle says in Rom. 9:16: "it is not of him that willeth, nor of him that runneth, but of God that sheweth mercy." Augustine, also, says that "men do absolutely nothing good without grace, whether by thought, will, love, or deed" (*De Corrept. et Grat.* 2).

I answer: man's nature may be considered in two ways, either in its purity, as it was in our first parent before sin, or as corrupt, as it is in ourselves after the sin of our first parent. In either state, human nature needs divine help in order to do or to will any good, since it needs a first mover, as we said in the preceding article. In regard to the sufficiency of his operative power, man in the state of pure nature could will and do, by his own natural power, the good proportionate to his nature, such as the good of acquired virtue, though not surpassing good such as the good of infused virtue. In the state of corrupt nature he falls short of what nature makes possible, so that he cannot by his own power fulfil the whole good that pertains to his nature. Human nature is not so entirely corrupted by sin, however, as to be deprived of natural good altogether. Consequently, even in the state of corrupt nature a

man can do some particular good by the power of his own
nature, such as build houses, plant vineyards, and things of
this kind. But he cannot achieve the whole good natural to him,
as if he lacked nothing. One who is infirm, similarly, can make
some movements by himself, but cannot move himself naturally
like a man in health, unless cured by the help of medicine.

Thus in the state of pure nature man needs a power added to
his natural power by grace, for one reason, namely, in order to
do and to will supernatural good. But in the state of corrupt
nature he needs this for two reasons, in order to be healed, and
in order to achieve the meritorious good of supernatural virtue.
In both states, moreover, he needs the divine help by which he
is moved to act well.

On the first point: it is because of the deliberation of his
reason, which can turn to one side or the other, that a man is
master of his actions, and of willing and not willing. But
although he is thus master, it is only through a previous
deliberation that he either deliberates or does not deliberate.
Since this regress cannot be infinite, we are finally driven to
say that a man's free will is moved by an external principle
higher than the mind of man, that is, by God. The philosopher
indeed proves this in his chapter on Good Fortune (7 *Mor.
Eudem.* 18). Thus even the mind of a healthy man is not so
thoroughly master of its actions that it does not need to be
moved by God. Much more so the free will of a man weakened
by sin and thereby hindered from good by the corruption of
nature.

On the second point: to sin is nothing other than to fall short
of the good which befits one according to one's nature. Now
just as every created thing has its being from another, and considered in itself is nothing, so also it must be preserved by
another in the good which befits its nature. It can nevertheless
through itself fall short of this good, just as it can through itself
cease to exist, if it is not providentially preserved.

On the third point: as we said in Art. 1, a man cannot even
know truth without divine help. Now his nature is impaired by
sin more in the desire for good than in the knowledge of
truth.

Article Three

WHETHER A MAN CAN LOVE GOD ABOVE ALL THINGS BY HIS NATURAL POWERS ALONE, WITHOUT GRACE

We proceed to the third article thus:

1. It seems that a man cannot love God above all things by his natural powers alone, without grace. To love God above all things is the proper and principal act of charity, and a man cannot have charity of himself, since "the love of God is shed abroad in our hearts by the Holy Ghost, which is given unto us" (Rom. 5:5). It follows that a man cannot love God above all things by his natural powers alone.

2. Again, no nature can rise above itself. But to love God more than oneself is to tend to what is above oneself. Hence no created nature can love God more than itself, without the help of grace.

3. Again, since God is the greatest good, we ought to give him the greatest love, which is to love him above all things. But without grace a man is not fit to give to God the greatest love, which we ought to give him, since it would be useless to add grace if he were so. It follows that a man cannot love God by his natural powers alone, without grace.

On the other hand: as some maintain, the first man was made with natural powers only, and it is obvious that in this state he loved God to some extent. But he loved God neither equally with himself nor less than himself, since he would have sinned in either case. He therefore loved God more than himself. It follows that man can love God more than himself and above all things by his natural powers alone.

I answer: as we said when we stated the various opinions about the natural love of angels (Pt. I, Q. 60, Art. 5), man in the state of pure nature could do such good as was natural to him by means of his natural power, without any superadded gift of grace, though not without the help of God moving him. To love God above all things is natural to man, and indeed to every creature, irrational as well as rational, and even to inanimate things, according to the manner of love of which each creature is capable. The reason for this is that it is natural for each thing to desire and to love something, according to what it is made fit to love, just as each thing acts as it is made fit to act, as is said in 2 *Physics*, text 78. Now it is clear that the good of the part is for the sake of the good of the whole. It follows that every particular thing, by its own natural desire or love, loves its own peculiar good for the sake of the common good of the whole universe, which is God. As Dionysius says, "God directs everything to love himself" (4 *Div. Nom.*, lect. 11). In the state of pure nature, accordingly, man subordinated his love of himself, and of all other things also, to love of God as its end. Thus he loved God more than himself, and above all things. But in the state of corrupt nature he falls short of this in the desire of his rational will, which through corruption seeks its own private good, unless it is healed by the grace of God.

We must say, accordingly, that in the state of pure nature man did not need a gift of grace added to his natural power, in order to love God above all things, although he did need the help of God moving him to do so. But in the state of corrupt nature he needs further help of grace, that his nature may be healed.

On the first point: charity loves God above all things more eminently than does nature. Nature loves God above all things because he is the beginning and the end of the good of nature. Charity loves God because he is the object of beatitude, and because man has spiritual fellowship with him. Moreover, charity adds an immediate willingness and joy to the natural love of God, just as the habit of virtue adds something to a good action which springs solely from the natural reason of a man who lacks the habit of virtue.

On the second point: when it is said that no nature can rise above itself, we must not understand that it cannot be drawn to what is above itself. For it is evident that the intellect can know, by natural knowledge, some things above itself, as it manifestly does in the natural knowledge of God. What we must understand is that a nature cannot be incited to an action which exceeds the proportion of its power. But to love God above all things is not such an action. This is natural to every created nature, as we have said.

On the third point: love is said to be greatest, not only on the ground of the degree of its affection, but also on the ground of the reason for it and the quality of it. On such grounds, the greatest love is the love with which charity loves God as him who leads us to beatitude, as we have said.

Article Four

WHETHER A MAN CAN FULFIL THE COMMANDMENTS OF THE LAW BY HIS NATURAL POWERS, WITHOUT GRACE

We proceed to the fourth article thus:

1. It seems that a man can fulfil the commandments of the law by his own natural powers, without grace. For the apostle says that "the Gentiles, which have not the law, do by nature the things contained in the law" (Rom. 2:14). But what a man does by nature he can do by himself, without grace. He can therefore keep the commandments of the law without grace.

2. Again, Hieronymus (Pelagius) says that "they speak ill who affirm that God has commanded anything impossible for man" (*Expositio Cath. Fidei, Epist. ad Damasc.*). Now what a man cannot fulfil is impossible for him. It follows that he can fulfil all the commandments of the law by himself.

3. Again, it is plain from Matt. 22:37 that the greatest commandment of all is this: "thou shalt love the Lord thy God with all thy heart." Now a man can fulfil this commandment by his natural powers alone, by loving God above all things, which the preceding article affirmed that he can do. He can therefore fulfil all the commandments of the law without grace.

On the other hand: Augustine says (*De Haer.* 88): "to believe that a man can fulfil all the divine commandments without grace is part of the Pelagian heresy."

I answer: there are two ways of fulfilling the commandments of the law. In the first place, one may actually do what the law commands, by performing acts of justice or fortitude, for example, or other acts of virtue. Man could fulfil all the commandments of the law in this way when he was in the state of pure nature, since he would not otherwise have been able to avoid sin, which is nothing other than transgression of the divine commandments. But a man in the state of corrupt nature cannot fulfil all the divine commandments without healing grace. In the second place, the law may be fulfilled not only in respect of what it commands, but also in respect of the manner of action. It is so fulfilled when actions are inspired by charity. A man cannot fulfil the law in this way without grace, whether in the state of pure nature or in the state of corrupt nature. For this reason, when Augustine said that men do absolutely nothing good without grace, he added: "not only do they know by grace what they ought to do, but they do it out of love by the aid of grace" (*De Corrept. et. Grat.*). In both states, moreover, men need the help of God moving them to fulfil his commandments, as we said in Art. 3.

On the first point: as Augustine says (*De Spiritu et Littera*, 27): "It should not disturb us that he said that these do by nature the things contained in the law. For this is wrought by the spirit of grace, to restore within us the image of God in which we were naturally made."

On the second point: what we can do by means of divine help is not absolutely impossible for us. As the philosopher says: "what we can do through our friends we can in a sense do ourselves" (3 *Ethics* 3). Hieronymus (Pelagius) accordingly confesses, in the passage quoted, that "our will is free enough to allow us to say that we always need God's help."

On the third point: it is clear from what was said in Art. 3 that a man cannot, by his natural powers alone, fulfil the commandment about love to God in the same way as it is fulfilled through charity.

Article Five

WHETHER A MAN CAN MERIT ETERNAL LIFE, WITHOUT GRACE

We proceed to the fifth article thus:

1. It seems that a man can merit eternal life without grace. Our Lord says (Matt. 19:17): "if thou wilt enter into life, keep the commandments"—whence it appears that whether a man enters into eternal life depends on his own will. Now we can do by ourselves what depends on our own will. It seems, therefore, that a man can merit eternal life by himself.

2. Again, God gives eternal life to men as a meed or reward, according to Matt. 5:12: "great is your reward in heaven," and Ps. 62:12 says that a meed or reward is rendered by God according to a man's works: "thou renderest to every man according to his work." Hence the attainment of eternal life seems to depend on a man's own power, since a man has control of his own works.

3. Again, eternal life is the ultimate end of human life. Now every natural thing can attain its end by its natural power. Much more then can man, who is of a higher nature, attain eternal life by his natural power, without any grace.

On the other hand: the apostle says: "the gift of God is eternal life" (Rom. 6:23), and the gloss by Augustine says:

"this means that God leads us to eternal life for his mercy's sake" (*De Grat. et Lib. Arb.* 9).

I answer: actions which lead to an end must be commensurate with the end. But no action transcends the limits of the principle by which a thing acts. Thus we see that no natural thing can produce, by its own action, an effect which is greater than its own active power, but only an effect commensurate with this power. Now eternal life is an end which exceeds what is commensurate with human nature, as is clear from what we said in Q. 5, Art. 5. It follows that a man cannot, by his natural powers, produce meritorious works commensurate with eternal life. A higher power is needed for this, namely, the power of grace. Hence a man cannot merit eternal life without grace, although he can perform works which lead to such good as is connatural to him, such as labour in the field, eat, drink, have friends, and so on, as is said by Augustine (or by another, in *Contra Pelagianos* 3; *Hypognosticon* 3, cap. 4).

On the first point: a man performs works deserving of eternal life by his own will. But as Augustine says in the same passage, his will must be prepared by God through grace.

On the second point: if one is to fulfil the commandments of the law in the adequate way which is meritorious, grace is indispensable. This agrees with what Augustine's gloss says on Rom. 6:23, "the gift of God is eternal life," namely that "it is certain that eternal life is the reward for good works, but works so rewarded are the result of God's grace" (*De Grat. et Lib. Arb.* 8). It also agrees with what we said in the preceding article.

On the third point: this objection argues from the end which is connatural to man. But the very fact that human nature is nobler than natural things means that it can be raised, at least through the help of grace, to an end higher than this, to which inferior natures can nowise attain. A man who can recover his health through the help of medicine is, similarly, nearer to health than another who can in nowise do so, as the philosopher remarks in 2 *De Coelo*, texts 64, 65.

Article Six

WHETHER WITHOUT GRACE A MAN CAN PREPARE HIMSELF FOR GRACE

We proceed to the sixth article thus:

1. It seems that a man can prepare himself for grace by himself, without the external help of grace. For nothing impossible

is laid upon man, as was said in Art. 4, and yet it is written in Zech. 1:3: "Turn ye unto me, and I will turn unto you." To prepare oneself for grace is nothing other than to turn unto God. It seems, therefore, that a man can prepare himself for grace by himself, without the help of grace.

2. Again, a man prepares himself for grace by doing what lies within him. For God will not refuse him grace if he does what lies within him, since Matt., ch. 7, says that "God gives his good spirit to them that ask him." Now what is said to lie within us is within our power. Hence it seems that to prepare ourselves for grace is within our power.

3. Again, if a man needs grace to prepare himself for grace, for the same reason he will need grace to prepare himself for this latter grace, and so on to infinity, which is impossible. It seems to hold good in the first instance, therefore, that without grace a man can prepare himself for grace.

4. Again, Prov. 16:1 says: "The preparations of the heart in man." [1] Now that is said to be of man which he can do by himself. Hence it seems that a man can prepare himself for grace by himself.

On the other hand: it is said in John 6:44: "no man can come to me, except the Father which hath sent me draw him." But a man would not need to be drawn by another if he could prepare himself for grace. Hence a man cannot prepare himself for grace without the help of grace.

I answer: the preparation of the human will for grace is two-fold. In the first place, the will must be prepared for good works, and for the enjoyment of God. Such preparation is impossible without an enduring gift of grace, grace being the principle of meritorious works, as we said in the preceding article. But we may have in mind, in the second place, the preparation of the will so that this enduring gift may follow. We do not need to suppose another enduring gift already in the soul, by means of which a man is enabled to receive this enduring gift, since this would go on to infinity. But we are bound to suppose the gift of God's help in moving the soul inwardly, and inspiring it to aim at good. For we need God's help in these two ways, as we said in Arts. 2 and 3. It is plain that we need the help of God as mover. Every agent acts for some definite end, and every cause is therefore bound to direct its effects to its own end. Since the hierarchy of ends is parallel to the hierarchy of agents, it follows that man must be directed to his ultimate end by the

[1] Migne: "It is of man to prepare the soul."

147

moving of the first mover, and to his penultimate end by the moving of lesser movers, just as a soldier's mind is set on victory by the influence of the army commander, and on following a standard by the influence of a captain. Now since God is the absolute first mover, it is by God's moving that all things are directed to him, in accordance with the universal tendency to good by which each thing strives to resemble God after its own fashion. As Dionysius says: "God turns all things to himself" (4 *Div. Nom.*, lect. 11). But God turns just men to himself as the special end which they seek, and to which they desire to cleave as to their true good, in accordance with Ps. 73:28: "It is good for me to draw near to God." A man cannot therefore turn to God except through God turning him to himself. To turn to God is to prepare oneself for grace, just as one whose eyes are turned away from the light of the sun prepares himself to receive its light by turning his eyes towards the sun. It is clear, then, that a man cannot prepare himself for the light of grace without the gracious help of God, who moves him inwardly.

On the first point: a man turns to God of his own free will. Hence he is bidden to do so. But his free will can turn to God only through God turning it to himself, according to Jer. 31:18: "turn thou me, and I shall be turned; for thou art the Lord my God," and also Lam. 5:21: "Turn thou us unto thee, O Lord, and we shall be turned."

On the second point: a man can do nothing unless he is moved by God, as is said in John 15:5: "without me ye can do nothing." When a man is said to do what lies within him, this is said to be within his power as moved by God.

On the third point: this objection argues from habitual[1] grace, which needs preparation, since every form requires an amenable disposition. But no other previous moving is needed in order that a man may be moved by God, since God is the first mover. There is therefore no infinite regress.

On the fourth point: it is for man to prepare his soul, since he does this by his own free will. Yet he does not do so without God helping him as mover, and drawing him to himself, as we have said.

[1] I.e. a habit which is a gift of grace. Cf. Art. 9, *infra.*

Article Seven

WHETHER A MAN CAN RISE FROM SIN WITHOUT THE HELP OF GRACE

We proceed to the seventh article thus:

1. It seems that a man can rise from sin without the help of grace. For what grace presupposes occurs without grace, and the light of grace presupposes that we rise from sin, according to Eph. 5:14: "arise from the dead, and Christ shall give thee light." It follows that a man can rise from sin without grace.

2. Again, it was said in Q. 71, Art. 1, that sin is opposed to virtue as disease is opposed to health. Now a man may recover from illness by his natural strength, without the artificial aid of medicine, if there remains within him the principle of life on which the natural process depends. It seems then that for a similar reason he may recover from a state of sin, and return to a state of justice, without the external help of grace.

3. Again, every natural thing can of itself recover the action which befits its nature. Thus water, when heated, returns to its natural coolness of its own accord, and a stone thrown upwards returns to its natural movement. Now sin is action contrary to nature, as the Damascene shows (2 *De Fid. Orth.* 30). It seems, then, that a man can of himself return from sin to a state of justice.

On the other hand: as the apostle says in Gal. 2:21: "If righteousness come by the law, then is Christ dead in vain," that is, to no purpose. But by the same reasoning Christ is dead in vain, that is, to no purpose, if man possesses a nature through which he can become just. It follows that a man cannot become just through himself, that is, cannot return from a state of guilt to a state of justice.

I answer: a man can in no wise rise from sin by himself, without the help of grace. Sin endures as guilt, though it is transient as an action. (Q. 87, Art. 6.) To rise from sin, therefore, is not the same as to cease from the action of sin, but involves the restoration of what a man has lost through sinning. We have already shown that a man incurs a threefold loss through sin, namely, the stain on the soul, the corruption of natural good, and the debt of punishment (Qq. 85, 86, 87, Arts. 1). He incurs a stain, since the deformity of sin deprives him of the comeliness of grace; natural good is corrupted, since his nature is deranged by the insubordination of his will to the will of God, which disruption of the order of things leaves his whole nature disordered; finally, by mortal sin he merits eternal damnation as the debt of punishment. Now it is obvious that none of these can be restored except by God. The comeliness of grace cannot be restored unless God sheds his light anew, since it is derived from the shining of the divine light, and therefore depends on an enduring gift of the light of grace. Neither can the natural order of things be restored, in which a man's will is subordinated to the will of God, unless God draws his will to himself, as we said in the preceding article. Nor can the debt of punishment be forgiven save by God alone, against whom the offence is committed, and who is the judge of men. The help of grace is therefore indispensable if a man is to rise from sin. It is needed both as an enduring gift and as the inward moving of God.

On the first point: what a man is bidden to do pertains to the act of free will which his recovery from sin involves. When it is said "arise, and Christ shall give thee light," we must understand not that the whole recovery from sin precedes the light of grace, but that when a man strives to rise from sin of his own free will as moved by God, he receives the light of justifying grace.

On the second point: natural reason is not the sufficient principle of the health which is in a man through justifying grace. The principle of this is the grace which has been taken away on account of sin. A man cannot then restore himself, but needs the light of grace shed on him anew, like a soul re-entering a dead body to bring it back to life.

On the third point: when nature is unimpaired, it can restore itself to what befits it as commensurate with it, though it cannot without external help be restored to what exceeds this. But when human nature is impaired by sin, so that it is no longer pure, but corrupt, as we said in Q. 85, it cannot even restore itself to the good which is natural to it, much less to the supernatural good of justice.

Article Eight

WHETHER A MAN CAN AVOID SIN, WITHOUT GRACE

We proceed to the eighth article thus:

1. It seems that a man can avoid sin without grace. Augustine says that "no man sins in respect of what he cannot avoid" (*De Duab. Animabus*, 10, 11; 3 *De Lib. Arb.* 18). Hence it appears

that if a man cannot avoid sin while he lives in mortal sin, he does not sin while he sins. But this is impossible.

2. Again, one is chastised in order that one may not sin. But if a man who lived in mortal sin were unable to avoid sin, it seems that it would be useless to chastise him. But this is impossible.

3. Again, it is said in Ecclesiasticus 15:17: "Before man are life and death, good and evil; whatsoever he shall choose shall be given him." But when a man sins, he does not cease to be a man. It is therefore still within his power to choose either good or evil. Hence one who lacks grace can avoid sin.

On the other hand: Augustine says (*De Perf. Just.* 21): "Whosoever denies that we ought to pray 'lead us not into temptation' (and he denies this who argues that a man does not need the help of God's grace in order not to sin) should assuredly be removed from every ear and anathematized by every mouth."

I answer: we may speak of man in two ways; either as in the state of pure nature, or as in the state of corrupt nature. In the state of pure nature, man could avoid both mortal and venial sin, without grace. For to sin is nothing other than to fall short of what befits one's nature, and a man in the state of pure nature could avoid this. Yet he could not avoid it without the help of God preserving him in good, without which help his nature itself would have ceased to exist. But in the state of corrupt nature a man needs grace to heal his nature continually, if he is to avoid sin entirely. In our present life this healing is accomplished first in the mind, the appetite of the flesh being not yet wholly cured. Hence the apostle, speaking as one who is restored, says in Rom. 7:25: "with the mind I myself serve the law of God, but with the flesh the law of sin." A man in this state can avoid all mortal sin, which has to do with his reason, as we said in Q. 74, Art. 5. But he cannot avoid all venial sin, owing to the corrupt sensuality of his lower appetite. Reason can indeed suppress the urges of the lower appetite severally, wherefore they are sinful and voluntary. But it cannot suppress all of them. For while a man endeavours to suppress one of them, another may arise. Moreover, as we said in Q. 74, Art. 10, reason cannot always be vigilant enough to suppress such urges.

But before his reason is restored through justifying grace, a man can likewise avoid severally, for some time, the mortal sins which have to do with his reason, since he is not bound by necessity actually to sin at all times. But he cannot continue without mortal sin for long. As Gregory says, "a sin which is not instantly blotted out by repentance drags us down to another by its weight" (*Hom. in Ezech.* 11; 25 *Moral.* 9). This is because reason ought to be subject to God, and ought to find in God the end which it desires, just as the lower appetite ought to be subject to reason. Every human action, indeed, ought to be regulated by this end, just as the urges of the lower appetite ought to be regulated by the judgment of reason. There are therefore bound to be many untoward actions of reason itself when reason is not entirely subject to God, just as there are bound to be uncontrolled movements of the sensitive appetite when the lower appetite is imperfectly subject to reason. When a man's heart is not so firmly fixed on God that he is unwilling to be separated from him for the sake of any good, or to avoid any evil, he forsakes God, and breaks his commandments in order to gain or to avoid many things. He thus sins mortally, especially since "he acts according to his preconceived end and previous habit whenever he is caught off his guard," as the philosopher says in 3 *Ethics* 8. Premeditation may perhaps enable him to do something better than his preconceived end requires, and better than that to which his habit inclines. But he cannot be always premeditating, and will not perchance continue for long before suiting his action to a will which is not controlled by God, unless he is quickly restored to right order by grace.

On the first point: as we have said, a man can avoid sinful actions taken singly, but he cannot avoid all of them, unless through grace. Yet his sin is not to be excused on the ground that he cannot avoid it without grace, because it is due to his own fault that he does not prepare himself for grace.

On the second point: as Augustine says (*De Corrept. et Grat.* 6): "chastisement is useful in order that the desire for regeneration may arise out of the pain of it. While the noise of chastisement resounds without, God may work within by an unseen inspiration, that one should so desire, if one be a son of promise." Chastisement is necessary because a man must desist from sin of his own will. But it is not enough without the help of God. Wherefore it is said in Eccl. 7:13: "Consider the work of God: for who can make that straight which he hath made crooked?" [1]

On the third point: as Augustine says (or another, in *Hypognosticon* 3, cap. 1, 2), this saying must be understood as referring to man in the state of pure nature, not yet the slave of sin,

[1] Migne: "for no one can correct one whom he hath despised."

able both to sin and not to sin. Whatever a man then desires is given him. It is nevertheless by the help of grace that he desires what is good.

Article Nine

WHETHER, AFTER RECEIVING GRACE, A MAN CAN DO GOOD AND AVOID SIN, WITHOUT FURTHER HELP OF GRACE

We proceed to the ninth article thus:

1. It seems that one who has already received grace can do good and avoid sin by himself, without further help of grace. For if anything does not achieve that for which it is given, either it is given in vain, or it is imperfect. Now grace is given to enable us to do good and avoid sin. Hence if one who has received grace is unable to do this, either grace is given in vain, or it is imperfect.

2. Again, the Holy Spirit dwells in us by grace, according to I Cor. 3:16: "Know ye not that ye are the temple of God, and that the Spirit of God dwelleth in you?" Now the Holy Spirit is omnipotent, and therefore sufficient to make us do good and to keep us from sin. It follows that a man who has received grace can do both of these things, without further help of grace.

3. Again, if a man who has received grace needs further help of grace in order to live rightly and avoid sin, by the same reasoning he will need yet further help of grace after receiving this further grace, and so on to infinity, which is impossible. One who is already in grace, therefore, does not need further help of grace in order to do good and avoid sin.

On the other hand: Augustine says (*De Nat. et Grat.* 26): "just as even the healthiest eye of the body cannot see unless aided by the radiance of light, so even the most perfectly justified man cannot live rightly unless aided by the eternal light of heavenly righteousness." Now justification is by grace, according to Rom. 3.24: "Being justified freely by his grace." Hence even a man who has already received grace needs further help of grace in order to live rightly.

I answer: as we said in Art. 5, a man needs help from God in two ways, in order to live rightly. First, he needs a habitual gift by which his corrupt nature may be healed, and thereafter raised to perform works such as merit eternal life, which exceed what is commensurate with his nature. Secondly, he needs the help of grace by which God moves him to act. Now a man already in grace does not need further grace in the form of another infused habit. But there are two reasons why he needs the help of grace in the second way, if he is to act rightly. He needs it for the general reason that no creature can act at all except by the divine moving, as we said in the first article. He also needs it for the special reason that the natural condition of human nature remains corrupt and infected in the flesh, with which it serves the law of sin, according to Rom. 7:25, even though it be healed in the spirit through grace. There remains also a darkness of ignorance in the intellect, on account of which "we know not what we should pray for as we ought," as it is said in Rom. 8:26. We cannot fully know what is for our good, because of the unpredictable course of events, and because we do not even know ourselves perfectly. As it is said in Wisdom 9:14: "the deliberations of mortals are hesitant, and our counsels uncertain." We must therefore be guided and protected by God, who knows and can do all things. Hence even those who are reborn through grace as sons of God ought to pray "and lead us not into temptation," and also "Thy will be done on earth, as it is in heaven," and whatever else in the Lord's prayer is relevant.

On the first point: a gift of habitual grace is not given so that we may dispense with any further divine help, since every creature must be preserved by God in the good which it receives from him. We cannot then conclude that grace is given in vain, or that it is imperfect, from the fact that a man in grace needs divine help in this way. A man will need divine help even in the state of glory, when grace will be perfect in every sense, whereas in this life grace is in one sense imperfect, in that it does not heal a man entirely, as we have said.

On the second point: the operation of the Holy Spirit, which inspires and perfects us, is not confined to the provision of the habitual gift which it causes in us. Together with the Father and the Son, it also inspires and protects us.

On the third point: this reasoning shows that a man needs no further habitual grace.

Article Ten

WHETHER A MAN IN GRACE NEEDS THE HELP OF GRACE IN ORDER TO PERSEVERE

We proceed to the tenth article thus:

1. It seems that a man in grace does not need the help of

grace in order to persevere. Perseverance, like continence, is something less than a virtue, as the philosopher explains in 7 *Ethics* 7 and 8. Now a man does not need any help of grace in order to possess the virtues on account of which he is justified by grace. Much less, then, does he need the help of grace in order to persevere.

2. Again, the virtues are all bestowed at the same time, and it is maintained that perseverance is a virtue. Hence it seems that perseverance is bestowed along with the other virtues infused by grace.

3. Again, as the apostle says in Rom., ch. 5, more was given back to man by the gift of Christ than he had lost through Adam's sin. But Adam received what enabled him to persevere. Much more, then, does the grace of Christ restore to us the ability to persevere. Hence a man does not stand in need of grace, in order to persevere.

On the other hand: Augustine says (*De Persev.* 2): "Why is perseverance asked of God, if it is not given by God? Is it not a supercillious request, to ask him for something which we know he does not give, but which is in our power without his giving it?" Moreover, perseverance is asked for even by those who are sanctified through grace. This is what we mean when we say "Hallowed be thy name," as Augustine confirms by the words of Cyprian (*De Corrept. et Grat.* 12). Thus even a man in grace needs that perseverance be given him by God.

I answer: we speak of perseverance in three senses. In one sense, it means the habit of mind by which a man stands firm, and is not dissuaded from what virtue demands by sudden tribulations. Perseverance in this sense is related to tribulations as continence is related to desires and pleasures, as the philosopher says in 7 *Ethics* 7. In a second sense, it means the habit by which a man maintains his intention of persevering in good to the last. Perseverance in both senses is bestowed along with grace, as are also continence and the other virtues. In a third sense, it means the actual continuing in good to the end of life. A man does not need any other habitual grace in order to persevere in this sense. But he does need the help of God to direct him, and to guard him from the shocks of temptation, as is apparent from the preceding article. It is therefore necessary for him to ask God for this gift of perseverance even after he has been justified by grace, so that he may be delivered from evil until the end of life. For there are many to whom grace is given, to whom it is not given to persevere in grace.

On the first point: this objection argues from the first meaning of perseverance, just as the second objection argues from the second meaning. The answer to the second objection is then obvious.

On the third point: as Augustine says (*De Nat. et Grat.* 43; *De Corrept. et Grat.* 12): "in his original state man received a gift whereby he might persevere, but not whereby he actually should persevere." Now by the grace of Christ many receive a gift of grace whereby they may persevere, while it is also given them to do so. The gift of Christ is thus greater than Adam's sin. But a man in the state of innocence, with no warring of the flesh against the spirit, could persevere by means of this gift of grace more easily than we can now, when regeneration by the grace of Christ, although begun in the mind, is not yet complete in regard to the flesh, as it shall be in heaven, when man shall be not only able to persevere, but unable to sin.

Question One Hundred and Ten

THE ESSENCE OF GOD'S GRACE

We must now consider the essence of God's grace, concerning which there are four questions. 1. Whether grace denotes something in the soul. 2. Whether grace is a quality. 3. Whether grace differs from infused virtue. 4. Concerning the subject of grace.

Article One

WHETHER GRACE DENOTES SOMETHING IN THE SOUL

We proceed to the first article thus:

1. It seems that grace does not denote anything in the soul. One is said to have the grace[1] of a man, just as one is said to have the grace of God. Thus it is said in Gen. 39:21: "the Lord gave Joseph favour in the sight of the keeper of the prison." Now to say that one man has the favour of another is not to denote anything in him who has the favour, but to denote acceptance in him whose favour he enjoys. To say that a man has the grace of God, therefore, is not to denote anything in his soul, but merely to affirm that God accepts him.

[1] The Latin words for "grace," "favour," "freely," "thanks," "gratitude," all have the same root—*gratia, gratis, gratias agere, gratiarum actio.*

2. Again, God enlivens the soul in the same way as the soul enlivens the body. Thus it is said Deut. 30:20: "He is thy life." Now the soul enlivens the body immediately. Hence there is nothing which stands as a medium between God and the soul. It follows that grace does not denote anything created in the soul.

3. Again, the gloss on Rom. 1:7, "Grace to you and peace . . .," says: "grace, i.e., the remission of sins." But the remission of sins does not denote anything in the soul. It signifies only that God does not impute sin, in accordance with Ps. 32:2: "Blessed is the man unto whom the Lord imputeth not iniquity." Neither then does grace denote anything in the soul.

On the other hand: light denotes something in what is illumined, and grace is a light of the soul. Thus Augustine says (*De Nat. et Grat.* 22): "The light of truth rightly deserts him who falsifies the law, and he who is thus deserted is left blind." Hence grace denotes something in the soul.

I answer: there are three things commonly meant by grace, as the word is used in ordinary speech. First, it means someone's love, as when we say that a certain soldier has the king's favour, i.e., that the king holds him in favour. Secondly, it means a gift freely given, as when we say: "I do you this favour." Thirdly, it means the response to a gift freely given, as when we are said to give thanks for benefits received. The second of these depends on the first, since it is out of love for another whom one holds in favour that one freely bestows a gift upon him. The third likewise depends on the second, since gratitude is due to gifts freely given.

Now if grace is understood according to either of the two latter meanings, it is obvious that it leaves something in the recipient of grace—the gift freely given, or the acknowledgment of it. But if grace means someone's love, we must observe the difference between the grace of God and the favour of a man. For the good which is in a creature is due to the will of God, and therefore some of the good in a creature is due to the love of God, who wills the good of the creature. The will of a man, on the other hand, is moved by good which already exists in things, so that his approval does not wholly cause the good in a thing, but presupposes it, partially or wholly. It is plain, then, that God's love invariably causes some good to be in the creature at some time, although such good is not co-eternal with his eternal love. God's love to creatures has then two aspects, on account of this special kind of good. It is universal, in so far as God gives to created things their natural being. As it is said in Wisdom, ch. 11: "He loves all things that are." It is also special, in so far as God raises a rational creature above its natural state, to share in divine good. It is in this special sense of love that God is said to love someone absolutely, since it is by this special love that he wills for a creature, absolutely, the eternal good which is himself. To say that a man has the grace of God, therefore, is to say that there is something supernatural in him, which God bestows.

Sometimes, however, the grace of God means God's eternal love, as it does when we speak of the grace of predestination, which signifies that God predestines or elects some by grace, and not on account of merit, as according to Eph. 1:5–6: "Having predestinated us unto the adoption of children . . . to the praise of the glory of his grace."

On the first point: even when a man is said to have the favour of another man, something is understood to be in him which pleases the other. So also when one is said to have the grace of God, but with this difference, that whereas a man's approval presupposes that which pleases him in another, God's love causes that which pleases him in a man, as we have said.

On the second point: God is the life of the soul as its efficient cause, whereas the soul is the life of the body as its formal cause.[1] There is no medium between a form and its matter, because a form determines the formation of its matter, or subject, by means of itself. But an agent does not determine a subject by means of its own substance. It does so by means of the form which it causes to be in the matter.

On the third point: Augustine says (1 Retract. 5): "when I say that grace is for the remission of sins, and peace for reconciliation to God, I do not mean that peace and reconciliation are outside the scope of grace, but that the name of grace signifies the remission of sins especially." There are thus many other gifts of God which pertain to grace, besides the remission of sins. Indeed there is no remission of sin without some effect divinely caused within us, as will be explained in Q. 113, Art. 2.

[1] For the distinction between final, formal, efficient, and material cause, see 22ae, Q. 27, Art. 3; cf. Aristotle's *Physics*, bk. 2, ch. 3 (194b), ch. 7 (198a); also *Metaph. A*, ch. 3 (983a), *D*, ch. 2 (1013a–b).

Article Two

WHETHER GRACE IS A QUALITY OF THE SOUL

We proceed to the second article thus:

1. It seems that grace is not a quality of the soul. No quality acts on the subject to which it belongs. If it did, the subject would have to act on itself, since there is no action of a quality without the action of its subject. But grace acts on the soul, in justifying it. It follows that grace is not a quality.

2. Again, a substance is nobler than its quality. But grace is nobler than the soul's nature, since we can do many things by grace which we cannot do by nature, as was said in Q. 109, Arts. 1, 2, and 3. It follows that grace is not a quality.

3. Again, no quality persists after it ceases to be in its subject. But grace persists, since it is not corrupted. If grace were corrupted it would be reduced to nothing, since it is created out of nothing—wherefore it is called a "new creature" in Galatians. It follows that grace is not a quality.

On the other hand: the gloss by Augustine on Ps. 104:15, "Oil to make his face to shine," says that "grace is a beauty of the soul, which wins the divine love." Beauty of soul is a quality, just as comeliness of body is a quality. It follows that grace is a quality.

I answer: as we maintained in the preceding article, to say that a man has the grace of God is to say that there is within him an effect of God's gracious will. Now God's gracious will helps a man in two ways, as we said in Q. 109, Art. 1. In the first place, a man's mind is helped by God to know, to will, or to act. Such an effect of grace is not a quality, but a movement of the soul, since "in the moved, the act of the mover is a movement," as is said in 3 *Physics*, text 18. Secondly, God infuses a habitual gift into the soul, for the reason that it would not be fitting that God should give less to those whom he loves in order that they may attain supernatural good, than he gives to creatures whom he loves in order that they may attain only natural good. Now God provides for natural creatures not only by moving them to their natural actions, but by endowing them with forms and powers which are the principles of actions, so that they may incline to such movements of their own accord. In this way the movements to which God moves them become natural to creatures, and easy for them, in accordance with Wisdom 8:1: ". . . and disposes all things sweetly." Much more, then, does God infuse certain forms or supernatural qualities into those whom he moves to seek after supernatural and eternal good, that they may be thus moved by him to seek it sweetly and readily. The gift of grace, therefore, is a certain quality.

On the first point: as a quality, grace is said to act on the soul not as an efficient cause, but as a formal cause, as whiteness makes things white, or as justice makes things just.

On the second point: any substance is either the nature of that of which it is the substance, or a part of its nature. In this sense, matter and form are both called "substance." But grace is higher than human nature. It cannot then be its substance, nor yet the form of its substance. Grace is a form accidental to the soul. What exists as substance in God occurs as accident in the soul which shares in divine good, as is obvious in the case of knowledge. But since the soul shares in divine good imperfectly, this participation itself, which is grace, exists in the soul in a less perfect mode than that in which the soul exists in itself. Such grace is nevertheless nobler than the soul's nature, in so far as it is an expression or sharing of the divine goodness, even though it is not nobler than the soul in respect of its mode of being.

On the third point: as Boethius says (*Isagogue Porphyri*): "the being of an accident is to inhere." Thus an accident is said to "be," not as if it existed by itself, but because some subject "is" through possessing it. It is thus affirmed of an existence, rather than affirmed to be an existence, as is said in 7 *Metaph.*, text 2. Now since coming to be and passing away are affirmed of what exists, properly speaking no accident comes to be or passes away. But an accident is said to come to be or to pass away when its subject begins or ceases to be actualized through possession of it. In this sense, grace is said to be created when it is men who are created in grace, i.e., when they are created anew out of nothing, and not on account of merit, according to Eph. 2:10: "created in Christ Jesus unto good works."

Article Three

WHETHER GRACE IS THE SAME AS VIRTUE

We proceed to the third article thus:

1. It seems that grace is the same as virtue. For Augustine says "operative grace is faith that works by love" (*De Spiritu et*

Littera 14, 32). But faith that works by love is a virtue. Therefore grace is a virtue.

2. Again, whatever a definition fits, fits the thing defined.
Now the definitions of virtue fit grace, whether they are given
by saints or by philosophers—"it makes him who possesses it
good, and his work good," "it is a good quality of mind,
whereby one lives rightly," etc. Therefore grace is a virtue.

3. Again, grace is a quality of some kind. But it manifestly
does not belong to the fourth species of quality, which comprises
"the form or unchanging pattern of things." Neither does it
belong to the third species, since it is neither a "passion" nor a
"passionate quality." These belong to the sensitive part of the
soul, as is proved in 8 *Physics*, text 14, whereas grace is principally in the mind. Nor does it belong to the second species,
which includes "natural power and impotence." It must therefore belong to the first species, which is that of "habit" or
"disposition." But habits of mind are virtues, since even
knowledge is in a sense a virtue. Hence grace is the same as
virtue.

On the other hand: if grace is a virtue, it must certainly be
one of the three theological virtues. But grace is neither faith nor
hope, since these occur without sanctifying grace. Nor is it
charity, since "grace precedes charity," as Augustine says (*De
Dono Persev.* 16). Hence grace is not a virtue.

I answer: some have held that grace and virtue differ only as
different aspects of one identical essence, which we call grace
in so far as it is freely given, or makes men pleasing to God, and
which we call virtue in so far as it perfects us in well-doing. So
indeed the Master[1] seems to have thought, in 2 *Sent., Dist.* 26.
But this cannot be maintained if one pays due attention to the
meaning of virtue. As the philosopher says in 7 *Physics*, text 17:
"virtue is the disposition of the perfect, and I call that perfect
which is disposed according to nature." This makes it clear that
the virtue of any particular thing is determined by a nature
which is prior to it, and means the disposition of all its elements
according to what is best for its nature. Now the virtues which
a man acquires through practice, of which we spoke in Q. 55 ff.,
are obviously dispositions by which he is disposed in a manner
which befits his nature as a man. But the infused virtues dis-
pose men in a higher way to a higher end, and therefore

---

[1] Peter the Lombard, to whom the title refers throughout this volume;
generally known as "Magister Sententiarum," or the "Master of Sentences,"
from his work *Libri Sententiarum*.

according to a higher nature, indeed according to the divine nature in which he participates. We call this participation "the light of grace," on account of what is said in II Peter 1:4: "Whereby are given unto us exceeding great and precious promises: that by these ye might be partakers of the divine nature." It is in fact as receiving this nature that we are said to be born again as sons of God. Hence just as the natural light of reason is something over and above the acquired virtues, which are called virtues because they are ordered by this light, so the light of grace, which is a partaking of the divine nature, is something over and above the infused virtues, which are derived from it and ordered by it. Thus the apostle says in Eph. 5:8: "For ye were sometimes darkness, but now are ye light in the Lord: walk as children of light." Just as the acquired virtues enable a man to walk by the natural light of reason, so do the infused virtues enable him to walk by the light of grace.

On the first point: Augustine gives the name of grace to "faith that works by love" because the act of faith which works by love is the first act in which sanctifying grace is manifest.

On the second point: the term "good," as used in the definition of virtue, means conformity with a nature which is either prior, essential, or partaken. It is not applied in this sense to grace, but to the root of goodness in man, as we have said.

On the third point: grace belongs to the first species of quality. But it is not the same as virtue. It is the disposition which the infused virtues presuppose as their principle and root.

Article Four

WHETHER GRACE IS IN THE SOUL'S ESSENCE AS ITS SUBJECT, OR IN ONE OF ITS POWERS

We proceed to the fourth article thus:

1. It seems that grace is not in the soul's essence as its subject, but in one of its powers. For Augustine says (or another, in *Hypognosticon* 3): "grace is to the will, or free will, as a rider to his horse," and it was said in Q. 88, Art. 2, that the will, or the free will, is a power. It follows that grace is in a power of the soul as its subject.

2. Again, Augustine says (*De Grat. et Lib. Arb.* 4): "a man's merits arise out of grace." But merit consists in action, and action proceeds from a power. It seems, then, that grace is a power of the soul.

3. Again, if the essence of the soul is the proper subject of grace, every soul which has an essence ought to be capable of receiving grace. But this is false, since it would follow that every soul was capable of receiving grace. Hence the essence of the soul is not the proper subject of grace.

4. Again, the soul's essence is prior to its powers, and what is prior can be conceived apart from that which depends on it. If grace were in its essence, therefore, we could conceive of a soul which possessed grace without possessing any part or any power, whether will, intellect, or anything of the kind. But this is impossible.

On the other hand: it is through grace that we are regenerated as sons of God. Now generation reaches the essence before it reaches the powers. It follows that grace is in the soul's essence before it is in its powers.

I answer: this question depends on the preceding question. If grace is the same as virtue, it must be in one of the soul's powers as its subject, since the proper subject of virtue is a power of the soul. But we cannot say that a power of the soul is the subject of grace if grace is not the same as virtue, because every perfection of a power of the soul has the nature of virtue, as we said in Qq. 55, 56. Now grace is prior to virtue, and accordingly has a subject which is prior to the powers of the soul, such as the essence of the soul. Just as it is through the virtue of faith that a man partakes of the divine knowledge by means of the power of his intellect, and through the virtue of charity that he partakes of the divine love by means of the power of his will, so is it through regeneration or recreation of his soul's nature that he partakes of the divine nature by way of a certain likeness.

On the first point: just as the soul's essence is the source of the powers which are its principles of action, so is grace the source of the virtues which enter the powers of the soul, and move them to act. Hence grace is related to the will as a mover to a thing moved, which is the relation of a rider to his horse, not as an accident to its subject.

The answer to the second point is then clear. Grace is the principle of meritorious works through the medium of the virtues, just as the soul's essence is the principle of its vital operations through the medium of its powers.

On the third point: the soul is the subject of grace because it belongs to the species of the intellectual, or rational. But it is not on account of any of its powers that it belongs to this species. The powers of the soul are its natural properties, and are therefore consequential to its species. Because of its essence, the soul belongs to a different species from other souls, such as irrational animals and plants. That the human soul should be the subject of grace does not then imply that every soul should be so. A soul can be the subject of grace only if it is of a certain kind.

On the fourth point: since the powers of the soul are natural properties consequential to its species, a soul cannot exist without them. But supposing that it did exist without them, the soul would still be said to belong to the species of the intellectual, or rational, not as actually possessing such powers, but on the ground that its species was of the kind from which such powers are derived.

Question One Hundred and Eleven

THE DIVISIONS OF GRACE

We must now consider the division of grace, concerning which there are five questions. 1. Whether grace is appropriately divided into free grace and sanctifying grace. 2. Of the division of sanctifying grace into operative and co-operative grace. 3. Of the division of the same into prevenient and subsequent grace. 4. Of the division of free grace. 5. How sanctifying grace compares with free grace.

Article One

WHETHER GRACE IS APPROPRIATELY DIVIDED INTO SANCTIFYING GRACE AND FREE GRACE

We proceed to the first article thus:

1. It seems that grace is not appropriately divided into sanctifying grace and free grace.[1] What was said in Q. 110 makes it clear that grace is a gift of God. Now a man is not pleasing to God because God has given him something. On the contrary, God freely gives him something because he is pleasing to God. There is therefore no grace which sanctifies.

2. Again, whatever is not given on account of previous merit, is freely given. Now the good of nature is given to man without

[1] The Latin phrases are *gratia gratum faciens*, and *gratia gratis data*.

any previous merit, since merit presupposes nature. Nature is therefore a free gift of God, and it belongs to a different genus from grace. Since the character of gratuitousness thus occurs outside the genus of grace, it is an error to regard it as a character which distinguishes grace from grace.

3. Again, every division ought to be between opposites. But even the sanctifying grace by which we are justified is freely extended to us by God, according to Rom. 3:24: "being justified freely by his grace." Sanctifying grace should not then be contrasted with free grace.

On the other hand: the apostle attributes both things to grace, affirming that it sanctifies and also that it is freely given. In Eph. 1:6 he affirms that it sanctifies: "he hath made us accepted in the beloved," and in Rom. 11:6 he affirms that it is freely given: "And if by grace, then it is no more of works; otherwise grace is no more grace." Grace may therefore be differentiated as either having one of these characters only, or having both characters.

I answer: as the apostle says in Rom. 13:1, "the powers that be are ordained of God." [1] Now the order of things is such that some things are led to God by means of others, as Dionysius says (Coel. Hier. 6, 7, 8). Hence grace, which is ordained to lead men to God, works in accordance with a certain order, in such a way that some men are led to God by means of other men. Grace is therefore twofold. There is grace through which a man is himself united to God, which is called sanctifying grace. There is also grace whereby one man co-operates with another to lead him to God. This latter gift is called "free grace," since it is beyond the capacity of nature to give, and beyond the merit of him to whom it is given. But it is not called sanctifying grace, since it is not given in order that a man may himself be justified by it, but in order that he may co-operate towards the justification of another. It is of such grace that the apostle speaks in I Cor. 12:7: "But the manifestation of the Spirit is given to every man to profit withal," that is, for the benefit of others.

On the first point: grace is said to make one pleasing, not efficiently, but formally, since one is justified by it, and so made worthy to be called pleasing to God. As it is said in Col. 1:12: "which hath made us meet to be partakers of the inheritance of the saints in light."

On the second point: since grace is freely given, it excludes

1 Migne: "The things which are of God are ordained" (ordinata—ordered).

the idea of debt. Now debt can be understood in two ways. In one sense it is the correlative of merit, applicable to a person upon whom it is incumbent to achieve works of merit, as in Rom. 4:4: "Now to him that worketh is the reward not reckoned of grace, but of debt." In a second sense it refers to the condition which is natural to one, as when we say that a man "ought" to have reason, and other things pertaining to human nature. In neither sense, however, does debt imply that God owes anything to a creature. Rather does it mean that a creature ought to be subject to God, so that there may be realized within it the divine order according to which a given nature has certain conditions and properties, and attains certain ends by means of certain activities. It follows that the gifts of nature exclude debt in the first sense. But they do not exclude debt in the second sense. Supernatural gifts, on the other hand, exclude debt in both senses, and thus warrant the title of grace in a manner peculiar to themselves.

On the third point: sanctifying grace adds to the notion of free grace something integral to the meaning of grace itself, in that it makes a man pleasing to God. Free grace does not do this, but nevertheless retains the common name, as often happens. The two parts of the division thus stand in contrast, as grace which sanctifies and grace which does not sanctify.

Article Two

WHETHER GRACE IS APPROPRIATELY DIVIDED INTO OPERATIVE AND CO-OPERATIVE GRACE

We proceed to the second article thus:

1. It seems that grace is not appropriately divided into operative and co-operative grace. It was said in the preceding article that grace is an accident, and no accident can act on its subject. Hence no grace should be called operative.

2. Again, if grace works anything in us, it assuredly works justification. But grace does not work this by itself. For on John 14:12, "the works that I do shall he do also," Augustine says: "He who created thee without thyself will not justify thee without thyself" (implicitly in *Tract. 72 in Joan.*, explicitly in *De Verb. Apost.*, *Sermo* 15, cap. 2). Hence no grace should be called operative simply.

3. Again, co-operation would seem to be appropriate to a subsidiary agent, but not to a principal agent. Now grace works in us more fundamentally than does free will, according

to Rom. 9:16: "it is not of him that willeth, nor of him that runneth, but of God that sheweth mercy." Grace should not then be called co-operative.

4. Again, a division should be between opposites. But operative and co-operative grace are not opposites, since the same agent can both operate and co-operate. Hence grace is not appropriately divided into operative and co-operative grace.

On the other hand: Augustine says (*De Grat. et Lib. Arb.* 17): "God perfects within us by co-operation what he initiates by operation. For he operates first to make us will, and co-operates with those who will to make them perfect." Now the operations by which God moves us to good are operations of grace. Grace is therefore appropriately divided into operative and co-operative grace.

I answer: as we said in Q. 110, Art. 2, grace may be understood in two ways, as the divine help by which God moves us to do and to will what is good, and as a habitual gift divinely bestowed on us. In either sense grace is appropriately divided into operative and co-operative grace. An operation which is part of an effect is attributed to the mover, not to the thing moved. The operation is therefore attributed to God when God is the sole mover, and when the mind is moved but not a mover. We then speak of "operative grace." But when the soul is not only moved but also a mover, the operation is attributed to the soul as well as to God. We then speak of "co-operative grace." In this case there is a twofold action within us. There is an inward action of the will, in which the will is moved and God is the mover, especially when a will which previously willed evil begins to will good. We therefore speak of "operative grace," since God moves the human mind to this action. But there is also an outward action, in which operation is attributed to the will, since an outward action is commanded by the will, as we explained in Q. 17, Art. 9. We speak of "co-operative grace" in reference to actions of this kind, because God helps us even in outward actions, outwardly providing the capacity to act as well as inwardly strengthening the will to issue in act. Augustine accordingly adds, to the words quoted, "he operates to make us will, and when we will, he co-operates with us that we may be made perfect." Hence if grace is understood to mean the gracious moving by which God moves us to meritorious good, it is appropriately divided into operative and co-operative grace.

If, on the other hand, grace is understood to mean a habitual gift, there is then a twofold effect of grace, as there is of any other form. There is an effect of "being" and an effect of "operation." The operation of heat is to make a thing hot, and also to cause it to emit heat. So likewise, grace is called "operative" in so far as it heals the soul, and in so far as it justifies the soul or makes it pleasing to God; and "co-operative" in so far as it is also the principle of meritorious action by the free will.

On the first point: as an accidental quality of the soul, grace acts on the soul not efficiently, but formally, in the way in which whiteness makes things white.

On the second point: God does not justify us without ourselves, since when we are justified we consent to his justice by a movement of our free will. This movement, however, is not the cause of grace, but the result of it. The whole operation is therefore due to grace.

On the third point: one is said to co-operate with another not only as an agent subsidiary to a principal agent, but also as contributing to an end which is preconceived. Now man is helped by God's operative grace to will what is good, and this end is already conceived. Hence grace co-operates with us.

On the fourth point: operative and co-operative grace are the same grace. They are nevertheless distinguished by their different effects, as is clear from what we have said.

Article Three

WHETHER GRACE IS APPROPRIATELY DIVIDED INTO PREVENIENT AND SUBSEQUENT GRACE

We proceed to the third article thus:

1. It seems that grace is not appropriately divided into prevenient and subsequent grace. For grace is an effect of God's love, and God's love is never subsequent, but always prevenient, according to I John 4:10: "not that we loved God, but that he loved us." Grace should not therefore be described as prevenient and subsequent.

2. Again, sanctifying grace in man is one, since it is sufficient, according to II Cor. 12:9: "My grace is sufficient for thee." But the same thing cannot be both prior and posterior. Grace is therefore inappropriately divided into prevenient and subsequent grace.

3. Again, grace is known by its effects. Now the effects of

grace are infinite in number, and one effect precedes another. It seems, therefore, that the species of grace will also be infinite in number, if grace is divided into prevenient and subsequent grace in respect of each of its effects. But what is infinite in number is ignored by every art. The division of grace into prevenient and subsequent grace is therefore not appropriate.

On the other hand: God's grace is the outcome of his mercy. Now on the one hand we read in Ps. 59:10: "The God of my mercy shall prevent me," and on the other hand in Ps. 23:6: "mercy shall follow me." Grace is therefore appropriately divided into prevenient and subsequent grace.

I answer: just as grace is divided into operative and co-operative grace on account of its different effects, so is it divided into prevenient and subsequent grace on the same grounds. There are five effects of grace in us: first, that the soul is healed; second, that it wills what is good; third, that it carries out what it wills; fourth, that it perseveres in good; and fifth, that it attains to glory. Since grace causes the first effect in us, it is called prevenient in relation to the second effect. Since it causes the second effect in us, it is called subsequent in relation to the first effect. And since any particular effect follows one effect and precedes another, grace may be called both prevenient and subsequent in regard to the same effect as related to different effects. This is what Augustine is saying in *De Nat. et Grat.* 31, and 2 *ad Bonif.* 9,[1] "Grace precedes, that we may be healed; it follows, that being healed we may be quickened; it precedes, that we may be called; it follows, that we may be glorified."

On the first point: since God's love means something eternal, it can never be called other than prevenient. Grace, however, signifies an effect in time, which can precede one effect and follow another. It may therefore be called both prevenient and subsequent.

On the second point: grace is not divided into prevenient and subsequent grace in respect of its essence, but solely in respect of its effects, as we said also in regard to operative and co-operative grace. Even as it pertains to the state of glory, subsequent grace is not numerically different from the prevenient grace by which we are now justified. The charity of the way is not annulled in heaven, but perfected, and we must

---

[1] In full, *Contra Pelagios ad Bonifacium.* Leonine Ed. implies that Aquinas did not give this reference.

say the same of the light of grace, since neither of them can mean anything imperfect.

On the third point: although the effects of grace may be as infinite in number as the deeds of men, they are all reducible to what is determinate in species. Moreover, they are all alike in that one precedes another.

Article Four

WHETHER FREE GRACE IS APPROPRIATELY DIVIDED BY THE APOSTLE

We proceed to the fourth article thus:

1. It seems that free grace is not appropriately distinguished by the apostle. For every gift which God freely gives us may be called a free grace, and the gifts which God freely give us, other than sanctifying gifts, are infinite in number. The free graces cannot then be comprehended under any precise division of grace.

2. Again, free grace is distinguished from sanctifying grace. Now faith pertains to sanctifying grace, since we are justified by it, according to Rom. 5:1: "being justified by faith." It is therefore inappropriate to include faith among the free graces, especially when other virtues such as hope and charity are not included.

3. Again, the work of healing, and speaking with diverse kinds of tongues, are miracles. Further, the interpretation of tongues depends either on wisdom or on knowledge, according to Dan. 1:17: "God gave them knowledge and skill in all learning and wisdom." The gifts of healing and kinds of tongues are therefore inappropriately distinguished from the working of miracles, and likewise the interpretation of tongues from the word of wisdom and the word of knowledge.

4. Again, understanding, counsel, piety, fortitude, and fear are gifts of the Holy Spirit no less than wisdom and knowledge, as we said in Q. 68, Art. 4. All of these should therefore be included among the free graces.

On the other hand: the apostle says (I Cor. 12:8–10): "For to one is given by the Spirit the word of wisdom; to another the word of knowledge by the same Spirit; to another faith by the same Spirit; to another the gifts of healing by the same Spirit; to another the working of miracles; to another prophecy; to another discerning of spirits; to another diverse kinds of tongues; to another the interpretation of tongues."

I answer: as we said in the first article, free grace is given in order that one man may co-operate with another to lead him to God. Now a man cannot contribute to this end by moving another inwardly (only God can do this), but only by outwardly teaching or persuading him. Free grace accordingly contains all that a man requires in order to instruct another in divine things which transcend reason. Three things are required for this. 1. He must have a full knowledge of divine things, so as to be able to teach others. 2. He must be able to verify or prove what he says, otherwise his teaching will be ineffective. 3. He must be able to convey his knowledge to others in a suitable manner.

1. We know from ordinary teaching that three things are essential for the first of these requirements. He who would instruct another in any science must first of all be firmly convinced of the principles of that science. Corresponding to this is faith, the certainty of the unseen things which are maintained as principles in catholic doctrine. Secondly, a teacher must have a correct knowledge of the principal conclusions of his science. Corresponding to this is the "word of wisdom," which is the knowledge of divine things. Thirdly, he must have a wealth of examples, and must be thoroughly acquainted with the effects by means of which he will sometimes have to demonstrate causes. Corresponding to this is the "word of knowledge," which is the knowledge of human things, since it is said in Rom. 1:20: "the invisible things of God . . . are clearly seen, being understood by the things that are made."

2. Such matters as are within the scope of reason are proved by means of argument. But divine revelations which transcend reason are proved by means peculiar to the divine power, and this in two ways. In one way, they are proved by the teacher of sacred doctrine carrying out what only God can do, in such miraculous works as healing the body, for which is given the "gift of healing"; or again in such as are intended solely to manifest the divine power, for example, that the sun should stand still or darken, or the sea be divided, for which the "working of miracles" is given. In another way, they are proved by his declaring things which only God can know, such as contingent events of the future, for which "prophecy" is given; or the hidden things of the heart, for which is given the "discerning of spirits."

3. The capacity to speak may be concerned either with the idioms which enable one to be understood by others, for which

are "kinds of tongues," or with the sense of what is conveyed, for which is the "interpretation of tongues."

On the first point: as we said in the first article, the blessings which are divinely bestowed upon us are not all called free graces, but only those which are beyond the power of nature, such as that a fisherman should be filled with the word of wisdom and the word of knowledge, and other things of the same kind. It is such that are here included under free grace.

On the second point: the faith which is here included among the free graces is not the virtue by which a man is himself justified, but the faith which possesses that supereminent certainty which makes him worthy to instruct others in matters pertaining to the faith. Hope and charity are concerned with the appetitive power by which it is ordained that a man shall seek God.

On the third point: the gift of healing is distinguished from the general working of miracles because it leads to faith in a special way. A man is more readily brought to faith if he acquires the blessing of bodily health through the power of faith. "Speaking with diverse tongues" and "interpretation of tongues" also lead to faith in special ways. They are accordingly regarded as free graces of a special kind.

On the fourth point: wisdom and knowledge are not included among the free graces on the ground that they are numbered with the gifts of the Holy Spirit, on the ground, that is, that men are readily brought by the Holy Spirit to matters of wisdom and knowledge. They are indeed gifts of the Holy Spirit, as we said in Q. 68, Arts. 1 and 4. But they are included among the free graces, because they provide a wealth of knowledge and wisdom which enables a man not only to discern divine things aright for himself, but also to instruct others and refute adversaries. The "word of wisdom" and the "word of knowledge" are therefore included with some point. As Augustine says, "It is one thing to know what a man must believe in order to attain to the life of the blessed. It is another thing to know how this helps the pious, and how it may be defended against the impious" (14 *De Trin.* 1).

Article Five

WHETHER FREE GRACE IS NOBLER THAN SANCTIFYING GRACE

We proceed to the fifth article thus:

1. It seems that free grace is nobler than sanctifying grace. For the philosopher says that "the good of the race is better

than the good of the individual" (1 *Ethics* 2), and sanctifying grace is ordained only for the good of the individual, whereas free grace is ordained for the common good of the whole Church, as was said in Arts. 1 and 4. Free grace is therefore nobler than sanctifying grace.

2. Again, a power which can act upon something else is greater than a power which is merely perfect in itself. Light which can illumine objects, for example, is greater than light which shines itself but cannot illumine objects. For this reason the philosopher says that "justice is the noblest of the virtues" (5 *Ethics* 1), since justice enables a man to behave rightly towards others. Now by sanctifying grace a man is made perfect in himself. But by free grace he contributes to the perfection of others. Free grace is therefore nobler than sanctifying grace.

3. Again, what is peculiar to those who are better is nobler than what is common to all. Thus reason, which is peculiar to man, is nobler than feeling, which is common to all animals. Now sanctifying grace is common to all members of the Church, whereas free grace is a special gift to its worthier members. Free grace is therefore nobler than sanctifying grace.

On the other hand: after numbering the free graces, the apostle says (I Cor. 12:31): "and yet show I unto you a more excellent way"—and what follows clearly shows that he here speaks of charity, which belongs to sanctifying grace. Sanctifying grace is therefore more excellent than free grace.

I answer: a power is the more excellent the higher is the end for which it is ordained. For an end is always more important than the means to it. Now sanctifying grace is ordained to unite man directly with his final end, whereas the free graces are ordained to prepare him for his final end; prophecy, miracles, and the like being the means whereby he is put in touch with it. Sanctifying grace is therefore more excellent than free grace.

On the first point: as the philosopher says in 12 *Metaph.*, text 52, the good of a multitude, such as an army, is twofold. There is the good which is in the multitude itself, such as the orderliness of an army. But there is also the good of its leader. This is separate from the multitude, and is the greater good, since the former is ordained for the sake of it. Now free grace is ordained for the common good of the Church, which consists in ecclesiastical order. But sanctifying grace is ordained for the common good which is separate, which is God himself. Sanctifying grace is therefore the nobler.

On the second point: if free grace could bring about in

another what a man himself obtains through sanctifying grace, it would follow that free grace was the nobler, just as the light of the sun which illumines is greater than the light of the object which it illumines. But free grace does not enable a man to bring about in another the fellowship with God which he himself shares through sanctifying grace, although he creates certain dispositions towards it. Hence free grace is not bound to be the more excellent, any more than the heat in a fire, which reveals the specific nature by which it produces heat in other things, is nobler than its own substantial form.

On the third point: feeling is subservient to reason as its end. Hence reason is the nobler. But in this instance things are reversed. What is special is ordained to serve what is common. There is therefore no similarity.

Question One Hundred and Twelve

THE CAUSE OF GRACE

We must now consider the cause of grace, concerning which there are five questions. 1. Whether God is the sole efficient cause of grace. 2. Whether any disposition for grace is required on the part of the recipient, by an act of free will. 3. Whether such a disposition can ensure grace. 4. Whether grace is equal in everyone. 5. Whether any man can know that he has grace.

Article One

WHETHER GOD IS THE SOLE CAUSE OF GRACE

We proceed to the first article thus:

1. It seems that God is not the sole cause of grace. For it is said in John 1:17 that "grace and truth came by Jesus Christ," and the name Jesus Christ means the creaturely nature assumed as well as the divine nature which assumed it. It follows that what is creaturely can be the cause of grace.

2. Again, the sacraments of the new law are said to differ from those of the old in this respect, namely that the sacraments of the new law are causes of the grace which those of the old law only signify. Now the sacraments of the new law are visible elements. It follows that God is not the sole cause of grace.

3. Again, according to Dionysius (*Coel. Hier.* 3, 4): "angels purge, enlighten, and perfect both lesser angels and men." But rational creatures are purged, enlightened, and perfected through grace. It follows that God is not the sole cause of grace.

On the other hand: it is said in Ps. 84:11: "the Lord will give grace and glory."

I answer: nothing can act upon what is above its own species, since a cause must always be greater than its effect. Now the gift of grace exceeds every capacity of nature, since it is none other than a participation of the divine nature, which exceeds every other nature. It is therefore impossible for any creature to be a cause of grace. Hence it is just as inevitable that God alone should deify, by communicating a sharing of the divine nature through a participation of likeness, as it is impossible that anything save fire alone should ignite.

On the first point: the humanity of Christ is "an organ of his divinity," as the Damascene says (3 *De Fid. Orth.* 15). Now an instrument carries out the action of a principal agent by the power of the principal agent, not by its own power. Thus the humanity of Christ does not cause grace by its own power, but by the power of the divinity conjoined with it, through which the actions of the humanity of Christ are redemptive.

On the second point: just as in the person of Christ humanity is the cause of our salvation through the divine power which operates as the principal agent, so it is with the sacraments of the new law. Grace is caused instrumentally by the sacraments themselves, yet principally by the power of the Holy Spirit operating in the sacraments.

On the third point: an angel purges, enlightens, and perfects an angel or a man by instruction, not by justification through grace. Wherefore Dionysius says (*Coel. Hier.* 7): "this kind of purging, enlightening, and perfecting is nothing other than the acquisition of divine knowledge."

Article Two

WHETHER A PREPARATION OR DISPOSITION FOR GRACE IS REQUIRED ON THE PART OF MAN

We proceed to the second article thus:

1. It seems that no preparation or disposition for grace is required on the part of man. For the apostle says (Rom. 4:4): "Now to him that worketh [1] is the reward not reckoned of grace,

1 *qui operatur.*

but of debt." But a man could not of his own free will prepare himself for grace, unless by an operation. The meaning of grace would then be taken away.

2. Again, a man who walks in sin does not prepare himself for grace. Yet grace is given to some while they walk in sin. This is evident in the case of Paul, who received grace while "breathing out threatenings and slaughter against the disciples of the Lord" (Acts. 9:1). Hence no preparation for grace is required on the part of man.

3. Again, an agent whose power is infinite does not need any disposition of matter, since he does not even need matter itself, as is obvious in creation. Now grace is likened to creation, being called a new creature in Gal., ch. 6, and it was said in the preceding article that God, whose power is infinite, is the sole cause of grace. It follows that no preparation for receiving grace is required on the part of man.

On the other hand: it is said in Amos 4:12: "prepare to meet thy God, O Israel," and in I Sam. 7:3: "prepare your hearts unto the Lord."

I answer: as we said in Q. 111, Art. 2, grace may be understood in two ways. Sometimes it means a habitual gift which God bestows. At other times it means the help of God, who moves the soul to good. Now some preparation is required for grace as a habitual gift, since a form can exist only in matter which is disposed to it. But no previous preparation is required on the part of man if we are speaking of grace as the help of God, by which he moves him to good. Rather is any preparation which can take place within him due to the help of God, who thus moves him. Even the good action of his free will, by which he is made ready to receive the gift of grace, is an action of his free will as moved by God. Hence a man is said to prepare himself. As it is said in Prov. 16:1: "the preparations of the heart in man."[1] But since his free will is moved by God as principal agent, his will is also said to be prepared by God, and his steps guided by the Lord.

On the first point: there is a preparation of oneself for grace which is simultaneous with the infusion of grace. This is indeed a meritorious work. But it merits the glory which a man does not yet possess, not the grace which he now has. There is also an incomplete preparation for grace which sometimes precedes sanctifying grace, though nevertheless due to God as mover. But this last is not sufficient for merit, since there is as yet no

[1] Migne: "It is of man to prepare the soul."

justification by grace. As we shall show in Q. 114, Art. 2, there is no merit except by grace.

On the second point: since a man cannot prepare himself for grace unless God first moves him to good, it is immaterial whether one is perfectly prepared all at once, or little by little. As it is said in Ecclesiasticus 11:21: "In the eyes of God, it is easy for a poor man suddenly to become rich." Sometimes God moves a man to good, but not perfectly. This is a preparation which precedes grace. At other times he moves a man to good both instantaneously and perfectly, and such a one then receives grace suddenly, after the manner spoken of in John 6:45: "Every man therefore that hath heard, and hath learned of the Father, cometh unto me." This is what happened to Paul, whose heart was suddenly moved by God to hear, to learn, and to come, even while he yet walked in sin. He thus received grace suddenly.

On the third point: an agent whose power is infinite needs neither matter nor a disposition of matter provided by the action of any other cause. Such an agent is nevertheless bound to cause both the matter in a thing and a disposition favourable to its form, according to the condition of the thing to be made. So likewise when God infuses grace into the soul, no preparation is required which God does not himself achieve.

Article Three

WHETHER GRACE IS BOUND TO BE GIVEN TO ONE WHO PREPARES HIMSELF FOR GRACE, OR WHO DOES WHAT HE CAN

We proceed to the third article thus:

1. It seems that grace is bound to be given to one who prepares himself for grace, or who does what he can. For a gloss on Rom. 3:21, "the righteousness of God . . . is manifested," says: "God receives him who flies to him, since otherwise he would be unjust." It is impossible that God should be unjust, and consequently impossible that he should not receive one who flies to him. Such a one is therefore bound to receive grace.

2. Again, Anselm says (*De Casu Diaboli* 3): "the reason why God does not extend grace to the devil is that he was neither willing nor prepared to receive it." But if a cause be removed, its effect is also removed. If anyone is willing to receive grace, therefore, he is bound to receive it.

3. Again, "good diffuses itself," as Dionysius explains (4 *Div. Nom.*, lect. 3), and the good of grace is better than the good of nature. Now a natural form is bound to be received by matter which is disposed to it. Much more, then, is grace bound to be given to one who prepares himself for it.

On the other hand: man is to God as clay to the potter, according to Jer. 18:6: "as the clay is in the potter's hand, so are ye in mine hand." But clay is not bound to receive a form from the potter, however much it may be prepared. Neither then is a man bound to receive grace from God, however much he may prepare himself.

I answer: preparation for grace may be considered under two aspects, since a man's preparation for it is due to God as mover, and also to his own free will as moved by God, as we said in the preceding article. In so far as preparation for grace is due to a man's own free will, there is no necessity why grace should follow it. The gift of grace exceeds any preparation by human power. But in so far as it is due to the moving of God, what God intends by such moving is bound to be achieved, since God's purpose cannot fail. As Augustine says: "whosoever will be set free by the blessings of God will most certainly be set free (*De Dono Persev.* 14). Hence if a man whose heart is moved receives grace by the intention of God who moves him, he receives grace inevitably, in accordance with John 6:45: "Every man therefore that hath heard, and hath learned of the Father, cometh unto me."

On the first point: this gloss refers to one who flies to God by a meritorious action of free will which has already been brought to its form by means of grace. If such a one did not receive grace, this would be contrary to the justice which God has himself ordained. Or, if it refers to an action of free will which precedes grace, it assumes that such flight to God is due to the moving of God, which moving ought not in justice to fail.

On the second point: the first cause of the absence of grace lies with ourselves, whereas the first cause of the bestowal of grace lies with God. Thus it is said in Hos. 13:9: "O Israel, thou hast destroyed thyself; but in me is thine help."

On the third point: a disposition of matter does not ensure the reception of a form, even in natural things, unless through the power of the agent which caused the disposition.

Article Four

WHETHER GRACE IS GREATER IN ONE MAN THAN IN
ANOTHER

We proceed to the fourth article thus:
1. It seems that grace is not greater in one man than in another. For it was said in Q. 110, Art. 1, that grace is caused in us by God's love, and according to Wisdom 6:7, "He made both the small and the great, and cares equally for all." It follows that all receive grace equally.
2. Again, whatever is said to be the greatest possible does not admit of more and less. Now grace is said to be the greatest possible, since it unites us with our final end. It does not then admit of more and less. It follows that it is not greater in one man than in another.
3. Again, it was said in Q. 110, Arts. 1, 2, and 4, that grace is the life of the soul. But life does not admit of more and less. Neither then does grace.

On the other hand: it is said in Eph. 4:7: "But unto every one of us is given grace according to the measure of the gift of Christ." Now what is given according to measure is not given equally to all. It follows that everyone does not have equal grace.

I answer: as we said in Q. 52, Arts. 1 and 2, a habit can have magnitude in two ways: in respect of its end or object, as when we say that one virtue is nobler than another because it is directed to a greater good; and in respect of its subject, as when we say that one who possesses a habit possesses it in greater or less degree. Now sanctifying grace cannot admit of more and less in respect of its end or object, since grace by its very nature unites a man with the greatest possible good, which is God. But grace does admit of more and less in respect of its subject, since one man may be more enlightened by the light of grace than another. Such diversity is partly due to him who prepares himself for grace, since he who prepares himself the more receives the greater fullness of grace. But we cannot accept this as the primary reason for it, because it is only in so far as his free will is itself prepared by God that a man prepares himself for grace. We must acknowledge that the primary reason for this diversity lies with God. For God distributes his gracious gifts diversely, to the end that the beauty and perfection of the Church may ensue from their diversity, even as he instituted the various degrees of things to the end that the universe might be perfect. Wherefore the apostle, having said: "unto every one of us is given grace according to the measure of the gift of Christ," thereafter enumerates the various graces, adding the words "for the perfecting of the saints . . . for the edifying of the body of Christ" (Eph. 4:12).

On the first point: the divine care may mean either of two things. It may mean the divine act itself, which is simple and uniform. If it means this, the divine care is equally towards all, since God bestows both the greater and the less by one, simple act. But if it means the gifts which creatures receive as the result of God's care, there is then diversity, since God bestows greater gifts on some, and lesser gifts on others.

On the second point: natural life cannot admit of more and less, because it belongs to man's essential being. But man participates in the life of grace accidentally, and may therefore do so in greater or in less degree.

Article Five

WHETHER A MAN CAN KNOW THAT HE HAS GRACE

We proceed to the fifth article thus:

1. It seems that a man can know that he has grace. For grace is in the soul through its essence, and the most certain knowledge that the soul can have is of what is in itself through its own essence (as Augustine proves in 12 *Gen. ad Litt.* 31). Grace can therefore be known by him who has grace, with the greatest possible certainty.

2. Again, as knowledge is a gift from God, so also is grace. Now whosoever receives knowledge from God knows that he has knowledge, according to Wisdom 7:17: "the Lord hath given me true knowledge of the things that are." For a like reason, therefore, whosoever receives grace from God knows that he has grace.

3. Again, light is more easily known than darkness, since "whatsoever doth make manifest is light," [1] as the apostle says (Eph. 5:13). But sin, which is spiritual darkness, can be known with certainty by him who has sin. Much more then can grace, which is spiritual light.

4. Again, the apostle says (I Cor. 2:12): "Now we have received, not the spirit of the world, but the spirit which is of God; that we might know the things that are freely given to us

[1] Migne: "All that is made manifest is light."

of God." Now grace is the first gift of God. A man who has received grace through the Holy Spirit therefore knows that grace is given to him.

5. Again, the Lord himself said to Abraham: "now I know that thou fearest God" (Gen. 22:12), that is, "I have made thee to know"—and this is the fear of reverence, for which grace is essential. A man can therefore know that he has grace.

On the other hand: it is said in Eccl. 9:1: "no man knoweth either love or hatred by all that is before them."[1] Now sanctifying grace makes a man worthy of the love of God. It follows that no man can know whether he has sanctifying grace.

I answer: there are three ways by which a thing may be known. One way is by revelation. A man may know by revelation that he has grace, since there are times when God reveals this to some as a special privilege, thus engendering within them the joy of security, even in this present life, in order that they may the more confidently and wholeheartedly carry out noble works, and withstand the evils of this present life. Thus was it said to Paul: "My grace is sufficient for thee" (II Cor. 12:9).

In another way, a man may know something by himself, and that with certainty. But no man can know, in this way, that he has grace. For we can be certain of something only if we apprehend it through its own proper principle. In knowledge of this kind, we are certain of conclusions which can be demonstrated from indemonstrable and universal principles. But no one can be sure that he knows any conclusion if he does not know its principle. Now the principle of grace is God himself, who is also its object, and God is unknown by us on account of his excellence. As Job says: "Behold, God is great, and we know him not" (36:26). Neither his presence in us nor his absence can be known with certainty. As Job says again: "Lo, he goeth by me, and I see him not: he passeth on also, but I perceive him not" (9:11). It follows that a man cannot judge with certainty whether he has grace. As it is said in I Cor. 4:3-4: "yea, I judge not mine own self . . . but he that judgeth me is the Lord."

In a third way, we may know something conjecturally by means of signs. Anyone may know, after this manner, that he has grace, in as much as he perceives that he delights in God and loves not the world, and in as much as he is not aware of any mortal sin within him. We may understand in this wise what is said in Rev. 2:17: "To him that overcometh will I give

[1] Migne: "No man knoweth whether he is worthy of hate or of love."

to eat of the hidden manna . . . which no man knoweth, saving he that receiveth it." But such knowledge is imperfect, wherefore it is said by the apostle in I Cor. 4:4: "I know nothing by myself; yet am I not hereby justified," and also in Ps. 19:12–13: "Who can understand his errors? cleanse thou me from secret faults. Keep back thy servant also from presumptuous sins."

On the first point: what is in the soul through its essence is known by way of experimental awareness, in so far as a man knows inward principles through actions. We know the will through willing, for example, and we know life through the functions of life.

On the second point: certainty of what we know is essential to science. Certainty of what we hold in faith is likewise essential to faith. The reason for this is that certainty is a perfection of the intellect, in which such gifts exist. Whosoever has either knowledge or faith, therefore, is certain that he has it. But it is otherwise with grace and charity, and the like, because these are perfections of the appetitive power.

On the third point: the principle and the object of sin both consist in changeable good, which we know. But the object and end of grace is unknown to us on account of the immensity of its light, of which 1 Tim. 6:16 says: "the light which no man can approach unto."

On the fourth point: the apostle is here speaking of the gifts of glory, the hope of which is given unto us. We know such things assuredly through faith, although we do not know assuredly that we have grace whereby we may merit them.

On the fifth point: what was said to Abraham may have referred to his experimental awareness, which his actions revealed. Abraham could have known, experimentally through his actions, that he feared God. Or it may refer to a revelation.

Question One Hundred and Thirteen

THE EFFECTS OF GRACE

We must now inquire into the effects of grace. We shall inquire first into the justification of the ungodly, which is the effect of operative grace, and second into merit, which is the effect of co-operative grace.

There are ten questions concerning the justification of the ungodly. 1. What is the justification of the ungodly. 2. Whether an infusion of grace is required for it. 3. Whether any movement of the free will is required for it. 4. Whether a movement of faith is required for the justification of the ungodly. 5. Whether a movement of the free will against sin is required for it. 6. Whether the remission of sins is to be numbered with these requirements. 7. Whether the justification of the ungodly is gradual or instantaneous. 8. Concerning the natural order of things required for justification. 9. Whether the justification of the ungodly is the greatest work of God. 10. Whether the justification of the ungodly is miraculous.

Article One

WHETHER THE JUSTIFICATION OF THE UNGODLY IS THE REMISSION OF SINS

We proceed to the first article thus:

1. It seems that the justification of the ungodly is not the remission of sins. It is clear from what was said in Q. 71, Arts. 1 and 2, that sin is opposed not only to justice, but to all virtues. Now justification means a movement towards justice. Hence not every remission of sin is justification, since every movement is from one contrary to its opposite.

2. Again, it is said in 2 *De Anima*, text 49, that each thing should be denominated by what is most prominent in it. Now the remission of sins is brought about primarily by faith, according to Acts 15:9; "purifying their hearts by faith," and also by charity, according to Prov. 10:12: "love covereth all sins." It should therefore be denominated by faith, or by charity, rather than by justice.

3. Again, the remission of sins seems to be the same as calling, since one who is called is at a distance, and since we are separated from God by sin. Now according to Rom. 8:30: "whom he called, them he also justified," calling comes before justification. It follows that justification is not the remission of sins.

On the other hand: a gloss on Rom. 8:30, "whom he called, them he also justified," says: "that is, by the remission of sins." It follows that the remission of sins is justification.

I answer: understood passively, justification means the movement towards justice, in the same way as to be heated means the movement towards heat. But justice, considered in its own nature, means a certain right order, and may be understood in two senses. In one sense it means the right order of a man's action. Such justice is reckoned as one of the virtues, either as particular justice, which regulates a man's action in relation to another individual, or as legal justice, which regulates his action in relation to the good of the community, as explained in 5 *Ethics* 1. In a second sense it means the right order of a man's inward disposition, signifying the subordination of his highest power to God, and the subordination of the lower powers of his soul to the highest, which is reason. The philosopher calls this "metaphorical justice," in 5 *Ethics* 11.

Now justice of this latter kind may be brought about in two ways. It may be brought about by simple generation, which is from privation to form. Justification in this wise may happen even to one who is not in sin, through his receiving justice from God, as Adam is said to have received original justice. But it may also be brought about by movement from contrary to contrary. When it is brought about in this latter way, justification means the transmutation from a state of injustice to the state of justice which we have mentioned. It is this that we mean when we speak here of the justification of the ungodly, in agreement with the apostle's words in Rom. 4:5: "But to him that worketh not, but believeth on him that justifieth the ungodly, his faith is counted for righteousness." And since a movement is denominated from its *terminus ad quem* rather than from its *terminus a quo*, the transmutation, wherein one is transmuted by remission of sin from a state of injustice to a state of justice, is called "the justification of the ungodly."

On the first point: every sin involves the disorder of a man's insubordination to God. Every sin may therefore be called an injustice, and consequently a contrary of justice. As it is said in I John 3:4: "Whosoever committeth sin transgresseth also the law: for sin is the transgression of the law." Deliverance from any sin is therefore called justification.

On the second point: faith and charity subordinate man's mind to God in specific ways, in respect of the intellect and in respect of the will. But justice means right order in general, and the transmutation referred to is therefore denominated by justice, rather than by faith or charity.

3. Again, "calling" refers to the help of God, who moves the mind from within and excites it to renounce sin. This moving of God is not itself remission of sin, but the cause of it.

Article Two

WHETHER AN INFUSION OF GRACE IS REQUIRED FOR THE REMISSION OF GUILT, WHICH IS THE JUSTIFICATION OF THE UNGODLY

We proceed to the second article thus:

1. It seems that an infusion of grace is not required for the remission of guilt, which is the justification of the ungodly. For if there is a mean between two contraries, it is possible to be delivered from one of them without being brought to the other. Now there is a mean between the state of guilt and the state of grace, namely the state of innocence, in which one has neither grace nor guilt. One may therefore be forgiven one's guilt without being brought to grace.

2. Again, remission of guilt consists in divine forbearance to impute it, according to Ps. 32:2: "Blessed is the man unto whom the Lord imputeth not iniquity." Infusion of grace, on the other hand, denotes something within us, as was maintained in Q. 110, Art. 1. It follows that an infusion of grace is not required for the remission of guilt.

3. Again, no one can be subject to two contraries at once. Now certain sins are contraries, like prodigality and parsimony. Whoever is subject to the sin of prodigality cannot then be subject to the sin of parsimony at the same time, although he may have been subject to it previously. Hence he is set free from the sin of parsimony through sinning by the vice of prodigality. Thus a sin is remitted without grace.

On the other hand: it is said in Rom. 3:24: "Being justified freely by his grace."

I answer: it is clear from what we said in Q. 71, Art. 5, that when a man sins, he offends God. Now an offence is not remitted unless the mind of the offended one is pacified towards the offender. Our sin is accordingly said to be remitted when God is pacified towards us. This peace is one with the love with which God loves us. But although the love of God is eternal and unchangeable as a divine action, the effect which it impresses upon us is intermittent, since we sometimes lose it and recover it again. Moreover, the effect of the divine love which we forfeit through sin is grace, and grace makes a man worthy of the eternal life from which mortal sin excludes him. The remission of sin would therefore be meaningless if there were no infusion of grace.

On the first point: to forgive an offender for an offence demands more than is required merely to feel no hatred towards one who does not offend. For it can happen with men that one man neither loves not hates another, and yet will not forgive an offence if the other should offend him, unless through exceptional good will. Now God's good will to man is said to be renewed by a gift of grace. Hence although a man may have been without either grace or guilt before he sins, he cannot be without guilt after he sins, unless he has grace.

On the second point: just as God's love not only consists in a divine act of will, but also implies some effect of grace, as we said in Q..110, Art. 1, so also the divine forbearance to impute sin implies some effect in him to whom God does not impute it. For God's forbearance to impute sin is an expression of his love.

On the third point: as Augustine says (1 *De Nup. et Concup.* 26): "If to be sinless were merely to desist from sin, it would be enough if the scriptural warning were this—'My son, thou hast sinned. Do it not again.' But this is not enough, wherefore there is added 'and pray that thy former sins may be forgiven thee.'" Now sins endures as guilt, though it is transient as an action, as we said in Q. 87, Art. 6. Hence although a man ceases from the action of his former sin when he passes from the sin of one vice to the sin of a contrary vice, he does not cease to bear the guilt of it. Indeed, he bears the guilt of both sins simultaneously. Moreover, sins are not contrary to each other in respect of turning away from God, which is the very reason why sin involves guilt.

Article Three

WHETHER A MOVEMENT OF THE FREE WILL IS REQUIRED FOR THE JUSTIFICATION OF THE UNGODLY

We proceed to the third article thus:

1. It seems that a movement of the free will is not required for the justification of the ungodly. For we see that infants are justified through the sacrament of Baptism without any movement of the free will, and sometimes adults also. Augustine indeed says that when one of his friends lay sick of a fever, "he lay for long unconscious in a deathly sweat, and when given up in despair, was baptized without his knowing it, and was regenerated" (4 *Confessions*, cap. 4). Now regeneration is by justifying grace. But God does not confine his power to the

sacraments. He can therefore justify a man not only without any movement of the free will, but without the sacraments.

2. Again, a man does not have the use of his reason while asleep, and there cannot be a movement of the free will without the use of reason. Yet Solomon received the gift of wisdom from God while he slept (I Kings, ch. 3, and II Chron., ch. 1). It is just as reasonable that a man should sometimes receive the gift of justifying grace from God without a movement of the free will.

3. Again, grace is conserved and begun by the same cause. Hence Augustine says: "a man ought to turn to God, so that he may at all times be justified by him" (8 *Gen. ad Litt.* 10, 12). Now grace is conserved in a man without a movement of the free will. It can therefore be infused initially without a movement of the free will.

On the other hand: it is said in John 6:45: "Every man that hath heard, and hath learned of the Father, cometh unto me." Now one cannot learn without a movement of the free will, since the learner gives his consent to the teacher. It follows that no man comes to God through justifying grace without a movement of the free will.

I answer: the justification of the ungodly is achieved through God moving a man to justice, as Rom., ch. 3 affirms. Now God moves each thing according to its own manner. We see in natural things that what is heavy is moved by God in one way, and what is light in another way, on account of the different nature of each. He likewise moves a man to justice in a manner which accords with the condition of his human nature, and it is proper to the nature of man that his will should be free. Consequently, when a man has the use of his free will, God never moves him to justice without the use of his free will. With all who are capable of being so moved, God infuses the gift of justifying grace in such wise that he also moves the free will to accept it.

On the first point: infants are incapable of a movement of free will. God therefore moves them to justice solely by moulding their souls. But this is possible only by means of a sacrament, because grace comes to them through spiritual regeneration by Christ; just as the original sin from which they are justified came to them through their carnal origin, not through their own will. It is the same with maniacs and morons, who have never had the use of their free will. But if anyone should lose the use of his free will either through infirmity or sleep, having formerly had the use of it, such a one does not receive justifying grace through the outward administration of Baptism, or of any other sacrament, unless he previously intended to partake of it, which he could not do without the use of his free will. The friend of whom Augustine speaks was regenerated in this way because he assented to Baptism, both previously and subsequently.

On the second point: Solomon neither merited wisdom nor received it while he slept. But it was declared to him while he slept that God would infuse wisdom, because of his previous desire for it. Wisdom 7:7 accordingly puts these words in his mouth: "I desired, and understanding was given unto me." Or it may be that his was not natural sleep, but the sleep of prophecy referred to in Num. 12:6: "If there be a prophet among you, I the Lord will make myself known unto him in a vision, and will speak unto him in a dream." If so, his free will could have been used. But we must observe that the gifts of wisdom and of justifying grace are not alike. The gift of justifying grace directs a man especially to good, which is the object of the will, and therefore moves him to good by a movement of the will, which is a movement of his free will. Wisdom, on the other hand, perfects the intellect, which is more fundamental than the will, and can therefore be enlightened by the gift of wisdom without any complete movement of the free will. Some things are revealed in this way to men while they sleep, as we see from Job 33:15–16: "In a dream, in a vision of the night, when deep sleep falleth upon me, in slumberings upon the bed; Then he openeth the ears of men, and sealeth their instruction."

On the third point: in the infusion of justifying grace there is a transmutation of the human soul. A movement proper to the human soul is therefore required, in order that the soul may be moved according to its own manner. But in the preservation of grace there is no transmutation. Consequently, no movement is required on the part of the soul, but only a continuation of divine inspiration.

Article Four

WHETHER A MOVEMENT OF FAITH IS REQUIRED FOR THE JUSTIFICATION OF THE UNGODLY

We proceed to the fourth article thus:

1. It seems that a movement of faith is not required for the justification of the ungodly. For a man is justified by other

things besides faith. He is justified by fear, for example, of which Ecclesiasticus says (1:21): "The fear of the Lord driveth out sin, for he who is without fear cannot be justified"; and by charity, according to Luke 7:47: "Her sins, which are many, are forgiven, for she loved much"; and by humility, according to James 4:6: "God resisteth the proud, but giveth grace unto the humble"; and also by mercy, according to Prov. 16:6: "By mercy and truth iniquity is purged."[1] Hence a movement of faith is no more required for the justification of the ungodly than is a movement of the virtues named.

2. Again, justification requires an act of faith only in so far as a man knows God through faith. But a man can know God in other ways. He can know him through natural knowledge, for example, or by means of the gift of wisdom. It follows that an act of faith is not required for the justification of the ungodly.

3. Again, there are several articles of faith. Hence if an act of faith is required for the justification of the ungodly, it seems that a man must contemplate all the articles of faith at the time when he is first justified. But this is impossible, because such contemplation would take a long time. It seems, therefore, that an act of faith is not required for the justification of the ungodly.

On the other hand: it is said in Rom. 5:1: "Therefore being justified by faith, we have peace with God. . . ."

I answer: as we said in the preceding article, the justification of the ungodly requires a movement of the free will, since God moves a man's mind. Now God moves a man's soul by turning it to himself, according to Ps. 85:7: "Thou wilt turn us, O God, and bring us to life" (Septuagint). Hence justification requires the movement of the mind by which it turns to God. But the mind turns to God in the first instance by faith, according to Heb. 11:6: "he that cometh to God must believe that he is." A movement of faith is therefore required for the justification of the ungodly.

On the first point: a movement of faith is not perfect unless it is formed by charity. There is, therefore, a movement of charity in the justification of the ungodly, simultaneous with the movement of faith. There is also an act of filial fear, and an act of humility. Provided that it can be directed to diverse ends, one and the same act of the free will can be the act of diverse virtues, one of which commands while the others obey. An act of mercy, however, either operates like a satisfaction for sin, in which case it follows justification, or serves as a preparation

1 Migne: "By mercy and faith sins are purged."

for justification, as it does when the merciful obtain mercy. It can therefore precede justification, contributing towards it simultaneously with the virtues mentioned, as it does when mercy is included in love to one's neighbour.

On the second point: when a man knows God through natural knowledge, he is not turned to God as the object of blessedness and cause of justification. His knowledge is therefore insufficient for justification. The gift of wisdom presupposes faith, as we explained in Q. 68, Art. 4, ad 3.

On the third point: the apostle says (Rom. 4:5): "to him . . . that believeth on him that justifieth the ungodly, his faith is counted for righteousness."[1] This makes it plain that an act of faith is required in the justification of the ungodly to this extent —that a man believe that God is the justifier of men through the mystery of Christ.

Article Five

WHETHER A MOVEMENT OF THE FREE WILL AGAINST SIN IS REQUIRED FOR THE JUSTIFICATION OF THE UNGODLY

We proceed to the fifth article thus:

1. It seems that a movement of the free will against sin is not required for the justification of the ungodly. According to Prov. 10:12: "love covereth all sins," charity alone is enough to blot out sin. But charity is not concerned with sin as its object. It follows that a movement of the free will against sin is not required for the justification of the ungodly.

2. Again, one who is pressing forward should not look behind him, according to Phil. 3:13–14: "forgetting those things which are behind, and reaching forth unto those things which are before, I press toward the mark for the prize of the high calling. . . ." Now the previous sins of one who is on the way to righteousness are behind him. He should therefore forget them, and not turn back to them by a movement of the free will.

3. Again, in the justification of the ungodly, one sin is not forgiven without another. "It is impious to expect half a pardon from God" (*Sunt Plures, Dist. 3 de Poenit.*). A man would therefore have to reflect upon every one of his sins, if the justification of the ungodly required a movement of the free will against sin. But this seems impossible. For a man would need a long time for such reflection. Neither could he be forgiven for the sins

[1] Migne adds: ". . . according to the purpose of God's grace."

which he had forgotten. It follows that a movement of the free will against sin is not required for the justification of the ungodly.

On the other hand: it is said in Ps. 32:5: "I said, I will confess my transgressions unto the Lord; and thou forgavest the iniquity of my sin."

I answer: as we said in the first article, the justification of the ungodly is a movement, in which the human mind is moved by God from a state of sin to a state of justice. It is therefore necessary that a man's mind should relate itself to both states by a movement of the free will, just as a body which moves away from one point is related to both the points between which it moves. When a body moves in space, it obviously moves from a *terminus a quo* and approaches a *terminus ad quem*. When a human mind undergoes justification, it must both abandon sin and approach justice by a movement of the free will.

This movement of recoil and approach on the part of the free will means abhorrence and yearning. Hence in his exposition of John 10:13, "the hireling fleeth," Augustine says: "our feelings are the movements of our souls; joy is the soul's overflowing; fear is its flight; when you yearn, the soul advances; when you fear, it flees" (*Tract. in Joan.* 46). The justification of the ungodly thus requires a twofold movement of the free will. It must yearn for the justice which is of God. It must also abhor sin.

On the first point: it is by the same virtue that we strive towards one contrary and recoil from its opposite. It is thus by charity that we delight in God, and by charity also that we abhor the sins which separate us from God.

On the second point: when a man has put things behind him, he should not revert to them out of love for them. Rather should he forget them, lest he be drawn to them. But he ought to take note of them in thought as things to be abhorred, for thus does he forsake them.

On the third point: in the period before justification, a man must feel a loathing for the sins which he remembers having committed. From such preliminary meditation there ensues in the soul a movement of general loathing for all sins committed, including those which are buried in the past. For a man in this state would repent of the sins which he does not remember, if they were present to his memory. This movement contributes to his justification.

Article Six

WHETHER THE REMISSION OF SINS SHOULD BE NUMBERED WITH THE THINGS REQUIRED FOR THE JUSTIFICATION OF THE UNGODLY

We proceed to the sixth article thus:

1. It seems that the remission of sins should not be numbered with the things required for the justification of the ungodly. For the substance of a thing is not numbered with the things required for it. A man, for example, should not be numbered together with his soul and his body. Now it was said in the first article that the justification of the ungodly itself is the remission of sins. The remission of sins should not therefore be numbered with the things required for it.

2. Again, infusion of grace and remission of sin are the same thing, just as illumination and the dispelling of darkness are the same thing. But what is identical should not be numbered together with itself. Remission of guilt should not then be numbered together with infusion of grace.

3. Again, the remission of sins follows the movement of the free will toward God and against sin, as an effect follows its cause. For sins are forgiven as a result of faith and contrition. But an effect should not be numbered together with its cause, since things which are numbered as belonging to the same class are simultaneous by nature. The remission of guilt should not then be numbered with the things required for the justification of the ungodly.

On the other hand: since the end is paramount in all things, we should not omit to take account of the end in enumerating the things which are required for something. Now the remission of sins is the end in the justification of the ungodly, since it is said in Isa. 27:9: "and this is all the fruit to take away his sin." [1] The remission of sins should not therefore be omitted in the enumeration of things required for the justification of the ungodly.

I answer: four things are accounted necessary for the justification of the ungodly—an infusion of grace, a movement of the free will toward God in faith, a movement of the free will in recoil from sin, and the remission of guilt. The reason for this is that justification is a movement in which the soul is moved by God from a state of guilt to a state of justice. Three things

[1] Migne: "and this is all the fruit, that his sin should be taken away."

are necessary for any movement in which one thing is moved by another: first, the motion of the mover itself; second, the movement of the thing moved; and third, the consummation of the movement, or the attainment of the end. Now the infusion of grace is the motion of God, and the twofold movement by which the free will abandons a *terminus a quo* and approaches a *terminus ad quem* is the movement of the thing moved. But the consummation of the movement, or attainment of the end, lies in the remission of guilt. For therein is justification consummated.

On the first point: the justification of the ungodly is said to be itself the remission of sins because every movement takes its species from its end. But many other things are also required for the attainment of the end, as is clear from the preceding article.

On the second point: the infusion of grace and the remission of guilt may be considered in two ways. They are identical as referring to the substance of the act, since God bestows grace and forgives guilt by one and the same act. But they differ as referring to their objects, since the guilt removed and the grace infused are not the same; just as the generation and corruption of natural things differ, even though the generation of one may be identical with the corruption of another.

On the third point: this is not a classification according to genus and species, in which things classed together must be simultaneous. It is an enumeration of the different things required in order to complete something. It may therefore include one thing which precedes and another which follows, since one of the principles or parts of a composite thing may be prior to another.

Article Seven

WHETHER THE JUSTIFICATION OF THE UNGODLY IS ACHIEVED
INSTANTANEOUSLY OR GRADUALLY

We proceed to the seventh article thus:

1. It seems that the justification of the ungodly is not instantaneous, but gradual. For it was said in Art. 3 that justification requires a movement of the free will, and the action of the free will is that of choice, which presupposes thoughtful deliberation, as was said in Q. 13, Art. 1. Now deliberation implies a certain amount of reasoning, and reasoning involves a degree of succession. It seems, therefore, that the justification of the ungodly is gradual.

2. Again, there is no movement of the free will without actual consideration, and it was said in Q. 85, Art. 4 that we cannot actually understand many things at the same time. Now the justification of the ungodly requires a movement of the free will in different directions—in relation to God, and in relation to sin. It seems, therefore, that the justification of the ungodly cannot be instantaneous.

3. Again, a form which admits of more and less is received by its subject gradually, as is obvious in the case of whiteness or blackness. Now it was said in Q. 112, Art. 4, that grace admits of more and less. Hence grace is not received suddenly. Since the justification of the ungodly requires an infusion of grace, it seems that it cannot be instantaneous.

4. Again, the movement of the free will which contributes to the justification of the ungodly is meritorious. It must therefore have its origin in grace, since there is no merit without grace (as will be shown later, Q. 114, Art. 2). Now a thing receives its form before it acts by means of it. Grace must therefore be first of all infused, and the movement of the free will in relation to God and sin must follow. Hence justification is not entirely instantaneous.

5. Again, if grace is infused into the soul, there must be a first instant in which it is present in the soul, and if guilt is remitted, there must likewise be a last instant in which one is under guilt. Now these instants cannot be the same, since opposites would be in the same thing at the same time if they were so. There must therefore be two successive instants, and these must have a period of time between them, as the philosopher explains in 6 *Physics*, text 2. It follows that justification is achieved not instantaneously, but gradually.

On the other hand: the justification of the ungodly is by the grace of the Holy Spirit, which justifies us. Now the Holy Spirit comes to the minds of men suddenly, according to Acts 2:2: "And suddenly there came a sound from heaven, as of a rushing mighty wind," on which the gloss says: "the grace of the Holy Spirit knows no tardy travail" (and also a gloss by Ambrose on Luke 4:1: "he was led by the Spirit into the wilderness"). The justification of the ungodly is therefore instantaneous, not gradual.

I answer: the justification of the ungodly in its entirety has its origin in the infusion of grace. The free will is moved by grace, and guilt is removed by grace. Now the infusion of grace takes place in an instant, without any succession. For if any form is not imprinted on its subject suddenly, the reason is that its subject is not disposed to it, and that the agent needs time to make it so. Hence we see that a substantial form is received by matter at once, whenever matter becomes disposed to it through preliminary alteration. Hence also the atmosphere is at once illuminated by a body which is actually bright, since it is of its own accord disposed to receive light. Now we have already said that God needs no disposition, other than that which he himself creates, in order to infuse grace into the soul. As we said in Q. 112, Art. 2, he sometimes creates a disposition sufficient for the reception of grace all at once, sometimes by gradual degrees. A natural agent cannot adapt matter in an instant, because there is something in matter which resists his power. Matter is consequently adapted the more quickly the stronger is the power of the agent, as we may observe. The divine power can therefore adapt any created matter whatsoever instantly to its form, since the divine power is infinite. Much more can it so adapt the free will, the movement of which can be instantaneous by nature. The justification of the ungodly is therefore achieved by God in an instant.

On the first point: the movement of the free will which contributes to the justification of the ungodly is the consent to abhor sin and adhere to God. This consent is instantaneous. Deliberation may sometimes precede consent. But this is a way to justification, not the substance of it, just as local movement is a way to light, and change a way to generation.

On the second point: as we said in Pt. I, Q. 85, Art. 5, there is nothing to prevent us from understanding two things at the same time provided that they are in some way one. We understand a subject and a predicate simultaneously, since they are unified in a single affirmation. The free will can likewise be moved in two ways at the same time, provided that the one movement is subservient to the other. Now the movement of the free will in relation to sin is subservient to its movement in relation to God, since a man abhors sin because it is opposed to God, to whom he wills to adhere. Thus in the justification of the ungodly the free will abhors sin and turns to God simultaneously, just as a body simultaneously removes from one place and approaches another.

On the third point: there is no reason why a form which admits of more and less should not be received by matter instantaneously. If this were impossible, light could not be suddenly received by air, which can be illuminated in greater or in less degree. The explanation of this is to be found in the disposition of the matter or subject, as we have said.

On the fourth point: a thing begins to act by its form in the same instant in which the form is received. Fire moves upwards immediately it is kindled, and its upward movement would be completed at the same instant, if it were instantaneous. Now the movement of the free will, which is to will, is instantaneous, not gradual. The justification of the ungodly cannot therefore be gradual.

On the fifth point: the succession of two opposites in one subject which is in time must be considered differently from their succession in supra-temporal things. With things in time, there is no last instant in which a previous form inheres in its subject, although there is a last period of time in which it does so, and a first instant in which a succeeding form inheres in the matter, or subject. The reason for this is that there cannot be in time one instant which immediately precedes another, because instants are not continuous in time, any more than points are continuous in a line, as is proved in 6 *Physics*, text 1. A period of time, however, terminates at an instant, and hence a thing is under one opposite form during the whole period of time which precedes its movement to the other. But in the instant in which this period ends and the following period begins, it has the form which it attains by this movement.

But it is otherwise with supra-temporal things. For if there is any succession of affections or intellectual conceptions in them (e.g., in angels), this succession is measured by time which is discrete, not continuous, as we explained in Q. 53, Arts. 2 and 3. In such succession there is a last instant in which the former was, and also a first instant in which that which follows is. But there cannot be any intervening period of time, because there is no continuous time which could require it.

Now the mind of man which is justified is in itself supra-temporal. But it is in time accidentally, in so far as it understands things under the aspect of continuous time, in terms of the phantasms by means of which it appreciates intelligible species, as we said in Pt. I, Q. 85, Arts. 1 and 2. It is according to this latter context, therefore, that we must judge of its change from one condition to another by movement in time. We must say, accordingly, that although there is a last period of time, there is no last instant in which guilt inheres; but that there is a first instant in which grace inheres, and that guilt inheres during the whole of the preceding period.

Article Eight

WHETHER THE INFUSION OF GRACE IS THE FIRST OF THE THINGS REQUIRED FOR THE JUSTIFICATION OF THE UNGODLY, ACCORDING TO THE ORDER OF NATURE

We proceed to the eighth article thus:

1. It seems that the infusion of grace is not the first of the things required for the justification of the ungodly, according to the order of nature. For according to Ps. 34:14: "Depart from evil, and do good," departure from evil comes before approach to good. Now remission of guilt pertains to departure from evil, and infusion of grace pertains to the pursuit of good. Hence remission of guilt is naturally prior to infusion of grace.

2. Again, a disposition naturally precedes the form to which it is disposed, and the movement of the free will is a disposition towards the reception of grace. It therefore precedes grace naturally.

3. Again, sin prevents the soul from freely inclining to God. Now what prevents a movement must be removed first, before the movement can follow. The remission of guilt, and the movement of the free will in recoil from sin, are therefore naturally prior to the movement of the free will toward God, and also to the infusion of grace.

On the other hand: a cause naturally precedes its effect. Now we said in the preceding article that the infusion of grace is the cause of all other things which are necessary for the justification of the ungodly. It is therefore naturally prior to them.

I answer: as we said in the preceding article, the justification of the ungodly is not gradual. It follows that the four things which we said were required for it (Art. 6) are simultaneous in time. But one of them is nevertheless prior to another in the order of nature. In the order of nature, the infusion of grace is first, the movement of the free will toward God is second, its recoil from sin is third, and the remission of guilt is last. The reason for this is that, according to the order of nature, the motion of the mover is first in any movement. The adaptation of the matter, or the movement of the thing moved, is naturally second, and the end or termination of the movement, in which the motion of the mover finds its completion, is last. Now the motion of God, who is the mover, is the infusion of grace, as we said in Art. 6, and the movement or adaptation of the thing moved is the twofold movement of the free will. We also made it clear that the termination or end of the movement is the remission of guilt. Hence in the justification of the ungodly, the infusion of grace is first in the order of nature, the movement of the free will toward God second, and its recoil from sin third. The movement of the free will toward God precedes its recoil from sin as its ground and cause, since he who is justified abhors sin on the ground that it is opposed to God. Fourth and last is the remission of guilt, which is the end for which this transmutation is ordained, as we said in Arts. 1 and 6.

On the first point: departure from one term and approach to another may be considered in two ways. If we consider them on the part of a subject which is moved, departure from one term naturally comes before approach to another, because the one contrary which a subject abandons is in it first, and the other contrary which it acquires as the result of movement is in it afterwards. But if we consider them on the part of an agent, this order is reversed. It is because a form is already in it that an agent acts to repel a contrary form. For example, it is because of its light that the sun acts to repel darkness. On the part of the sun itself, illumination is prior to the expelling of darkness. But on the part of the air which it illuminates, liberation from darkness is naturally prior to the reception of light. Yet these are simultaneous. Now if we are speaking of infusion of grace and remission of guilt as on the part of God who justifies, the infusion of grace is naturally prior to the remission of guilt. But if we are looking at them from the point of view of a man who is justified, this order is reversed. Liberation from guilt is then naturally prior to the reception of justifying grace. Or we may say that guilt is the *terminus a quo* of justifying grace, and justification its *terminus ad quem*, and that grace is the cause both of the remission of guilt and of the acquisition of justice.

On the second point: the disposition of a subject is naturally prior to its reception of a form. But it follows the action of the agent whereby the subject becomes thus disposed. In the order of nature, therefore, the movement of the free will precedes the reception of grace, but follows the infusion of grace.

On the third point: as it is said in 2 *Physics*, text 89, "the first movement of the soul is essentially that which relates to the principle of speculation, or to the end of action." Outwardly, the removal of an obstacle precedes the pursuit of the end. But the movement of the free will is a movement of the soul. Its movement toward God as its end therefore precedes its movement in removing the obstacle of sin, according to the order of nature.

Article Nine

WHETHER THE JUSTIFICATION OF THE UNGODLY IS THE GREATEST WORK OF GOD

We proceed to the ninth article thus:

1. It seems that the justification of the ungodly is not the greatest work of God. By the justification of the ungodly one obtains the grace of the wayfarer. But by glorification one obtains the grace of heaven, which is greater. The glorification of men and angels is therefore a greater work than the justification of the ungodly.

2. Again, the justification of the ungodly is ordained for the particular good of an individual man. But the good of the universe is greater than the good of an individual man, as is clear from 1 *Ethics* 2. The creation of heaven and earth is therefore a greater work than the justification of the ungodly.

3. Again, to make something out of nothing, when there is nothing which co-operates with the agent, is greater than to make something out of something else with the co-operation of the subject. Now in the work of creation something is made out of nothing, and there is consequently nothing which can co-operate with the agent. In the justification of the ungodly, on the other hand, something is made out of something else. That is, God makes a just man out of an ungodly man, who, moreover, co-operates by the movement of his free will, as was said in Art. 3. Hence the justification of the ungodly is not the greatest work of God.

On the other hand: it is said in Ps. 145:9: "his tender mercies are over all his works," and the collect says: "O God, who declarest thy Almighty power especially by pardon and mercy." Further, expounding John 14:12, "and greater works than these shall he do," Augustine says: "that a just man should be made out of an ungodly man is a greater work than the creation of heaven and earth" (*Tract. 72 in Joan.*).

I answer: a work may be said to be great in two ways. It may be said to be great in respect of the manner of action. In this respect, the greatest work is the work of creation, in which something is made out of nothing. But a work may also be said to be great in respect of what it achieves. Now the justification of the ungodly terminates in the eternal good of participation in the divine nature. It is therefore greater in respect of what it achieves than the creation of heaven and earth, which terminates in the good of changeable nature. Hence, when Augustine says: "that a just man should be made out of an ungodly man is a greater work than the creation of heaven and earth," he adds: "for heaven and earth shall pass away, but the salvation and justification of the predestined shall remain."

But we must observe that there are two senses in which a thing is said to be great. The first sense is that of absolute quantity. In this sense, the gift of glory is greater than the gift of grace which makes an ungodly man just, and the glorification of the just is a greater work than the justification of the ungodly. The second sense is that of relative quantity, in respect of which we may say that a mountain is small, and a millet great. In this sense, the gift of grace which makes the ungodly just is greater than the gift of glory which beatifies the just. For the gift of grace exceeds the worthiness of an ungodly man, who is worthy of punishment, by more than the gift of glory exceeds the worthiness of a just man, who is worthy of glory since he is justified. Hence Augustine says in the same passage: "Let him judge who can whether it is greater to create just angels than to justify the ungodly. If these are equal in respect of power, the latter is assuredly greater in mercy."

From this the answer to the first point is obvious.

On the second point: the good of the universe is greater than the good of an individual man, if we consider them as in the same genus. But the good of the grace given to one man is greater than the good of the whole natural universe.

On the third point: this reasoning argues about the manner of the agent's action. The creation is the greatest work of God in this respect.

Article Ten

WHETHER THE JUSTIFICATION OF THE UNGODLY IS A MIRACLE

We proceed to the tenth article thus:

1. It seems that the justification of the ungodly is a miracle. For miracles are greater than works which are not miraculous, and the justification of the ungodly is a greater work than some others which are miraculous, as the passage from Augustine quoted in the preceding article makes clear. It follows that the justification of the ungodly is a miracle.

2. Again, the movement of the will in the soul is like the natural inclination in natural things. Now when God causes something to happen in natural things contrary to their natural inclination, e.g., when he causes the blind to see, or raises the dead to life, it is a miracle. It seems then that the justification of the ungodly is a miracle. For the will of an ungodly man inclines to evil, and God moves him to good when he justifies him.

3. Again, as wisdom is a gift of God, so also is justice. Now it is miraculous that any man should receive wisdom from God suddenly, without study. It is therefore miraculous also that any ungodly man should be justified by him.

On the other hand: miraculous works are beyond the power of nature. But the justification of the ungodly is not beyond the power of nature, since Augustine says: "the capacity to have faith is of the nature of man, as is also the capacity to have charity. But to have both faith and charity is of the grace of the faithful" (*De Praed. Sanct.* 5). It follows that the justification of the ungodly is not miraculous.

I answer: three things are usually to be found in miracles. The first concerns the power of the agent. Miracles can be wrought only by the power of God, and are therefore absolutely mysterious, having a cause which is hidden, as we said in Pt. I, Q. 105, Art. 7. In this respect, the justification of the ungodly is just as miraculous as the creation of the world, or indeed any work whatever which can be wrought by God alone. Secondly, in some miracles there is a form induced which is beyond the natural capacity of the matter. When one who is dead is brought to life, for example, life is beyond the capacity of a body in that state. The justification of the ungodly is not miraculous in this respect, because the soul is naturally capable of receiving grace. As Augustine says, the soul is capable of God by the very fact that it is made in the image of God (*loc. cit.*). Thirdly, there is something in miracles over and above the normal and usual order of cause and effect. For example, one who is infirm suddenly acquires perfect health in a manner outside the normal order of recovery, whether by natural or artificial means. The justification of the ungodly is sometimes miraculous in this respect, and sometimes not. The normal and usual course of justification is that God moves the soul from within, turning a man to himself at first by an imperfect conversion, to the end that his conversion may thereafter become perfect. As Augustine says: "charity begun deserves to be increased, so that it may deserve to be perfected when it is increased" (*Tract. 5 in Joan.*). But there are times when God moves the soul with such force that it immediately attains the perfection of justice. This is what happened in the conversion of Paul, together with a miraculous outward prostration. The conversion of Paul is accordingly commemorated in the Church as a miracle.

On the first point: some miracles are inferior to the justification of the ungodly in respect of the good which they achieve. They are nevertheless outside the causal order through which such effects are normally produced, and consequently have more of the nature of miracle.

On the second point: it is not always miraculous that a natural thing should be moved in a way contrary to its natural inclination. If this were the case, it would be miraculous that water should be heated, or that a stone should be thrown upwards. Such an event is miraculous only when it is brought about by some cause other than that which is naturally its proper cause. Now there is no cause, other than God, which can justify the ungodly, just as there is no cause other than fire which can heat water. It follows that the justification of the ungodly is not miraculous in this respect.

On the third point: man is born to acquire wisdom and knowledge from God through his own diligence and study. It is therefore miraculous that he should become wise and learned in any other way. He is not born to acquire grace by his own work, but by the work of God. There is therefore no comparison.

Question One Hundred and Fourteen

CONCERNING MERIT, WHICH IS THE EFFECT OF CO-OPERATIVE GRACE

We must now consider merit, which is the effect of co-operative grace. There are ten questions concerning merit. 1. Whether a man can merit anything from God. 2. Whether without grace one can merit eternal life. 3. Whether through grace one can merit eternal life condignly. 4. Whether grace is the principle of merit, through charity as the principal medium. 5. Whether a man can merit the grace first given to himself. 6. Whether he can merit it on behalf of another. 7. Whether anyone can merit for himself restoration after a lapse. 8. Whether anyone can merit for himself an increase of grace, or of charity. 9. Whether anyone can merit for himself perseverance to the end. 10. Whether temporal goods can be merited.

Article One

WHETHER A MAN CAN MERIT ANYTHING FROM GOD

We proceed to the first article thus:

1. It seems that a man cannot merit anything from God. No one merits a reward by repaying what he owes to another. But we cannot even fully repay what we owe to God, by all the good that we do. For we always owe him more than this, as the philosopher says in 8 *Ethics* 14. Hence it is said in Luke 17:10: "when ye shall have done all those things which are commanded you, say, We are unprofitable servants: we have done that which was our duty to do." It follows that a man cannot merit anything from God.

2. Again, it seems that a man merits nothing from God if he profits himself, but profits God nothing. Now by good work a man profits himself or another man, but not God. For it is said in Job 35:7: "If thou be righteous, what givest thou him? Or what receiveth he of thine hand?" It follows that a man cannot merit anything from God.

3. Again, whoever merits anything from another makes that other his debtor, since he who owes a reward ought to render it to him who merits it. But God is a debtor to no one, wherefore it is said in Rom. 11:35: "Or who hath first given to him, and it shall be recompensed unto him again?" It follows that no one can merit anything from God.

On the other hand: it is said in Jer. 31:16: "thy work shall be rewarded." Now a reward means something given for merit. Hence it seems that a man can merit something from God.

I answer: merit and reward mean the same thing. We call it a reward when it is given to someone in return for his work or labour, as a price for it. Now to give a reward for work or labour is an act of justice, just as to give a fair price for something received from another is an act of justice, and justice, as the philosopher says in 5 *Ethics* 4, is a kind of equality. Justice obtains absolutely between those between whom equality obtains absolutely. It does not obtain absolutely between those between whom equality does not obtain absolutely, but there may nevertheless be a kind of justice between them, since we speak of the "right" of a father, or of a master, as the philosopher says in ch. 6 of the same book. Merit and reward have accordingly an absolute meaning where justice obtains absolutely. But in so far as the meaning of justice remains where justice obtains relatively and not absolutely, the meaning of merit is relative though not absolute, such as is applicable to a son who deserves something from his father, or to a slave who deserves something from his master.

Now there is obviously a very great inequality between God and man. The gulf betwixt them is indeed infinite. Moreover, all the good that is in a man is due to God. The kind of justice which obtains where there is absolute equality cannot therefore obtain between man and God. There obtains only the justice which is relative to the proportion of what is wrought by each, according to their own mode. But since both the mode and the manner of man's virtue are due to God, it is only by a previous divine ordination that a man can merit anything from God. That is, a man can receive as a reward from God only what God has given him the power to work for by his own effort; just as natural things attain, by their own movements and activities, that to which they are divinely ordained. There is this difference, however. A rational creature moves itself to its action by its free will, and its action is therefore meritorious. This is not the case with other creatures.

On the first point: a man has merit in so far as he does what he ought by his own will. The act of justice whereby one repays a debt would not otherwise be meritorious.

On the second point: God does not seek to gain anything from our good works. He seeks to be glorified by them, i.e., that his goodness should be shown forth. He seeks this by his own works also. Neither does anything accrue to God from our worship of him, but to ourselves. Hence we merit something from God not because our works profit him, but because we work to his glory.

On the third point: our own action is meritorious only by reason of a previous divine ordination. It does not follow, therefore, that God becomes a debtor to ourselves simply. Rather does he become a debtor to himself, in so far as it is right that what he has ordained should be fulfilled.

Article Two

WHETHER ONE CAN MERIT ETERNAL LIFE WITHOUT GRACE

We proceed to the second article thus:

1. It seems that one can merit eternal life without grace. It was said in the preceding article that a man merits from God that to which he is divinely ordained. Now it is of the very nature of man that he is ordained to blessedness as his end, which is indeed the reason why he naturally seeks to be blessed. A man can therefore merit blessedness, which is eternal life, by his own natural powers and without grace.

2. Again, a work is the more meritorious the less it is incumbent upon one, and a good work is the less incumbent if it is done by him who has received the fewer benefits. Now a man who has only his own natural good has received less from God than one who has received gifts of grace in addition. His work is therefore the more meritorious in God's sight. Hence if one who has grace can in any wise merit eternal life, much more can one who is without grace.

3. Again, the mercy and liberality of God are infinitely greater than the mercy and liberality of man. Now one man can merit something from another, even though he has never had his grace. Much more, then, does it seem that a man without grace can merit eternal life from God.

On the other hand: the apostle says (Rom. 6:23): "the gift of God is eternal life."

I answer: there are two states of man without grace, as we said in Q. 109, Art. 2. One is the state of pure nature, such as was in Adam before his sin. The other is the state of corrupt nature, such as is in ourselves before restoration through grace. If we are speaking of man in the first of these states, there is one reason why he cannot merit eternal life by his natural powers alone, and that is that his merit depends on a divine preordination. No action of anything whatsoever is divinely ordained to that which exceeds what is commensurate with the power which is its principle of action. It is indeed an ordinance of divine providence that nothing shall act beyond its own power. Now eternal life is a good which exceeds what is commensurate with created nature, since it transcends both natural knowledge and natural desire, according to I Cor. 2:9: "Eye hath not seen, nor ear heard, neither have entered into the heart of man. . . ." No created nature, therefore, can suffice as the principle of an action which merits eternal life, unless there is added to it a supernatural gift, which we call grace. But if we are speaking of man as he exists in sin, there is a second reason why this is so, namely, the impediment of sin. Sin is an offence against God which excludes us from eternal life, as we said in Q. 71, Art. 6, and Q. 113, Art. 2. Hence no one who lives in sin can merit eternal life unless he is first reconciled to God by the remission of sin. Now sin is remitted by grace, since the sinner merits not life but death, according to Rom. 6:23: "the wages of sin is death."

On the first point: God has ordained that human nature shall attain the end of eternal life by the help of grace, not by its own power. Its own action can merit eternal life by the help of grace.

On the second point: a man without grace cannot have it in him to perform a work equal to that which proceeds from grace, since action is the more perfect the more perfect is its principle. This reasoning would be valid, however, if such works were equal in each case.

On the third point: the first reason to which we have referred relates to God and to man in dissimilar ways. For it is from God, and not from man, that a man has every power of well-doing which he possesses. He cannot therefore merit anything from God except by means of God's gift. The apostle expresses this pointedly when he says: "who hath first given to him, and it shall be recompensed unto him again?" (Rom. 11:35). The second reason, on the other hand, which is concerned with the impediment of sin, relates to man and to God in a similar way, since one man cannot merit anything even from another man whom he has offended, unless he first makes retribution, and is reconciled to him.

Article Three

WHETHER A MAN IN GRACE CAN MERIT ETERNAL LIFE CONDIGNLY

We proceed to the third article thus:

1. It seems that a man in grace cannot merit eternal life condignly. For the apostle says (Rom. 8:18): "the sufferings of this present time are not worthy to be compared with the glory which shall be revealed in us." Now the sufferings of the saints seem to be the worthiest of all meritorious works. Hence no works of men can merit eternal life condignly.

2. Again, a gloss by Augustine on Rom. 6:23: "the gift of God is eternal life," says: "He could have said with truth 'the wages of justice is eternal life.' But he preferred to say 'the gift of God is eternal life,' in order that we might understand that God leads us to eternal life for his mercy's sake, and not for the sake of our merits." Now what is merited condignly is received for the sake of merit, not for mercy's sake. It seems, therefore, that a man cannot merit eternal life condignly through grace.

3. Again, merit would seem to be condign if it is equal to the reward. But no action in this present life can be equal to eternal life. For eternal life transcends our knowledge and our desire, and even the charity and love of the wayfarer, just as it transcends nature. It follows that a man cannot merit eternal life condignly through grace.

On the other hand: that which is given in accordance with a righteous judgment would seem to be a condign reward. Now God gives eternal life in accordance with a righteous judgment, since it is said in II Tim. 4:8: "Henceforth there is laid up for me a crown of righteousness, which the Lord, the righteous judge, shall give me at that day." It follows that a man merits eternal life condignly.

I answer: a man's meritorious work may be considered in two ways; in so far as it proceeds from his own free will, and in so far as it proceeds from the grace of the Holy Spirit. There cannot be condignity if a meritorious work is considered as it is in its own substance, and as the outcome of a man's own free will, since there is then extreme inequality. There is, however, congruity, since there is a certain relative equality. For it seems congruous that if a man works according to his own power, God should reward him according to the excellence of his power. But if we are speaking of a meritorious work as proceeding from the grace of the Holy Spirit, it merits eternal life condignly. For the degree of its merit then depends on the power of the Holy Spirit which moves us to eternal life, according to John 4:14: ". . . shall be in him a well of water springing up into everlasting life." A man's work is therefore rewarded according to the worth of the grace by which he is made a partaker of the divine nature, and adopted as a son of God to whom the inheritance is due by right of adoption, according to Rom. 8:17: ". . . and if children, then heirs."

On the first point: the apostle is speaking of the sufferings of the saints according to what they are in their own substance.

On the second point: this gloss is to be understood as referring to the first cause of the attainment of eternal life, which is the mercy of God. Our merit is nevertheless the secondary cause.

On the third point: the grace of the Holy Spirit which we have in this life is not equal to glory in actuality. But it is equal to it in power, like a seed which contains the power to become the whole tree. Thus does the Holy Spirit dwell in a man by grace as the efficient cause of eternal life, wherefore it is called the earnest of our inheritance in II Cor. 1:22.

Article Four

WHETHER GRACE IS THE PRINCIPLE OF MERIT THROUGH CHARITY MORE PRINCIPALLY THAN THROUGH OTHER VIRTUES

We proceed to the fourth article thus:

1. It seems that grace is not the principle of merit through charity more principally than through other virtues. Labour is worthy of its hire, according to Matt. 20:8: "call the labourers, and give them their hire." But every virtue is the principle of some labour, since a virtue is a habit of action, as was said in Q. 55, Art. 2. Every virtue is therefore equally a principle of merit.

2. Again, the apostle says (I Cor. 3:8): "and every man shall receive his own reward, according to his own labour." But charity lightens labour rather than increases it, since "love makes every hard and heavy task easy, and almost as nothing," as Augustine says (*De Verb. Dom., Sermo* 9; *De Tempt., Sermo* 49). Charity is not then the principle of merit more principally than other virtues.

3. Again, the virtue which is most principally the principle of merit would seem to be the virtue whose actions are the most meritorious. Now the most meritorious actions seem to be those of faith and patience, or fortitude. This is apparent from the martyrs, who for their faith remained stedfast unto death with patience and fortitude. Other virtues are therefore the principle of merit more principally than charity.

On the other hand: our Lord says: "he that loveth me shall be loved of my Father, and I will love him, and will manifest myself to him" (John 14:21). Now eternal life consists in the manifest knowledge of God, according to John 17:3: "this is life eternal, that they might know thee the only true God." The meriting of eternal life therefore depends principally on charity.

I answer: there are two sources from which the meritorious

character of a human action is derived, as may be understood from what we said in the first article. First and foremost, there is the divine ordination. This is the ground upon which an action is said to merit the good to which a man is divinely ordained. Secondly, there is the free will of man, which gives him the power to act voluntarily on his own part, more than any other creature. In regard to either source, the principle of merit depends especially on charity. For we must observe in the first place that eternal life consists in the enjoyment of God. The movement of man's mind towards the enjoyment of divine good is the proper action of charity, and it is the action of charity that directs all actions of the other virtues to this end, since charity commands the other virtues. The meriting of eternal life therefore depends primarily on charity, and secondarily on other virtues, in so far as their actions are directed by charity. It is apparent, also, that we do most willingly what we do out of love. Even in respect of the voluntary character essential to its nature, therefore, merit depends principally on charity.

On the first point: since charity has the ultimate end as its object, it moves the other virtues to act. A habit which relates to an end always commands the habits which relate to the means to it, as we explained in Q. 9, Art. 1.

On the second point: there are two ways in which a work may be laborious and difficult. It may be so because of its magnitude, which increases its merit. Charity does not lighten labour in this respect. On the contrary, it causes us to undertake the greatest works. As Gregory says, "charity is such that it does great works" (*Hom. in Evang.* 30). But a work may also be laborious and difficult because of a fault in him who labours. Anything can be hard and difficult if it is not done readily and with a will. Such labour lessens merit, and is removed by charity.

On the third point: an act of faith is not meritorious unless faith works by love, as is said in Gal. 5. Neither is an act of patience and fortitude meritorious unless performed through charity, according to I Cor. 13:3: "though I give my body to be burned, and have not charity, it profiteth me nothing."

Article Five

WHETHER A MAN CAN MERIT THE FIRST GRACE FOR HIMSELF

We proceed to the fifth article thus:

1. It seems that a man can merit the first grace for himself.

For Augustine says that "faith merits justification" (*Praef. Ps. 32*), and a man is justified by the grace first given to him. It follows that a man can merit the first grace for himself.

2. Again, God gives grace only to those who are worthy. But we do not say that anyone is worthy of something good unless he has merited it condignly. It follows that one can merit the first grace condignly.

3. Again, with men, one can merit a gift which has already been received. One who has been given a horse by his master, for example, may deserve it through using it well in his master's service. Now God is more generous than a man. Much more, then, can a man merit the first grace which he has already received from God, by reason of his subsequent works.

On the other hand: the very meaning of grace excludes the notion of reward for works, according to Rom. 4:4: "Now to him that worketh is the reward not reckoned of grace, but of debt." But what a man merits is credited to him as a reward for works. Hence he cannot merit the first grace.

I answer: we may think of a gift of grace in two ways. If we are thinking of the gratuitous character of the gift, it is obvious that all merit is opposed to grace, since the apostle says: "and if by grace, then it is no more of works" (Rom. 11:6). If, on the other hand, we are thinking of the nature of what is given, such a gift cannot be merited by one who does not have grace. For not only does grace exceed what is commensurate with nature, but a man in the state of sin before grace is prevented from meriting grace by the impediment of sin. Neither can grace already possessed be merited subsequently, since a reward is the outcome of work, and grace is the principle of all our good works, as we said in Q. 109. Finally, if one should merit another gratuitous gift by virtue of grace already received, this would not be the first grace. It is apparent, then, that no man can merit the first grace for himself.

On the first point: as Augustine says in 1 *Retract.* 23, he was at one time deceived in this matter, when he believed that the beginning of faith lay with ourselves, although its consummation was a gift of God. He retracts this belief, but it is apparently on this assumption that he declares that faith merits justification. But if we suppose that faith is begun in us by God, this being indeed a truth of faith, then even the act of faith follows the first grace. It cannot then merit the first grace. Hence a man is justified by faith not in the sense that he merits justification by believing, but in the sense that he believes while he is being justified. This movement of faith is required for the justification of the ungodly, as we said in Q. 113, Art. 4.

On the second point: the reason why God gives grace only to the worthy is not that they were previously worthy, but that by grace God makes them worthy, who alone "can bring a clean thing out of an unclean" (Job. 14:4).

On the third point: every good work which a man does proceeds from the first grace as its principle. But it does not proceed from any gift of man. We cannot therefore argue in the same way about a gift of grace and a gift of man.

Article Six

Whether a Man can Merit the First Grace for Another

We proceed to the sixth article thus:

1. It seems that a man can merit the first grace for another. For the gloss on Matt. 9:2, "and Jesus, seeing their faith," etc., says: "How much is our own faith worth in the sight of God, if he values the faith of one so highly that he heals another both inwardly and outwardly!" Now it is by the first grace that a man is healed inwardly. One man can therefore merit the first grace for another.

2. Again, the prayers of the righteous are not in vain, but effectual, according to James 5:16: "the effectual fervent prayer of a righteous man availeth much." Now he has just said: "pray for one another, that ye may be healed," and a man can be healed only through grace. It seems, therefore, that one man can merit the first grace for another.

3. Again, it is said in Luke 16:9: "Make to yourselves friends of the mammon of unrighteousness; that, when ye fail, they may receive you into everlasting habitations." But no one is received into everlasting habitations otherwise than through grace, through which alone one can merit eternal life, as was said in Art. 2, and also in Q. 109, Art. 5. It follows that one man can acquire the first grace for another by merit.

On the other hand: it is said in Jer. 15:1: "Though Moses and Samuel stood before me, yet my mind could not be toward this people."

I answer: as we have explained already in Arts. 1, 2, and 4, there are two sources from which our works derive their meritorious character. In the first place, they have merit because God moves us. This merit is condign. In the second place, they have merit as proceeding from the free will, in so far as we do something willingly. This merit is congruous, since when a man makes good use of his own power, it is congruous that God should perform works that are more excellent, according to the surpassing excellence of his power. Now this makes it clear that none save Christ alone can merit the first grace for another condignly. For by the gift of grace each one of us is so moved by God that he may attain to eternal life, and eternal life cannot be merited condignly by anything other than God's moving. But God moved the soul of Christ by grace not only that he might attain eternal life himself, but also that he might lead others to it, as the Head of the Church and the Captain of our salvation, according to Heb. 2:10: "bringing many sons unto glory, to make the captain of their salvation perfect through sufferings."

But one man can merit the first grace for another by congruous merit. A man in grace fulfils the divine will, and it is congruous, according to the relation of friendship, that God should fulfil his desire by saving another. There may sometimes be an obstacle, however, on the part of him whose justification a sanctified man desires. The passage quoted from Jeremiah refers to such a case.

On the first point: the faith of some avails for the healing of others by congruous merit, not by condign merit.

On the second point: intercessory prayer depends on mercy, whereas merit depends on condign justice. Hence a man obtains many things through prayer, by the mercy of God, which are not justly merited. As it is said in Dan. 9:18: "For we do not present our supplications before thee for our righteousnesses, but for thy great mercies."

On the third point: the poor who receive alms are said to receive others into everlasting habitations either because they intercede for their forgiveness by prayer, or because they merit it congruously by other good works. Or else this is a metaphorical way of saying that one deserves to be received into everlasting habitations for the sake of one's deeds of pity towards the poor.

Article Seven

WHETHER A MAN CAN MERIT HIS RESTORATION AFTER A LAPSE

We proceed to the seventh article thus:

1. It seems that a man can merit his restoration after a lapse. For a man can merit what he can justly ask of God, and nothing

can be more justly asked of God than to be restored after a lapse, as Augustine says in his commentary on Ps. 71:9: "forsake me not when my strength faileth." A man can therefore merit his restoration after a lapse.

2. Again, a man's own works profit himself more than another. But he can merit restoration after a lapse for another, in the same manner in which he can merit the first grace for him. Much more, therefore, can he merit restoration after a lapse for himself.

3. Again, it was explained in Art. 2, and also in Q. 109, Art. 5, that a man who has once been in grace has merited eternal life for himself by his good works. But he cannot attain eternal life unless he is restored through grace. It seems, therefore, that he has merited his restoration through grace.

On the other hand: it is said in Ezek. 18:24: "But when the righteous turneth away from his righteousness, and committeth iniquity . . . All his righteousness that he hath done shall not be mentioned." His previous merits shall thus be of no avail for his restoration. Hence no man can merit restoration after a future lapse.

I answer: no man can merit his restoration after a future lapse, either by condign or by congruous merit. He cannot merit it condignly, because condign merit depends essentially on the gracious moving of God, and this is impeded by subsequent sin. Merit cannot then be the reason for any of the benefits which a man later receives from God for his restoration, since the previous gracious moving of God does not extend to them. On the other hand, congruous merit, by which one merits the first grace for another, is prevented from realizing its effect by an impediment of sin in him on whose behalf it is merited. Much more, then, is congruous merit made ineffective when the impediment is in him who merits, since the impediment then counts twice in the one person. Hence no man can in any wise merit his own restoration after a lapse.

On the first point: the desire by which one desires to be restored after a lapse is said to be just. So likewise a prayer for such restoration is called just, since it tends to justice. But it depends entirely on mercy, not on justice to merit.

On the second point: one can merit the first grace for another because there is no impediment, at least on the part of him who merits, such as there is in one who has lapsed from the state of justice after once possessing the merit of grace.

On the third point: some have said that no one merits eternal life absolutely, but only on condition that he perseveres, except when one merits it by an act of final grace. But this is unreasonable, since an act of final grace may sometimes be less meritorious than previous acts of grace, owing to the stricture of illness. We must therefore say that any act of charity merits eternal life absolutely. But subsequent sin puts an obstacle in the way, which prevents the effect of previous merit from being realized; just as natural causes fail to produce their effect because some obstacle intervenes.

Article Eight

WHETHER A MAN CAN MERIT AN INCREASE OF GRACE OR CHARITY

We proceed to the eighth article thus:

1. It seems that a man cannot merit an increase of grace or charity. For when one has received the reward which one has merited, one is not entitled to any other reward. Thus it is said of some in Matt. 6:2: "They have their reward." Hence if anyone were to merit an increase of grace or charity, it would follow that he could not expect any other reward, once this increase was granted. But this is impossible.

2. Again, nothing acts beyond its own species. Now it is clear from what was said in Arts. 2 and 4 that the principle of merit is either grace or charity. It follows that no man can merit grace or charity greater than that which he already possesses.

3. Again, everything that a man merits, he merits by each and every act which proceeds from grace or charity, since each and every such act merits eternal life. Hence if a man merits an increase of grace or charity, it seems that he merits it by any act of charity whatsoever: and if subsequent sin does not prevent it, everything that is merited is inevitably received from God, since it is said in II Tim. 1:12: "I know whom I have believed, and am persuaded that he is able to keep that which I have committed unto him." It follows that grace or charity must be increased by each and every meritorious action. But this seems impossible, since meritorious actions are sometimes not very fervent, and insufficient for an increase of charity. Increase of charity cannot therefore be merited.

On the other hand: Augustine says (*Tract. 5 in Joan.*): "Charity deserves to be increased, so that when increased it may deserve to be perfected." Increase of grace or charity is therefore merited.

I answer: as we said in Arts. 6 and 7, that to which the moving of grace extends is merited condignly. Now the moving of a mover extends not only to the final term of a movement, but also to the whole progress of the movement. The final term of the movement of grace is eternal life, and progress in this movement is by increase of charity or grace, according to Prov. 4:18: "the path of the just is as the shining light, that shineth more and more unto the perfect day." It follows that increase of grace is merited condignly.

On the first point: reward is indeed the final term of merit. But there are two kinds of term in a movement. There is a final term, and also a mediate term which is both beginning and term at once. Now the reward of an increase of grace or charity is a mediate term. But a reward of man's favour is a final term for those who set their heart on it. That is why they receive no other reward.

On the second point: an increase of grace is not beyond the power of grace already received, although it is quantitatively greater, just as a tree is not beyond the power of its seed, although greater in size.

On the third point: a man merits an increase of grace by each and every meritorious action, just as he thereby merits the consummation of grace, which is eternal life. But just as eternal life is granted not immediately, but in its own time, so is an increase of grace granted not immediately, but in its own time, that is, when a man is sufficiently well disposed to receive it.

Article Nine

WHETHER A MAN CAN MERIT PERSEVERANCE

We proceed to the ninth article thus:

1. It seems that a man can merit perseverance. For a man in grace can merit what he obtains through petition, and men obtain perseverance through petition, since otherwise perseverance would be asked of God in vain by the petition of the Lord's prayer, as Augustine says (2 *De Bono Persev.*).[1] It follows that perseverance can be merited by a man in grace.

2. Again, to be unable to sin is more than not to sin. Now to be unable to sin can be merited, since one merits eternal life, which is by its very nature impeccable. Much more, then, can one merit to live without sin, that is, to persevere.

[1] Cf. *De Corrept. et Gratia*, 6, §10. The petition referred to is "Hallowed be thy name."

3. Again, an increase of grace is more than perseverance in the grace which one already possesses. Now it was said in the preceding article that a man can merit an increase of grace. Much more, then, can he merit perseverance in the grace which he already possesses.

On the other hand: unless sin prevents it, a man receives from God everything that he merits. Now many who perform works of merit do not receive perseverance. But we cannot attribute this to sin, since God would not allow anyone who merited perseverance to fall into sin, for the very reason that sin is opposed to perseverance. It follows that perseverance cannot be merited.

I answer: since the free will with which he is naturally endowed can turn either to good or to evil, there are two ways in which a man may obtain from God perseverance in good. He may obtain it through the consummation of grace whereby his will is finally turned to good, as it shall be in heaven. He may also obtain it through a divine moving which inclines him to good till the end. Now as we explained in Arts. 6, 7, and 8, a man merits what is related to the movement of his free will as the final term to which God's moving directs it. But he does not merit what is related to the movement of his free will as its principle. This makes it clear that the perseverance which belongs to glory is merited, since it is the final term of the movement of man's free will. But the perseverance of the wayfarer is not merited, since it depends entirely on the moving of God, which is the principle of all merit. God nevertheless bestows the gift of perseverance freely, on whomsoever he bestows it.

On the first point: through petitionary prayer we receive many things which we do not merit. For God hears even the prayers of sinners who ask for the forgiveness which they do not deserve, as Augustine says (*Tract. 44 in Joan.*) on John 9:31: "we know that God heareth not sinners." Were it not so, the publican would have said in vain: "God be merciful to me a sinner." So also may one obtain the gift of perseverance through asking it of God, either for oneself or for another, even though it cannot be merited.

On the second point: the perseverance which belongs to glory is related to the meritorious actions of the free will as their final term. But the perseverance of the wayfarer is not so related to them, as we have said. The third point concerning the increase of grace is similarly answered, as will be clear from this and the preceding article.

Article Ten

WHETHER TEMPORAL GOODS CAN BE MERITED

We proceed to the tenth article thus:

1. It seems that temporal goods can be merited. For what is promised as a reward for righteousness is merited, and it appears from Deut., ch. 28, that temporal goods were promised as a reward for righteousness under the old Law. Thus it seems that temporal goods can be merited.

2. Again, it seems that what God gives to a man in return for a service is merited. Now God sometimes rewards men for their services to him with temporal goods. For it is said in Ex. 1:21: "And it came to pass, because the midwives feared God, that he made them houses," and the gloss by Gregory says: "their good will might have earned the reward of eternal life, but the guilt of their deceit earned a reward that was temporal." Further, it is said in Ezek. 29:18: "the king of Babylon caused his army to serve a great service against Tyrus: . . . yet he had no wages," to which is added "and it shall be the wages for his army. I have given him the land of Egypt . . . because they wrought for me." Thus temporal goods can be merited.

3. Again, evil is to demerit as good is to merit. Now some are punished by God for the demerit of sin by temporal punishments, as were the Sodomites (Gen., ch. 19). Temporal goods, accordingly, may be merited.

4. On the other hand: things which are merited do not come alike to all. But temporal good and evil come alike to the righteous and to the unrighteous, according to Eccl. 9:2: "All things come alike to all; there is one event to the righteous, and to the wicked; to the good and to the clean, and to the unclean; to him that sacrificeth and to him that sacrificeth not." Thus temporal goods are not merited.

I answer: what is merited is a recompense or reward, and a recompense or reward has the nature of a good. Now the good of man is of two kinds, absolute and relative. The good of man which is absolute is his final end, according to Ps. 73:28: "it is good for me to draw near to God," together with all that is ordained to lead him to it. This good is merited absolutely. The good of man which is relative, and not absolute, is what is good for him at the present time, or what is good for him in certain circumstances. Accordingly, if it is their usefulness for the virtuous works through which we are brought to eternal

217

life that we have in mind, we must say that temporal goods are merited; just as increase of grace is merited, and indeed everything else that follows the grace first received and helps a man on his way to blessedness. For God gives to just men as much of temporal goods, and of temporal evils also, as will help them to attain to eternal life, and such temporal things are so far good absolutely. Hence it is said in Ps. 34:10: "they that seek the Lord shall not want any good thing," and also in Ps. 37:25: "yet have I not seen the righteous forsaken." Considered in themselves, however, such temporal goods are not the good of man absolutely, but only relatively. They are therefore merited not absolutely, but only relatively. That is, they are merited in so far as men are moved by God to do certain temporal things, wherein they achieve what God sets before them, and through God's favour. We have already explained that eternal life is in an absolute sense the reward of works of justice, since it is related to the divine moving in a certain way (Arts. 6 and 8). So also may temporal goods, considered in themselves, derive the character of reward from their relation to the divine moving by which the wills of men are moved to seek them. But men do not always seek them with the right motive.

On the first point: as Augustine says: "these promised temporal things contained the symbols of spiritual things to be fulfilled in us in time to come. But this carnal people held fast to what was promised for this present life, and not only their speech but their very life was prophetic." (4 *Contra Faustum* 2.)

On the second point: these retributions are said to have been divinely wrought because they were the result of the divine moving, not because of their connection with wilful deceit. This is especially the case with regard to the king of Babylon, who besieged Tyre with the intention of usurping the throne, rather than of serving God. Neither had the midwives any integrity of will, since they fabricated falsehoods, even though their will did happen to be good when they liberated the children.

On the third point: temporal evils are inflicted on the ungodly as punishments, in so far as they do not help them to attain to eternal life. But they are not punishments to the just, who are helped by them. Rather are they as medicines, as we said in Q. 87, Art. 8.

On the fourth point: all things come alike to the good and to the wicked as regards the substance of temporal goods and evils, but not as regards the end. For the good are guided to blessedness by them, whereas the wicked are not.

Treatise on the Theological Virtues

I. On Faith.   Secunda Secundae, Questions 1—7

Question One

THE OBJECT OF FAITH

THE FIRST OF THE THEOLOGICAL VIRTUES WHICH we must consider is faith. The second is hope, and the third is charity. Concerning faith, we shall consider first the object of faith, secondly the act of faith, and thirdly the habit of faith.

There are ten questions concerning the object of faith. 1. Whether the object of faith is the first truth. 2. Whether the object of faith is that which is simple or that which is complex, i.e., whether it is the reality itself or what can be said about it. 3. Whether what is false can be believed by faith. 4. Whether the object of faith can be something that is seen. 5. Whether it can be something known scientifically. 6. Whether matters of faith ought to be divided into certain articles. 7. Whether the same articles are articles of faith for all time. 8. Concerning the number of articles. 9. Concerning the manner of setting forth the articles in a symbol. 10. As to who is entitled to draw up a symbol of the faith.

Article One

WHETHER THE OBJECT OF FAITH IS THE FIRST TRUTH

We proceed to the first article thus:

1. It seems that the object of faith is not the first truth. For whatever is proposed for our belief would seem to be the object of faith, and there are proposed for our belief not only things pertaining to the Godhead, which is the first truth, but also things pertaining to the humanity of Christ, to the sacraments of the Church, and to the condition of creatures. Hence not only the first truth is the object of faith.

2. Again, faith and unbelief have the same object, since they are opposites. Now there can be unbelief concerning everything in sacred Scripture, since a man is called an unbeliever if he disbelieves anything which is therein contained. It follows that faith is likewise concerned with everything in sacred Scripture, which contains many things relating to men, and to other creatures also. Hence the object of faith is not only the first truth, but also the truth about creatures.

3. Again, it was said in 12ae, Q. 62, Art. 3, that faith is condivided with charity. Now by charity we not only love God, who is the supreme good, but love our neighbour also. Hence the object of faith is not only the first truth.

On the other hand: Dionysius says (7 *Div. Nom.*, lect. 5): "Faith is in the simple and eternal truth." Now this is the first truth. The object of faith is therefore the first truth.

I answer: the object of any cognitive habit is twofold. It includes what is known materially as a material object, and also that through which it is known, this being the formal meaning of its object. In the science of geometry, for example, the conclusions are known materially, while the principles of demonstration whereby the conclusions are known are the formal meaning of the science. Now if we are thinking of the formal meaning of the object of faith, this is nothing other than the first truth. For the faith of which we are speaking does not assent to anything except on the ground that it is revealed by God. The ground upon which faith stands is therefore divine truth. But if we are thinking in a concrete way about the things to which faith gives its assent, these include not only God himself, but many other things. Such other things, however, are held in faith only because they relate to God in some way, that is to say, in so far as certain effects of the Godhead are an aid to man in his endeavour after the enjoyment of God. Thus the object of faith is still in a sense the first truth, since nothing is an object of faith unless it relates to God; just as the object of medicine is health, since nothing is considered to be medicine unless it relates to health.

On the first point: the things which pertain to the humanity of Christ, or to the sacraments of the Church, or to any creature whatsoever, are included in the object of faith in so far as we are directed by them to God, and in so far as we assent to them on account of the divine truth.

The second point, concerning all the matters related in sacred Scripture, is answered in the same way.

On the third point: by charity we love our neighbour for God's sake. Hence the object of charity is properly God, as we shall affirm later.

Article Two

WHETHER THE OBJECT OF FAITH IS SOMETHING COMPLEX, IN THE FORM OF A PROPOSITION

We proceed to the second article thus:

1. It seems that the object of faith is not something complex, in the form of a proposition. For the object of faith is the first truth, as was maintained in the first article, and the first truth is simple. Hence the object of faith is not something complex.

2. Again, the exposition of the faith is contained in the symbol. [1] Now the symbol does not affirm the propositions, but the reality. For it does not say that God is almighty, but declares: "I believe in God . . . Almighty." Thus the object of faith is not the proposition, but the reality.

3. Again, faith is followed by vision, according to I Cor. 13:12: "For now we see through a glass, darkly; but then face to face: now I know in part; but then shall I know even as also I am known." Now the heavenly vision is of what is simple, since it is the vision of the divine essence itself. Hence the faith of the wayfarer is likewise in what is simple.

On the other hand: faith is a mean between knowledge and opinion. Now a mean and its extremes belong to the same genus, and since knowledge and opinion are about propositions, it seems that faith is also about propositions. But if faith is about propositions, the object of faith is something complex.

I answer: things known are in the knower according to the manner in which he knows them. Now the characteristic way in which the human intellect knows truth is by means of the combination and separation of ideas, as we said in Pt. I, Q. 85, Art. 5. It is therefore with a measure of complexity that the human intellect knows things which are in themselves simple; just as, conversely, the divine intellect knows without complexity things which are in themselves complex.

The object of faith may then be understood in two ways. If we are referring to the thing itself which is believed, the object of faith is something simple, namely, the thing itself in which we have faith. But from the point of view of the believer the object of faith is something complex, in the form of a proposition.

[1] I.e., the Nicene Creed.

Both opinions have been held true by the ancients, and both are true conditionally.

On the first point: this reasoning argues from the object of faith considered as the thing itself which is believed.

On the second point: it is clear from the very manner of speaking that the things in which faith believes are affirmed in the symbol, in so far as the act of the believer terminates in them. Now the act of the believer terminates in the reality, not in the proposition. For we formulate propositions only in order to know things by means of them, in faith no less than in science.

On the third point: the heavenly vision will be the vision of the first truth as it is in itself, according to I John 3:2: "but we know that, when he shall appear, we shall be like him; for we shall see him as he is." This vision will not then be by way of propositions, but by simple understanding. By faith, on the other hand, we do not apprehend the first truth as it is in itself. We cannot therefore argue about faith in the same way.

Article Three

WHETHER WHAT IS FALSE CAN BE HELD IN FAITH

We proceed to the third article thus:

1. It seems that what is false can be held in faith. Faith is condivided with hope and charity. Now what is false can be hoped for, since many hope for eternal life although they will not attain it. In regard to charity, similarly, many are loved as if they were good although they are not good. Hence what is false can similarly be held in faith.

2. Again, Abraham believed that Christ would be born, according to John 8:56: "Your father Abraham rejoiced to see my day; and he saw it, and was glad." But after Abraham's time it was possible that God should not become incarnate, since he was incarnate purely by reason of God's will. What Abraham believed about Christ would then have been false. Hence it is possible that what is false should be held in faith.

3. Again, those of old believed that Christ would be born in the future, and many continued to believe this until the time when the Gospel was proclaimed. But after Christ had been born, and before the proclamation began, it was false that Christ would be born in the future. Hence what is false can be held in faith.

4. Again, it is one of the things pertaining to faith, that a man

should believe that the true body of Christ is contained in the sacrament of the altar. Yet it might happen that the true body of Christ was not present, but only the bread, if it had not been properly consecrated. Hence what is false can be held in faith.

On the other hand: no virtue which perfects the intellect embraces what is false, since the false is the evil of the intellect, as the philosopher says (6 *Ethics* 2). Now faith is a virtue which perfects the intellect, as we shall show later (Q. 4, Arts. 2, 5). What is false cannot therefore be held in faith.

I answer: nothing can come under any power, habit, or act, except through the medium of that which its object formally signifies. Thus colour cannot be seen except through the medium of light, and a conclusion cannot be known except through the medium of demonstration. Now we said in Art. 1 that the object of faith formally signifies the first truth. Hence nothing can be held in faith except in so far as it stands under the first truth. But nothing which is false can stand under the first truth, any more than not-being can stand under being, or evil under goodness. It follows that what is false cannot be held in faith.

On the first point: the true is the good of the intellect, but not of any appetitive virtue. Hence all virtues which perfect the intellect entirely exclude the false, since it is the nature of a virtue to embrace only what is good. On the other hand, the virtues which perfect the appetitive part of the soul do not entirely exclude the false. One may act in accordance with justice and temperance even though one holds a false opinion about what one is doing. Now since faith perfects the intellect, whereas hope and charity perfect the appetitive part of the soul, we cannot argue about them in the same way. Yet neither is hope directed to what is false. For one does not hope to attain eternal life by means of one's own power (which would be presumption), but by means of the help of grace, and one will assuredly and infallibly attain it through grace, if one perseveres. Similarly, since charity loves God in whomsoever he may be, it makes no difference to charity whether God is or is not present in him who is loved for God's sake.

On the second point: considered in itself, "that God should not become incarnate" was possible even after the time of Abraham. But as we said in Pt. I, Q. 14, Arts. 13 and 15, the incarnation has a certain infallible necessity since it stands under the foreknowledge of God, and it is thus that it is held in faith. In so far as it is held in faith, therefore, it cannot be false.

On the third point: after Christ was born, the believer believed by faith that he would be born at some time. But it was due to human conjecture, not to faith, that there was error in the determination of the time. It is indeed possible for a believer to judge wrongly by human conjecture. But it is impossible to judge wrongly by reason of faith.

On the fourth point: by faith one does not believe that the bread is in the one state or the other, but that the true body of Christ is under the sensible appearance of the bread when it has been properly consecrated. Hence if it is not properly consecrated, nothing false is held by faith in consequence.

Article Four

WHETHER THE OBJECT OF FAITH CAN BE SOMETHING SEEN

We proceed to the fourth article thus:

1. It seems that the object of faith is something which is seen. For our Lord said to Thomas: "Thomas, because thou hast seen me, thou hast believed." Thus the same thing is both seen and believed.

2. Again, the apostle says in I Cor. 13:12: "For now we see through a glass, darkly"—and he is speaking of the knowledge of faith. Hence what is believed is seen.

3. Again, faith is a kind of spiritual light. Now by light of any kind, something is seen. Hence faith is of things that are seen.

4. Again, as Augustine says (*De Verb. Dom., Sermo. 33*, cap. 5): "Every sense is called sight." Now faith is of things that are heard, according to Rom. 10:17: "faith cometh by hearing." Hence faith is of things that are seen.

On the other hand: the apostle says: "Faith is . . . the evidence of things not seen" (Heb. 11:1).

I answer: faith implies intellectual assent to that which is believed. But there are two ways in which the intellect gives its assent. In the first way, it is moved to give its assent by the object itself, which is either known in itself, as first principles are obviously known, since the intellect understands them, or known through something else that is known, as are conclusions which are known scientifically. In the second way, the intellect gives its assent not because it is convinced by the object itself, but by voluntarily preferring the one alternative to the other. If it chooses with hesitation, and with misgivings about the other alternative, there will be opinion. If it chooses with assurance, and without any such misgivings, there will be faith. Now those things are said to be seen which of themselves move our intellect or sense to know them. Hence it is clear that neither faith nor opinion can be of things that are seen, whether by sense or by the intellect.

On the first point: Thomas "saw one thing and believed another." When he said: "my Lord and my God," he saw a man. But by faith he confessed God.

On the second point: things which are held in faith may be considered under two aspects. If we consider them in their particularity, they cannot be both seen and believed at the same time, as we have said above. But if we consider them in their general aspect as things which can be believed, they are seen by him who believes them. For a man would not believe them if he did not see that they were to be believed, either on the evidence of signs, or on some other similar evidence.

On the third point: the light of faith enables us to see what we believe.[1] Just as the habit of any other virtue enables a man to see what is becoming for him in respect of it, so does the habit of faith incline a man's mind to assent to such things as are becoming for true faith, but not to other things.

On the fourth point: it is the words signifying the things of faith that are heard, not the things of faith themselves. Hence it does not follow that these things are seen.

Article Five

WHETHER THE THINGS OF FAITH CAN BE KNOWN SCIENTIFICALLY

We proceed to the fifth article thus:

1. It seems that the things of faith can be known scientifically.[2] We are ignorant of what we do not know scientifically, since ignorance is the opposite of science. But we are not ignorant of the things of faith, since ignorance is unbelief, according to I Tim. 1:13: "I did it ignorantly in unbelief." Hence the things of faith can be known scientifically.

2. Again, science is acquired through the giving of reasons. Now the sacred writers give reasons for the things of faith. Hence the things of faith can be known scientifically.

3. Again, whatever is proved by demonstration is known scientifically, since "demonstration is making known by syllogism." Now some of the things of faith are demonstratively

---

[1] *Cod. Alcan. et Camer.*: "to see that the things believed are." In margin *Alcan.*: "to see that the things believed are true."

[2] I.e., understood through their cause, so as to be demonstrable.

proved by the philosophers, for example, that God exists, that he is one, and the like. Hence things of faith can be known scientifically.

4. Again, opinion is farther removed from science than is faith, since faith is said to be a mean between opinion and science. But it is said in 1 *Post. An.*, text *ult.*, that there can, in some way, be opinion and science about the same thing. Hence there can also be faith and science about the same thing.

On the other hand: Gregory says (*Hom. in Evang.* 21): "they do not have faith in things which are seen, but perceive them." Hence they do not perceive things which are of faith. But they do perceive what is known scientifically. There cannot then be faith in what is known scientifically.

I answer: every science depends upon principles which are known in themselves, and which are consequently seen. Everything which is known scientifically, therefore, is in a manner seen. Now we said in the preceding article that it is impossible for the same thing to be both seen and believed by the same person. It is nevertheless possible for the same thing to be seen by one person and believed by another. We hope that we shall some time see what we now believe about the Trinity, in accordance with I Cor. 13:12: "now we see through a glass, darkly; but then face to face." But the angels already have this vision. Hence what we believe, they see. It is also possible that what is seen or known scientifically by one man, even while he is a wayfarer, should be believed by another who has no demonstrative knowledge of it. But all men are without scientific knowledge of the things which are proposed for the belief of all alike. Such things are entirely matters of faith. Hence faith and scientific knowledge are not of the same thing.

On the first point: unbelievers are ignorant of the things of faith because they neither see or know them in themselves, nor are aware that they can be believed. Believers do not have demonstrative knowledge of them, yet they know them in so far as the light of faith enables them to see that they are to be believed, as we said in the preceding article.

On the second point: the reasons which are adduced by holy men in order to prove the things of faith are not demonstrative reasons. They are either persuasive, showing that what faith believes is not impossible, or else, as Dionysius says (2 *Div. Nom.* 1, lect. 1), they are grounded on principles of the faith itself, such as the authority of sacred Scripture. These principles are sufficient to prove something for believers, just as the principles of natural knowledge prove something for all men. In this way, theology is indeed a science, as we said at the beginning of this work (Pt. I, Q. 1, Art. 2).

On the third point: things which can be proved by demonstration are included among the things to be believed in faith. This is not because all men believe them purely by faith, but because they are necessary presuppositions to what is believed by faith, and must initially be believed at least by way of faith by those who have no demonstrative knowledge of them.

On the fourth point: as the philosopher says in the same passage: "there can assuredly be scientific knowledge and opinion about the same thing, in different men." This is what we have just said concerning scientific knowledge and faith. But one and the same man can have scientific knowledge and also faith about the same subject in different respects, although not in the same respect. For it is possible to know one thing scientifically, and to hold an opinion about something else, in relation to one and the same thing. Similarly, it is possible to know through demonstration that God is one, and at the same time to believe by faith that he is Triune. But one man cannot have scientific knowledge of the same thing in the same respect, and simultaneously either hold an opinion about it, or believe it by faith—for different reasons. There cannot be scientific knowledge simultaneously with opinion about the same thing, since it is essential to science that one should be convinced that what is known scientifically cannot possibly be otherwise; whereas it is essential to opinion that one should be aware that its object may be otherwise than it is thought to be. One is equally convinced that what is held in faith cannot possibly be otherwise, owing to the certainty of faith. But the reason why there cannot be scientific knowledge simultaneously with belief about the same thing in the same respect is this—that to know scientifically is to see, whereas to believe is not to see, as we have already said.

Article Six

WHETHER MATTERS OF FAITH OUGHT TO BE DIVIDED INTO CERTAIN ARTICLES

We proceed to the sixth article thus:

1. It seems that matters of faith ought not to be divided into certain articles. For we ought to have faith in all things contained in sacred Scripture, and these cannot be reduced to any

definite number of articles, owing to their multitude. It seems superfluous, therefore, to distinguish articles of faith.

2. Again, art should ignore material distinctions, since they may be endless. Now it was said in the first article that the formal meaning of the object of faith is one and indivisible, since it is the first truth, from which it follows that matters of faith cannot be distinguished in respect of their formal meaning. The material distinction between them by means of articles should therefore be omitted as superfluous.

3. Again, it is said by some that "an article is an indivisible truth about God, which constrains us to believe." But belief is voluntary, since Augustine says "no man believes, unless he wills to believe" (*Tract. 24 in Joan.*). Hence it seems unfitting that matters of faith should be divided into articles.

On the other hand: Isodorus says: "an article is a perception of the divine truth, to which it tends." Now it is only through making distinctions that we can perceive the divine truth, since the truth which is one in God is many in our intellect. Matters of faith should therefore be divided into articles.

I answer: the term "article" appears to be derived from the Greek. Now the Greek ἄρθρον, which in Latin is *articulus*, signifies the putting together of several distinct parts. Thus the small parts of the body which fit neatly together are called the articles of the limbs. In Greek grammar, similarly, the parts of speech which combine with others to denote gender, number, and case are called articles. In rhetoric, also, certain ways of combining parts of speech are called articles. For Tullius says (4 *Rhet. ad Heren.*): "it is called an article when the single words which compose an utterance are separated by intervals, in this wise—'By your bitterness, by your voice, by your bearing, you have terrified your adversaries.'"

Hence the Christian belief also is said to be divided into articles, in so far as it is divided into parts which fit together. We said in Art. 4 that the object of faith is something unseen which relates to divine things. Now wherever something is unseen for a special reason, there is a special article. But separate articles are not to be distinguished where many things are known or unknown for the same reason. For example, there is one difficulty in seeing how God could suffer, and a different difficulty in seeing how he could rise from the dead. There are accordingly separate articles on the Passion and on the Resurrection. But that he suffered, was dead, and was buried, present the same difficulty, so that if one is accepted, there is no difficulty in accepting the others. These are accordingly all contained in the one article.

On the first point: some matters of belief belong to the faith by reason of what they are in themselves, while some matters belong to it not by reason of what they are in themselves, but only because they relate to other things; just as some propositions are put forward in science for the sake of their own meaning, and others merely as illustrations. Now faith is primarily concerned with what we hope to see in the hereafter, according to Heb. 11:1: "faith is the substance of things hoped for." Hence those matters which directly order us to eternal life belong to faith by reason of what they are in themselves. Such are the three persons of God Almighty, the mystery of the incarnation of Christ, and the like, for each of which there is a separate article. Other things in sacred Scripture are proposed for belief not as if their meaning were fundamental, but in order to manifest the aforesaid—for example, that Adam had two sons; that a dead man was brought to life at a touch of the bones of Eliseus; and such things as are related in order to manifest the glory of God, or the incarnation of Christ. There is no need for separate articles corresponding to them.

On the second point: the formal meaning of the object of faith can be understood in two ways. If it refers to the reality itself in which we believe, the formal meaning of all matters of faith is one, since it is the first truth, and the articles of faith are not distinguished in respect of it. But the formal meaning of matters of faith can also be understood in relation to ourselves. So understood, the formal meaning of a matter of faith is that it is "not seen." It is in this latter regard that the articles of faith are distinguished, as has been shown.

On the third point: this definition of an article is the result of attending to the etymology of the word as if it were derived from the Latin, instead of attending to its true meaning as derived from the Greek. It has therefore no great weight. But it may be said that although no one is constrained to believe by any irresistible compulsion, since belief is voluntary, we are nevertheless constrained by a necessity which derives from the end. For as the apostle says: "he that cometh to God must believe that he is," and "without faith it is impossible to please him" (Heb. 11:6).

Article Seven

WHETHER THE ARTICLES OF FAITH HAVE INCREASED WITH THE PASSING OF TIME

We proceed to the seventh article thus:

1. It seems that the articles of faith have not increased with the passing of time. The apostle says in Heb. 11:1, "faith is the substance of things hoped for." Now the same things are to be hoped for at all times. It follows that the same things are to be believed at all times.

2. Again, as the philosopher explains in 1 *Metaph.*, texts 1 and 2, the sciences which men have devised have grown because of the limited knowledge of those who invented them. But the doctrine of the faith was not invented by man, since it is a bequest from God. As it is said in Eph. 2:8, "it is the gift of God." Knowledge of the things of faith must therefore have been perfect from the beginning, since there cannot be any limitation of knowledge in God.

3. Again, the operation of grace is not less orderly than the operation of nature. Now nature always begins from the perfect, as Boethius says (3 *De Consol.* 10). It seems, then, that the work of grace must have begun from the perfect. Hence those who first handed down the faith must have known it perfectly.

4. Again, just as the faith of Christ was delivered unto us by the apostles, so in the old Testament was knowledge of the faith handed down by the earlier fathers to those who came after them, according to Deut. 32:7: "ask thy father, and he will show thee." Now the apostles were thoroughly instructed in the mysteries, since they received them "more fully than others, just as they received them earlier," as the gloss says on Rom. 8:23: "but ourselves also, which have the first fruits of the Spirit." Hence it seems that knowledge of the faith has not increased with the passing of time.

On the other hand: Gregory says (*Hom. in Ezech.* 16), and also Hugo St. Victor (1 *De Sacrament.*, Part 10, cap. 6): "the knowledge of the holy fathers increased with the fullness of time, . . . and the nearer they were to the coming of the Saviour, the more fully did they understand the sacraments of salvation."

I answer: in the doctrine of the faith, the articles of faith have the same relative status as self-evident principles in the doctrines of natural reason. Now there is a certain order in these principles. Some of them are implicitly contained in others, and all of them depend on this as the first, namely, "it is impossible to affirm something and to deny it at the same time," as the philosopher explains in 4 *Metaph.*, text 9. In a similar way, all the articles are implicitly contained in certain fundamental matters of faith, such as that God is, and that he cares for the salvation of men. This is in accordance with Heb. 11:6: "he that cometh to God must believe that he is, and that he is a rewarder of them that diligently seek him." The "being" of God includes all things which we believe to exist eternally in God, and in which our blessedness consists. Faith in providence embraces all that God provides in time for the salvation of men, and which leads to blessedness. The other articles are consequential to these, and some of them are contained in others. For example, faith in the incarnation of Christ, and in his passion, and all matters of this kind, is implicitly contained in faith in the redemption of man.

It must therefore be said that the articles of faith have not increased in substance with the passing of time. Everything that the later fathers have believed was contained, at least implicitly, in the faith of the earlier fathers. But the number of explicit articles has increased, since some things of which the earlier fathers had no explicit knowledge were known explicitly by the later fathers. Thus the Lord said to Moses: "I am the Lord: And I appeared unto Abraham, unto Isaac, and unto Jacob, . . . but by my name Jehovah was I not known to them" (Ex. 6:2–3).[1] Thus also David says in Ps. 119:100: "I understood more than the ancients," and the apostle in Eph. 3:5: "Which in other ages was not made known [the mystery of Christ] . . ., as it is now revealed unto his holy apostles and prophets by the Spirit."

On the first point: the same things are to be hoped for from Christ at all times. But since it is only through Christ that men have come to hope for them, the further they have been removed from Christ in time, the further have they been from receiving them. Thus the apostle says (Heb. 11:13): "These all died in faith, not having received the promises, but having seen them afar off." Now the greater is the distance from which a thing is seen, the less clearly is it seen. The good things to be hoped for were therefore known more distinctly by those who lived near the time of Christ.

[1] Migne: "I am the God of Abraham, the God of Isaac, the God of Jacob; and my name Adonai have I not shown unto them."

On the second point: there are two ways in which knowledge progresses. The knowledge of the teacher progresses as time goes on, be he one or many. That is the reason why sciences invented by human reason increase. But there is also the knowledge of the learner. A master who knows the whole art does not impart it to his pupil all at once, since he could not absorb it, but imparts it gradually, in accordance with his pupil's capacity. Now it is as learners that men have progressed in knowledge of the faith with the passing of time. Hence the apostle likens the Old Testament to childhood, in Gal. 3:24.

On the third point: two causes are required for natural generation, namely, an active cause, and a material cause. According to the order of the active cause, the more perfect is naturally prior. Hence in respect of the active cause nature begins with what is perfect, since it is only through something perfect which already exists that the imperfect can be brought to perfection. According to the order of the material cause, on the other hand, the imperfect comes first, and nature advances from the imperfect to the perfect. Now in the manifestation of the faith, God is as the active cause, having perfect knowledge from eternity, while man is as the material cause, receiving the influence of God as the active cause. Hence in men, knowledge of the faith was bound to progress from the imperfect to the perfect. Yet some men have been like an active cause, as teachers of the faith. For the manifestation of the Spirit is given to some to profit withal, as it is said in I Cor. 12:7. Thus the fathers who formulated the faith were given such knowledge of it as could be profitably imparted to the people of their time, either openly or by way of metaphor.

On the fourth point: the final consummation of grace was achieved through Christ, whose time is consequently called "the fullness of time" in Gal. 4:4. Hence those who were nearer to Christ in time, whether earlier like John the Baptist, or later like the apostles, had a fuller knowledge of the mysteries of the faith. We see the same thing with regard to a man's condition, which is perfect in his youth, and more nearly perfect the nearer he is to his youth, whether before it or after it.

Article Eight

WHETHER THE ARTICLES OF FAITH ARE APPROPRIATELY ENUMERATED

We proceed to the eighth article thus:

1. It seems that the articles of faith are not appropriately enumerated. For it was said in Art. 5 that things which can be known through demonstrative reasoning do not belong to faith as matters of belief for all. Now it can be shown by demonstration that God is one. The philosopher proves this in 12 *Metaph.* 52, and many other philosophers have added their proofs. "There is one God" should not therefore be an article of faith.

2. Again, it is just as necessary for faith that we should believe that God is omniscient, and that he cares for all, as that we should believe that he is almighty. Moreover, some have erred on both points. The wisdom and providence of God should therefore be mentioned in the articles of faith, as well as his omnipotence.

3. Again, according to John 14:9: "he that hath seen me hath seen the Father," our knowledge of the Father is the same as our knowledge of the Son. There should therefore be only one article on the Father and the Son—and the Holy Spirit, for the same reason.

4. Again, the Person of the Father is not less than the Persons of the Son and of the Holy Spirit. Now there are several articles on the Person of the Holy Spirit, and several on the Person of the Son. There should therefore be several articles on the Person of the Father.

5. Again, just as something is attributed to the Person of the Father and to the Person of the Holy Spirit in respect of their divinity, so also is something attributed to the Son in respect of his divinity. Now in the articles of faith there is a work attributed to the Father, namely the work of creation, and also a work attributed to the Holy Spirit, namely that "he spoke by the prophets." The articles ought therefore to include a work attributed to the Son in respect of his divinity.

6. Again, the sacrament of the Eucharist has a special difficulty of its own, which is distinct from the difficulties of the many articles. There should therefore be a special article on the Eucharist. Hence it seems that there are not a sufficient number of articles.

On the other hand: the articles are enumerated as they are by authority of the Church.

I answer: as we said in Arts. 4 and 6, the things which belong to faith by reason of what they are in themselves are the things which we shall enjoy in eternal life, together with the means whereby we are brought to eternal life. Now we are told that we shall see two things, namely, the hidden Godhead, the vision of which is our blessedness, and the mystery of the humanity of Christ, through whom we have access into the glory of the sons of God, as it is said in Rom. 5:2. Hence it is said also in John 17:3: "And this is life eternal, that they might know thee the only true God, and Jesus Christ, whom thou hast sent." The first distinction for faith, consequently, is between what pertains to the majesty of the Godhead and what pertains to the mystery of the manhood of Christ, which is called "the mystery of godliness" in I Tim. 3:16.

Three things are proposed for our belief concerning the majesty of the Godhead: first, the Unity of the Godhead, to which the first article refers; second, the Trinity of the Persons, on which there are three articles corresponding to the three Persons; third, the works proper to the Godhead. The first of these works is the "order" of nature, concerning which the article on the creation is proposed to us. The second is the "order" of grace, concerning which all that relates to the salvation of man is proposed to us in one article. The third is the "order" of glory, concerning which there is another article on the resurrection of the body and on eternal life. There are thus seven articles pertaining to the Godhead.

There are likewise seven articles concerning the humanity of Christ, of which the first refers to the incarnation, or the conception of Christ, the second to his virgin birth, the third to his passion, death, and burial, the fourth to his descent into hell, the fifth to his resurrection, the sixth to his ascension, and the seventh to his coming in judgment. There are thus fourteen articles in all.

Some, however, distinguish twelve articles of faith, six pertaining to the Godhead, and six pertaining to the humanity. They combine the three articles on the three Persons into one, on the ground that our knowledge of the three Persons is the same. They divide the article on the work of glorification into two, which refer respectively to the resurrection of the body and to the glory of the soul. They similarly combine into one the articles on the conception and on the nativity.

On the first point: by faith we hold many things concerning God which the philosophers have been unable to discover by natural reason, such as the providence and omnipotence of God, and that God alone is to be worshipped. These are all contained in the article on the unity of God.

On the second point: as we said in Pt. I, Q. 13, Art. 8, the very name "Godhead" implies providence of some kind. Further, in intellectual beings, power does not operate otherwise than in accordance with will and knowledge. Hence the omnipotence of God in a manner includes both knowledge and providence in relation to all things. For God could not do all that he wills among lower creatures, did he not both know them and care for them.

On the third point: in respect of the unity of their essence, we have but one knowledge of the Father, of the Son, and of the Holy Spirit, and the first article refers to it. With regard to the distinction of the persons, which is according to their relations of origin, knowledge of the Son is in a manner included in knowledge of the Father. For God would not be Father unless he had a Son, the Holy Spirit being the bond which unites them. Those who formulated one article on the three Persons were therefore well guided. Three articles can nevertheless be formulated on the three Persons, since there are points which must be observed concerning each of them, and about which error is possible. Arius indeed believed in the Father Almighty and Eternal, but he did not believe that the Son is coequal and consubstantial with the Father. It was therefore necessary to add an article on the Person of the Son, to settle this point. For the same reason, it was necessary to include a third article on the Person of the Holy Spirit, in view of Macedonius. Similarly, the conception and nativity of Christ may be comprehended in one article, and likewise the resurrection and eternal life, on the ground that they are ordained to the same end. But they may also be distinguished, on the ground that each has its own special difficulty.

On the fourth point: it pertains to the Son and to the Holy Spirit to be sent for the sanctification of creatures. Now there are several things to be believed about this. There are accordingly more articles on the Persons of the Son and the Holy Spirit than on the Person of the Father, who is never sent, as we said in Pt. I, Q. 43, Art. 4.

On the fifth point: the sanctification of a creature through grace, and its consummation in glory, are brought about by means of the gift of charity, which is attributed to the Holy Spirit; and also by means of the gift of wisdom, which is attributed to the Son. Hence either work pertains both to the Son and to the Holy Spirit, being attributable to each for a different reason.

On the sixth point: there are two points to consider about the sacrament of the Eucharist. One is that it is a sacrament. As such, it has the same nature as other effects of sanctifying grace. The other point is that the body of Christ is miraculously contained therein. This is included under omnipotence, just as all other miracles are attributed to omnipotence.

Article Nine

WHETHER THE ARTICLES OF FAITH ARE APPROPRIATELY SET FORTH IN A SYMBOL

We proceed to the ninth article thus:

1. It seems that the articles of faith are not appropriately set forth in a symbol. For sacred Scripture is the rule of faith, and nothing should be added to it or taken from it. As it is said in Deut. 4:2, "Ye shall not add unto the word which I command you, neither shall ye diminish ought from it." It was therefore unlawful to draw up any symbol as a rule of faith, once sacred Scripture had been written.

2. Again, in Eph. 4:5 the apostle says "one faith." Now a symbol is a profession of the faith. It is therefore inappropriate that there should be many symbols.

3. Again, the confession of faith contained in the symbol is for all the faithful. Now the faithful are not all capable of believing in God, but only those whose faith is formed. It is therefore inappropriate that the symbol of the faith should be expressed in such words as "I believe in one God."

4. Again, it was said in the preceding article that the descent into hell is one of the articles of faith. But there is no mention of the descent into hell in the symbol of the Fathers, which therefore seems to be incomplete.

5. Again, in his exposition of John 14:1, "ye believe in God, believe also in me," Augustine says: "we believe Peter or Paul, but we say that we believe 'in' God only." Now the catholic Church is merely something that is created. It seems inappropriate, therefore, to say "in one holy, catholic, and apostolic Church."

6. Again, a symbol is drawn up as a rule of faith. Now a rule

of faith ought to be set before everyone, publicly. Every symbol should accordingly be sung at mass, like the symbol of the Fathers. It seems inappropriate, therefore, to edit the articles of faith in the form of a symbol.

On the other hand: the universal Church cannot err, since it is governed by the Holy Spirit, which is the Spirit of truth. For this was the promise which our Lord gave to the disciples when he said: "when he, the Spirit of truth, is come, he will guide you into all truth" (John 16:13). Now the symbol is published by the universal Church. It therefore contains nothing inappropriate.

I answer: as the apostle says in Heb. 11:6: "he that cometh to God must believe." Now no one can believe, unless the truth which he may believe is proposed to him. It was therefore necessary that the truth of faith should be collected into one, that it might the more easily be proposed to all, lest any should default from the truth through ignorance of the faith. It is as such a collection of pronouncements of the faith that the "symbol" is so named.

On the first point: the truth of faith is contained in sacred Scripture diffusely and in various modes, in some of which it is obscure. To elicit the truth from sacred Scripture consequently requires prolonged study and training. This is not possible for all of those who must know the truth of faith, many of whom are busy with other matters, and cannot find the time for study. It was therefore necessary to put together a clear summary of the pronouncements of sacred Scripture, and to propose this for the belief of all. This is not an addition to sacred Scripture, but rather an extract from it.

On the second point: it is the same truth of faith that is taught by every symbol. But it is necessary to explain the truth of faith more thoroughly whenever errors arise, lest the faith of the simple minded should be corrupted by heretics, and several symbols have had to be devised for this reason. But they differ only in that what is implicit in one is made more explicit in another, in order to counter the menace of heresies.

On the third point: the confession of faith is expressed in the symbol on behalf of the whole Church, which is united by the faith. Now the faith of the Church is formed faith, for such is the faith of all who belong to the Church worthily, and not as numbers. Hence the confession of faith is expressed in the symbol in a manner befitting faith which is formed, while it also enables those whose faith is unformed to study to conform to it.

On the fourth point: there was no need to make the descent into hell more explicit, since no error concerning it had arisen among heretics. Hence it is not reaffirmed in the symbol of the Fathers, but assumed as settled by the earlier symbol of the apostles. A later symbol does not however cancel an earlier one, but makes it explicit, as we said in reply to the second point.

On the fifth point: if we say "in the holy catholic Church," it is to be understood that our faith refers to the Holy Spirit who sanctifies the Church, so that we mean "I believe in the Holy Spirit who sanctifies the Church." It is better, however, and also customary, to omit the word "in," and to say simply "the holy catholic Church," as did Pope Leo (according to Rufinus in his exposition of the symbol, among the works of Cyprian).

On the sixth point: the symbol of the Fathers is sung publicly at mass because it is a declaration of the symbol of the apostles, and because it was formulated at a time when the faith had already been manifested, and when the Church had peace. The symbol of the apostles, on the other hand, is said secretly at Prime and Compline as if it were a protection against the shadows of past and future errors, because it was formulated in time of persecution, when the faith had not yet been made public.

Article Ten

Whether it is for the Chief Pontiff to Draw Up the Symbol of the Faith

We proceed to the tenth article thus:

1. It seems that it is not for the chief pontiff to draw up the symbol of the faith. For it is in order to make the articles of faith explicit that a new edition of the symbol is required, as was said in the preceding article. Now in the Old Testament, the articles of faith became more and more explicit as time went on, because the truth of faith became more apparent as the time of Christ drew near, as was said in Art. 7. But this reason ceased when the New Law came. There is consequently no need for the articles of faith to be made more and more explicit. It seems, therefore, that the chief pontiff has no authority to draw up a new edition of the symbol.

2. Again, no man is entitled to do what has been forbidden by the universal Church under penalty of anathema. Now a new edition of the symbol was forbidden by the universal Church under penalty of anathema. For it is stated in the acts

of the first synod of Ephesus (p. 2, act. 6 *in decreto de fide.*): "After the Nicene Symbol had been read, the holy synod decreed that it was unlawful for anyone to proffer, write, or compose any other faith than that defined by the holy Fathers who assembled in the Holy Spirit at Nicaea," and this was forbidden under penalty of anathema. Moreover, the same is reaffirmed in the acts of the synod of Chalcedon (p. 2, act. 5). Hence it seems that the chief pontiff has no authority to draw up a new edition of the symbol.

3. Again, Athanasius was not a chief pontiff, but patriarch of Alexandria. Yet he formulated a symbol, and it is sung in the Church. Thus it seems that the right to draw up a symbol does not belong to the chief pontiff any more than to others.

On the other hand: the edition of the symbol was formulated in a general synod. Now a general synod can be assembled only by authority of the chief pontiff, as stated in the *Decretals*, Dist. 17, chs. 4 and 5. The authority to draw up a symbol therefore lies with the chief pontiff.

I answer: as the first point affirms, a new edition of the symbol is necessary when incipient errors have to be avoided. The authority to draw up a new edition of the symbol therefore lies with him who has authority to determine matters of faith with finality, so that everyone may hold them in faith with confidence. Now authority to do this lies with the chief pontiff, to whom the major and more difficult problems of the Church are referred, as stated in the *Decretals* (*extra. de Baptismo*, cap. *Majores*). Thus the Lord said to Peter, whom he made chief pontiff, "I have prayed for thee, that thy faith fail not: and when thou art converted, strengthen thy brethren" (Luke 22:32). The reason for this is that there ought to be only one faith of the whole Church, in accordance with I Cor. 1:10: "that ye all speak the same thing, and that there be no divisions among you." Now this is possible only if a question which arises concerning the faith is settled by him who rules over the whole Church, and his pronouncement firmly maintained in the whole Church. Hence the chief pontiff alone has authority to draw up a new edition of the symbol, just as he alone has authority in any other matter which affects the whole Church, such as the calling of a general synod, and the like.

On the first point: the truth of faith is sufficiently explicit in the teaching of Christ and the apostles. But since perverse men pervert the apostolic teaching, and also other doctrines and scriptures unto their own destruction, according to II Pet. 3:16, it has been necessary in later times to make the faith explicit, against incipient errors.

On the second point: this prohibition and pronouncement of the synod referred to private individuals, who have no authority to determine matters concerning the faith. But such a pronouncement by a general synod did not deny the right of a future synod to make a new edition of the symbol—not indeed containing a new faith, but expounding the same faith more fully. Indeed every synod has observed that a future synod would expound something more fully than a previous synod, should some heresy arise to make it necessary. This is consequently a matter for the chief pontiff, who has the authority to call a general synod, and also to confirm its pronouncements.

On the third point: it is clear from its very manner of expression that Athanasius did not compose his declaration of faith as a symbol, but rather as a doctrine. But because his doctrine contained the pure truth of faith in a concise form, it was accepted as a rule of faith by authority of the chief pontiff.

Question Two

THE ACT OF FAITH

We must now consider the act of faith, first the inward act, and second the outward act. There are ten questions concerning the inward act of faith. 1. In what belief consists, which is the inward act of faith. 2. In how many ways one may speak of belief. 3. Whether, for salvation, it is necessary to believe anything which is beyond natural reason. 4. Whether it is necessary to believe such things as are attainable by natural reason. 5. Whether, for salvation, it is necessary to believe anything explicitly. 6. Whether explicit belief is required of all men equally. 7. Whether, for salvation, it is always necessary to have explicit belief concerning Christ. 8. Whether explicit belief in the Trinity is necessary for salvation. 9. Whether the act of faith is meritorious. 10. Whether a human reason diminishes the merit of faith.

Article One

WHETHER TO BELIEVE IS TO THINK WITH ASSENT

We proceed to the first article thus:

1. It seems that to believe is not to think with assent. For "to think" implies inquiry of some kind, the word being a contraction of "to consider together" (*cogitare = coagitare = simul agitare*). But the Damascene says that "faith is assent without inquiry" (4 *De Fid. Orth.* 1). It follows that the act of faith does not involve thinking.

2. Again, it will be shown in Q. 4, Art. 2, that faith belongs to reason. But it was said in Pt. I, Q. 78, Art. 4, that thinking is an act of the cogitative power, which belongs to the sensitive part of the soul.[1] It follows that faith does not involve thinking.

3. Again, belief is an act of the intellect, since the object of belief is the true. Now it was said in 12ae, Q. 15, Art. 1, ad. 3 that assent is not an act of the intellect, but an act of the will, just as consent is an act of the will. It follows that to believe is not to think with assent.

On the other hand: "to believe" is thus defined by Augustine. (*De Praed. Sanct.* 2.)

I answer: "to think" can mean three things. Firstly, it means any deliberative intellectual act in general. This is what Augustine has in mind in 14 *De Trin.* 7, when he says: "what I now call understanding is that whereby we understand when we think." Secondly, and more precisely, it means the kind of intellectual deliberation which involves a degree of questioning, and which occurs before the intellect reaches perfection through the certainty of vision. This is what Augustine has in mind in 15 *De Trin.* 16, where he says: "The Son of God is not called the Thought of God, but the Word of God. When our thought has reached what we know and become formed by it, it becomes our word. The Word of God should therefore be conceived as without the thought of God, since it contains nothing which remains to be formed, and which could be unformed." In this sense, thought properly means the movement of a soul which deliberates, and which is not yet perfected by a

---

[1] The sensitive power operates through a corporeal organ, through which it perceives things which are actually present. The cogitative power perceives and preserves the "intention" or practical significance of particular things present or absent, by means of collating ideas. It is also called the "particular reason."

full vision of the truth. But since such movement may be either deliberation about universal meanings, which are the concern of the intellect, or deliberation about particular meanings, which are the concern of the sensitive part of the soul, the word "to think" is used in this second sense to mean the intellectual act of deliberation, and in yet a third sense to mean an act of the cogitative power.

Now if "to think" is understood in the first or general sense, "to think with assent" does not express the whole meaning of "to believe." For a man thinks in this way even about what he knows and understands in science, and also gives his assent. But if it is understood in the second sense, then by means of this expression we understand the whole nature of the act of belief. There are some acts of the intellect, such as those whereby one contemplates what one knows and understands in science, in which assent is given with confidence, without any deliberation. There are also others in which thought is unformed, and in which there is no firm assent. One may incline to neither alternative, as one who doubts. Or one may incline to the one rather than to the other on the strength of slight evidence, as does one who suspects. Or, again, one may choose one alternative with misgivings about the other, as does one who holds an opinion. Now the act which is "to believe" holds firmly to the one alternative. In this respect, belief is similar to science and understanding. Yet its thought is not perfected by clear vision, and in this respect belief is similar to doubt, suspicion, and opinion. To think with assent is thus the property of one who believes, and distinguishes the act of "belief" from all other acts of the intellect which are concerned with truth or falsity.

On the first point: faith does not make use of inquiry by natural reason to demonstrate what it believes. But it does inquire into the evidence by which a man is induced to believe, for example, into the circumstance that such things are spoken by God and confirmed by miracles.

On the second point: as we have said above, the word "to think" is here understood as it applies to the intellect, not as meaning an act of the cogitative power.

On the third point: the intellect of the believer is determined by the will, not by reason. Hence assent is here understood to mean the act of the intellect as determined by the will.

Article Two

WHETHER TO BELIEVE GOD, TO BELIEVE THAT THERE
IS A GOD, AND TO BELIEVE IN GOD ARE RIGHTLY
DISTINGUISHED AS ACTS OF FAITH

We proceed to the second article thus:

1. It seems that to believe God, to believe that there is a God, and to believe in God are not rightly distinguished as acts of faith. For only one act springs from a single habit, and faith is a single habit, since it is a single virtue. It is therefore wrong to attribute several acts to faith.

2. Again, what is common to all acts of faith should not be regarded as an act of faith of a particular kind. Now "to believe God" is common to all acts of faith, since faith takes its stand on the first truth. It seems wrong, therefore, to distinguish this from other acts of faith.

3. Again, we cannot regard anything as an act of faith, if it can be affirmed even of unbelievers. Now even unbelievers "believe that there is a God." We should not, therefore, regard this as an act of faith.

4. Again, movement towards an end is an act of the will, the object of which is the good, or the end, whereas belief is an act of the intellect, not of the will. Now "to believe in God" implies movement towards an end. It should not then be regarded as one distinguishable kind of belief.

On the other hand: Augustine makes this distinction in *De Verbis Domini* (*Sermo* 61, cap. 2), and also in *Tract. 29 in Joan.*

I answer: the act of any power or habit is understood from the relation of that power or habit to its object. Now the object of faith may be considered in three ways. As we said in reply to the third point in the preceding article, to believe is an act of the intellect as moved by the will to give its assent. The object of faith may therefore be understood either in relation to the intellect itself, or in relation to the will which moves the intellect, and there are two ways in which the object of faith is related to the intellect, as we said in Q. 1, Art. 1. In the first place, it is the material object of faith. The act of faith is then "to believe that there is a God," since nothing is an object of faith unless it relates to God, as we said also. In the second place, the object of faith may be understood in its formal meaning, as the ground upon which the intellect assents to something as a matter to be believed. The act of faith is then "to believe God," since the formal object of faith is the first truth, on which a man takes his stand when he assents to what he believes on the strength of it. Finally, the object of faith may be considered in relation to the intellect as moved by the will. The act of faith is then "to believe in God," since the first truth is referred to the will, having the character of an end.

On the first point: these three do not denote different acts of faith, but one and the same act in different relations to the object of faith. The reply to the second point is then obvious.

On the third point: unbelievers do not "believe that there is a God" in the sense in which this can be regarded as an act of faith. They do not believe that God exists under the conditions which faith defines. Hence they do not really believe that there is a God. As the philosopher says (9 *Metaph.*, text 22), "with incomposites, to know them imperfectly is not to know them at all."

On the fourth point: as we said in 12ae, Q. 9, Art. 1, the will moves the intellect and the other powers of the soul to the end. In this regard the act of faith is said to be "to believe in God."

Article Three

WHETHER, FOR SALVATION, IT IS NECESSARY TO BELIEVE ANYTHING WHICH IS BEYOND NATURAL REASON

We proceed to the third article thus:

1. It seems that for salvation it is not necessary to believe anything which is beyond natural reason. For it seems that what naturally belongs to a thing is sufficient for its salvation and perfection. Now the things of faith are beyond natural reason, since they are unseen, as was said in Q. 1, Art. 4. To believe in them is therefore unnecessary for salvation.

2. Again, it is precarious for a man to give his assent when he cannot judge whether what is proposed to him is true or false. As it is said in Job 12:11: "Doth not the ear try words?" Now a man cannot so judge of the things of faith, because he cannot see how they are derived from their first principles, which is the way in which we judge of all things. To believe such things is therefore precarious, and consequently unnecessary for salvation.

3. Again, according to Ps. 37:39: "the salvation of the righteous is of the Lord," man's salvation consists in God. Now it is said in Rom. 1:20: "the invisible things of him . . . are clearly seen, being understood by the things that are made,

even his eternal power and Godhead." But things which are clearly seen by the intellect are not believed. For salvation, therefore, it is unnecessary to believe anything.

On the other hand: it is said in Heb. 11:6: "without faith it is impossible to please him."

I answer: throughout the natural order, two things concur towards the perfection of a lower nature. One of these is its own movement. The other is the movement of a higher nature. Thus water moves towards the centre by its own movement, but moves round the centre, ebbing and flowing, owing to the movement of the moon. The planets, similarly, move from west to east by their own movement, but move from east to west owing to the movement of the first heaven. Now it is only rational created nature that is immediately related to God. Other creatures do not attain to anything universal, but only to what is particular. They share in the divine goodness only in so far as they "are," as in the case of inanimate things; or in so far as they "live, and know singulars," as in the case of plants and animals. But a rational nature is related immediately to the universal principle of all being, in as much as it knows the universal meaning of "good" and of "being." The perfection of a rational creature therefore consists not only in what belongs to it in consequence of its own nature, but also in what it derives from a certain participation in the divine goodness. The ultimate blessedness of man accordingly consists in a supernatural vision of God, as we said in 12ae, Q. 3, Art. 8. Now a man cannot attain to this vision unless he learns from God who teaches him, according to John 6:45: "Every man therefore that hath heard, and hath learned of the Father, cometh unto me." But he does not become a partaker of this learning all at once. He attains it gradually, according to the mode of his nature. Anyone who learns in this way is bound to believe, if he is to attain to perfect knowledge. Thus even the philosopher observes that "it behoves the learner to believe" (1 *Elenchi*, ch. 2). Hence if a man is to attain to the perfect vision of blessedness, it is essential that he should first believe God, as a learner believes the master who teaches him.

On the first point: man's nature depends on a higher nature. His natural knowledge is consequently insufficient for his perfection, for which something supernatural is required, as we have said.

On the second point: by the natural light of reason, a man assents to first principles. By the habit of a virtue, similarly, a virtuous man rightly judges what is becoming for that virtue. In this same way, by the divinely infused light of faith a man assents to the things of faith, but not to what is contrary to faith. There is therefore nothing precarious in such assent, and no condemnation to them which are in Christ Jesus.

On the third point: in many respects, faith perceives the invisible things of God in a way higher than that of natural reason as it reaches towards God from creatures. Hence it is said in Ecclesiasticus 3:23: "Many things beyond human understanding have been revealed unto thee."

Article Four

Whether it is Necessary to Believe such Things as can be Proved by Natural Reason

We proceed to the fourth article thus:

1. It seems that it is not necessary to believe such things as can be proved by natural reason. There is nothing superfluous in the works of God—much less than in the works of nature. Now when a thing can already be done in one way, it is superfluous to add another. It would therefore be superfluous to accept by faith what can already be known by natural reason.

2. Again, things which are accepted by faith must necessarily be believed. Now it was said in Q. 1, Arts. 4 and 5 that there cannot be both faith and scientific knowledge of the same thing. But there is scientific knowledge of all things which can be known by natural reason. It seems, therefore, that there cannot be any obligation to believe such things as can be proved by natural reason.

3. Again, all things which can be known by natural reason would seem to be of one kind. Hence if some of them are proposed for belief, it seems that it is necessary to believe all of them. But this is false. It follows that it is not necessary to believe such things as can be proved by natural reason.

On the other hand: it is necessary to believe that God is one and incorporeal, and philosophers have proved this by natural reason.

I answer: it is necessary for man to accept by way of faith not only such things as are beyond reason, but also such things as reason can know, and this on three grounds. First, it is necessary in order that he may the more quickly attain to a knowledge of divine truth. For the demonstrative knowledge by which one can prove that God exists, and other things about God, comes last of all things which men may learn, presupposing many other sciences. Hence it is only after a long period of life that a man can attain to the knowledge of God in this way. Secondly, it is necessary in order that the knowledge of God may be the more widespread. For there are many who cannot become proficient in the sciences, either owing to natural limitation of mind, or on account of laziness in learning. All such would be deprived altogether of the knowledge of God, if divine things were not proposed to them by the way of faith. Thirdly, it is necessary for the sake of certainty. For human reason is very defective in divine things. A sign of this is that philosophers have gone wrong in many ways, and have contradicted each other, in their investigations by means of natural inquiry into human things. It was therefore necessary that divine things should be proposed to men by the way of faith, in order that they might have confident and certain knowledge of God. That is, it was necessary that such things should be proposed to them as spoken by God, who cannot speak false.

On the first point: inquiry by natural reason does not suffice to give mankind a knowledge of divine things, even of such things as can be proved by reason. Hence it is not superfluous that these other matters should be believed by the way of faith.

On the second point: the same man cannot have both scientific knowledge and faith concerning the same thing. But what is known scientifically by one can be believed by another, as we said (Q. 1, Art. 5).

On the third point: although things which can be known scientifically are alike in their scientific character, they are not alike in equally directing men to blessedness. Hence they are not all equally proposed for belief.

Article Five

WHETHER A MAN IS REQUIRED TO BELIEVE ANYTHING EXPLICITLY

We proceed to the fifth article thus:

1. It seems that a man is not required to believe anything explicitly. For no man is required to do what is not within his power, and it is not within a man's power to believe anything explicitly, since it is said in Rom. 10:14–15: "how shall they believe in him of whom they have not heard? and how shall they hear without a preacher? And how shall they preach

except they be sent?" Hence a man is not required to believe
anything explicitly.

2. Again, just as we are directed to God by faith, so are we
directed to him by charity. Now a man is not required to fulfil
the precepts of charity. It is enough that he should be mentally
prepared to fulfil them. This is clear from our Lord's commandment in Matt. 5:39: "whosoever shall smite thee on thy
right cheek, turn to him the other also," and from other
similar passages, as Augustine observes (*Sermo. Dom. in monte,*
19). Neither then is a man required to believe anything
explicitly. It is enough that he should be mentally prepared to
believe such things as are proposed by God.

3. Again, the good of faith consists in obedience, according to
Rom. 1:5: "for obedience to the faith among all nations." But
obedience to the faith does not require that a man should obey
any particular precept. It is enough that he should be ready to
obey, in accordance with Ps. 119:60: "I made haste, and
delayed not to keep thy commandments." Hence it seems to
be enough for faith that a man should have a mind ready to
believe whatever may be divinely proposed to him, without
believing anything explicitly.

On the other hand: it is said in Heb. 11:6: "he that cometh to
God must believe that he is, and that he is a rewarder of them
that diligently seek him."

I answer: the precepts of the law, which a man is required to
fulfil, are concerned with the acts of the virtues, which are a
way of attaining salvation. Now as we said in 12ae, Q. 60,
Art. 9, the act of a virtue depends on the relation of its habit to
its object. But there are two things to be considered concerning
the object of any virtue: first, that which in itself is properly the
object of the virtue, and which is essential to its every act;
second, whatever attaches accidentally or consequentially to
what we mean by its proper object. To face the danger of
death, and to attack the enemy in spite of danger for the
common good, in itself belongs to the proper object of fortitude.
But that a man should be armed, or that he should smite
another with his sword in a just war, or do something of the
kind, is related to the proper object of fortitude accidentally
only.

Now a precept requires that a virtuous action should terminate in its essential and proper object, just as it requires the
virtuous action itself. But it is only at given times, and in given
circumstances, that a precept requires that a virtuous action

should terminate in what belongs to its object accidentally or secondarily. We must therefore observe that, as we said in Q. 1, Art. 8, what helps a man to attain blessedness belongs to the object of faith by reason of what it is in itself, whereas all things divinely revealed to us in sacred Scripture belong to its object accidentally or secondarily, such as that Adam had two sons, that David was the son of Jesse, and other things of this kind.

Accordingly, a man is required to believe explicitly such primary matters as are articles of faith, just as he is required to have faith. He is not however required to believe other matters explicitly, but only implicitly, or by preparedness of mind, that is, by being prepared to believe whatever sacred Scripture contains. He is required to believe such things explicitly only when he is aware that they are included in the doctrine of the faith.

On the first point: if a thing is said to be within a man's power when he can do it without the aid of grace, then there are many things required of him which are not within his power, unless he is healed by grace, such as to love God and his neighbour, and likewise to believe the articles of faith. But he can do these things through the aid of grace, of which Augustine says: "to whomsoever it is given, it is given in mercy; from whomsoever it is withheld, it is withheld in justice, in consequence of previous sins, or at least in consequence of original sin" (*De Corrept. et Grat.* 5 and 6).

On the second point: a man is required to love explicitly that which properly and in itself is the object of charity, namely, God and his neighbour. This objection argues from the precepts of charity which pertain to the object of charity consequentially.

On the third point: the virtue of obedience properly resides in the will. Readiness of will to obey one who commands is therefore sufficient for obedience, since this is properly and in itself the object of obedience. But one precept or another is accidental or consequential to its proper object.

Article Six

Whether all Men Equally are required to have Explicit Faith

We proceed to the sixth article thus:

1. It seems that all men equally are required to have explicit faith. For it is clear from the precepts of charity that all men

are required to believe such things as are necessary for salvation, and it was said in the preceding article that explicit belief in some matters is necessary for salvation. It follows that all men equally are required to have explicit faith.

2. Again, no one should be examined in what he is not required to believe explicitly. But simpletons are sometimes examined on the most meticulous points of faith. Everyone, therefore, is required to believe all things explicitly.

3. Again, if the more simple minded are not required to have explicit faith, but only implicit faith, they must have faith implicit in the faith of the wiser. But this is precarious, for the wiser may happen to be wrong. It seems, therefore, that even the more simple minded ought to have explicit faith. Hence all men equally are required to believe explicitly.

On the other hand: it is said in Job 1:14: "The oxen were ploughing, and the asses feeding beside them." According to Gregory, this means that in matters of faith the simpler minded, who are signified by the asses, ought to follow the wiser, who are signified by the oxen.

I answer: matters of faith are made explicit by revelation, since they are beyond reason. Now divine revelation reaches lower creatures through higher creatures, in a certain order. It is given to men through the angels, and to lower angels through higher angels, as Dionysius explains (*Coel. Hier.*, caps. 4, 7). In the same way, it is through wiser men that the faith must be made explicit for the simpler. Hence just as higher angels have a fuller knowledge of divine things than the lower angels whom they enlighten, so also are wiser men, to whom it pertains to instruct others, required to have a fuller knowledge of what ought to be believed, and to believe it more explicitly.

On the first point: explicit understanding of what ought to be believed is not equally necessary for the salvation of all men. For wiser men, whose office is to instruct others, are required to believe more things explicitly than others.

On the second point: the simple minded are not examined in the subtleties of the faith unless there is a suspicion that they have been perverted by heretics, who have a habit of perverting the faith of the simple minded on subtle points. But if they do not hold tenaciously to a perverse doctrine, and if their error is due to their simplicity, they are not blamed for it.

On the third point: the simple minded have faith implicit in the faith of the wiser only to the extent to which the wiser adhere to the divine teaching. Hence the apostle says: "Wherefore I beseech you be ye followers of me" (I Cor. 4:16). Thus it is not human knowledge that is the rule of faith, but divine truth. If some of the wiser should err therein, this will not prejudice the faith of the simpler minded who believe that they have a true faith, unless they hold pertinaciously to their particular errors in opposition to the faith of the universal Church, which cannot err, since the Lord said: "I have prayed for thee [Peter], that thy faith fail not" (Luke 22:32).

Article Seven

WHETHER EXPLICIT BELIEF IN THE MYSTERY OF THE INCARNATION OF CHRIST IS NECESSARY FOR THE SALVATION OF EVERYBODY

We proceed to the seventh article thus:

1. It seems that explicit belief in the mystery of the incarnation of Christ is not necessary for the salvation of everybody. A man is not required to have explicit belief in matters of which angels are ignorant, since the faith is made explicit by divine revelation, which reaches men through the medium of angels, as was said in the preceding article. Now even angels have been ignorant of the mystery of the incarnation of Christ, since they asked: "Who is this king of glory?" (Ps. 24:8), and "Who is this that cometh from Edom?" as Dionysius observes (*Coel. Hier.* 7). Hence men are not required to believe explicitly in the mystery of the incarnation of Christ.

2. Again, it is obvious that the blessed John the Baptist was one of the wise, and that he was very near to Christ. For the Lord said of him: "Among them that are born of women there hath not arisen a greater." But even John the Baptist does not seem to have known the mystery of the incarnation of Christ explicitly, since he inquired of Christ: "Art thou he that should come, or do we look for another?" (Matt. 11:3). Thus even the wise are not required to have explicit faith concerning Christ.

3. Again, according to Dionysius (*Coel. Hier.* 9, 4), many of the Gentiles obtained salvation through the ministry of angels. Now it appears that the Gentiles had neither explicit nor implicit faith concerning Christ, since no revelation of the faith was given unto them. Thus it seems that explicit faith in the mystery of the incarnation of Christ has not been necessary for the salvation of everybody.

On the other hand: Augustine says (*De Corrept. et Grat.* 7,

Epist. 190): "That faith is sound by which we believe that no man, whether old or young, is set free from the contagion of death or from the debt of sin, except by the one mediator of God and men, Jesus Christ."

I answer: that through which we attain to blessedness, as we said in Art. 5, and in Q. 1, Art. 8, properly and in itself belongs to the object of faith. Now our way to blessedness is the mystery of the incarnation and passion of Christ. For it is said in Acts 4:12: "there is none other name under heaven given among men, whereby we must be saved." Hence some kind of belief in the mystery of the incarnation of Christ has been necessary for all men at all times, although the manner of belief required has been different for different persons at different times.

Before he was in the state of sin, man had explicit faith in the mystery of the incarnation of Christ as the means of his consumation in glory, but not as the means of liberation from sin through the passion and resurrection, since he was not aware of sin to come. It appears that he had foreknowledge of Christ's incarnation, since according to Gen. 2:24 he said: "Therefore shall a man leave his father and his mother, and shall cleave unto his wife," on which passage the apostle says: "This is a great mystery: but I speak concerning Christ and the Church" (Eph. 5:32). We cannot then believe that the first man was ignorant of this mystery.

After sin, men believed explicitly in the mystery of the incarnation of Christ, including not only his incarnation, but also his passion and resurrection, through which the human race is set free from sin and death. For they would not otherwise have foreshown the passion of Christ in certain sacrifices, both before the Law and under the Law. The wiser among them knew the meaning of these sacrifices explicitly. The simpler minded believed that under the veil of such sacrifices were contained divine preparations for the coming of Christ, of which they were dimly aware. Further, as we said in Q. 1, Art. 7, ad 1 and 4, the nearer men have been to Christ, the more distinctly have they known the things which pertain to the mysteries of Christ.

But now that grace has been revealed, wise and simple alike are required to have explicit faith in the mysteries of Christ, especially in such things as are universally solemnized in the Church, and publicly proposed, such as the articles on the incarnation, of which we spoke in Q. 1, Art. 8. With regard to subtle points connected with the articles on the incarnation, however, some are required to believe them more or less explicitly, according to the status and office of each.

On the first point: the mystery of the kingdom of God was not altogether hidden from the angels, as Augustine says (5 *Gen. ad Litt.* 19), although their knowledge of it was in some respects more perfect after it had been revealed by Christ.

On the second point: John the Baptist did not inquire about the coming of Christ in the flesh as one who did not know of it, since he had openly confessed it, saying: "And I saw, and bare record that this is the Son of God" (John 1:34). Thus he did not say: "Art thou he that has come?" but "Art thou he that should come?" His question related to the future, not to the past. Nor are we to believe that he was ignorant of Christ's coming passion, since he said: "Behold the Lamb of God, which taketh away the sin of the world!" thus foretelling his approaching sacrifice. There have also been other prophets who were not ignorant of it, as is clear from Isa. ch. 53. We may therefore say with Gregory (*Hom. in Evang.* 6) that he asked this question because he did not know whether Christ would descend into hell in his own person. For he knew that the power of his passion would reach to those who were detained in hell, according to Zech. 9:11: "As for thee also, by the blood of thy covenant I have sent forth thy prisoners out of the pit wherein is no water." [1] But he was not required to believe explicitly, before it was fulfilled, that Christ would descend into hell himself. Or we may say with Ambrose (on Luke 7) that he asked this question out of piety, not out of doubt or ignorance. Or we may say with Chrysostom (*Hom. in Matt.* 37) that he asked this question not because he did not know, but in order that his disciples might be convinced by Christ himself, and that Christ directed his reply to John's disciples, pointing to his works as signs.

On the third point: it is evident from their predictions that many of the Gentiles received a revelation concerning Christ. Thus it is said in Job 19:25: "I know that my Redeemer liveth." The sibyl also predicted certain things of Christ, as Augustine says (13 *Contra Faustum* 15). Histories of the Romans also tell us that a tomb was discovered in the days of Constantine Augustus and his mother Irene, in which there lay a man on whose breast was a plate of gold, inscribed with the words "Christ will be born of a virgin, and I believe in him. O Sun, thou shalt see me again, in the time of Irene and

---

[1] Migne: "thou hast sent forth."

Constantine." (*Vid. Baron. ad annum Christi* 780). If, on the other hand, there have been some who have been saved without a revelation, these were not saved without faith in a Mediator. For although they did not have explicit faith, they believed that God was the deliverer of mankind in whatsoever ways might please him, accordingly as the Spirit should reveal the truth to such as should have knowledge of it. This was in accordance with Job. 35:11: "Who teacheth us more than the beasts of the earth . . .?"

Article Eight

Whether Explicit Belief in the Trinity is Necessary for Salvation

We proceed to the eighth article thus:

1. It seems that explicit belief in the Trinity has not been necessary for salvation. The apostle indeed says in Heb. 11:6: "he that cometh to God must believe that he is, and that he is a rewarder of them that diligently seek him." But one can believe this without believing in the Trinity. Hence it has not been necessary to believe in the Trinity explicitly.

2. Again, in John 17:6 the Lord says: "I have manifested thy name unto the men which thou gavest me." Expounding this, Augustine says: "Not thy name whereby thou art called God, but thy name whereby thou art called my Father," and he adds later: "He is known among all nations as the God who made the world; he is known in Judea as the God who is not to be worshipped together with false Gods; but he has not manifested unto men this name which was formerly hidden from them, by which he is called the Father of this Christ through whom he taketh away the sin of the world" (*Tract 106 in Joan.*). Thus it was not known, before the coming of Christ, that both Fatherhood and Sonship were in the Godhead. Hence the Trinity was not believed explicitly.

3. Again, what we are required to believe explicitly about God is that the object of blessedness is in God. Now the object of blessedness is the supreme good, and we can understand that this is in God without distinguishing between the Persons. Hence it has not been necessary to believe in the Trinity explicitly.

On the other hand: the Trinity of the Persons is expressed in many ways in the Old Testament. It is said at the very beginning of Genesis, for example, in order to express the Trinity,

"Let us make man in our image, after our likeness" (Gen. 1:26). Explicit belief in the Trinity has therefore been necessary for salvation from the very beginning.

I answer: it is impossible to believe explicitly in the mystery of the incarnation of Christ without faith in the Trinity. For the mystery of the incarnation of Christ includes that the Son of God took flesh, that he made the world new through the grace of the Holy Spirit, and that he was conceived by the Holy Ghost. Hence just as before the time of Christ the mystery of his incarnation was believed explicitly by the wise, and implicitly and as it were obscurely by the simple, so also was the mystery of the Trinity believed in the same manner. But now that grace has been revealed, it is necessary for everybody to believe in the Trinity explicitly. Moreover, all who are born again in Christ are reborn through invocation of the Trinity, in accordance with Matt. 28:19: "Go ye therefore, and teach all nations, baptizing them in the name of the Father, and of the Son, and of the Holy Ghost."

On the first point: to believe these two things has been necessary for all men at all times. But it is not sufficient for all men at all times.

On the second point: before the coming of Christ, faith in the Trinity was hidden in the faith of the wise. But it was made manifest to the world through Christ, and also through the apostles.

On the third point: without the Trinity of the Persons, the supreme goodness of God can be understood as we now understand it through its effects. But without the Trinity of the Persons it cannot be understood as it is in itself, and as it will be seen by the blessed. Moreover, it is the sending of the divine Persons that brings us to blessedness.

Article Nine

WHETHER TO BELIEVE IS MERITORIOUS

We proceed to the ninth article thus:

1. It seems that to believe is not meritorious. It was said in 12ae, Q. 114, Art. 4, that the principle of merit is charity. Now faith is a preamble to charity, just as nature is a preamble. But a natural action is not meritorious, since we merit nothing by our natural powers. Neither then is the act of faith meritorious.

2. Again, belief is a mean between opinion and science, or

the study of what is known scientifically. Now the study of science is not meritorious, and neither is opinion. Neither, then, is it meritorious to believe.

3. Again, he who assents to anything by faith either has a sufficient reason for believing, or does not. If he has a sufficient reason, his assent is no credit to him, since he is not then free to believe or not to believe. If he does not have a sufficient reason, he believes lightly, in the manner referred to in Ecclesiasticus 19:4: "he that believes in haste is light in heart" —which does not appear to be meritorious. Hence in no wise is it meritorious to believe.

On the other hand: it is said in Heb. 11:33: "Who through faith . . . obtained promises." Now this would not have been, had they not merited by believing. To believe is therefore meritorious.

I answer: as we said in 12ae, Q. 114, Arts. 3 and 4, our actions are meritorious in so far as they proceed from the free will as moved by God through grace. It follows that any human action which depends on the free will can be meritorious, provided that it is related to God. Now "to believe" is the act of the intellect as it assents to divine truth at the command of the will as moved by God through grace. It is therefore an act commanded by the free will as ordered to God. The act of faith can therefore be meritorious.

On the first point: nature is related to charity, which is the principle by which we merit, as matter is related to its form. Faith, on the other hand, is related to charity as a disposition is related to the ultimate form which it precedes. Now it is obvious that a subject, or matter, cannot act except by the power of its form. Neither can a preceding disposition act before its form is received. Once the form has been received, however, a subject and a preceding disposition alike act by the power of the form, and the form is the main principle of action. The heat of a fire, for example, acts by the power of its substantial form. Thus without charity, neither nature nor faith can produce a meritorious action. But when charity supervenes, the act of faith becomes meritorious through charity, just as a natural action thereby becomes meritorious, including a natural action of the free will.

On the second point: two things may be considered in regard to science, namely, the assent of the knower to what he knows, and his study of it. The assent of one who knows scientifically does not depend on his free will, since the cogency of demonstration compels him to give it. Hence in science, assent is not meritorious. The actual study of a scientific matter, however, does depend on his free will, since it lies within his power whether to study or not to study. The study of science can therefore be meritorious if it is referred to the end of charity, that is, to the honour of God, or to the service of one's neighbour. In faith, on the other hand, both assent and practice depend on the free will. The act of faith can therefore be meritorious in both respects. Opinion does not involve firm assent. It is indeed feeble and infirm, as the philosopher says in *Post. An.*, text 44. Hence it does not appear to proceed from a complete volition, nor, therefore, to have much of the nature of merit in respect of its assent, although it may be meritorious in respect of actual study.

On the third point: he who believes has a sufficient reason for believing. He is induced to believe by the authority of divine teaching confirmed by miracles, and what is more, by the inward prompting of divine invitation. Hence he does not believe lightly. But he does not have a reason such as would suffice for scientific knowledge. Thus the character of merit is not taken away.

Article Ten

WHETHER A REASON IN SUPPORT OF THE THINGS OF FAITH DIMINISHES THE MERIT OF FAITH

We proceed to the tenth article thus:

1. It seems that a reason in support of the things of faith diminishes the merit of faith. For Gregory says: "Faith has no merit when human reason proves it by test" (*Hom. in Evang.* 26). Thus a human reason excludes the merit of faith altogether, if it provides an adequate proof. It seems, therefore, that any kind of human reason in support of the things of faith diminishes the merit of faith.

2. Again, as the philosopher says in 1 *Ethics* 9, "happiness is the reward of virtue." Hence anything which diminishes the nature of a virtue diminishes the merit of it. Now a human reason seems to diminish the nature of the virtue of faith. For it is of the very nature of faith that its object is unseen, as was said in Q. 1, Arts. 4 and 5, and the more reasons are given in support of something, the less does it remain unseen. A human reason in support of the things of faith therefore diminishes the merit of faith.

3. Again, the causes of contraries are themselves contrary. Now anything which conduces to the contrary of faith, whether it be persecution in order to compel one to renounce it, or reasoning in order to persuade one to renounce it, increases the merit of faith. A reason which encourages faith therefore diminishes the merit of faith.

On the other hand: it is said in I Peter 3:15: "be ready always to give an answer to every man that asketh you a reason of the hope that is in you." [1] Now the apostle would not have given this advice if the merit of faith were to be diminished as a result of it. Hence a reason does not diminish the merit of faith.

I answer: as we said in the preceding article, the act of faith can be meritorious inasmuch as it depends on the will, in respect of assent and not only of practice. Now a human reason in support of the things of faith may relate to the will of the believer in two ways. In the first place, it may precede the will to believe, as it does when a man has no desire to believe, or has not a ready will to believe, unless he is induced to do so by some human reason. If it precedes in this way, a human reason diminishes the merit of faith. We have already said that a passion which precedes choice in moral virtues diminishes the worth of a virtuous action (12ae, Q. 24, Art. 4, ad 1; Q. 77, Art. 6, ad 6). Just as a man ought to perform acts of moral virtue on account of reasoned judgment, and not on account of passion, so ought he to believe the things of faith on account of divine authority, and not on account of human reason.

In the second place, a human reason may follow the will to believe. When a man has a ready will to believe, he rejoices in the truth which he believes, thinks about it, and turns it over in his mind to see whether he can find a reason for it. A human reason which thus follows the will to believe does not exclude merit. Rather is it a sign of greater merit, just as a passion which follows the will in moral virtues is a sign of greater readiness of will, as we said in 12ae, Q. 24, Art. 3, ad 1. This is the import of the words of the Samaritan to the woman, who signifies human reason (John 4:42): "Now we believe, not because of thy saying."

On the first point: Gregory is speaking of such as have no desire to believe the things of faith otherwise than on the evidence of reason. But when a man is willing to believe them on the authority of God alone, the merit of faith is neither

1 Migne: "of that faith and hope which is in you."

excluded nor diminished if he also has demonstrative proof of some of them, such as that God is one.

On the second point: the reasons which are given in support of the authority of faith are not demonstrative reasons, such as could lead the human intellect to intellectual vision. Hence the things of faith do not cease to be unseen. Such reasons remove hindrances to faith, showing that what is proposed in faith is not impossible. They consequently diminish neither the nature nor the merit of faith. But although demonstrative reasons brought in support of the preambles to faith (not in support of the articles) may diminish the nature of faith by causing what is proposed to be seen, they do not diminish the nature of charity, through which the will is ready to believe the things of faith even though they should remain unseen. Hence the nature of merit is not diminished.

On the third point: whatever is hostile to the faith, whether it be the reasoning of a man or outward persecution, increases the merit of faith in so far as it shows that the will is readier and stronger in the faith. Martyrs had greater merit of faith, since they did not renounce the faith on account of persecutions. Men of wisdom also have greater merit, when they do not renounce it on account of reasons brought against it by philosophers or heretics. But things which encourage faith do not always diminish the readiness of the will to believe. Neither, therefore, do they always diminish the merit of faith.

Question Three

THE OUTWARD ACT OF FAITH

We must now consider the outward act of faith, that is, confession. Two questions are asked concerning confession. 1. Whether confession is an act of faith. 2. Whether confession of faith is necessary for salvation.

Article One

WHETHER CONFESSION IS AN ACT OF FAITH

We proceed to the first article thus:

1. It seems that confession is not an act of faith. For the same act does not belong to different virtues, and confession belongs

to penance, of which it is a part. It follows that confession is not an act of faith.

2. Again, sometimes a man is prevented from confessing the faith by fear, or by self-consciousness. Thus even the apostle asks others to pray that it may be given unto him "that I may open my mouth boldly, to make known the mystery of the gospel" (Eph. 6:19). Now it is through fortitude, which restrains both audacity and fear, that one does not shrink from what is good through either self-consciousness or fear. Hence it seems that confession is an act of fortitude, or of constancy, rather than an act of faith.

3. Again, the fervour of faith causes some to perform other outward good works, just as it causes them to confess the faith. Thus Gal. 5:6 speaks of "faith which worketh by love." Yet these other outward works are not regarded as acts of faith. Hence neither is confession an act of faith.

On the other hand: a gloss on II Thess. 1:11, "and the work of faith with power," says: "that is, confession, which is properly the work of faith."

I answer: outward acts are properly the acts of that virtue to whose end they refer by reason of their specific nature. For example, fasting is an act of abstinence, since it refers by reason of its specific nature to the end of abstinence, which is to curb the flesh. Now the end to which confession of faith refers by reason of its specific nature is the end of faith, according to II Cor. 4:13: "having the same spirit of faith . . . we also believe, and therefore speak." For outward speaking is intended to convey what is conceived in the heart. Hence just as the inward conception of the things of faith is properly an act of faith, so likewise is the outward confession of them.

On the first point: the Scriptures commend three kinds of confession: first, confession of the things of faith, which is the proper act of faith, since it relates to the end of faith, as we have said; second, confession as an act of thanksgiving or praise, which is an act of glorification, since it is ordained for the outward honour of God, which is the end of glorification; third, the confession of sins, which is part of penance, since it is ordained for the blotting out of sin, which is the end of penance.

On the second point: that which removes an obstacle is not an essential cause, but only an accidental cause, as the philosopher explains in 8 *Physics*, text 32. Now fortitude removes an obstacle to confession of faith, whether it be fear or a feeling of shame. It is thus as it were only an accidental cause, not the proper and essential cause of confession of faith.

On the third point: inward faith works by love, through which it causes every outward act of virtue by means of the other virtues, which it commands but does not compel. But it produces confession as its own proper act, without any other virtue as a medium.

Article Two

Whether Confession of Faith is Necessary for Salvation

We proceed to the second article thus:

1. It seems that confession of faith is not necessary for salvation. For that whereby a man attains the end of a virtue would seem to be sufficient for salvation. Now the proper end of faith is that a man's mind should become one with the divine truth. But this can be attained without confession. Hence confession is not necessary for salvation.

2. Again, by outward confession a man declares his faith to another. But this is necessary only for those whose duty it is to instruct others. Hence it appears that the simple minded are not required to confess their faith.

3. Again, nothing is necessary for salvation if it is liable to be an offence to others, or liable to create a disturbance. For the apostle says in I Cor. 10:32: "Give none offence, neither to the Jews, nor to the Gentiles, nor to the church of God." Now a confession of faith sometimes raises a disturbance among unbelievers. It follows that confession of faith is not necessary for salvation.

On the other hand: the apostle says in Rom. 10:10: "For with the heart man believeth unto righteousness; and with the mouth confession is made unto salvation."

I answer: such things as are necessary for salvation are enjoined by the precepts of the divine law. But since confession of faith is something positive, it can be enjoined only by an affirmative precept. It is therefore necessary for salvation only to the extent to which it is enjoined by an affirmative precept of the divine law. Now we have already said that affirmative precepts are not binding for all times, although they are always binding[1] (12ae, Q. 71, Art. 5, ad 3; Q. 88, Art. 1, ad 2). They are binding only for particular times and places, in accordance with other circumstances to which a man's action must have due

[1] Cf. *supra*, 22ae, Q. 2, Art. 5.

regard, if it is to be a virtuous action. Hence it is not necessary for salvation to confess one's faith at all times and places, but only at particular times and places—when God would be deprived of honour, or when the good of one's neighbour would be imperilled, if one did not confess it. One is bound to confess one's faith, for example, if one's silence when asked about it would give the impression either that one had no faith, or that one did not believe the faith to be true; or if it would turn others away from the faith. In such circumstances, confession of faith is necessary for salvation.

On the first point: the end of faith, and of the other virtues also, ought to be referred to the end of charity, which is to love God and one's neighbour. A man ought not therefore to be content to be one with divine truth through faith, but ought to confess his faith outwardly whenever the honour of God or the good of his neighbour demands it.

On the second point: everyone ought to confess their faith openly whenever some danger to the faith makes it necessary, whether it be to instruct other believers, or to strengthen them in the faith, or to set at naught the taunts of unbelievers. But it is not the duty of all to instruct others in the faith at other times.

On the third point: if an open confession of faith would cause a disturbance among unbelievers, without any good ensuing to the faith or to the faithful, public confession of faith is not to be commended. Thus our Lord says in Matt. 7:6: "Give not that which is holy unto the dogs, neither cast ye your pearls before swine, lest they trample them under their feet, and turn again and rend you." But if any good is to be hoped for, or if there is any need, a man ought to ignore any such disturbance and openly confess his faith. Thus it is said in Matt. 15:12–14: "Then came his disciples, and said unto him, Knowest thou that the Pharisees were offended, after they heard this saying? But he answered . . . Let them alone [that is, do not disturb them]: they be blind leaders of the blind."

Question Four

THE VIRTUE ITSELF OF FAITH

We must now consider the virtue itself of faith. We shall consider first faith itself, secondly those who have faith, thirdly the cause of faith, and lastly the effects of faith. Eight questions are asked concerning faith itself. 1. What faith is. 2. In which power of the soul it inheres. 3. Whether its form is charity. 4. Whether formed and unformed faith are numerically the same. 5. Whether faith is a virtue. 6. Whether it is a single virtue. 7. How faith is related to the other virtues. 8. How the certainty of faith compares with the certainty of the intellectual virtues.

Article One

WHETHER THIS IS A SATISFACTORY DEFINITION OF FAITH: FAITH IS THE SUBSTANCE OF THINGS HOPED FOR, THE EVIDENCE OF THINGS NOT SEEN

We proceed to the first article thus:

It seems that the apostle's definition of faith (Heb. 11:1) is not satisfactory—"Faith is the substance of things hoped for, the evidence of things not seen." For no quality is a substance, and it was said in 12ae, Q. 72, Art. 3, that faith is a quality, since it is a theological virtue. It follows that faith is not a substance.

2. Again, different objects belong to different virtues. Now a thing hoped for is the object of hope. Hence it should not be included in the definition as if it were the object of faith.

3. Again, faith is made perfect by charity, rather than by hope. For charity is the form of faith, as will be shown in Art. 3. "Things loved" should therefore be included in the definition, rather than "things hoped for."

4. Again, the same thing should not be included in different genera. Now "substance" and "evidence" are different genera, and neither is intended as a subalternative. It is therefore wrong to define faith as both "substance" and "evidence." Hence faith is improperly described.

5. Again, evidence makes apparent the truth of that in evidence of which it is brought. Now when the truth about a thing is apparent, the thing is said to be seen. It is therefore contradictory to speak of "the evidence of things not seen," since evidence causes something to be seen which was previously unseen. It is therefore wrongly said "of things not seen." Hence faith is improperly described.

On the other hand: the authority of the apostle is sufficient.

I answer: there are some who say that these words of the apostle are not a definition of faith, on the ground that definition exhibits the "what," or essence of a thing, as is maintained in 6 *Metaph.*, text 19. But if anyone consider the matter aright, he will see that this description indicates everything by means of which faith could be defined, even though it is not expressed in the form of a definition. Philosophers indicate the principles of syllogism in a similar way, without making use of the syllogistic form.

To make this clear, we may observe that faith is bound to be defined in terms of its own proper act in relation to its own proper object. For faith is a habit, and habits are known through their acts, which are known through their objects. Now as we said in Q. 2, Arts. 2 and 3, the act of faith is to believe, and belief is an act of the intellect as directed to one object by the will. The act of faith is therefore related both to the object of the will, which is the good and the end, and to the object of the intellect, which is the truth. Further, since faith is a theological virtue, as we said in 12ae, Q. 92, Art. 3, it has the same thing for its object as it has for its end. Consequently, the object of faith is bound to correspond, relatively,[1] to the end of faith. Now we have already said that the object of faith is the unseen first truth, together with what is consequential to the first truth (Q. 1, Arts. 1 and 4). It must therefore be as something unseen that the first truth relates to the act of faith as its end. Such is the nature of things hoped for. As the apostle says: "we hope for that we see not" (Rom. 8:25). To see the truth is to possess it, whereas no one hopes for what he already possesses, since we hope for what we do not possess, as we observed in 12ae, Q. 67, Art. 4. The way in which the act of faith is related to the end of faith as the object of the will is accordingly indicated by the words: "faith is the substance of things hoped for." We often apply the name "substance" to the origin from which something is derived, especially when all that derives therefrom is virtually contained therein, as in a first principle. For example, we might say that its primary indemonstrable principles are the substance of a science, since they are the first things that we understand about the science, and since the whole science is virtually contained in them. It is in this sense that faith is said to be "the substance of things hoped for." For the first beginning of things hoped for arises in us as a result of the assent of faith, which virtually contains everything that is hoped for. We hope for the blessedness in which we shall see, face to face, the truth to which we now unite ourselves by the way of faith, as we said when speaking of blessedness in 12ae, Q. 3, Art. 8; Q. 4, Art. 3.

[1] or "proportionately."

The way in which the act of faith relates to the object of faith as the object of the intellect, on the other hand, is indicated by the words "the evidence of things not seen," "evidence" standing for the result of evidence. The firm adherence of the intellect to the unseen truth of faith is here called "evidence" because evidence leads the intellect to accept something in a final manner. Thus another version reads "conviction," as in Augustine's *Tract. 79 in Joan.*, since the intellect is convinced by divine authority when it assents to what it does not see. Hence if anyone wishes to reduce these words to the form of a definition, he may say: "faith is a habit of the mind, whereby eternal life is begun in us, and which causes the intellect to assent to things not seen."

Thus faith is distinguished from everything else that pertains to the intellect. By what is meant by "evidence," it is distinguished from opinion, suspicion, and doubt, whereby the intellect does not adhere firmly to anything. By what is meant by "things not seen", it is distinguished from science and understanding, through which a thing becomes seen. As "the substance of things hoped for," the virtue of faith is also distinguished from what is commonly called faith, but is not directed to the hope of blessedness.

All other definitions of faith are explanations of that given by the apostle. The definitions given by Augustine (*Tract. 79 in Joan*: 2 *Quaest. Evang.*, Q. 39): "faith is the virtue by which we believe things not seen," by the Damascene (4 *De Fid. Orth.* 12): "faith is assent without inquiry," and by others: "faith is certainty of mind concerning things which are absent, more than opinion, but less than science," affirm what the apostle means by "the evidence of things not seen." The definition given by Dionysius (7 *Div. Nom.*, lect. 5): "faith is the enduring foundation of believers, by which they are devoted to the truth, and the truth shown forth in them," affirms what he means by "the substance of things hoped for."

On the first point: "substance" does not here mean the highest genus as distinguished from other genera. It denotes that wherein every genus bears a likeness to a substance, in that what is primary therein virtually contains the rest, and is accordingly said to be the substance of the rest.

On the second point: since faith pertains to the intellect as commanded by the will, the end of faith must include the objects of the virtues by which the will is perfected. Now hope is one of these virtues, as we shall show in Q. 18, Art. 1, and its object is included in the definition for this reason.

On the third point: love can be of things seen as well as of things not seen, and of things present as well as of things absent. Things loved are therefore not so appropriate to faith as things hoped for, since hope is always for the absent and unseen.

On the fourth point: as they are used in the definition, "substance" and "evidence" do not mean different genera, nor even different acts. They indicate different relations of the same act to different objects, as is plain from what we have said.

On the first point: when evidence is drawn from the proper principles of something, it causes the thing itself to be seen. But the evidence of divine authority does not make the thing itself to be seen, and such is the evidence of which the definition speaks.

Article Two
WHETHER FAITH IS IN THE INTELLECT AS ITS SUBJECT

We proceed to the second article thus:

1. It seems that faith is not in the intellect as its subject. For Augustine says (implicitly in *De Praed. Sanct.* 5): "faith depends on the will of those who believe." But the will is a power distinct from the intellect. It follows that faith is not in the intellect as its subject.

2. Again, assent to matters of faith is the outcome of a will obedient to God. Hence the praiseworthiness of faith seems to lie entirely in obedience. Now obedience is in the will. It follows that faith also is in the will, not in the intellect.

3. Again, the intellect is either speculative or practical. Now faith is not in the speculative intellect. For faith "worketh by love" (Gal. 5:6), whereas the speculative intellect is not a principle of action, since it has nothing to say about what we ought to shun or avoid, as is said in 3 *De Anima*, texts 34, 35. Yet neither is it in the practical intellect, the object of which is some contingent truth about something which can be made or done, whereas the object of faith is eternal truth, as was explained in Q. 1, Art. 1. It follows that faith is not in the intellect as its subject.

On the other hand: faith is succeeded in heaven by vision, according to I Cor. 13:12: "Now we see through a glass, darkly; but then face to face." Now vision is in the intellect. So also, therefore, is faith.

I answer: since faith is a virtue, the act of faith must be perfect. Now the perfection of an act which springs from two active principles requires the perfection of both these principles. For one cannot saw well unless one knows the art of sawing, and unless the saw is also well adapted for sawing. Further, when a disposition to act well exists in powers of the soul which tend to do the opposite, such a disposition is a habit, as we explained in 12ae, Q. 49, Art. 4, ad, 1, 2, and 3. An act which springs from two such powers can be perfect, therefore, only if such a habit already exists in both of them. Now to believe is an act of the intellect as moved to assent by the will, as we said in Q. 2, Arts. 1 and 2. Thus the act of belief springs both from the intellect and from the will, and each of these two powers is such that it is perfected by means of some habit, as we have explained.[1] Hence if the act of faith is to be perfect, there must be a habit in the will as well as in the intellect; just as there must be a habit of prudence in the reason, and also a habit of temperance in the faculty of desire, if an act of desire is to be perfect. Nevertheless, the act of belief is immediately an act of the intellect, since the object of belief is "the true," which properly pertains to the intellect. Faith must therefore be in the intellect as its subject, since it is the proper principle of the act of belief.

On the first point: by faith Augustine means the act of faith, which is said to depend on the will of believers in as much as the intellect assents to matters of faith by command of the will.

On the second point: not only must the will be ready to obey, but the intellect must also be disposed to follow the command of the will, just as desire must be well disposed to follow the direction of reason. There must therefore be a habit in the intellect which assents, as well as in the will which commands the intellect.

On the third point: it is quite clear from the object of faith that faith is in the intellect as its subject. Yet since the first truth, which is the object of faith, is the end of all our desires and actions (as Augustine explains in 1 *De Trin.* 8), faith works by love, just as "the speculative intellect becomes practical by extension," as it is said in 3 *De Anima*, text 49.

[1] 12ae, Q. 49. A habit is necessary whenever a power, in spite of possessing its form to the full, may tend to diverse objects, such as good and evil.

Article Three

WHETHER CHARITY IS THE FORM OF FAITH

We proceed to the third article thus:

1. It seems that charity is not the form of faith. The species of each thing is derived from its own form. One thing cannot then be the form of another, if the two are distinguished as separate species of one genus. Now in I Cor., ch. 13, faith and charity are distinguished as separate species of virtue. Hence charity is not the form of faith.

2. Again, a form and that of which it is the form are in the same thing, since that which arises out of them is one absolutely. But faith is in the intellect, whereas charity is in the will. Hence charity is not the form of faith.

3. Again, the form of a thing is the principle of it. Now in so far as belief is due to the will, its principle would seem to be obedience rather than charity, according to Rom. 1:5: "for obedience to the faith among all nations." Obedience is therefore the form of faith, rather than charity.

On the other hand: everything works by means of its form. Now faith worketh by love. The love of charity is therefore the form of faith.

I answer: as we explained in 12ae, Q. 1, Art. 3, and Q. 17, Art. 6, voluntary acts take their species from the object to which the will is directed as an end. Now things derive their species from the manner in which a form exists in natural things. The form of any voluntary act is therefore in a sense the end to which it is directed, both because it takes its species from this end, and because its manner of action is bound to correspond to the end proportionately. It is also clear from what we said in the first article that the object of will which the act of faith seeks as an end is the good, and that this good is the divine good, which is the proper object of charity. Charity is accordingly said to be the form of faith, because it is through charity that the act of faith is made perfect, and brought to its form.

On the first point: charity is said to be the form of faith in the sense that it brings the act of faith to its form. There is nothing to prevent one act being brought to its form by different habits, and consequently classified under different species when human actions in general are being discussed, as we said in 12ae, Q. 18, Arts. 6, 7; Q. 61, Art. 2.

On the second point: this objection argues from the intrinsic form. Charity is not the intrinsic form of faith, but that which brings the act of faith to its form, as we have said.

On the third point: even obedience itself, like hope and any other virtue which can precede the act of faith, is brought to its true form by charity, as we shall explain in Q. 23, Art. 8. Charity is named as the form of faith for this reason.

Article Four

WHETHER UNFORMED FAITH CAN BECOME FORMED, OR VICE VERSA

We proceed to the fourth article thus:

1. It seems that unformed faith cannot become formed, nor formed faith unformed. It is said in I Cor. 13:10: "when that which is perfect is come, then that which is in part shall be done away." Now in comparison with formed faith, unformed faith is imperfect. It will therefore be done away when formed faith is come. It follows that it cannot be numerically one habit with formed faith.

2. Again, the dead does not become the living. Unformed faith is dead, according to James 2:20: "faith without works is dead." It follows that unformed faith cannot become formed.

3. Again, when God's grace is bestowed on a believer, its effect is not less than when it is bestowed on an unbeliever. Now it causes a habit of faith in an unbeliever. It must therefore cause another habit of faith in a believer, who already has the habit of unformed faith.

4. Again, as Boethius says, "accidents cannot be altered." Faith is an accident. It follows that the same faith cannot be formed at one time and unformed at another.

On the other hand: a gloss on James 2:20, "faith without works is dead," says: "by works it is revived." Thus faith which was once dead and unformed becomes formed and living.

I answer: opinion has varied on this matter. Some have said that the habit of formed faith is not the same habit as that of unformed faith; that unformed faith is done away when formed faith comes; and similarly that when a man whose faith is formed sins mortally, God infuses another habit of unformed faith. But it does not seem possible that a gift of grace should expel another gift of God, nor that any gift of God should be infused in consequence of mortal sin. Others have said that although the habits of formed and unformed faith are different habits, the habit of unformed faith is not done away, but remains together with the habit of formed faith in the same person. But it seems no less impossible that the habit of unformed faith should remain, inactive, in one who has faith that is formed.

We must therefore say, as against such views, that the habit of formed and of unformed faith is the same habit. The reason for this is that a habit is differentiated by what belongs to it essentially. What pertains to the intellect belongs to faith essentially, since faith is a perfection of the intellect. But what pertains to the will does not belong to faith essentially, and cannot therefore justify a distinction within it. Now the distinction between formed and unformed faith depends on charity, which pertains to the will, not on anything which pertains to the intellect. Hence formed and unformed faith are not different habits.

On the first point: the apostle means that when imperfection is essential to the nature of that which is imperfect, that which is imperfect shall be done away when that which is perfect is come. For example, when open vision is come, faith shall be done away, which is essentially "of things not seen." But when imperfection is not essential to the nature of that which is imperfect, that which was imperfect and becomes perfect is numerically the same. For example, it is numerically the same person who was a boy and becomes a man, since boyhood is not essential to the nature of manhood. The unformed condition of faith is not essential to faith itself, but is accidental to it, as we have said. Hence it is the same faith which was unformed and becomes formed.

On the second point: what makes an animal alive belongs to its essence, since it is its essential form, namely, the soul. It is for this reason that the dead cannot become the living, and that the dead and the living differ in kind. But what brings faith to its form, or makes it alive, does not belong to the essence of faith. The two cannot then be compared.

On the third point: grace causes faith so long as faith endures, not only when it is newly begun in a man. For God works a man's justification continually, as we said in Pt. I, Q. 104, Art. 1, and 12ae, Q. 109, Art. 9, just as the sun continually illumines the atmosphere. Hence grace does not do less for the believer than for the unbeliever, since it causes faith in both. It confirms and perfects faith in the one, and creates it anew in the other. Or we might say that it is accidental, as due to the nature of the subject, that grace does not cause faith to arise in one who already has faith; just as it is accidental, conversely, that a second mortal sin does not deprive a man of grace if he has already lost it through a previous mortal sin.

On the fourth point: when formed faith becomes unformed, it is not faith itself that is altered, but the subject of faith, that is, the soul, which at one time has faith with charity, at another faith without charity.

Article Five

WHETHER FAITH IS A VIRTUE

We proceed to the fifth article thus:

1. It seems that faith is not a virtue. Virtue is "that which makes its subject good," as the philosopher says in 2 *Ethics* 6, and is therefore directed to the good, whereas faith is directed to the true. It follows that faith is not a virtue.

2. Again, an infused virtue is more perfect than an acquired virtue. Now as the philosopher says in 6 *Ethics* 3, faith is not regarded as one of the acquired intellectual virtues, owing to its imperfection. Much less, then, can it be regarded as an infused virtue.

3. Again, it was said in the preceding article that formed and unformed faith are of the same species. But unformed faith is not a virtue, since it has no connection with other virtues. Hence neither is formed faith a virtue.

4. Again, the freely given graces are distinct from the virtues, and so is the fruit of the Spirit. Now in I Cor. 12:9 faith is included among the freely given graces, and in Gal. 5:22 it is included in the fruit of the Spirit. Hence faith is not a virtue.

On the other hand: a man is made just by means of the virtues. For "justice is the whole of virtue," as it is said in 5 *Ethics* 1. But he is justified by faith, according to Rom. 5:1: "Therefore being justified by faith, we have peace with God. . . ." Hence faith is a virtue.

I answer: it is plain from what we said in 12ae, Q. 55, Arts. 3 and 4, that human virtue is that which makes human actions good. Any habit which is invariably the principle of a good action may therefore be called a human virtue. Now formed faith is such a habit. Two things are necessary, however, if the act of belief is to be perfect, since it is the act wherein the intellect finally gives its assent at the command of the will. The intellect must be infallibly directed to its object, which is the truth, and the will must be infallibly directed to the ultimate end, for the sake of which assent is finally given. Now both of these conditions are fulfilled in the act of formed faith. It is of the very nature of faith that the intellect should be in the way of truth at all times, since faith cannot believe what is false, as we said in Q. 1, Art. 3. The will of the soul is likewise infallibly directed to the ultimate good by charity, which brings faith to its form. Formed faith is therefore a virtue.

Unformed faith, on the other hand, is not a virtue, since even though it should have the perfection which is necessary on the part of the intellect, it would still lack the perfection which is necessary on the part of the will; just as we said that temperance would not be a virtue if prudence were wanting in the reason, even though there should be temperance in the concupiscible element. (12ae, Q. 58, Art. 4; Q. 55, Art. 1.) An act of temperance requires an act of reason as well as an act of the concupiscible element. So likewise does the act of faith require an act of the will as well as an act of the intellect.

On the first point: "the true" is itself the good of the intellect, since it is the perfection of the intellect. Faith is consequently directed to the good in so far as the intellect is directed to truth by faith. Faith is further directed to the good in so far as it is brought to its form by charity, since the good is then the object of the will.

On the second point: the philosopher is speaking of the faith which trusts in human reason when it accepts a conclusion which does not necessarily follow, and which may be false. Faith of this kind is not a virtue. We are speaking of the faith which trusts in divine truth, which is infallible, and cannot be false. This faith can, therefore, be a virtue.

On the third point: formed and unformed faith do not differ in species as belonging to different species. They differ, however, as the perfect and the imperfect within the same species. Thus unformed faith lacks the perfect nature of a virtue because it is imperfect, virtue being a kind of perfection, as is said in 7 *Physics*, texts 17 and 18.

On the fourth point: some say that the faith included among the freely given graces is unformed faith. But this is not well said. For the graces mentioned are not common to all members of the Church, wherefore the apostle says: "there are diversities of gifts," and again, "to one is given this, to another that." Unformed faith, on the other hand, is common to all members of the Church. Lack of form is not a part of its substance, whereas a gift is gratuitous by its substance. We must therefore say that in this passage faith stands for some excellence of faith, such as constancy, as the gloss says, or the "word of faith." Faith is also included in the fruit of the Spirit, because it rejoices in its own act, on account of its certainty. As numbered with the fruits in Gal., ch. 5, faith is accordingly explained as "certainty of things not seen."

Article Six

Whether Faith is a Single Virtue

We proceed to the sixth article thus:

1. It seems that faith is not a single virtue. For just as faith is a gift of God, according to Eph. 2:8, so also are wisdom and understanding clearly reckoned as gifts of God, according to Isa. 11:2. Now wisdom and knowledge are different, in that wisdom is of things eternal, whereas understanding is of things temporal. Hence since faith is of things eternal, and also of some things which are temporal, it seems that it is not single, but divided into parts.

2. Again, it was said in Q. 3, Art. 1 that confession is an act of faith. But confession is not the same for all. We confess as having happened in the past what the ancient fathers confessed as about to happen in the future, as is plain from Isa. 7:14: "Behold, a virgin shall conceive." Hence faith is not single.

3. Again, faith is common to all who believe in Christ. But a single accident cannot be in different subjects. There cannot then be one faith for everybody.

On the other hand: the apostle says (Eph. 4:5): "One Lord, one faith."

I answer: if we are speaking of the habit of faith, this may be considered either in respect of its object, or in respect of its subject. Faith is one in respect of its object, since its formal object is the first truth, in believing which we believe everything contained in the faith. But it is diverse in respect of its subject, since it occurs in different persons. Now it is obvious that faith, like any other habit, takes its species from what we mean by its formal object, while it is individualized by its subject. Consequently, if by faith we mean the habit whereby we believe, faith is one in species, even though it is numerically different in different persons. If, on the other hand, we mean that which is believed, then again, faith is one, since it is the same thing that is believed by all. For even though the matters of faith which all believe in common are diverse, they are all reducible to one.

On the first point: such temporal things as are proposed to faith are the object of faith only in so far as they relate to what is eternal, namely, to the first truth, as we said in Q. 1, Art. 1. Faith is therefore one, whether of things eternal or temporal. But it is otherwise with wisdom and understanding, which are concerned with the eternal and the temporal according to their different natures.

On the second point: the difference between past and future is not a difference within what is believed, but a difference in the relation of believers to the one thing which is believed, as we said in 12ae, Q. 103, Art. 4; Q. 107, Art. 1, ad 1.

On the third point: this objection argues from the numerical diversity of faith.

Article Seven

Whether Faith is the First of the Virtues

We proceed to the seventh article thus:

1. It seems that faith is not the first of the virtues. For a gloss by Ambrose on Luke 12:4, "I say unto you, my friends . . .," says that fortitude is the foundation of faith. A foundation is prior to what is founded upon it. Hence faith is not the first of the virtues.

2. Again, a gloss (Cassiod.) on the words "trust in the Lord," [1] in the psalm "Fret not" (Ps. 37) says: "hope leads to faith." Now it is to be explained later that hope is a virtue (Q. 17, Art. 1). Hence faith is not the first of the virtues.

3. Again, it was said in Art. 2 that the intellect of the believer is inclined to assent to the things of faith by obedience to God. Now obedience is a virtue. Hence faith is not the first of the virtues.

4. Again, a gloss on I Cor. 3:11, "For other foundation can no man lay . . .," says that formed faith is the foundation, not unformed faith (Augustine, *De Fide et Operibus* 16). Now it was said in Art. 1 that faith is brought to its form by charity. It is therefore through charity that faith is made the foundation, so that charity is the foundation rather than faith: and since the foundation is the first part of the building, it seems that charity is prior to faith.

5. Again, we understand the order of habits from the order of

[1] Migne: "Hope in the Lord."

their acts. Now in the act of faith, the act of the will, which is made perfect by charity, precedes the act of the intellect, which is made perfect by faith, as the cause which precedes its effect. It follows that charity precedes faith. Hence faith is not the first of the virtues.

On the other hand: the apostle says (Heb. 11:1): "Faith is the substance of things hoped for." Now a substance is first by nature. Faith is therefore the first of the virtues.

I answer: one thing may precede another in two ways, either essentially or accidentally. Essentially, faith is the first of all the virtues. The theological virtues are bound to be prior to the others, since their object is the final end, the end being the principle of action in all practical matters, as we said in 12ae, Q. 13, Art. 3; and Q. 34, Art. 4, ad. 1. Further, the final end itself must be in the intellect before it is in the will, since the will cannot intend anything which is not first apprehended by the intellect. Faith must then be the first of all the virtues. For the final end is in the intellect through faith, whereas it is in the will through hope and charity. Neither can natural knowledge attain to God as the object of blessedness, as he is sought by hope and charity.

Some other virtues, however, may precede faith accidentally. For an accidental cause is accidentally prior. As the philosopher explains in 8 *Physics*, text 32, the removal of a hindrance is accidentally part of the cause, and we may say that other virtues may be prior to faith in this way, in so far as they remove hindrances to belief. Fortitude, for example, removes irrational fear, which is a hindrance to faith, and humility removes pride, through which the intellect scorns to submit to the truth of faith. The same may also be said of certain other virtues, although they are not genuine virtues unless faith is presupposed, as Augustine says (4 *Cont. Julian. 3*).

The reply to the first point is thus obvious.

On the second point: hope does not always lead to faith. One cannot hope for eternal blessedness unless one believes it to be possible, since one cannot hope for what is impossible, as we said in 12ae, Q. 40, Art. 1. But hope may lead one to persevere in faith, or to remain steadfast in faith. It is in this sense that it is said to lead to faith.

On the third point: there are two senses in which we may speak of obedience. In the first place, we may mean the inclination of the will to obey the divine commandments. This is not in itself a special virtue. It is common to all virtues, since all virtues are commanded by the precepts of the divine law, as we said in 12ae, Q. 100, Art. 2. In this sense, obedience is necessary for faith. Secondly, we may mean the inclination of the will to obey the divine commandments as a duty. Understood in this sense, obedience is a special virtue, and part of justice, since it renders to a superior what is his due, by obeying him. Such obedience, however, is consequential to faith, since it is faith that enables a man to know that God is his superior who ought to be obeyed.

On the fourth point: the nature of a foundation requires not only that a thing should be first, but also that it should be a bond for the other parts of the building. For nothing is a foundation unless the other parts of the building hold together upon it. Now the spiritual edifice is bound together by charity, according to Col. 3:14: "above all these things put on charity, which is the bond of perfectness." Thus it is true that faith cannot be the foundation without charity. But this does not mean that charity is prior to faith.

On the fifth point: faith does presuppose an act of will, but not an act of will which has been brought to its form by charity. Such an act presupposes faith, since the will cannot seek God with perfect love unless the intellect has a right belief about God.

Article Eight

WHETHER FAITH IS MORE CERTAIN THAN SCIENCE AND THE OTHER INTELLECTUAL VIRTUES

We proceed to the eighth article thus:

1. It seems that faith is not more certain than science and the other intellectual virtues. For doubt is opposed to certainty, wherefore that is apparently the more certain which is the less open to doubt, just as that is the whiter which is the less mixed with black. Now understanding and science, and even wisdom, have no doubts about their objects. But one who believes may be subject to intermittent doubt, and may have doubts concerning matters of faith. It follows that faith is not more certain than the intellectual virtues.

2. Again, vision is more certain than hearing. Now it is said in Rom. 10:17 that "faith cometh by hearing." In understanding, science, and wisdom, on the other hand, there is a kind of intellectual vision. It follows that science, or understanding, is more perfect than faith.

3. Again, in matters pertaining to the intellect, things are

more certain if they are more perfect. Now understanding is more perfect than faith, since we advance to understanding through faith, according to Isa. 7:9: "Except ye believe, ye shall not understand" (Septuagint). Moreover, Augustine says that "faith is strengthened by science" (14 *De Trin.* 1). Hence it appears that science and understanding are more certain than faith.

On the other hand: the apostle says in I Thess. 2:13: "when ye received the word of God which ye heard of us," that is, through faith, "ye received it not as the word of men, but, as it is in truth, the word of God." Now nothing is more certain than the word of God. Hence neither science nor anything else is more certain than faith.

I answer: as we said in 12ae, Q. 62, Art. 4, ad. 2, two of the intellectual virtues, namely prudence and art, are concerned with the contingent. Faith is more certain than either of these by reason of its very matter, since it is concerned with the eternal, which cannot be other than it is. There remain, then, the three intellectual virtues of wisdom, science, and understanding, which are concerned with the necessary, as we said in 12ae, Q. 57, Arts. 2 and 3. We must observe, however, that wisdom, science, and understanding may be understood in two ways. As understood by the philosopher in 6 *Ethics* 3, 6, and 7, they denote intellectual virtues. But they also denote gifts of the Holy Spirit.

There are two kinds of certainty which belong to them as intellectual virtues. In the first place, a thing is said to be more certain if the cause of certainty is itself more certain. Faith is in this sense more certain than the three virtues named, since it relies on divine truth, whereas they rely on human reason. Secondly, the assurance of the subject is more certain when the intellect grasps a thing more fully. In this sense, faith is less certain than these virtues, since the things of faith transcend the intellect of man, whereas the virtues named are concerned with what does not transcend it. Now a thing is judged absolutely by reference to its cause, and relatively by reference to the disposition of the subject. In the absolute sense, therefore, faith is the more certain, although these others are more certain relatively, that is, from the point of view of ourselves.

The case is similar if these three are understood to denote divine gifts given to us in this present life. Faith is more certain than such gifts, since they presuppose faith as their principle.

On the first point: this doubt does not pertain to the cause of faith. It pertains to ourselves, in so far as the intellect does not fully grasp the things of faith.

On the second point: other things being equal, vision is more certain than hearing. But if he from whom one hears greatly surpasses the vision of him who sees, hearing is more certain than vision. Indeed, anyone who has a little learning is more certain of what he hears from a scientist than of what he perceives by his own reason. Much more, then, is a man more certain of what he hears from God, which cannot be false, than of what he perceives by his own reason, which is liable to err.

On the third point: as divine gifts, perfect understanding and knowledge surpass the knowledge of faith in clarity, but not in certainty. For their certainty is the outcome of the certainty of faith, just as certainty of a conclusion is the outcome of certainty of the premises. As intellectual virtues, on the other hand, knowledge, wisdom, and understanding depend on the natural light of reason, which falls short of the certainty of the word of God, on which faith relies.

Question Five

OF THOSE WHO HAVE FAITH

We must now inquire concerning those who have faith. Four questions are asked. 1. Whether angels and man had faith in their first state. 2. Whether devils have faith. 3. Whether heretics who err in one article of faith have faith in the other articles. 4. Whether, of those who have faith, one has greater faith than another.

Article One

WHETHER ANGELS AND MAN HAD FAITH IN THEIR FIRST STATE

We proceed to the first article thus:

1. It seems that neither angels nor man had faith in their first state. For Hugo St. Victor says (*Sentent.* 1; 10 *De Sacrament.* 2): "it is because the eye of contemplation is not open that man cannot see God, or what is in God." But the eye of contemplation was open in angels in their first state, before their confirmation or their lapse. As Augustine says, they "saw the realities in the word" (2 *Gen. ad Litt.* 8). It seems, also, that the eye of contemplation was open in the first man during his state

of innocence, since Hugo St. Victor says in the same work (6, cap. 14): "in his first state, man knew his Creator not with the knowledge wherein the gate is open to hearing only, but with the knowledge which is of inward inspiration; not with the knowledge of those who by faith seek God while he is absent, but with clear vision of God as present to their contemplation." Hence neither men nor the angels had faith in their first state.

2. Again, the knowledge of faith is dark and dim, according to I Cor. 13:12: "now we see through a glass, darkly." But in their first state there was dimness neither in man nor in the angels, since darkness was the penalty of sin. Hence neither man nor the angels can have had faith in their first state.

3. Again, the apostle says in Rom. 10:17: "faith cometh by hearing, and hearing by the word of God." But there was no place for this in the first state of man or the angels, since they did not hear anything from another. Neither then was there faith in this state, whether of man or of angels.

On the other hand: the apostle says (Heb. 11:6): "he that cometh to God must believe that he is, and that he is a rewarder of them that diligently seek him." Now in their first state, angels and man were coming to God. It follows that they had need of faith.

I answer: some say that the angels did not have faith before their confirmation or lapse, nor man before his sin, on account of their clear contemplation of divine things. But the only manifestation which excludes the character of faith is that wherein the principal object of faith is made apparent, or seen. For as the apostle says: "faith is the evidence of things not seen" (Heb. 11:1), and as Augustine says in *Tract. 40 in Joan.*, and in *2 Quaest. Evang.*, Q. 39, "by faith we believe what we do not see." Now the principal object of faith is the first truth, the vision of which makes us blessed, and supersedes faith. But neither the angels before confirmation nor man before sin were in the state of blessedness wherein God is seen in his essence. It is obvious, therefore, that they did not have the clear knowledge which would exclude the character of faith. Hence if they did not have faith, this could only be because they were entirely ignorant of the object of faith. If man and the angels had been created in the purely natural state, as some say they were, one might have maintained that neither angels before confirmation nor man before sin had faith. For the knowledge of faith is beyond the natural knowledge of God, with angels no less than with men. But as we said in Pt. I, Q. 62, Art. 3, and Q. 91, Art. 1, the gift of grace was given to man and to angels at the time when they were created.

We must therefore say that the hope of blessedness began in man and in the angels in consequence of the grace which they received, before this grace was consummated. Now as we said in Q. 4, Art. 7, this hope is begun in the intellect through faith, while it is begun in the will through hope and charity. Hence we are bound to say that the angels had faith before they were confirmed, and that man had faith before he sinned. But we must bear in mind that the object of faith has a formal aspect, as the first truth which transcends the natural knowledge of any creature, and also a material aspect, as that to which we assent when we acknowledge the first truth. In its formal aspect, faith is the same for all who know God by way of acknowledging the first truth, while future blessedness is as yet unattained. Of the things which are materially proposed for belief, however, some are believed by one and clearly known by another, even in this present state, as we said in Q. 1, Art. 5, and Q. 2, Art. 4, ad 2. We may accordingly say that angels before confirmation and man before sin had to some extent a clear knowledge of the divine mysteries, which we can know only by faith.

On the first point: although these words of Hugo St. Victor are the words of a master, and have the force of authority, it may be said that the contemplation which makes faith unnecessary is the contemplation of heaven, whereby supernatural truth is seen in its essence. Now the angels did not have contemplation of this kind before confirmation. Neither did man before he sinned. Their contemplation was nevertheless of a higher order than our own. For it brought them nearer to God, and thereby gave them a clear knowledge of more things concerning the divine effects and mysteries than is possible for ourselves. Hence they did not have faith such as ours, which seeks God while he is absent, since God was more present to them by the light of wisdom than he is to us. But he was not present to them as he is present to the blessed by the light of glory.

On the second point: in their first state, man and the angels were not affected by any darkness of guilt or punishment. There was nevertheless in them a certain natural dimness of the intellect, since every creature is dim compared with the immensity of the divine light. Such dimness was sufficient to make faith necessary.

On the third point: although man in his first state did not

hear anything outwardly, God inspired him inwardly. The prophets also heard in this way, according to Ps. 85:8: "I will hear what God the Lord will speak."

Article Two

Whether Devils Have Faith

We proceed to the second article thus:

1. It seems that devils do not have faith. For Augustine says that "faith depends on the will of those who believe" (*De Praed. Sanct.* 5). Now the will whereby one wills to believe in God is good. But there is no deliberate good will in devils. Hence it seems that devils do not have faith.

2. Again, faith is a gift of grace, according to Eph. 2:8: "For by grace ye are saved through faith . . . it is the gift of God." Now the gloss on Hosea 3:1, "who look to other gods, and love flagons of wine," says that the devils forfeited the gift of grace by their sin. It follows that faith did not remain in them after their sin.

3. Again, unbelief seems to be one of the more serious sins, according to what Augustine says (*Tract. 9 in Joan.*) on John 15:22: "If I had not come and spoken unto them, they had not had sin: but now they have no cloak for their sin." Now some men are guilty of the sin of unbelief. Their sin would then be worse than that of devils, if devils had faith. But this is impossible. Therefore devils do not have faith.

On the other hand: it is said in James 2:19: "the devils also believe, and tremble."

I answer: as we said in Q. 1, Art. 2, and Q. 2, Art. 1, the intellect of the believer assents to what he believes neither because he sees the thing as it is in itself, nor because he understands it through its first principles seen as they are in themselves, but because his will moves his intellect to give its assent. Now there are two ways in which the will may move the in-intellect to give its assent. In the first place, the will may be directed to the good, in which case belief is a praiseworthy act. Secondly, the intellect may be sufficiently convinced to judge that what is said ought to be believed, without being convinced by any evidence of the thing itself. Thus if a prophet should predict something as by the word of God, and if he should also give a sign by raising one who was dead, the intellect of one who saw would be convinced by the sign, and he would know assuredly that this was spoken by God who does not lie, even though what was predicted was not apparent. The character of faith would then remain.

Hence we must say that the faith of those who believe in Christ is praised as being of the first kind. Devils, on the other hand, do not have faith of this kind, but only of the second kind. For they see many unmistakable signs by which they know that the doctrine of the Church is given by God, although they do not see the things themselves which the Church teaches, for example, that God is Three and also One, and the like.

On the first point: the faith of devils is such as the evidence of signs compels. Their belief is therefore no credit to their will.

On the second point: even though it should be unformed, faith which is the gift of grace inclines a man to believe out of regard for what is good. The faith of devils is therefore not the gift of grace. Rather are they compelled to believe by what they perceive by their natural intellect.

On the third point: devils are displeased by the very obviousness of the signs which compel them to believe. Hence the evil in them is not diminished by their belief.

Article Three

WHETHER ONE WHO DISBELIEVES ONE ARTICLE OF FAITH CAN HAVE UNFORMED FAITH IN THE OTHER ARTICLES

We proceed to the third article thus:

1. It seems that a heretic who disbelieves one article of faith can have unformed faith in the other articles. For the natural intellect of a heretic is no better than that of a catholic, and the intellect of a catholic needs the help of the gift of faith in order to believe in any of the articles. It seems, then, that neither can heretics believe in any articles of faith, unless through the gift of unformed faith.

2. Again, the faith contains many articles, just as a single science, such as geometry, contains many conclusions. Any man can have a scientific knowledge of geometry in respect of some geometrical conclusions, even though he is ignorant of others. Similarly, any man can have faith in some of the articles of faith, even though he does not believe the others.

3. Again, just as a man obeys God in believing the articles of faith, so does he obey him in keeping the commandments of the law. He may be obedient in regard to some of the commandments, and not in regard to others. He may therefore have faith in regard to some of the articles, and not in regard to others.

On the other hand: as mortal sin is contrary to charity, so is disbelief in one article contrary to faith. Now charity does not remain after a single mortal sin. Neither then does faith remain after disbelief in a single article.

I answer: neither formed faith nor unformed faith remains in a heretic who disbelieves one article. The reason for this is that the species of any habit depends on what we mean by its formal object, and cannot remain if this is taken away. Now the formal object of faith is the first truth, as manifested in the sacred Scriptures and the doctrine of the Church, which proceeds from the first truth. Hence anyone who does not adhere, as to an infallible and divine rule, to the doctrine of the Church, which proceeds from the first truth manifested in the sacred Scriptures, does not possess the habit of faith, even if he maintains the things of faith otherwise than by faith. It is similarly obvious that one who maintains a conclusion without knowing the premise by means of which it is demonstrated has no scientific knowledge of it, but only an opinion. It is plain, on the other hand, that one who adheres to the doctrine of the Church as an infallible rule assents to everything that the Church teaches. For if he were to maintain such doctrines of the Church as he might choose, and not such as he did not wish to maintain, he would not adhere to the doctrine of the Church as an infallible rule, but only in accordance with his own will. It is clear then, that a heretic who persists in disbelieving one article of faith is not prepared to follow the doctrine of the Church in all matters. If he did not so persist, he would not be a heretic, but merely one who erred. It is thus apparent that one who is a heretic in one article does not have faith in the other articles, but holds an opinion in accordance with his own will.

On the first point: a heretic does not maintain the other articles of faith, in which he does not err, as a faithful man maintains them, that is, through adherence to the first truth, to which a man is bound to adhere if the habit of faith is in him. He maintains the things of faith according to his own will and judgment.

On the second point: the different conclusions of a science are proved by means of different premises, one of which may be known apart from the others. A man may therefore have scientific knowledge of some conclusions of a science without knowing others. Faith, however, accepts all the articles of faith on the ground of a single premise, namely, the first truth proposed to us in the Scriptures, according to the doctrine of the Church, which understands it properly. He who rejects this premise is therefore altogether without faith.

On the third point: the several commandments of the law may be considered in reference to their several proximate motives, in respect of which one of them may be kept and not another. But they may also be considered in reference to their single primary motive, which is perfect obedience to God, in which anyone fails who transgresses any one commandment, according to James 2:10: "whosoever shall keep the whole law, and yet offend in one point, he is guilty of all."

Article Four

WHETHER FAITH CAN BE GREATER IN ONE THAN IN ANOTHER

We proceed to the fourth article thus:

1. It seems that faith cannot be greater in one than in another, since the quantity of a habit is determined by reference to its object. Anyone who has faith has faith in all that the faith contains, since he who disbelieves in a single point is altogether without faith, as was said in the preceding article. Hence it seems that faith cannot be greater in one than in another.

2. Again, that which depends on what is greatest does not admit of more and less. Now faith depends on what is greatest, since it demands that a man adhere to the first truth before all things. It follows that faith does not admit of more and less.

3. Again, it was said in Q. 1, Art. 7, that the articles of faith are the first principles of the knowledge which is of grace. In the knowledge which is of grace, therefore, faith has the same relative status as has the understanding of principles in natural knowledge. Now the understanding of principles occurs equally in all men. Hence faith likewise occurs equally in all who believe.

On the other hand: wherever there is little and great, there is greater and less. Now there is little and great in faith. For the Lord said to Peter, "O thou of little faith, wherefore didst thou doubt?" (Matt. 14:31), and to the woman, "O woman, great is thy faith" (Matt. 15:28). Thus faith can be greater in one than in another.

I answer: as we said in 12ae, Q. 52, Arts. 1 and 2, and Q. 112, Art. 4, the magnitude of a habit may be considered in two ways; in respect of its object, and in respect of the subject who possesses it. Faith may be considered in two ways in respect of its object, which includes what we mean by the formal object of faith, and also things materially proposed for belief. It cannot be different in different persons in respect of its formal object, since this is one and indivisible, as we said in Q. 1, Art. 1. In this respect, faith is the same in all men, as we said in Q. 4, Art. 6. But the things which are materially proposed for belief are many, and can be accepted either more or less explicitly. Hence one man can believe explicitly more things than another. Faith may therefore be greater in one man than in another, in as much as it may be more explicit.

In respect of the person who possesses it, faith may again be considered in two ways, since the act of faith proceeds from the intellect and also from the will, as we said in Q. 2, Arts. 1 and 2, and in Q. 4, Art. 2. Faith may accordingly be said to be greater in one man than in another either when there is greater certainty and firmness on the part of the intellect, or when there is greater readiness, devotion, or confidence on the part of the will.

On the first point: he who persistently disbelieves any one of the things contained in the faith does not possess the habit of faith. But he who does not believe all things explicitly, yet is prepared to believe all of them, does possess the habit of faith. In respect of the object of faith, therefore, one man can have greater faith than another, in as much as he believes more things explicitly, as we have said.

On the second point: it belongs to the very nature of faith to put the first truth before all other things. Yet some of those who put it before all other things submit to it with greater assurance and devotion than others. In this way, faith is greater in one than in another.

On the third point: the understanding of principles is due to human nature itself, which occurs in all men equally. But faith is due to the gift of grace, which is not given to all men equally, as we said in 12ae, Q. 112, Art. 4. We cannot then argue about them in the same way. Moreover, one man may know the truth of principles better than another, if he has more intelligence.

Question Six

THE CAUSE OF FAITH

We must now consider the cause of faith, concerning which there are two questions. 1. Whether faith is infused into man by God. 2. Whether unformed faith is a gift of God.

Article One

WHETHER FAITH IS INFUSED INTO MAN BY GOD

We proceed to the first article thus:

1. It seems that faith is not infused into man by God. For Augustine says (14 *De Trin.* 1): "by knowledge is faith begotten, nourished, defended, and strengthened in us." Now what is begotten in us by knowledge would seem to be acquired, rather than infused. Thus it appears that faith is not in us by divine infusion.

2. Again, what a man attains through hearing and seeing would seem to be acquired. Now a man comes to believe both through seeing miracles and through hearing the doctrine of the faith. Thus it is said in John 4:53: "So the father knew that it was at the same hour in which Jesus said unto him, Thy son liveth: and himself believed, and his whole house," and in Rom. 10:17: "faith cometh by hearing." Hence faith can be acquired.

3. Again, a man can acquire what depends on his will, and Augustine says that "faith depends on the will of those who believe" (*De Praed. Sanct.* 5). It follows that a man can acquire faith.

On the other hand: it is said in Eph. 2:8–9: "by grace are ye saved through faith; and that not of yourselves; it is the gift of God: . . . lest any man should boast."

I answer: for faith, two things are required. In the first place, the things which a man is to believe must be proposed to him. This is necessary if anything is to be believed explicitly. Secondly, the believer must give his assent to what is proposed. Now faith is bound to be from God as regards the first of these conditions. For the things of faith are beyond human reason, so that a man cannot know them unless God reveals them. They are revealed by God immediately to some, such as the apostles and the prophets, and mediately to others, through preachers of the faith who are sent by God according to Rom. 10:15: "And how shall they preach except they be sent?" The cause of the believer's assent to the things of faith is twofold. There is in the first place an external cause which induces him to believe, such as the sight of a miracle, or the persuasion of another who leads him to the faith. But neither of these is a sufficient cause. For of those who see one and the same miracle, or who hear the same prophecy, some will believe and others will not believe. We

286

must therefore recognize that there is also an inward cause, which moves a man from within to assent to the things of faith.

The Pelagians attributed this inward cause solely to a man's own free will, and said accordingly that the beginning of faith lies with ourselves, since we prepare ourselves to assent to the things of faith, although the consummation of faith lies with God, who proposes to us such things as we ought to believe. But this is false. For when a man gives his assent to the things of faith, he is raised above his own nature, and this is possible only through a supernatural principle which moves him from within. This principle is God. The assent of faith, which is the principal act of faith, is therefore due to God, who moves us inwardly through grace.

On the first point: faith is begotten by knowledge, and is nourished by the external persuasion which knowledge provides. But the principal and proper cause of faith is that which inwardly moves us to give our assent.

On the second point: this reasoning argues from the cause whereby the things of faith are externally proposed, or whereby one is persuaded to believe them by means of word or deed.

On the third point: to believe does depend on the will of those who believe. But a man's will must be prepared by God through grace, in order that he may be raised to things which are above nature, as we have said, and as we said also in Q. 2, Art. 3.

Article Two

WHETHER UNFORMED FAITH IS A GIFT OF GOD

We proceed to the second article thus:

1. It seems that unformed faith is not a gift of God. For it is said in Deut. 32:4: "His work is perfect." But unformed faith is imperfect. It is therefore not the work of God.

2. Again, just as an act is said to be deformed because it lacks the form which it ought to have, so is faith said to be unformed because it lacks the form which it ought to have. Now it was said in 12ae, Q. 79, Art. 2, that a deformed act of sin is not due to God. Neither then is unformed faith due to God.

3. Again, whomsoever God heals, he heals completely. For it is said in John 7:23: "If a man on the sabbath day receive circumcision, that the law of Moses should not be broken; are ye angry at me, because I have made a man every whit whole on the sabbath day?" Now by faith a man is healed of infidelity.

Hence anyone who receives the gift of faith from God is healed of all his sins. But this is possible only by means of faith which is formed. Formed faith only, therefore, is a gift of God. It follows that unformed faith is not a gift of God.

On the other hand: the gloss by Augustine on I Cor., ch. 13, says that "the faith which lacks charity is a gift of God" (*Sermo* 5).

I answer: lack of form is a kind of privation. A privation sometimes belongs to the specific nature of a thing. At other times it does not, but is merely added to something which already conforms to its specific nature. For example, deficiency in the balance of the fluids of the body belongs to the specific nature of sickness, whereas darkness does not belong to the specific nature of the atmosphere, but is something added to it. Now when we assign a cause to anything, what we understand to be assigned as its cause is that which causes the thing to be of its own specific nature. Hence we cannot say that anything is the cause of a thing to whose specific nature a privation belongs, if it is not the cause of this privation itself. We cannot, for example, say that anything is the cause of bodily sickness, if it is not the cause of unbalance in the fluids of the body. On the other hand, we can say that something is the cause of the atmosphere, even if it is not the cause of its darkness.

Now in faith, lack of form is not a privation which belongs to the specific nature of faith itself. For faith is said to be unformed because it lacks a form which is added to it from without, as we said in Q. 4, Art. 4. The cause of unformed faith is therefore that which is the cause of faith simply as faith, and this, as we said in the preceding article, is God. Unformed faith is therefore a gift of God.

On the first point: although unformed faith lacks the perfection which pertains to it as a virtue, it is nevertheless perfect in the perfection which suffices for the nature of faith.

On the second point: as we said in Pt. I, Q. 48, Art. 1, *ad* 2, and in 12ae, Q. 71, Art. 6, the deformity of an act belongs to its specific nature as a moral act. For an act is said to be deformed when it lacks the form which is intrinsically right for it, in view of the circumstances in which it is performed. Hence we cannot say that God is the cause of an act which is deformed, because he is not the cause of its deformity. But he is nevertheless the cause of the act, considered as an act. Or we may say that deformity not only implies lack of the form which a thing ought to have, but also implies a contrary disposition, so that deformity in an act is like falsehood in faith. Just as an act which is deformed is not due to God, neither is a faith which is false. But acts which are good in themselves are due to God even when they lack the form of charity, as often happens among sinners; just as unformed faith is due to God.

On the third point: one who receives faith from God without receiving charity is not entirely healed of infidelity, since the guilt of his former infidelity is not removed. He is healed partially only, so that he ceases from such sin. For it often happens that a man desists from one act of sin through God causing him to do so, but is prevented from desisting from another by the impulsion of his own iniquity. Thus God sometimes gives a man the gift of faith without the gift of charity, just as he gives to some men the gift of prophecy, or something similar, without charity.

Question Seven

THE EFFECT OF FAITH

We must now consider the effects of faith, concerning which there are two questions. 1. Whether fear is an effect of faith. 2. Whether purification of the heart is an effect of faith.

Article One

WHETHER FEAR IS AN EFFECT OF FAITH

We proceed to the first article thus:

1. It seems that fear is not an effect of faith. For an effect does not precede its cause. But fear precedes faith, since it is said in Ecclesiasticus 2:8: "Ye that fear God, believe in him." Hence fear is not an effect of faith.

2. Again, the same thing is not the cause of contrary effects. Now it was said in 12ae, Q. 23, Art. 2, that fear and hope are contraries, and the gloss on Matt. 1:2, "Abraham begat Isaac," says that "faith begets hope." It follows that faith is not the cause of fear.

3. Again, one contrary is not the cause of another. Now the object of faith is something good, namely, the first truth. But it was said in 12ae, Q. 18, Art. 2, that the object of fear is something evil,[1] while it was also affirmed in the same passage

[1] Cf. 22ae, Q. 19, Art. 1.

that actions take their species from their objects. It follows that faith is not the cause of fear.

On the other hand: it is said in James 2:19: "the devils also believe, and tremble."

I answer: fear is a movement of the appetitive power, as we said in 12ae, Q. 22, Art. 2, and Q. 42, Art. 1, and the principle of all appetitive movements is some good or evil which is apprehended. The principle of fear, as of all appetitive movements, must therefore be some apprehension. Now through faith we apprehend certain evils which follow divine judgment as punishments. In this way, faith is the cause of the servile fear whereby one fears the punishment of God. But it is also the cause of the filial fear whereby one fears to be separated from God, and whereby one does not presume to make oneself equal with God, but holds him in reverence. For by faith we know that God is great and good, that the worst evil is to be separated from him, and that it is evil to wish to be equal with God. Unformed faith is the cause of servile fear. Formed faith is the cause of filial fear, since it is through charity that faith causes a man to adhere to God, and to be subject to him.

On the first point: fear of God cannot always precede faith, since we would not fear God at all if we were entirely ignorant of the rewards and punishments which he disposes, and of which we learn through faith. But if there is already faith in some of the articles of faith, such as the divine excellence, the fear of reverence follows, through which in turn a man submits his intellect to God, thereby believing in all of the divine promises. Hence the passage quoted continues "and your reward will not become void."

On the second point: the same thing can be the cause of contraries in relation to contraries, though not in relation to the same thing. Thus faith begets hope by causing us to appreciate the rewards which God bestows on the just, and begets fear by causing us to appreciate the punishments which he wills to inflict on sinners.

On the third point: the primary and formal object of faith is something good, namely, the first truth. But the material object of faith includes what is evil, for example, that it is evil not to be subject to God, or to be separated from him; and that sinners will endure the evils of divine punishment. In this way, faith can be the cause of fear.

Article Two

WHETHER PURIFICATION OF THE HEART IS AN EFFECT OF FAITH

We proceed to the second article thus:

1. It seems that purification of the heart is not an effect of faith. Purity of heart pertains mainly to the affections. But faith is in the intellect. Hence faith does not cause purification of the heart.

2. Again, that which causes purification of the heart cannot exist together with impurity. But faith exists together with the impurity of sin, as is obvious in those whose faith is unformed. Hence faith does not purify the heart.

3. Again, if faith were to purify the heart in any way, it would purify the intellect especially. But faith does not purify the intellect of dimness, since it knows things darkly. Hence faith does not purify the heart in any way.

On the other hand: it is said by Peter (Acts 15:9): "purifying their hearts by faith."

I answer: the impurity of anything consists in its being mixed with meaner things. We do not say that silver is impure if it is mixed with gold, but only if it is mixed with lead, or with tin. Now it is obvious that a rational creature is of greater worth than all temporal and corporeal creatures. A rational creature therefore becomes impure if it subjects itself to temporal things through love of them. But when it turns to what is above itself, that is, to God, it is purified from this impurity by movement in the opposite direction. The first beginning of this movement is faith. As it is said in Heb. 11:6: "he that cometh to God must believe that he is." The first beginning of purification of the heart is therefore faith, which purifies from the impurity of error. If faith is itself perfected by being brought to its form through charity, it purifies the heart completely.

On the first point: things which are in the intellect are the principles of things which are in the affections, since it is good understood that moves the affections.

On the second point: even unformed faith excludes such impurity as is opposed to itself, such as the impurity of error, which is due to the inordinate adherence of the human intellect to meaner things, and to the accompanying desire to measure divine things in terms of sensible things. But when faith is brought to its form by charity it tolerates no impurity, since "love covereth all sins," [1] as it is said in Prov. 10:12.

On the third point: the dimness of faith has nothing to do with the impurity of guilt, but is due to the natural limitation of the intellect of man in his present state.

[1] Migne: "charity makes all things to be loved."

Treatise on the Theological Virtues

II. On Hope. *Secunda Secundae, Questions 17–21*

Question Seventeen

OF HOPE, CONSIDERED IN ITSELF

A FTER CONSIDERING FAITH, WE MUST NOW CONSIDER
hope. We shall first consider hope itself, concerning
which there are eight questions. 1. Whether hope is a
virtue. 2. Whether the object of hope is eternal blessedness.
3. Whether by the virtue of hope one man can hope for the
blessedness of another. 4. Whether a man may legitimately
hope in man. 5. Whether hope is a theological virtue. 6. Of the
distinction of hope from the other theological virtues. 7. How
hope is related to faith. 8. How it is related to charity.

Article One

WHETHER HOPE IS A VIRTUE

We proceed to the first article thus:

1. It seems that hope is not a virtue. No one makes bad
use of a virtue, as Augustine says (2 *De Lib. Arb.* 18). But one
can make bad use of hope, since the passion of hope has extremes as well as a mean, just like other passions. It follows
that hope is not a virtue.

2. Again, no virtue is the result of merits, since Augustine
says that "God works virtue in us without ourselves" (on
Ps. 119, *Feci Iudicium*; and *De Grat. et Lib. Arb.* 17). But the
Master says that hope is the result of grace and of merits (3
Sent., Dist. 26). It follows that hope is not a virtue.

3. Again, it is said in 7 *Physics*, texts 17 and 18 that "virtue
is the disposition of the perfect." But hope is the disposition of
the imperfect, namely, of him who lacks what he hopes for. It
follows that hope is not a virtue.

On the other hand: Gregory says (1 *Moral.* 12, *olim* 28) that the three daughters of Job signify these three virtues: faith, hope, and charity. Hope is therefore a virtue.

I answer: as the philosopher says in 2 *Ethics* 6, "the virtue of each thing is that which makes its subject good, and its work good." Wherever a man's action is found to be good, therefore, it must correspond to some human virtue. Now with all things subject to rule and measure, a thing is called good because it attains its own proper rule. Thus we say that a garment is good when it neither exceeds nor falls short of its due measure. But there is a twofold measure of human actions, as we said in Q. 8, Art. 3. One is proximate and homogeneous, namely, reason. The other is supreme and transcendent, namely, God. Hence every human action which attains to reason, or to God himself, is good. The act of hope of which we are speaking attains to God. As we said when dealing with the passion of hope in 12ae, Q. 40, Art. 1, the object of hope is a future good which is difficult to obtain, yet possible. But there are two ways in which a thing may be possible for us. It may be possible through ourselves alone, or possible through others, as is said in 3 *Ethics* 3. When we hope for something which is possible for us through divine help, our hope attains to God, on whose help it relies. Hope is therefore clearly a virtue, since it makes a man's action good, and causes it to attain its due rule.

On the first point: in regard to the passions, the mean of virtue consists in attaining right reason. It is indeed in this that the essence of virtue consists. In regard to hope also, therefore, the good of virtue consists in a man's attaining his right rule, which is God, by way of hoping. Now no man can make bad use of the hope which attains God, any more than he can make bad use of a moral virtue which attains reason, since so to attain is itself a good use of virtue. But in any case the hope of which we are speaking is a habit of mind, not a passion, as we shall show in Q. 18, Art. 1.

On the second point: it is in respect of the thing hoped for that hope is said to be the result of merits, in the sense that one hopes to attain blessedness through grace and merits. Or this may be said of hope that is formed. But the habit of hope whereby one hopes for blessedness is not caused by merits. It is entirely the result of grace.

On the third point: he who hopes is indeed imperfect in respect of that which he hopes to obtain but does not yet possess. But he is perfect in that he already attains his proper rule, that is, God, on whose help he relies.

Article Two

WHETHER ETERNAL BLESSEDNESS IS THE PROPER OBJECT OF HOPE

We proceed to the second article thus:

1. It seems that eternal blessedness is not the proper object of hope. A man does not hope for that which is beyond every movement of his soul, since the action of hope is itself a movement of the soul. Now eternal blessedness is beyond every movement of the human soul, since the apostle says in I Cor. 2:9: "neither have entered into the heart of man . . ." It follows that blessedness is not the proper object of hope.

2. Again, petition is an expression of hope, since it is said in Ps. 37:5: "Commit thy way unto the Lord; trust also in him, and he shall bring it to pass." But it is plain from the Lord's Prayer that one may lawfully pray to God not only for eternal blessedness, but also for the good things of this present life, both spiritual and temporal, and for deliverance from evils which will have no place in eternal blessedness. It follows that eternal blessedness is not the proper object of hope.

3. Again, the object of hope is the arduous. But many other things are arduous for man, besides eternal blessedness. It follows that eternal blessedness is not the proper object of hope.

On the other hand: the apostle says in Heb. 6:19: "we have hope . . . which entereth," that is, which causes us to enter, "into that within the veil," that is, into heavenly blessedness, as the gloss says. The object of hope is therefore eternal blessedness.

I answer: as we said in the preceding article, the hope of which we are speaking attains to God, depending on his help in order to obtain the good for which it hopes. Now an effect must be proportionate to its cause. The good which we should properly and principally hope to receive from God is therefore the infinite good which is proportionate to the power of God who helps us, since it is proper to infinite power to lead to infinite good. This good is eternal life, which consists in the enjoyment of God. We ought indeed to hope for nothing less than himself from God, since the goodness by which he bestows good things on a creature is nothing less than his essence. The proper and principal object of hope is therefore eternal blessedness.

On the first point: eternal blessedness does not enter into the heart of man perfectly, in such a way that the wayfarer may know what it is, or of what kind it is. But a man can apprehend it under the universal idea of perfect good, and in this way the movement of hope arises. It is therefore with point that the apostle says in Heb. 6:19: "we have hope . . . which entereth into that within the veil," since what we hope for is yet veiled, as it were.

On the second point: we ought not to pray to God for any other good things unless they relate to eternal blessedness. Hope is therefore concerned principally with eternal blessedness, and secondarily with other things which are sought of God for the sake of it, just as faith also is concerned principally with such things as relate to God, as we said in Q. 1, Art. 1.

On the third point: all other things seem small to one who sets his heart on something great. To one who hopes for eternal life, therefore, nothing else appears arduous in comparison with this hope. But some other things can yet be arduous in relation to the capacity of him who hopes. There can accordingly be hope in regard to them, as things subservient to the principal object of hope.

Article Three

WHETHER ONE CAN HOPE FOR THE ETERNAL BLESSEDNESS OF ANOTHER

We proceed to the third article thus:

1. It seems that one can hope for the eternal blessedness of another. For the apostle says in Phil. 1:6: "Being confident of this very thing, that he which hath begun a good work in you will perform [1] it until the day of Jesus Christ." Now the perfection of that day will be eternal blessedness. One can therefore hope for the eternal blessedness of another.

2. Again, that for which we pray to God, we hope to obtain from him. We pray that God should bring others to eternal blessedness, in accordance with James 5:16: "pray for one another, that ye may be healed." [2] We can therefore hope for the eternal blessedness of others.

3. Again, hope and despair refer to the same thing. Now one can despair of the eternal blessedness of another, otherwise there would have been no point in Augustine's saying that one should despair of no man while he lives (*De Verb. Dom., Sermo*

1 Migne: "will perfect it."
2 Migne: "that ye may be saved."

71, cap. 13). One can therefore hope for eternal life for another.

On the other hand: Augustine says (*Enchirid.* 8): "hope is only of such things as pertain to him who is said to hope for them."

I answer: there are two ways in which one can hope for something. One can hope for something absolutely, such hope being always for an arduous good which pertains to oneself. But one can also hope for something if something else is presupposed, and in this way one can hope for what pertains to another. To make this clear, we must observe that love and hope differ in this, that love denotes a union of the lover with the loved one, whereas hope denotes a movement or projection of one's desire towards an arduous good. Now a union is between things which are distinct. Love can therefore be directly towards another person whom one unites to oneself in love, and whom one looks upon as oneself. A movement, on the other hand, is always towards a term which is its own, and which is related to that which moves. For this reason, hope is directly concerned with a good which is one's own, not with a good which pertains to another. But if it is presupposed that one is united to another in love, one can then hope and desire something for the other as if for oneself. In this way one can hope for eternal life for another, in so far as one is united to him in love. It is by the same virtue of hope that one hopes on behalf of oneself and on behalf of another, just as it is by the same virtue of charity that one loves God, oneself, and one's neighbour.

The answers to the objections are now obvious.

Article Four

WHETHER ONE MAY LAWFULLY HOPE IN MAN

We proceed to the fourth article thus:

1. It seems that one may lawfully hope in man. The object of hope is indeed eternal blessedness. But we are helped to attain eternal blessedness by the patronage of the saints, since Gregory says that "predestination is furthered by the prayers of the saints" (1 *Dialog.*, cap. 8). One may therefore hope in man.

2. Again, if it is not lawful to hope in man, it should not be regarded as a vice in a man, that one cannot hope in him. But this seems to have been regarded as a vice in some, as appears from Jer. 9:4: "Take ye heed every one of his neighbour, and

trust ye not in any brother." It is therefore lawful that one should hope in man.

3. Again, it was said in Art. 2 that petition is an expression of hope. Now a man may lawfully petition something of a man. It follows that he may lawfully hope in him.

On the other hand: it is said in Jer. 17:5: "Cursed be the man that trusteth in man."

I answer: as we said in 12ae, Q. 40, Art. 7, hope refers to two things, namely, to the good which one hopes to obtain, and to the help whereby one hopes to obtain it. The good which one hopes to obtain has the nature of a final cause.[1] The help whereby one hopes to obtain it has the nature of an efficient cause. Now each of these types of cause contains what is principal and what is secondary. The principal end is the final end, while the secondary end is such good as leads to the final end. Similarly, the principal efficient causal agent is the first agent, while the secondary efficient cause is the secondary and instrumental agent.

Now hope refers to eternal blessedness as the final end, and refers to God's help as the first cause which leads to it. Hence just as it is unlawful to hope for any good other than blessedness as a final end, but lawful to hope for it only as a means to final blessedness, so is it unlawful to hope in any man or any creature as if it were the first cause which brings us to blessedness. But one may lawfully hope in a man or in a creature as a secondary and instrumental agent, which helps one to obtain such good things as serve as a means to blessedness. It is in this way that we turn to the saints, and in this way that we petition things of men. This also explains why those are blamed who cannot be trusted to help.

The answers to the objections are now obvious.

Article Five

WHETHER HOPE IS A THEOLOGICAL VIRTUE

We proceed to the fifth article thus:

1. It seems that hope is not a theological virtue. A theological virtue is a virtue which has God as its object. But hope has not only God as its object, but other things also, which we hope to obtain from him. It follows that hope is not a theological virtue.

2. Again, it was said in 12ae, Q. 64, Art. 4, that a theological

[1] Cf. 22ae, Q. 27, Art. 3, infra.

virtue is not a mean between two vices. But hope is a mean between presumption and despair. It is therefore not a theological virtue.

3. Again, expectation pertains to longanimity, which is a species of fortitude. Now hope is a kind of expectation. It seems, therefore, that hope is a moral virtue, not a theological virtue.

4. Again, the object of hope is the arduous. To aim at the arduous is magnanimous, and magnanimity is a moral virtue. Hope is therefore a moral virtue, not a theological virtue.

On the other hand: in I Cor., ch. 13, hope is numbered together with faith and charity, which are theological virtues.

I answer: a genus is divided according to the natures which differentiate its species. In order to determine the division of virtue to which hope belongs, therefore, we must attend to the source from which it derives its character as a virtue. We said in the first article that hope has the character of a virtue because it attains the supreme rule of human actions. Hope attains this rule as its first efficient cause, in so far as it relies on its help. It also attains this rule as its ultimate final cause, in so far as it looks for blessedness in the enjoyment of it. This makes it plain that in so far as hope is a virtue, its principal object is God. Now it is the very meaning of a theological virtue, that it has God as its object, as we said in 12ae, Q. 62, Art. 1. It is obvious, then, that hope is a theological virtue.

On the first point: whatever else hope expects to obtain, it hopes for as subordinate to God as its final end, or to God as its first efficient cause, as we have said above.

On the second point: there is a mean in things which are ruled and measured, according to which they attain their proper rule and measure. Thus a thing is excessive if it exceeds its rule, and defective if it falls short of its rule. But there is neither a mean nor extremes in the rule or the measure itself. Now the proper object with which a moral virtue is concerned comprises things which are regulated by reason. It is therefore essentially the nature of a moral virtue to respect the mean in regard to its proper object. But the proper object with which a theological virtue is concerned is the first rule itself, which is not regulated by any other rule. It is consequently not essentially the nature of a theological virtue to respect a mean, although it may do so accidentally in regard to that which is subservient to its principal object. There can thus be neither a mean nor extremes in the trust of faith in the first truth, in which no man can trust too much, although there can be a mean and extremes in regard to the things which faith believes, since a truth is midway between two falsehoods. Similarly, there is neither a mean nor extremes in hope in regard to its principal object, since no man can trust too much in the help of God. There can be a mean and extremes, however, in regard to the things which one confidently expects to obtain, since one may either presume to obtain things which exceed what is proportionate to oneself, or despair of things which are proportionate to oneself.

On the third point: the expectation attributed to hope by definition does not imply deferment, as does the expectation of longanimity. It implies regard for divine help, whether what is hoped for be deferred or not.

On the fourth point: while magnanimity attempts what is arduous, it hopes to attain what is within one's own power. It is thus properly concerned in the doing of great things. But hope, as a theological virtue, looks upon the arduous as something to be attained through the help of another, as we said in the first article.

Article Six

WHETHER HOPE IS DISTINCT FROM THE OTHER THEOLOGICAL
VIRTUES

We proceed to the sixth article thus:

1. It seems that hope is not distinct from the other theological virtues. It was said in 12ae, Q. 54, Art. 2, that a habit is distinguished by its object. But the object of hope is identical with that of the other theological virtues. It follows that hope is not distinct from the other theological virtues.

2. Again, in the symbol of the faith, by which we profess our faith, it is said: "And I look for the Resurrection of the dead, And the life of the world to come." Now it was said in the preceding article that to look for future blessedness pertains to hope. It follows that hope is not distinct from faith.

3. Again, by hope man tends to God. But this properly pertains to charity. It follows that hope is not distinct from charity.

On the other hand: where there is no distinction, there is no number. But hope is numbered with the other theological virtues. For Gregory says that there are three virtues: hope, faith, and charity (1 *Moral.* 16). Hope is therefore a virtue distinct from other theological virtues.

I answer: a virtue is said to be theological on the ground that it has God as the object to which it adheres. Now there are two ways in which one may adhere to something. One may adhere to it for its own sake. One may also adhere to it for the sake of something else which is thereby attained. Charity causes a man to adhere to God for his own sake, uniting his mind to God through the affection of love. Hope and faith, on the other hand, cause him to adhere to God as the principle whereby other things are vouchsafed to us. For it is through God that we have knowledge of the truth, and through God that we attain to the perfection of goodness. Faith causes a man to adhere to God as the principle whereby we know the truth, since we believe those things to be true which God tells us. Hope causes him to adhere to God as the principle whereby we attain to the perfection of goodness, since by hope we depend on God's help in order to obtain blessedness.

On the first point: as we have said, God is the object of these virtues under different aspects. A different aspect of its object suffices to distinguish a habit, as we maintained in 12ae, Q. 54, Art. 2.

On the second point: expectation is mentioned in the symbol not because it is the proper act of faith, but inasmuch as the act of hope presupposes faith, as we shall show in the next article. The act of faith is manifest in the act of hope.

On the third point: hope causes a man to tend to God as the final good to be obtained, and as a helper strong to aid; whereas charity properly causes him to tend to God by uniting his affection to God, so that he lives for God and not for himself.

Article Seven

WHETHER HOPE PRECEDES FAITH

We proceed to the seventh article thus:

1. It seems that hope precedes faith. For the gloss on Ps. 37:3, "Trust in the Lord, and do good," says that "hope is the entrance to faith, and the beginning of salvation." But salvation is through faith, by which we are justified. Hence hope precedes faith.

2. Again, what is used in the definition of anything ought to be prior to it, and better known. Now hope is used in the definition of faith which is given in Heb. 11:1: "Faith is the substance of things hoped for." It is therefore prior to faith.

3. Again, hope precedes a meritorious act. For the apostle says in I Cor. 9:10: "he that ploweth should plow in hope." Now the act of faith is meritorious. Hence hope precedes faith.

On the other hand: it is said in Matt. 1:2: "Abraham begat Isaac," that is, "faith begat hope," as the gloss says.

I answer: in the absolute sense, faith precedes hope. The object of hope is a future good which is arduous yet possible to obtain. It is therefore necessary that the object of hope should be proposed to a man as something which is possible, in order that he may hope. Now as we said in the preceding article, the object of hope is in one way eternal blessedness, while in another way it is the divine help. These things are both proposed to us through faith, which enables us to know that it is possible to attain eternal life, and to know also that divine help has been prepared for us to this end, according to Heb. 11:6: "he that cometh to God must believe that he is, and that he is a rewarder of them that diligently seek him." This makes it clear that faith precedes hope.

On the first point: as the gloss says also, hope is said to be the "entrance to faith" in the sense that it is the entrance to the thing believed, since by hope we enter in to see what it is that we believe.

On the second point: the definition of faith makes use of "things hoped for" because the proper object of faith is not seen in itself. For this reason it was necessary to make use of a circumlocution, in terms of a consequence of faith.

On the third point: hope does not precede every meritorious act. It is enough if it accompanies such an act, or follows it.

Article Eight

WHETHER CHARITY IS PRIOR TO HOPE

We proceed to the eighth article thus:

1. It seems that charity is prior to hope. For on Luke 17:6, "If ye had faith as a grain of mustard seed . . .," the gloss by Ambrose says: "From faith issues charity, and from charity issues hope." But faith is prior to charity. Hence charity is prior to hope.

2. Again, Augustine says (14 *De Civ. Dei.* 9): "good movements and affections are derived from love, and from holy charity." Now to hope, as an act of hope, is a good movement of the soul. It is therefore derived from charity.

3. Again, the Master says that hope proceeds from merits, which not only precede the thing hoped for, but precede hope itself; also that charity precedes hope in the order of nature (3 *Sent.*, *Dist.* 26). Hence charity is prior to hope.

On the other hand: the apostle says (I Tim. 1:5): "Now the end of the commandment is charity out of a pure heart, and of a good conscience," that is, as the gloss says, "and of hope." Hope is therefore prior to charity.

I answer: there are two kinds of order. There is the order of generation and of nature,[1] according to which the imperfect is prior to the perfect. There is also the order of perfection and of form, according to which the perfect is naturally prior to the imperfect. According to the first of these orders, hope is prior to charity. This is obvious, since hope and every appetitive movement is derived from love, as we said in 12ae, Q. 55, Arts. 1 and 2, when speaking of the passions.

But love may be either perfect or imperfect. Perfect love is that wherewith a thing is loved for its own sake, as for example when one wills good for someone for his own sake, as a man loves a friend. Imperfect love, on the other hand, is love wherewith one loves a thing not for its own sake, but in order that one may have the good of it for oneself, as a man loves a thing which he covets. Now perfect love pertains to charity, which adheres to God for his own sake. But imperfect love pertains to hope, since one who hopes intends to obtain something for himself.

Thus according to the order of generation, hope is prior to charity. For just as a man is led to love God through desisting from sin for fear of being punished by him (*Tract. 9 in Joan.*), so also does hope engender charity, since one who hopes to be rewarded by God may come to love God and to obey his commandments. But charity is naturally prior according to the order of perfection. For this reason, hope is made more perfect by the presence of charity. Thus we hope supremely when we hope on behalf of our friends. It is in this way that "hope issues from charity," as Ambrose says.

The answer to the first point is thus obvious.

On the second point: hope and every appetitive movement of the soul is derived from love of some kind, since one loves the good for which one hopes. Not every hope, however, is derived from charity, but only the movement of hope that is formed, whereby one hopes for some good from God as a friend.

On the third point: the Master is speaking of hope that is formed, which is naturally preceded by charity, and also by the merits which result from charity.

[1] Nicolaius: *materiae* (for *naturae*).

Question Eighteen

THE SUBJECT OF HOPE

We must now consider the subject of hope, concerning which there are four questions. 1. Whether the virtue of hope is in the will as its subject. 2. Whether there is hope in the blessed. 3. Whether there is hope in the damned. 4. Whether the hope of wayfarers is certain.

Article One

WHETHER HOPE IS IN THE WILL AS ITS SUBJECT

We proceed to the first article thus:

1. It seems that hope is not in the will as its subject. It was said in the first article of the preceding question, and also in 12ae, Q. 40, Art. 1, that the object of hope is an arduous good. Now the arduous is not the object of the will, but of the irascible element. Hope is therefore not in the will, but in the irascible element.

2. Again, where one thing is sufficient, it is superfluous to add another. Now charity, which is the most perfect of the virtues, is sufficient to make the power of the will perfect. It follows that hope is not in the will.

3. Again, the same power cannot perform two acts simultaneously. The intellect, for example, cannot understand many things simultaneously. Now an act of hope can be simultaneous with an act of charity, and since the act of charity clearly belongs to the will, it follows that the act of hope does not belong to this same power. Thus hope is not in the will.

On the other hand: in 14 *De Trin.* 3 and 6, Augustine makes it clear that it is only in so far as it is composed of memory, understanding, and will that the soul can apprehend God. Now hope is a theological virtue, having God as its object. But it is neither in the memory nor in the understanding. It remains that hope is in the will as its subject.

I answer: habits are known through their acts, as is plain from what we said in Q. 4, Art. 1, and in Pt. I, Q. 87, Art. 2. Now the act of hope is a movement of the appetitive part of the soul, since its object is the good. But there are two kinds of appetite in man. There is the sensitive appetite, which includes both the irascible and concupiscible elements, and there is also the intellectual appetite which we call the will, as we said in Q. 82, Art. 5. The movements which belong to the lower appetite are mixed with passion, while the movements of the higher appetite are free from passion, as we said in Pt. I, Q. 85, Art. 5 *ad* 1, and in 12ae, Q. 22, Art. 3 *ad* 3. The act of the virtue of hope cannot belong to the sensitive appetite, since the good which is its principal object is not a sensible good, but a divine good. The subject of hope is therefore the higher appetite which we call the will, not the lower appetite to which the irascible element pertains.

On the first point: the object of the irascible element is something which is sensible and arduous. The object of hope is something which is intelligible and arduous, or rather, something which transcends the intellect.

On the second point: charity is sufficient to perfect the will in respect of one action, which is to love. But another virtue is required to perfect it in respect of its other action, which is to hope.

On the third point: it is clear from what we said in Q. 17, Art. 8, that the movement of hope and the movement of charity relate to the same thing. There is therefore no reason why both movements should not belong to the same power simultaneously. The intellect can likewise understand many things simultaneously, provided that they relate to the same thing, as we said in Pt. I, Q. 85, Art. 4.

Article Two

WHETHER THERE IS HOPE IN THE BLESSED

We proceed to the second article thus:

1. It seems that there is hope in the blessed. Christ was the perfect comprehensor from the moment of his conception, and he had hope, since it is said in his person in Ps. 31:1: "In thee, O Lord, have I hoped," as the gloss expounds it. There can therefore be hope in the blessed.

2. Again, just as to obtain blessedness is an arduous good, so is to continue in blessedness. Men hope to obtain blessedness before they obtain it. They can therefore hope to continue in blessedness after they obtain it.

3. Again, it was said in Art. 3 of the preceding question that by the virtue of hope one can hope for blessedness for others as well as for oneself. Now in heaven the blessed hope for the blessedness of others, since otherwise they would not pray for them. There can therefore be hope in the blessed.

4. Again, the blessedness of the saints means glory of the body as well as of the soul. But it appears from Rev., ch. 6, and also from what Augustine says in 12 *De Gen. ad Litt.* 35, that the souls of the saints in heaven still await the glory of the body. There can therefore be hope in the blessed.

On the other hand: the apostle says in Rom. 8:24: "for what a man seeth, why doth he yet hope for?" The blessed enjoy the vision of God. There is therefore no place in them for hope.

I answer: if that which determines the species of a thing is taken away, its species is taken away, and it cannot continue to be of the same species, any more than a natural body whose form has been removed. Now hope, like the other virtues, derives its species from its principal object, as we said in Q. 17, Arts. 5 and 6, and in Pt. I, Q. 54, Art. 2, and its principal object is eternal blessedness as possible through divine help, as we said in Q. 17, Arts. 1 and 2. But a good which is arduous yet possible can be hoped for only when it belongs to the future. There cannot then be hope for blessedness when it is no longer future, but present. Hope, like faith, is therefore done away in heaven, and there can be neither hope nor faith in the blessed.

On the first point: although Christ was a comprehensor, and therefore blessed in the enjoyment of God, he was nevertheless a wayfarer in respect of the passibility of nature, while subject to nature. He could therefore hope for the glory of impassibility and immortality. But he would not do so by the virtue of hope, the principal object of which is not the glory of the body, but the enjoyment of God.

On the second point: the blessedness of the saints is called eternal life because the enjoyment of God makes them in a manner partakers of the divine eternity, which transcends all time. There is therefore no distinction of past, present, and future in the continuation of blessedness. Hence the blessed do not hope for the continuation of blessedness, but have blessedness itself, to which futurity is not applicable.

On the third point: so long as the virtue of hope endures, it is by the same hope that one hopes for blessedness for oneself and for others. But when the hope with which the blessed hoped for blessedness for themselves is done away, they hope for blessedness for others by the love of charity, rather than by the virtue of hope. In a similar way, although one who has charity loves both God and his neighbour with the same charity, one who does not have charity can love his neighbour with a different kind of love.

On the fourth point: hope is a theological virtue which has God as its principal object. The principal object of hope is therefore the glory of the soul which consists of the enjoyment of God, not the glory of the body. Moreover, although glory of the body is arduous in relation to human nature, it is not arduous to one who has glory of the soul; not only because glory of the body is comparatively less than glory of the soul, but because one who has glory of the soul already possesses the sufficient cause of glory of the body.

Article Three

WHETHER THERE IS HOPE IN THE DAMNED

We proceed to the third article thus:

1. It seems that there is hope in the damned. For the devil is damned, and the prince of the damned, according to Matt. 25:41: "Depart from me, ye cursed, into everlasting fire, prepared for the devil and his angels." Yet the devil has hope, according to Job 41:9: "Behold, the hope of him is in vain." It seems, therefore, that the damned have hope.

2. Again, just as faith can be formed and unformed, so can hope. Now there can be unformed faith in devils and in the damned, according to James 2:19: "the devils also believe, and tremble." It seems, therefore, that there can be unformed hope in the damned.

3. Again, no man after death is credited either with a merit or with a demerit which he did not have in life, according to Eccl. 11:3: "and if the tree fall toward the south, or toward the north, in the place where the tree falleth, there it shall be." But many of the damned had hope in this life, and never despaired. They will therefore have hope in the life to come.

On the other hand: hope causes joy, according to Rom. 12:12: "Rejoicing in hope." Now the damned do not have joy, but rather sorrow and grief, according to Isa. 65:14: "Behold, my servants shall sing for joy of heart, but ye shall cry for sorrow of heart, and shall howl for vexation of spirit." There is therefore no hope in the damned.

I answer: it is of the essence of blessedness that the will should find rest in it. It is likewise of the essence of punishment that the will should find what is inflicted as punishment repugnant. Now when a thing is not known, the will can neither find rest in it nor find it repugnant. Hence Augustine says that the angels could not be perfectly content in their first state, before their confirmation or their lapse, because they were not aware of what was to happen to them (11 *De Gen. ad Lit.* 17, 19). For perfect and true blessedness, one must be certain of having it perpetually, since otherwise the will would not be at rest. Similarly, the eternity of damnation is part of the punishment of the damned, and it would not have the true nature of punishment unless it were repugnant to their will. Now the eternity of damnation would not be repugnant to their will unless the damned were aware that their punishment was everlasting. It is therefore a condition of their misery that they know that they can in no wise escape damnation and reach blessedness. As it is said in Job 15:22: "He believeth not that he shall return out of darkness." It is clear, then, that the damned cannot look upon blessedness as a good which is possible, any more than the blessed can look upon it as a good which is future. Hence there is hope neither in the blessed nor in the damned. Wayfarers, however, can hope both in this life and in purgatory, since in either state they look upon blessedness as a future good which it is possible to obtain.

On the first point: Gregory says that this is said of the devil's members, whose hope will be frustrated (33 *Moral.* 19). Or, if we take it as said of the devil himself, it may refer to the hope with which he hopes to vanquish the saints, in accordance with the preceding words: "he trusteth that he can draw up Jordan with his mouth" (Job 40:23). But this is not the hope of which we are speaking.

On the second point: as Augustine says: "faith is of things both bad and good, whether past, present, or future, whether pertaining to oneself or to another" (*Enchirid.* 8). But hope is only of good things of the future which pertain to oneself. It is therefore more possible that there should be unformed faith in the damned than that there should be unformed hope in them, since the good things of God are not possibilities for them, but things which they do not have.

On the third point: the absence of hope in the damned does not alter their demerit, any more than the cessation of hope in the blessed increases their merit. Such absence and cessation is due to the change of state in either case.

Article Four

WHETHER THE HOPE OF WAYFARERS IS CERTAIN

We proceed to the fourth article thus:

1. It seems that the hope of wayfarers is not certain. For hope is in the will as its subject, and certainty does not pertain to the will, but to the intellect. It follows that hope cannot be certain.

2. Again, it was said in Q. 17, Art. 4, that hope is the result of grace and of merits. But it was also said in 12ae, Q. 112, Art. 5, that in this life we cannot know with certainty that we have grace. It follows that the hope of wayfarers is not certain.

3. Again, there cannot be certainty of that which can fail. Now many hopeful wayfarers fail to attain blessedness. It follows that the hope of wayfarers is not certain.

On the other hand: the Master says that "hope is the sure expectation of future blessedness" (3 *Sent., Dist.* 26). This may also be taken to be the meaning of II Tim. 1:12: "I know whom I have believed, and am persuaded that he is able to keep that which I have committed unto him."

I answer: there are two ways in which certainty is found in something; essentially, and by participation. It is found in a cognitive power essentially, and by participation in everything that is moved infallibly to its end by a cognitive power. It is in this latter way that nature is said to be certain, since everything in nature is moved infallibly to its end by the divine intellect. It is in this way also that the moral virtues are said to be more certain in their operation than art, since they are moved to their actions by reason, after the manner of nature. In this way also, hope tends to its end with certainty, since it participates in the certainty of faith which is in the cognitive power.

The answer to the first point is thus obvious.

On the second point: hope does not depend principally on the grace which one already possesses, but on the divine omnipotence and mercy, through which even those who do not have grace may receive it, and thereby attain eternal life. Whosoever has faith is certain of the divine omnipotence and mercy.

On the third point: the reason why some who have hope fail to attain blessedness is that the deficiency of their free will puts an obstacle of sin in the way. Their failure is not due to any defect of the divine power or mercy on which hope is founded, and does not prejudice the certainty of hope.

Question Nineteen

THE GIFT OF FEAR

We must now consider the gift of fear, concerning which there are twelve questions. 1. Whether God ought to be feared. 2. Of the division of fear into filial, initial, servile, and worldly fear. 3. Whether worldly fear is always evil. 4. Whether servile fear is good. 5. Whether servile fear is substantially the same as filial fear. 6. Whether servile fear is excluded by charity. 7. Whether fear is the beginning of wisdom. 8. Whether initial fear is substantially the same as filial fear. 9. Whether fear is a gift of the Holy Spirit. 10. Whether fear increases together with charity. 11. Whether fear remains in heaven. 12. Of what corresponds to it in the beatitudes and the fruits.

Article One

WHETHER GOD CAN BE FEARED

We proceed to the first article thus:

1. It seems that God cannot be feared. It was said in 12ae, Q. 41, Arts. 2 and 3, that the object of fear is a future evil. But God is free of all evil, since he is goodness itself. It follows that God cannot be feared.

2. Again, fear is opposed to hope. But we hope in God. We cannot therefore fear him at the same time.

3. Again, the philosopher says that "we fear the things from which evil comes to us" (2 *Rhetoric* 5). Now evil does not come to us from God, but from ourselves, according to Hos. 13:9: "O Israel, thou hast destroyed thyself; but in me is thine help." It follows that God ought not to be feared.

On the other hand: it is said in Jer. 10:7: "Who would not fear thee, O King of nations?" and in Mal. 1:6: "if I be a master, where is my fear?"

I answer: just as hope has a twofold object, namely the future good which one hopes to obtain, and the help of another through which one hopes to obtain it, so also can fear have a twofold object, namely the evil which a man fears, and the source from which it can come to him. God cannot be the evil which a man fears, since he is goodness itself. But he can be the object of fear, in so far as some evil thing may threaten us from him, or from a divine source. The evil of punishment comes to

310

us from God. Yet this is not an evil absolutely, but only relatively Absolutely, it is a good. We say that a thing is good if it is ordered to an end, and evil implies privation of such order. Hence that is evil absolutely, which excludes the order which leads to the final end. This is the evil of guilt. The evil of punishment, on the other hand, is an evil only in so far as it deprives one of some particular good. It is a good absolutely, in so far as it belongs to the order which leads to the final end. Now the evil of guilt can come to us through our relationship to God, if we separate ourselves from him. In this way, God can and ought to be feared.

On the first point: this reasoning argues from the object of fear considered as the evil which a man fears.

On the second point: we must think both of the justice with which God punishes sinners and of the mercy with which he sets us free. The thought of God's justice causes us to fear, and the thought of his mercy causes us to hope. God is thus the object both of fear and of hope, under different aspects.

On the third point: God is not the source of the evil of guilt, but we ourselves, in so far as we separate ourselves from him. But God is the source of the evil of punishment in so far as it has the nature of a good, as a just punishment justly inflicted upon us. Punishment occurs, however, only because our sin merits it in the first place. Hence it is said in Wisdom 1:13: "God did not make death . . . but the ungodly have summoned it by their hands and by their words."

Article Two

Whether Fear is appropriately Divided into Filial, Initial, Servile, and Worldly Fear

We proceed to the second article thus:

1. It seems that fear is not appropriately divided into filial, initial, servile, and worldly fear. For in 2 *De Fid. Orth.* 15 the Damascene names six kinds of fear, including laziness and shame, which were discussed in 12ae, Q. 41, Art. 4. But these are not mentioned in this division, which therefore seems inappropriate.

2. Again, each of these fears is either good or evil. But there is a kind of fear, namely natural fear, which is neither good nor evil. For it is found in devils, according to James 2:19: "the devils believe, and tremble," and also in Christ, who "began to

be sore amazed, and very heavy," according to Mark 14:33. The foregoing division of fear is therefore inadequate.

3. Again, the relation of a son to his father, of a wife to her husband, and of a servant to his master, are severally different. Now filial fear, which is that of a son for his father, is distinguished from servile fear, which is that of a servant for his master. Chaste fear, which is seemingly that of a wife for her husband, ought then to be distinguished from all the fears mentioned.

4. Again, initial fear and worldly fear both fear punishment, as does servile fear. These should not therefore be distinguished from each other.

5. Again, fear is of evil things in the same way as desire is of good things. Now the "desire of the eyes," by which one desires worldly goods, is different from the "desire of the flesh," by which one desires one's own pleasure. Hence the worldly fear by which one fears to lose external good things is different from the human fear by which one fears harm to one's own person.

On the other hand: is the authority of the Master (3 *Sent.*, *Dist.* 34).

I answer: we are here speaking of fear in so far as we turn to God in fear, or turn away from him in fear. Now the object of fear is something which is evil. Hence a man sometimes turns away from God because he fears evil things. This is called human fear, or worldly fear. Sometimes, on the other hand, a man turns to God and adheres to him because he fears evil things. The evils which he then fears are of two kinds, namely, the evil of punishment, and the evil of guilt. If a man turns to God and adheres to him because he fears punishment, his fear is servile fear. If he does so because he fears guilt, his fear is filial fear, since what sons fear is to offend their fathers. Again, if a man turns to God for both of these reasons, his fear is initial fear, which is midway between these two. We have already discussed whether it is possible to fear the evil of guilt, in dealing with the passion of fear (12ae, Q. 42, Art. 3).[1]

On the first point: the Damascene divides fear as a passion of the soul. This division is concerned with fear in its relation to God, as we have said.

[1] The object of fear is a future evil which is not easily avoided. The evil of guilt is consequently an object of fear only in so far as it may be brought about through some external cause, such as the company of wicked men, not in so far as it may be directly due to a man's own will, which is its proper cause.

On the second point: moral good consists especially in turning to God, and moral evil in turning away from God. Hence each of the fears mentioned implies either moral evil or moral good. Natural fear is not included among these fears, because it is presupposed to moral good and evil.

On the third point: the relation of a servant to his master is founded on the power of a master over the servant who is subject to him. But the relation of a son to his father, or of a wife to her husband, is founded on the affection of the son who submits himself to his father, or on the affection of the wife who unites herself to her husband by the union of love. Filial fear and chaste fear therefore pertain to the same thing. For God is made our Father by reason of the love of charity, according to Rom. 8:15: "ye have received the Spirit of adoption, whereby we cry, Abba, Father," and is also called our spouse by reason of this same charity, as in II Cor. 11:2: "I have espoused you to one husband, that I may present you as a chaste virgin to Christ." Servile fear, on the other hand, pertains to something different, since it does not include charity in its definition.

On the fourth point: these three fears all fear punishment, but in different ways. Worldly or human fear fears the punishment which turns one away from God, and which the enemies of God sometimes inflict or threaten. Servile and initial fear, on the other hand, fear the punishment by which men are drawn to God, and which is inflicted or threatened by God. Servile fear fears such punishment principally, initial fear secondarily.

On the fifth point: it is all the same whether a man turns away from God through fear of losing his worldly goods or through fear for the safety of his body, because external goods pertain to the body. These fears are consequently here regarded as the same, even though the evils feared are different, just as the good things desired are different. Owing to their difference, the sins to which they give rise are different in species. They are nevertheless all alike in that they lead men away from God.

Article Three

WHETHER WORLDLY FEAR IS ALWAYS EVIL

We proceed to the third article thus:

1. It seems that worldly fear is not always evil. For regard for men appears to belong to human fear, and some are blamed because they have no regard for men, as for example the unjust

judge in Luke, ch. 18, who feared not God, neither regarded man. Hence it seems that worldly fear is not always evil.

2. Again, worldly fear, it seems, fears the punishments imposed by worldly powers. But we are induced by such punishments to do good, according to Rom. 13:3: "Wilt thou then not be afraid of the power? Do that which is good, and thou shalt have praise of the same." Hence worldly fear is not always evil.

3. Again, what is naturally in us does not seem to be evil, since what is natural is given us by God. Now it is natural that a man should fear harm to his own body, and natural also that he should fear loss of the worldly goods by which his present life is sustained. Hence it seems that worldly fear is not always evil.

On the other hand: our Lord says: "fear not them which kill the body," in Matt. 10:28, wherein worldly fear is forbidden. Now nothing is divinely forbidden unless it is evil. It follows that worldly fear is evil.

I answer: it is clear from what we said in 12ae, Q. 1, Art. 3; Q. 18, Art. 1; and Q. 54, Art. 2, that moral actions and moral habits take their name and their species from their objects. Now the proper object of an appetitive movement is the good which it seeks as an end, and each appetitive movement is accordingly named and specified by its proper end. It would therefore be a mistake for anyone to say that cupidity was love of work, on the ground that men work in order to serve their cupidity. For the covetous do not seek work as an end, but as the means to an end. They seek riches as an end, wherefore covetousness is rightly said to be the desire or love of riches, which is evil. Hence worldly love is correctly defined as the love whereby one trusts in the world as an end. It is consequently evil at all times. Now fear is born of love. For Augustine makes it clear that a man fears lest he should lose something which he loves (83 *Quaest. Evang.*, Q. 33). Worldly fear is therefore the fear which results from worldly love, as from an evil root. For this reason, worldly fear is always evil.

On the first point: there are two ways in which one may have regard for men. One may have regard for them because there is something divine in them, such as the good of grace or of virtue, or at least the image of God. Those who do not have regard for men in this way are blamed. But one may also have regard for men in their opposition to God. Those who do not have regard for men in this way are praised, as Elijah or Elisha is praised in Ecclesiasticus 48:12: "In his days he feared not the prince."

On the second point: when worldly powers impose punishments in order to restrain men from sin, they are ministers of God, according to Rom. 13:4: "for he is the minister of God, a revenger to execute wrath upon him that doeth evil." Fear of such worldly power is not worldly fear, but either servile or initial fear.

On the third point: it is natural that a man should fear harm to his own body, and the loss of temporal things. But to forsake justice on their account is contrary to natural reason. Hence the philosopher says in 3 *Ethics* I that there are certain things, such as deeds of sin, which a man ought not to contemplate on account of any fear, since to commit such sins is worse than to endure any penalties whatsoever.

Article Four

WHETHER SERVILE FEAR IS GOOD

We proceed to the fourth article thus:

1. It seems that servile fear is not good. If the use of a thing is evil, the thing itself is evil. Now the use of servile fear is evil, since "he who does something out of fear does not do well, even though that which is done be good," as the gloss says on Rom. ch. 8. It follows that servile fear is not good.

2. Again, that which has its origin in a root of sin is not good. Servile fear has its origin in a root of sin. For on Job 3:11, "Why died I not from the womb?" Gregory says: "when one fears the present punishment for one's sin, and has no love for the countenance of God which one has lost, one's fear is born of pride, not of humility." Hence servile fear is evil.

3. Again, servile fear seems to be opposed to chaste fear, just as mercenary love is opposed to the love of charity. Now mercenary love is always evil. Hence servile fear is likewise always evil.

On the other hand: nothing which is evil is of the Holy Spirit. But servile fear is of the Holy Spirit. For on Rom. 8:15, "For ye have not received the spirit of bondage again to fear . . .," the gloss (*ord. August. Tract. 9 in Joan.*) says: "It is the same Spirit which inspires both fears," that is, servile fear and chaste fear. Hence servile fear is not evil.

I answer: servile fear may be evil because of its servility. Since the free is "that which is the cause of itself," as it is said in 1 *Metaph.*, cap. 2, the slave is one who is not the cause of his own actions, but who is moved as by something external. Now whoever acts out of love acts as by himself, since he is moved to act by his own inclination. To act out of love is therefore opposed to the very nature of servility. Servile fear, in so far as it is servile, is therefore opposed to charity. Hence servile fear would be bound to be absolutely evil if servility belonged to its essential nature, just as adultery is absolutely evil because the element by which it is opposed to charity belongs to its specific nature. But the servility of which we are speaking does not belong to the specific nature of servile fear, any more than lack of form belongs to the specific nature of unformed faith. The species of a moral habit or action is determined by its object. But while its object is punishment, servile fear loves the good to which punishment is opposed, as the final end, and fears punishment consequentially, as the principal evil. So it is with one who does not have charity. Or again, servile fear may be directed to God as its end, in which case it does not fear punishment as a principal evil. Such fear is present in one who does have charity. For the species of a habit is not taken away by the circumstance that its object or end is subordinated to a more ultimate end. Servile fear is therefore substantially good, although its servility is evil.

On the first point: this saying of Augustine is to be understood as referring to one who does something out of servile fear because he is servile, that is, who has no love for justice, but merely fears punishment.

On the second point: servile fear is not born of pride in respect of its substance. But its servility is born of pride, in as much as a man is unwilling to subject his affection to the yoke of justice out of love.

On the third point: love is said to be mercenary when God is loved for the sake of temporal goods. This is in itself opposed to charity, and hence mercenary love is always evil. But fear which is substantially servile implies only fear of punishment, whether or not it be feared as the principal evil.

Article Five

WHETHER SERVILE FEAR IS SUBSTANTIALLY THE SAME AS FILIAL FEAR

We proceed to the fifth article thus:

1. It seems that servile fear is substantially the same as filial fear. Filial fear seems to be related to servile fear as formed faith is related to unformed faith, since the one is accompanied

by mortal sin, and the other is not. Now formed and unformed faith are substantially the same. Hence servile and filial fear are also substantially the same.

2. Again, habits are differentiated according to their objects. But servile and filial fear have the same object, since they both fear God. They are therefore substantially the same.

3. Again, just as a man hopes to enjoy God, and also to receive benefits from him, so does he fear to be separated from God, and also to be punished by him. Now the hope by which we hope to enjoy God is identical with the hope by which we hope to receive other benefits from him. The filial fear by which we fear to be separated from God is therefore identical with the servile fear by which we fear to be punished by him.

On the other hand: Augustine says that there are two kinds of fear, the one servile, the other filial or chaste (*Tract. 9 in Joan.*).

I answer: the proper object of fear is evil. But fears are bound to differ in kind if the evils which they fear are different, since actions and habits are distinguished according to their objects, as we said in 12ae, Q. 54, Art. 2. Now it is clear from what we said in Art. 2 that the evil of punishment, which is feared by servile fear, differs in kind from the evil of guilt, which is feared by filial fear. This makes it obvious that servile and filial fear are not substantially the same, but differ in their specific natures.

On the first point: formed and unformed faith do not differ in respect of their object, since they both believe in God, and believe God. They differ solely in what is extrinsic to them, namely, in the presence or absence of charity. Hence they do not differ in their substance. Servile and filial fear, on the other hand, differ in respect of their objects. They are therefore not of the same nature.

On the second point: servile and filial fear do not have regard to God in the same way. Servile fear looks upon God as the principal source of punishments. Filial fear does not look upon God as the principal source of guilt, but rather as the term from which it fears to be separated by guilt. These two fears do not then have the same specific nature on account of their object, since even natural movements have different specific natures if they are related to a term in different ways. The movement away from whiteness, for example, is not specifically the same as the movement towards it.

On the third point: hope looks to God principally, whether

in regard to the enjoyment of God or in regard to any other benefits. But it is not so with fear. We cannot therefore argue about them in the same way.

Article Six

WHETHER SERVILE FEAR REMAINS WHEN CHARITY IS PRESENT

We proceed to the sixth article thus:

1. It seems that servile fear does not remain when charity is present. For Augustine says: "when charity begins to dwell in us, it drives out the fear which has prepared a place for it" (*Tract 9 in Joan.*).

2. Again, "the love of God is shed abroad in our hearts by the Holy Ghost, which is given unto us" (Rom. 5:5). Now it is also said that "where the Spirit of the Lord is, there is liberty" (II Cor. 3:17), and since liberty excludes servitude, it seems that servile fear is expelled by the advent of charity.

3. Again, servile fear is caused by love of oneself, in as much as punishment diminishes the good of oneself. Now love to God expels love of oneself. It even causes one to despise oneself, according to Augustine, who says: "love of God to the contempt of self builds the city of God" (14 *De Civ. Dei.* 28; in *Ps. 65*). It seems, therefore, that servile fear is expelled by the advent of charity.

On the other hand: servile fear is a gift of the Holy Spirit, as was said in Art. 4. Now the gifts of the Holy Spirit are not taken away by the advent of charity, by which the Holy Spirit dwells in us. Hence servile fear is not taken away by the advent of charity.

I answer: servile fear is caused by love of oneself, since it is fear of the punishment which is detrimental to the good of oneself. Fear of punishment is therefore as compatible with charity as is love of oneself. For it amounts to the same thing whether a man desires his own good, or fears to be deprived of it.

There are three ways in which love of oneself may be related to charity. It may be opposed to charity, as it is when one makes love of oneself one's end. It may, on the other hand, be included within charity, as it is when a man loves himself for God's sake, and in God. It may, again, be distinct from charity and yet not opposed to charity, as for example when one loves oneself as one's own proper good, but without making one's own proper good one's end. One may similarly have a special love for one's neighbour, other than the love of charity which is founded upon God, and yet compatible with charity, loving him by reason of commodity, consanguinity, or some óther human circumstance.

Thus fear of punishment, likewise, may be included within charity. For to be separated from God is a kind of punishment, which charity naturally shuns. This pertains to chaste fear. It may also be opposed to charity, as it is when one fears punishment because it is contrary to one's own natural good, as the principal evil opposed to the good which one loves as an end. This fear of punishment is not compatible with charity. Again, fear of punishment may be substantially different from chaste fear. A man may fear punishment not because it means separation from God, but because it is harmful to his own good, yet without either making this good his end or consequently fearing the evil of punishment as the principal evil. Such fear of punishment is compatible with charity, but it is not called servile unless punishment is looked upon as the principal evil, as we explained in Arts. 2 and 3. Hence in so far as fear is servile, it cannot remain when charity is present. Yet the substance of fear can remain when charity is present, just as love of oneself can remain when charity is present.

On the first point: Augustine is here speaking of fear in so far as it is servile. The other two arguments speak of it in the same way.

Article Seven

WHETHER FEAR IS THE BEGINNING OF WISDOM

We proceed to the seventh article thus:

1. It seems that fear is not the beginning of wisdom. The beginning of a thing is a part of it. But fear is not a part of wisdom, since fear is in the appetitive power, whereas wisdom is in the intellectual power. Hence it seems that fear is not the beginning of wisdom.

2. Again, nothing is the beginning of itself. But it is said in Job 28:28: "Behold, the fear of the Lord, that is wisdom." Hence it seems that fear is not the beginning of wisdom.

3. Again, there is nothing prior to a beginning. But there is something prior to fear, since faith precedes fear. Hence it seems that fear is not the beginning of wisdom.

On the other hand: it is said in Ps. 111:10: "The fear of the Lord is the beginning of wisdom."

I answer: there are two ways in which we may say that something is the beginning of wisdom. We may mean that it is the beginning of wisdom in regard to its essence, or that it is the beginning of it in regard to its effect. We may similarly say that the principles upon which an art proceeds are the beginning of an art in regard to its essence, or again, that the foundation is the beginning of the art of building, since a builder begins his work with the foundation.

Now although wisdom is the knowledge of divine things, as we shall affirm later, we think of the knowledge of God in a different way from the philosophers. For us, life is ordained to the enjoyment of God, and ordered thereto by means of a certain participation in the divine nature through grace. Hence we do not think of wisdom merely as the knowledge of God, as do the philosophers. We think of it as directive of human life, which is ordered not only by human reasons, but by divine reasons also, as Augustine explains in 12 *De Trin.* 14.

It is therefore the first principles of wisdom that are the beginning of it in regard to its essence, and these are the articles of faith. In this way, accordingly, faith is said to be the beginning of wisdom. But in regard to its effect, the beginning of wisdom is that wherein wisdom begins to operate. In this way, fear is the beginning of wisdom, although servile fear is the beginning of it in a different way from filial fear. Servile fear is like an external principle which disposes one to wisdom, in as much as one is prepared for the effect of wisdom by refraining from sin through fear of punishment. As it is said in Ecclesiasticus 1:21: "The fear of the Lord driveth out sin." Chaste or filial fear, on the other hand, is the beginning of wisdom as the first effect of it. It pertains to wisdom to regulate human life according to divine reasons. Wisdom must therefore begin in this, that a man reverence God and submit himself to God. He will then be ruled by God in all things.

On the first point: this argument shows that fear is not the beginning of wisdom in regard to its essence.

On the second point: the fear of God is related to the whole of a human life which is ruled by God's wisdom, as is its root to a tree. Hence it is said in Ecclesiasticus 1:20: "The root of wisdom is to fear the Lord; for the branches thereof are longlived."

On the third point: as we have said above, faith is the beginning of wisdom in one way, and fear in another. Hence it is said in Ecclesiasticus 25:12: "The fear of God is the beginning of love; but the beginning of faith must be joined fast to it."

Article Eight

WHETHER INITIAL FEAR DIFFERS SUBSTANTIALLY FROM FILIAL FEAR

We proceed to the eighth article thus:

1. It seems that initial fear differs substantially from filial fear. For filial fear is caused by love, whereas initial fear is the beginning of love, according to Ecclesiasticus 25:12: "The fear of the Lord is the beginning of love." Initial fear is therefore other than filial fear.

2. Again, initial fear fears punishment, which is the object of servile fear. Thus it seems that initial fear is the same as servile fear. But servile fear is other than filial fear. Hence initial fear is substantially other than filial fear.

3. Again, a mean differs equally from both extremes. Now initial fear is a mean between servile fear and filial fear. It therefore differs from both of them.

On the other hand: the perfect and the imperfect do not diversify the substance of a thing. Now as Augustine explains (*Tract. 9 in Joan.*), initial and filial fear differ in respect of the perfection and the imperfection of charity. Hence initial fear does not differ substantially from filial fear.

I answer: fear is said to be initial because it is a beginning. Both servile fear and filial fear may in a manner be called initial, since each of them is in a manner the beginning of wisdom. Initial fear is not so called because it is distinct from servile and from filial fear. It is so called because it applies to the state of beginners, in whom filial fear is begun through the beginning of charity, but is not in them perfectly since they have not yet attained to the perfection of charity. Initial fear thus bears the same relation to filial fear as imperfect charity bears to perfect charity. Now perfect and imperfect charity do not differ in their substance, but only in their state. We must therefore say that initial fear, as we here understand it, does not differ substantially from filial fear.

On the first point: as Augustine says (*Tract. 9 in Joan.*), the fear which is the beginning of love is servile fear, which introduces charity, as the bristle introduces the thread. If this refers to initial fear, it means that fear is the beginning of love not absolutely, but in so far as it is the beginning of the state of perfect charity.

On the second point: initial fear does not fear punishment as its proper object. It fears punishment because something of servile fear is conjoined with it. When its servility has been removed, the substance of servile fear remains, together with charity. The act of servile fear remains, together with imperfect charity, in one who is moved to do well not only by love of justice, but also by fear of punishment. But this act ceases in one who has perfect charity, since "perfect love casteth out fear" (1 John 4:18).

On the third point: initial fear is a mean between servile and filial fear as the imperfect is a mean between perfect being and not-being, as it is said in 2 *Metaph.*, text 7, not as a mean between two things of the same genus. Imperfect being is the same in substance with perfect being, but differs altogether from not-being.

Article Nine

Whether Fear is a Gift of the Holy Spirit

We proceed to the ninth article thus:

1. It seems that fear is not a gift of the Holy Spirit. No gift of the Holy Spirit is opposed to a virtue, which is also from the Holy Spirit, since otherwise the Holy Spirit would be opposed to itself. But fear is opposed to hope, which is a virtue. It follows that fear is not a gift of the Holy Spirit.

2. Again, it is the property of a theological virtue that it has God as its object. Now fear has God as its object, in so far as it is God that is feared. Fear is therefore a theological virtue, not a gift.

3. Again, fear is the result of love. Now love is reckoned as a theological virtue. Fear is therefore a theological virtue also, since it pertains to the same thing.

4. Again, Gregory says that "fear is given as a protection from pride" (2 *Moral.* 26). Now the virtue of humility is opposed to pride. Hence fear is comprehended under a virtue.

5. Again, the gifts are more perfect than the virtues, since they are given in order to support the virtues, as Gregory says (2 *Moral., ibid.*). Now hope is a virtue, and it is more perfect than fear, since hope looks to what is good while fear looks to what is evil. Hence it should not be said that fear is a gift.

On the other hand: the fear of the Lord is numbered with the seven gifts of the Holy Spirit in Isa., ch. 11.

I answer: there are many kinds of fear, as we said in Art. 2. But as Augustine says, "human fear is not a gift of God" (*De Grat. et Lib. Arb.* 18). For this is the fear which caused Peter to deny Christ, whereas the fear which is a gift of God is that of which it is said in Matt. 10:28: "but rather fear him which is able to destroy both soul and body in hell." Neither is servile fear to be numbered with the seven gifts of the Holy Spirit, even though it may be due to the Holy Spirit. For servile fear can be combined with the will to sin, as Augustine says (*De Nat. et Grat.* 57), whereas gifts of the Holy Spirit cannot be combined with the will to sin, since they are not without charity, as we said in 12ae, Q. 68, Art. 5. It remains, therefore, that the fear of God which is numbered with the seven gifts of the Holy Spirit is filial fear, or chaste fear.

In 12ae, Q. 68, Arts. 1 and 3, we said that the gifts of the Holy Spirit are habitual perfections of the powers of the soul, in consequence of which these powers can be readily moved by the Holy Spirit, just as its appetitive powers can be readily moved by reason in consequence of the moral virtues. Now the first thing that is necessary if anything is to be readily moved by any mover is that it should be subject to the mover, and not repelled by it, since antipathy towards the mover on the part of the thing moved impedes the movement. This is achieved by filial or chaste fear, by which we reverence God and fear to be separated from him. Filial fear thus holds the first place in the ascending order of the gifts of the Holy Spirit, and the last place in their descending order, as Augustine says in 1 *Sermo Domini in monte,* cap. 4.

On the first point: filial fear is not opposed to the virtue of hope. For by filial fear we do not fear lest we should fail in that which we hope to obtain through divine help, but fear lest we should separate ourselves from this help. Filial fear and hope thus hold to one another, and perfect one another.

On the second point: the proper and principal object of fear is the evil which one fears. God cannot be the object of fear in this way, as we said in the first article. In this way he is the object of hope, and of the other theological virtues also. For by the virtue of hope we depend on God's help not only to obtain all other good things, but to obtain God himself as the principal good. The same is true of the other theological virtues.

On the third point: although love is the principle from which fear arises, it does not follow that fear of God is not a habit distinct from charity, which is love of God. Love is the principle of all affections, but we are nevertheless perfected in different affections by different habits. Love has more of the nature of a virtue than has fear. For it is plain from what we said in Pt. I, Q. 60, Arts. 3 and 4, that love looks to the good, to which virtue is principally ordained by its own nature. Hope is reckoned as a virtue for this same reason. Fear, on the other hand, looks principally to what is evil, and implies flight from it. It is therefore something less than a theological virtue.

On the fourth point: as it is said in Ecclesiasticus 10:12: "the beginning of man's pride is to stand apart from God," that is, to refuse to submit to God. This is opposed to filial fear, which reverences God, and is given as a protection from pride because it excludes the beginning of pride. Yet it does not follow that fear is the same as the virtue of humility, but rather that it is the beginning of this virtue. The gifts of the Holy Spirit are indeed the beginnings of the intellectual and moral virtues, as we said in 12ae, Q. 68, Arts. 5 and 8. But the theological virtues are the beginnings of the gifts, as we said in 12ae, Q. 69, Art. 4, *ad* 3.

From this the answer to the fifth point is clear.

Article Ten

WHETHER FEAR DIMINISHES AS CHARITY INCREASES

We proceed to the tenth article thus:

1. It seems that fear diminishes as charity increases. For Augustine says: "the more charity increases, the more fear decreases" (*Tract. 9 in Joan.*).

2. Again, fear diminishes as hope increases. Now it was said in Q. 17, Art. 8, that hope increases as charity increases. It follows that fear diminishes as charity increases.

3. Again, love implies union, and fear implies separation. Now separation diminishes as union increases. It follows that fear diminishes as the love of charity increases.

On the other hand: Augustine says: "the fear of God is not only the beginning of the wisdom whereby one loves God above all things and one's neighbour as oneself, but perfects it" (83 *Quaest. Evang.* Q. 36).

I answer: as we said in Arts. 2 and 4, there are two kinds of fear of God. There is the filial fear by which one fears to offend a father, or to be separated from him. There is also the servile fear by which one fears punishment. Filial fear is bound to increase as charity increases, as an effect increases along with its cause. For the more one loves someone, the more does one fear lest one should offend him, or be separated from him. The servility of servile fear is entirely removed by the advent of charity. Yet the substance of the fear of punishment remains, as we said in Art. 6. This last is diminished as charity increases, most of all in regard to its act. For the more one loves God, the less does one fear punishment: in the first place because one is the less concerned about one's own good, to which punishment is opposed; secondly because one is the more confident of one's reward the more firmly one adheres to God, and consequently has less fear of punishment.

On the first point: Augustine is speaking of the fear of punishment.

On the second point: it is the fear of punishment that decreases as hope increases. Filial fear increases as hope increases, since the more certainly one expects to obtain some good thing through the help of another, the more does one fear lest one should offend the other, or be separated from him.

On the third point: filial fear does not imply separation from God. Rather does it imply submission to God, and fears separation from submission to him. It implies separation in the sense that it does not presume to be equal with God, but submits to him. Separation in this sense is also found in charity, since charity loves God more than itself and above all things. Hence the reverence of fear does not diminish as the love of charity increases, but increases together with it.

Article Eleven

WHETHER FEAR REMAINS IN HEAVEN

We proceed to the eleventh article thus:

1. It seems that fear does not remain in heaven. For it is said in Prov. 1:33: ". . . shall dwell safely, and shall be quiet from fear of evil," and this is to be understood as referring to those who already enjoy wisdom in eternal blessedness. Now all fear is fear of evil, since evil is the object of fear, as was said in Arts. 2 and 5, and in 12ae, Q. 42, Art. 1. There will therefore be no fear in heaven.

2. Again, in heaven men will be like God, since it is said in I John 3:2: "when he shall appear, we shall be like him." But God fears nothing. In heaven, therefore, men will have no fear.

3. Again, hope is more perfect than fear, since hope looks to what is good, while fear looks to what is evil. But there will be no hope in heaven. Neither then will there be fear in heaven.

On the other hand: it is said in Ps. 19:9: "The fear of the Lord is clean, enduring for ever."

I answer: there will in no wise be servile fear in heaven, nor fear of punishment. Such fear is excluded by the security which belongs to blessedness by its very nature, as we said in 12ae, Q. 5, Art. 4. But filial fear will be made perfect when charity is made perfect, just as it increases when charity increases—wherefore its act will not be quite the same in heaven as it is now.

To make this clear, we must observe that the proper object of fear is a possible evil, just as the proper object of hope is a possible good. The movement of fear being similar to flight, fear implies flight from a possible and troublous evil, since small evils do not inspire fear. Now the good of each thing consists in remaining in its order, while its evil consists in abandoning its order, and the order of a rational creature consists in being subject to God, yet above other creatures. It is therefore an evil for a rational creature that it should presumptuously assume equality with God, or despise him, just as it is an evil for it that it should subject itself to a lower creature through love. Such evil is possible for a rational creature considered in its own nature, on account of the natural flexibility of its free will. But it is not possible for the blessed, owing to the perfection of glory. Flight from the evil of insubordination to God, which is possible for nature, will consequently be impossible for the blessedness of heaven. Hence in expounding Job 26:11, "The pillars of heaven tremble and are astonished at his reproof," Gregory says (17 *Moral. in fin*): "The heavenly powers which unceasingly behold him tremble while they contemplate. Yet their trembling is not of fear, lest it should be a punishment to them, but of wonder"—for they wonder at the incomprehensibility of God, whose being transcends them. Augustine likewise supposes that there is fear in heaven, although he leaves the matter open to doubt, in 14 *De Civ. Dei*. 9: "If this chaste fear which endures for ever is to endure in the life to come, it will not be the fear which fears an evil which may happen, but the fear which holds to a good which cannot be lost. For when love is unchangeable towards a good which has been obtained, fear is assuredly certain of avoiding evil, if we may so speak. By the name of chaste fear is signified a will whereby we shall of necessity be unwilling to sin, and whereby we shall be free of the anxiety of weakness lest perchance we should sin, avoiding sin with the tranquillity of charity. Or if no kind of fear is there present, it may be that fear is said to endure for ever because that to which fear leads us is everlasting."

On the first point: the fear which this passage excludes from the blessed is the anxious fear which takes precautions against evil, not the fear of security, of which Augustine speaks.

On the second point: as Dionysius says (9 *Div. Nom.*, lect. 3): "The same things are like God and unlike him. They are like him by reason of imitation of the inimitable"—that is, they imitate God in so far as they can, although he cannot be imitated perfectly; "they are unlike him, since they infinitely and immeasurably fall short of their cause, with which they cannot be compared."

On the third point: hope implies a defect, namely the futurity of blessedness, which will cease when blessedness is present. But fear implies a defect which is natural to a creature, since a creature is infinitely distant from God. This defect will remain in heaven. Hence fear will not be done away entirely.

Article Twelve

Whether Poverty of Spirit is the Beatitude which Corresponds to the Gift of Fear

We proceed to the twelfth article thus:

1. It seems that poverty of spirit is not the beatitude which corresponds to the gift of fear. For it was explained in Art. 7 that fear is the beginning of the spiritual life, whereas poverty of spirit pertains to the perfection of the spiritual life, according to Matt. 19:21: "If thou wilt be perfect, go and sell that thou hast, and give to the poor." Hence poverty of spirit does not correspond to the gift of fear.

2. Again, it is said in Ps. 119:120: "My flesh trembleth for fear of thee," from which it appears that fear mortifies the flesh. Now the beatitude of mourning seems to correspond to the mortification of the flesh. Hence the beatitude of mourning corresponds to the gift of fear, rather than poverty of spirit.

3. Again, it was said in Art. 9 that fear corresponds to the virtue of hope. Now hope seems to correspond especially to the last beatitude, which is: "Blessed are the peacemakers: for they shall be called the children of God," since it is said in Rom. 5:2: "we . . . rejoice in hope of the glory of God."[1] Hence this beatitude corresponds to the gift of fear, rather than poverty of spirit.

4. Again, it was said in 12ae, Q. 70, Art. 2, that the fruits of the Spirit correspond to the beatitudes. But there is nothing in

[1] Migne: ". . . in hope of the glory of the children [*filiorum*] of God."

the fruits which corresponds to the gift of fear. Neither then is there anything in the beatitudes which corresponds to it.

On the other hand: Augustine says (1 *Sermo Domini in monte*, cap. 4): "The fear of God befits the humble, of whom it is said 'Blessed are the poor in spirit.'"

I answer: poverty of spirit properly corresponds to fear. Reverence for God and submission to God belong to filial fear. What results from this submission therefore belongs to the gift of fear. When a man submits himself to God, he no longer seeks to glory in himself, nor in any other save God, since this would be incompatible with perfect submission to God. Thus it is said in Ps. 20:7: "Some trust in chariots, and some in horses; but we will remember the name of the Lord our God." Hence if any man fears God perfectly, he will not seek to glory in himself through pride, nor yet in external goods such as honours and riches. Now in either regard, such restraint pertains to poverty of spirit. For poverty of spirit can be understood to mean either the humiliation of a puffed up and haughty spirit, as Augustine interprets it (*loc. cit.*); or the renunciation of worldly things, which is of the spirit, that is, of our own will at the instigation of the Holy Spirit, as Ambrose says on Luke 6:20: "Blessed be ye poor," and as Hieronymus says also, in interpretation of Matt. 5:3.

On the first point: a beatitude is the actuality of a perfect virtue. Hence all the beatitudes belong to the perfection of spiritual life. But contempt of worldly goods would seem to be the beginning of this perfection, since it permits one to tend towards perfect participation in spiritual goods, just as fear comes first among the gifts of the Spirit. Renunciation of worldly goods is the way to perfection, even though perfection does not consist in the renunciation of them. Yet filial fear, to which the beatitude of poverty corresponds, is present in the perfection of wisdom, as we said in Arts. 7 and 10.

On the second point: undue glorification in oneself or in other things is more directly opposed to submission to God, which results from filial fear, than is love of external things. Love of external things is opposed to this fear consequentially, since one who reverences God and submits to him does not delight in things other than God. But such love does not pertain to the arduous, with which fear and glorification are concerned. Hence the beatitude of poverty corresponds to fear directly, while the beatitude of mourning corresponds to it consequentially.

On the third point: hope implies a movement towards the term to which it relates, whereas fear implies rather a movement away from the term to which it relates. Hence the last beatitude, which is the term of spiritual perfection, fittingly corresponds to hope in point of its ultimate object, while the first beatitude, which involves recoil from worldly things which hinder submission to God, fittingly corresponds to fear.

On the fourth point: those gifts of the Holy Spirit which relate to the moderate use of worldly things, or to abstention from them, such as modesty, continence, or chastity, do appear to correspond to the gift of fear.

Question Twenty

OF DESPAIR

We must now consider the vices opposed to the virtue of hope. The first of these is despair. The second is presumption. Four questions are asked concerning despair. 1. Whether despair is a sin. 2. Whether there can be despair without unbelief. 3. Whether despair is the greatest of sins. 4. Whether it is born of listlessness.

Article One

WHETHER DESPAIR IS A SIN

We proceed to the first article thus:

1. It seems that despair is not a sin. Augustine makes it clear that every sin turns to changeable good when it turns away from unchangeable good (De Lib. Arb., 1, cap. ult; 2, cap. 19). But despair does not turn to changeable good. Hence it is not a sin.

2. Again, that which springs from a good root would not seem to be a sin, since "a good tree cannot bring forth evil fruit" (Matt. 7:18). Now despair appears to spring from a good root, namely, from the fear of God, or from horror at the magnitude of one's own sins. Hence it is not a sin.

3. Again, if despair were a sin, it would be a sin for the damned to despair. Now their despair is not imputed to them as guilt, but rather as their damnation. Neither, then, is despair imputed to the wayfarer as guilt. Hence it is not a sin.

On the other hand: that by which men are led into sin would

seem to be not only a sin, but a principle of sins. Such is despair, since the apostle says: "Who being past feeling have given themselves over unto lasciviousness, to work all uncleanness with greediness" (Eph. 4:19). Despair is therefore not only a sin, but a principle of sins.

I answer: as the philosopher says in 6 *Ethics* 2, affirmation and negation in the intellect correspond to pursuit and avoidance in the appetite, while truth and falsity in the intellect correspond to what is good and to what is bad in the appetite. Hence every appetitive movement which corresponds to what is true in the intellect is good in itself, while every appetitive movement which corresponds to what is false in the intellect is bad in itself, and a sin. Now the true intellectual appreciation of God is of God as the source of man's salvation, and as the forgiver of sins, according to Ezek. 18:23: "Have I any pleasure at all that the wicked should die? saith the Lord God; and not that he should return from his ways, and live?" That God denies pardon to a penitent sinner, or that he does not turn sinners to himself by means of justifying grace, is a false opinion. Accordingly, just as the movement of hope, which corresponds to the true appreciation of God, is laudable and virtuous, so the opposite movement of despair, which corresponds to the false opinion about God, is vicious and sinful.

On the first point: every mortal sin turns away from unchangeable good in some way, and turns to changeable good in one way or another. Since the theological virtues have God as their object, the sins opposed to them consist principally in turning away from unchangeable good, and consequentially in turning to changeable good. Other sins consist principally in turning to changeable good, and consequentially in turning away from unchangeable good. One who commits fornication does not intend to separate himself from God, but seeks delight in carnal pleasure, of which separation from God is the consequence.

On the second point: there are two ways in which a thing may spring from a root of virtue. It may spring directly from the virtue itself, as an action springs from its habit. No sin can spring from a virtuous root in this way. It is indeed in this sense that Augustine says: "no man can make bad use of a virtue" (2 *De Lib. Arb.* 18, 19). But a thing may also spring from a virtue indirectly, or be occasioned by a virtue, and there is nothing to prevent a sin arising out of a virtue in this way. For example, men sometimes pride themselves on their virtues. As

Augustine says: "Pride lies in wait for good works, so that they perish" (*Epist.* 211 *olim* 109). In this way, despair can arise out of the fear of God, or out of horror at one's own sins, if a man makes bad use of these good things by turning them into an occasion for despair.

On the third point: the damned are not in a state which permits of hope, since it is impossible for them to return to blessedness. That they do not hope is consequently not imputed to them as guilt, but is part of their damnation. Neither is it imputed to a wayfarer as a sin, that he despairs of something which he is not born to attain, or of something which he is not under obligation to attain. It is not a sin, for example, if a doctor despairs of curing a sick man, or if one despairs of ever becoming rich.

Article Two

WHETHER THERE CAN BE DESPAIR WITHOUT UNBELIEF

We proceed to the second article thus:

1. It seems that there cannot be despair without unbelief. For the certainty of hope is founded on faith, and the effect cannot be removed so long as the cause remains. One cannot lose the certainty of hope through despair, therefore, unless one loses one's faith.

2. Again, to put one's own guilt before the goodness and mercy of God is to deny the infinite goodness or mercy of God, and this is unbelief. Now one who despairs puts his guilt before the mercy or goodness of God, in accordance with Gen. 4:13: "My punishment is greater than I can bear."[1] Anyone who despairs is therefore an unbeliever.

3. Again, anyone who falls into a condemned heresy is an unbeliever. Now one who despairs seems to fall into a condemned heresy, namely that of the Novatians, who say that sins cannot be forgiven after baptism. It seems, therefore, that anyone who despairs is an unbeliever.

On the other hand: the removal of a consequent does not imply the removal of what is prior to it. Now hope is a consequence of faith, as was said in Q. 17, Art. 7. Hence faith can remain when hope is removed. It does not then follow that whosoever despairs is an unbeliever.

I answer: unbelief belongs to the intellect, whereas despair

[1] Migne: "My iniquity is greater than that I should merit pardon."

belongs to the appetitive power. Further, the intellect is concerned with universals, whereas the appetitive power is moved
in relation to particulars, since appetitive movement is of the
soul towards things which are in themselves particular. Now
one who rightly appreciates something in its universal aspect
may yet be wrong in his appetitive movement, owing to a
faulty estimation of a particular instance of it. For one must pass
from appreciation of the universal to desire for the particular
through the medium of one's estimate of the particular, as is
said in 3 *De Anima*, text 58; just as one can infer a particular
conclusion from a universal proposition only through an
assumption about the particular. It is due to this circumstance
that one who rightly believes something in universal terms may
yet be wrong in his appetitive movement towards a particular
thing, if his estimate of the particular has been corrupted by
habit, or by passion. Thus the fornicator, who chooses fornication as something good for himself, has at the time a false
estimate of the particular, even though he may retain an
appreciation of the universal which is true as a belief, namely,
that fornication is a mortal sin. Similarly, one who continues to
believe truly, in universal terms, that the Church can remit
sins, may still undergo the movement of despair through having
a false estimate of the particular, namely, that he is in such a
state that he cannot hope for pardon. In this way there can be
despair without unbelief, just as there can be other mortal sins
without unbelief.

On the first point: an effect is removed not only if the first
cause is removed, but also if a secondary cause is removed.
Hence the movement of hope can be taken away not only by
the removal of the universal estimate of faith, which is as it
were the first cause of the certainty of faith, but also by the
removal of the particular estimate, which is as it were a
secondary cause.

On the second point: it would be unbelief to think, in universal terms, that the mercy of God was not infinite. But he
who despairs does not think thus. He supposes that there is no
hope of divine mercy for himself, owing to some particular
disposition.

The answer to the third point is similar. The Novatians
deny in universal terms that there is remission of sins in the
Church.

Article Three

WHETHER DESPAIR IS THE GREATEST OF SINS

We proceed to the third article thus:

1. It seems that despair is not the greatest of sins. For there can be despair without unbelief, as was said in the preceding article. Unbelief is the greatest of sins, since it corrupts the foundation of the spiritual edifice. Hence despair is not the greatest of sins.

2. Again, as the philosopher explains, the greatest good is opposed to the greatest evil (8 *Ethics* 10). Now it is said in I Cor., ch. 13, that charity is greater than hope. It follows that hatred of God is a greater sin than despair.

3. Again, the sin of despair involves nothing more than inordinately turning away from God. But other sins involve inordinately turning to other things, as well as inordinately turning away from God. Hence despair is not graver than other sins, but less grave.

On the other hand: the sin which is incurable would seem to be the gravest, according to Jer. 30:12: "Thy bruise is incurable, and thy wound is grievous." Now the sin of despair is incurable, according to Jer. 15:18: ". . . my wound incurable, which refuseth to be healed." It follows that despair is the gravest of sins.

I answer: the sins which are opposed to the theological virtues are graver than other sins, owing to their kind. For the theological virtues have God as their object, and the sins opposed to them consequently involve turning away from God, directly and principally. The principal evil and the gravity of every mortal sin consists in turning away from God, since it would not be a mortal sin to turn to changeable good, even inordinately, if this were possible without turning away from God. The gravest of mortal sins is therefore that which primarily and essentially turns away from God.

Unbelief, despair, and hatred of God are all opposed to theological virtues. If we compare them, we find that in themselves, that is, in their own specific nature, hatred and unbelief are graver than despair. Unbelief is due to a man's not believing the very truth of God. Hatred of God is due to his will being opposed to the very goodness of God. Despair, on the other hand, is due to a man's failure to hope that he will share in the goodness of God. Hence it is clear that unbelief and hatred of

God are opposed to God as he is in himself, whereas despair is opposed to him by way of being opposed to our participation in his good. In the absolute sense, therefore, to disbelieve the truth of God, or to harbour hatred of God, is a graver sin than not to hope to receive glory from him.

But if we compare despair with the other two sins from our own point of view, it is more dangerous. For by hope we are called back from evils and induced to strive for what is good, and if hope is lost, men fall headlong into vices, and are taken away from good works. Hence the gloss on Prov. 24:10, "If thou faint in the day of adversity, thy strength is small," says: "Nothing is more execrable than despair. For he who despairs loses his constancy in the daily labours of this life, and what is worse, loses his constancy in the endeavour of faith." Further, as Isodorus says in 2 *De Summo Bono* 14: "To commit a crime is death to the soul; but to despair is to descend into hell."

From this the answers to the objections are obvious.

Article Four

Whether Despair Arises from Listlessness

We proceed to the fourth article thus:

1. It seems that despair does not arise from listlessness. For the same thing does not result from different causes, and Gregory says that despair of the future life results from lust (31 *Moral.* 17). It does not then result from listlessness.

2. Again, as despair is opposed to hope, so is listlessness opposed to spiritual joy. Now spiritual joy is the result of hope, according to Rom. 12:12: "Rejoicing in hope." Hence listlessness is the result of despair, not *vice versa*.

3. Again, the causes of contraries are themselves contrary. Now hope is the contrary of despair, and hope seems to be caused by contemplation of the divine blessings, especially the incarnation. As Augustine says: "Nothing was so necessary in order to raise our hope, as that we should be shown how much God loves us. What could more plainly declare this to us than that the Son of God should deign to take our nature upon himself?" (13 *De Trin.* 10). Despair therefore results from neglect to think of these blessings, rather than from listlessness.

On the other hand: Gregory numbers despair among the results of listlessness (31 *Moral.* 17).

I answer: as we said in Q. 17, Art. 1, and in 12ae, Q. 40, Art. 1, the object of hope is a good which is arduous, and also possible to obtain. There are accordingly two ways in which one may fail in the hope of obtaining blessedness. One may fail to look upon it as an arduous good, and one may fail to look upon it as a good which it is possible to obtain, whether by oneself or through the help of another. It is especially through corruption of our affection by love of bodily pleasures, particularly those of sexuality, that we are brought to the point where spiritual goods do not savour of good, or do not seem to be very good. For it is due to love of such things that a man loses his taste for spiritual goods, and does not hope for them as arduous goods. In this way, despair arises from lust. But it is owing to excessive dejection that one fails to look upon an arduous good as possible to obtain, whether by oneself or through the help of another. For when dejection dominates a man's affection, it seems to him that he can never rise to anything good. In this way, despair arises from listlessness, since listlessness is the kind of sadness which casts down the spirit.

Now the proper object of hope is this—that a thing is possible to obtain. For to be good, or to be arduous, pertains to the object of other passions also. It is therefore from listlessness that despair arises the more especially, although it can also arise from lust, for the reason which we have stated.

From this the reply to the first point is plain.

On the second point: as the philosopher says in 1 *Rhetoric* 11, just as hope creates joy, so do men have greater hope when they live joyously. So likewise do they fall the more readily into despair when they live in sadness, according to II Cor. 2:7: "lest perhaps such a one should be swallowed up with overmuch sorrow." The object of hope is a good to which the appetite tends naturally, and from which it will not turn aside naturally, but only if some obstacle intervenes. Hence joy is more directly the result of hope, and despair more directly the result of sadness.

On the third point: neglect to think of the divine blessings is itself the result of listlessness. For a man who is affected by a passion thinks especially of the things which pertain to it. Hence it is not easy for a man who lives in sadness to contemplate any great and joyful things. He thinks only of things that are sad, unless he turns away from them by a great effort.

Question Twenty-One

OF PRESUMPTION

We must now consider presumption, concerning which there are four questions. 1. What is the object of presumption, on which it relies. 2. Whether presumption is a sin. 3. To what it is opposed. 4. From that it arises.

Article One

WHETHER PRESUMPTION RELIES ON GOD, OR ON ONE'S OWN POWER

We proceed to the first article thus:

1. It seems that presumption, which is a sin against the Holy Spirit, does not rely on God, but on one's own power. Sin is the greater, the lesser is the power in which one puts too much trust, and the power of man is less than the power of God. Hence one who presumes on the power of man is guilty of a greater sin than one who presumes on the power of God. Now sin against the Holy Spirit is the gravest of all sins. It follows that presumption, which is said to be a kind of sin against the Holy Spirit, relies on the power of man rather than on the power of God.

2. Again, other sins arise out of sin against the Holy Spirit. For sin against the Holy Spirit is called malice,[1] and through malice a man sins. Now it seems that other sins arise out of the presumption with which a man presumes on himself, rather than out of the presumption with which he presumes on God. For Augustine makes it clear that love of oneself is the beginning of sins (14 De Civ. Dei. 28). It appears, therefore, that the presumption which is a sin against the Holy Spirit relies especially on the power of man.

3. Again, sin is due to turning inordinately to changeable good. Now presumption is a sin. It is therefore due to turning to the power of a man, which is a changeable good, rather than to turning to the power of God, which is an unchangeable good.

On the other hand: by presumption one despises the divine

[1] To sin through malice is to sin against the Holy Spirit when it involves rejection, through contempt, of the protection from the choice of evil which is the effect of the Holy Spirit. (22ae, Q. 14, Art. 1).

justice which punishes sinners, just as by despair one despises the divine mercy on which hope relies. Now justice is in God, just as mercy is in God. Presumption therefore consists in turning to God in an inordinate manner, just as despair consists in turning away from him.

I answer: presumption seems to imply immoderate hope. The object of hope is a good which is arduous and yet possible, but there are two ways in which a thing may be possible for a man. It may be possible for him through his own power, and it may be possible only through the power of God. Now in either case there can be presumption through immoderate hope. The hope whereby one relies on one's own power is presumptuous, if one aims at a good beyond one's capacity as if it were possible for one to attain it, after the manner referred to in Judith 6:15 (Vulgate): "Thou humblest those that presume of themselves." Such presumption is opposed to the virtue of magnanimity, which holds to the mean in hope of this kind. But hope whereby one relies on the power of God can also be presumptuous through immoderation, if one looks for some good thing as if it were possible through the divine power and mercy, when it is not possible. It would be presumptuous, for example, for a man to hope to obtain pardon without penitence, or glory without merit. Such presumption is indeed a kind of sin against the Holy Spirit, since one who so presumes takes away or despises the aid whereby the Holy Spirit calls him back from sin.

On the first point: as we said in Q. 20, Art. 3, and in 12ae, Q. 73, Art. 3, a sin against God is more serious than other sins, owing to its kind. The presumption with which one relies on God in an inordinate manner is therefore a more serious sin than the presumption with which one relies on one's own power. To rely on the divine power for the purpose of obtaining what it is unbecoming for God to give is to deprecate the divine power, and it is obvious that one who deprecates the power of God sins more seriously than one who exalts his own power more than he ought.

On the second point: the presumption with which one presumes on God in an inordinate manner includes the love of oneself whereby one inordinately desires one's own good. For when we desire something excessively, we readily think that it is possible through others, when it is not so.

On the third point: presumption on the mercy of God includes turning to changeable good, in so far as it is the outcome of inordinate desire for one's own good. It also includes turning away from unchangeable good, in so far as it attributes to the divine power what is unbecoming to it. This means that a man turns away from the divine power.

Article Two

WHETHER PRESUMPTION IS A SIN

We proceed to the second article thus:

1. It seems that presumption is not a sin. No sin is a reason why a man should be heard by God. Yet some are heard by God on account of presumption, since it is said in Judith 9:17 (Vulgate): "Hear me, a miserable supplicant who presumes upon thy mercy." Hence presumption on the divine mercy is not a sin.

2. Again, presumption implies excessive hope. But the hope whereby we hope in God cannot be excessive, since his power and his mercy are infinite. Hence it seems that presumption is not a sin.

3. Again, a sin does not excuse sin. But presumption excuses sin, since the Master says (2 *Sent.*, *Dist.* 22): "Adam sinned the less, because he sinned in the hope of pardon," which would seem to be presumptuous. Hence presumption is not a sin.

On the other hand: presumption is said to be a kind of sin against the Holy Spirit.

I answer: as we said in the first article of the preceding question, every appetitive movement which corresponds to a falsity in the intellect is bad in itself, and a sin. Now presumption is an appetitive movement, since it involves inordinate hope. It also corresponds to a falsity in the intellect, as does despair. For just as it is false that God does not pardon the penitent, or that he does not turn sinners to penitence, so also is it false that he extends pardon to those who persevere in their sins, or that he gives glory to those who cease from good works. The movement of presumption corresponds to this opinion. Hence presumption is a sin. But it is a lesser sin than despair, since to have mercy and to spare is more becoming to God than to punish, on account of his infinite goodness. To have mercy and to spare is in itself becoming to God, whereas to punish becomes him by reason of our sins.

On the first point: presumption is sometimes used to denote hope, since even the hope in God which is justifiable seems presumptuous if measured by reference to the condition of man, although it is not presumptuous if we bear in mind the immensity of the divine goodness.

On the second point: the hope which presumption implies is not excessive in the sense that it expects too much from God, but in the sense that it expects something from God which is unbecoming to him. This is to expect too little from God, since it is a way of deprecating his power, as we said in the first article.

On the third point: to sin with the intention of persevering in sin, and in the hope of pardon, is presumptuous. Sin is thereby increased, not diminished. But to sin with the intention of refraining from sin, and in the hope that one will sometime be pardoned, is not presumptuous. This diminishes sin, since it seems to show that the will is less confirmed in sin.

Article Three

WHETHER PRESUMPTION IS OPPOSED TO FEAR RATHER
THAN TO HOPE

We proceed to the third article thus:

1. It seems that presumption is more opposed to fear than to hope. For inordinate fear is opposed to fear, and presumption seems to pertain to inordinate fear, since it is said in Wisdom 17:11: "a troubled conscience always presumes harsh things," and in the same passage "fear is the aid to presumption." Hence presumption is opposed to fear rather than to hope.

2. Again, those things are contrary which are farthest removed from each other. Now presumption is farther removed from fear than from hope. For presumption implies a movement towards something, as does hope also, whereas fear implies a movement away from something. Hence presumption is contrary to fear rather than to hope.

3. Again, presumption excludes fear entirely. It does not exclude hope entirely, but only the rightness of hope. Now things are opposed when they mutually exclude each other. Hence it seems that presumption is opposed to fear rather than to hope.

On the other hand: two contrary vices are opposed to the same virtue. Timidity and audacity, for example, are opposed to fortitude. Now the sin of presumption is the contrary of the sin of despair, and despair is directly opposed to hope. Hence it appears that presumption is also opposed to hope, more directly than to fear.

I answer: as Augustine says (4 *Cont. Julian.* 3): "with all virtues, there are not only vices which are clearly opposed to them, as temerity is clearly opposed to prudence. There are also vices which are akin to them, not truly, but with a false kind of similarity, such as astuteness bears to prudence." This is what the philosopher means when he says that a virtue seems to have more in common with one contrary vice than with another, as temperance seems to have the greater kinship with insensibility, and fortitude with audacity.

Presumption seems obviously opposed to fear, especially to servile fear, since servile fear is afraid of the punishment which comes from God's justice, while presumption hopes that this will be remitted. It is nevertheless more opposed to hope, by reason of the false similarity which it bears as a kind of inordinate hope in God. Things which belong to the same genus are more opposed than things which belong to different genera (since contraries belong to the same genus), and for this reason presumption is more opposed to hope than it is to fear. For presumption and hope look to the same object, in which they both trust. Hope trusts ordinately, and presumption inordinately.

On the first point: just as we speak of hope loosely in reference to what is evil, although rightly only in reference to what is good, so is it with presumption. It is in this loose way that inordinate fear is called presumption.

On the second point: things are contrary when they are farthest removed within the same genus. Now presumption and hope imply movements which belong to the same genus, and which may be either ordinate or inordinate. Presumption is therefore more directly contrary to hope than to fear. For it is contrary to hope by reason of its specific difference, as the inordinate is contrary to the ordinate, while it is contrary to fear by reason of the difference which distinguishes its genus (namely, by the anxiety which is of hope).[1]

On the third point: presumption is opposed to fear by reason of the difference which distinguishes its genus. But it is opposed to hope by reason of its own specific difference. Hence it is owing to the genus to which it belongs that presumption excludes fear entirely, while it excludes hope only to the extent to which its own specific difference excludes the ordinateness of hope.

[1] Added in some editions.

Article Four

WHETHER PRESUMPTION IS CAUSED BY VAINGLORY

We proceed to the fourth article thus:

1. It seems that presumption is not caused by vainglory. For presumption appears to trust especially in the divine mercy, and mercy relates to misery, which is the opposite of glory. Hence presumption is not the result of vainglory.

2. Again, presumption is the opposite of despair, and despair is caused by sadness, as was said in Q. 20, Art. 4, *ad* 2. Now the causes of opposites are themselves opposite. Hence it appears that presumption is due to pleasure, and therefore to carnal vices, which are more voluptuous than others.

3. Again, the vice of presumption consists in aiming at an impossible good as if it were possible. But it is due to ignorance that one thinks a thing to be possible when it is impossible. Hence presumption is the result of ignorance, rather than of vainglory.

On the other hand: Gregory says (31 *Moral.* 17): "the presumption of novelties is the child of vainglory."

I answer: as we said in the first article, there are two kinds of presumption. There is the presumption which trusts in one's own power, and which attempts what transcends one's power as if it were possible for oneself to attain it. Such presumption is obviously due to vainglory. For it is because a man has a great desire for glory that he attempts things beyond his power, especially novelties, which command more admiration. Hence Gregory says with point that the presumption of novelties is the child of vainglory. There is also the presumption which trusts inordinately in the divine mercy, or in the divine power, and by which one hopes to obtain glory without merit, or pardon without penitence. Presumption of this kind seems to arise directly out of pride. It is as if a man esteemed himself so highly as to think that God would neither punish him nor exclude him from glory, even though he should sin.

The answers to the objections are now obvious.

Treatise on the Theological Virtues

III. On Charity. Secunda Secundae. Questions 23, 27.

OF CHARITY, CONSIDERED IN ITSELF

THERE ARE EIGHT QUESTIONS CONCERNING CHARITY itself. 1. Whether charity is friendship. 2. Whether it is something created in the soul. 3. Whether it is a virtue. 4. Whether it is a particular kind of virtue. 5. Whether it is a single virtue. 6. Whether it is the greatest of the virtues. 7. Whether there can be any true virtue without charity. 8. Whether charity is the form of the virtues.

Article One

WHETHER CHARITY IS FRIENDSHIP

We proceed to the first article thus:

1. It seems that charity is not friendship. As the philosopher says in 8 *Ethics* 5, nothing is so characteristic of friendship as to live with a friend. But charity in man is toward God and the angels, "whose dwelling is not with flesh" according to Dan. 2:11. It follows that charity is not friendship.

2. Again, it is said in 8 *Ethics* 2 that there is no friendship where there is no return of affection. Now charity is extended even to enemies, according to Matt. 5:44: "Love your enemies." It follows that charity is not friendship.

3. Again, the philosopher says that there are three kinds of friendship, founded on the pleasant, on the useful, and on the good (8 *Ethics* 3). Now charity is not a friendship founded on the useful, or on the pleasant. As Hieronymus says in his letter to Paulinus, "it is a true friendship, sealed by the bond of Christ, in which men are united not by any commonplace usefulness, nor merely by bodily presence, nor yet by any subtle and soothing flattery, but by the fear of God and the study of the sacred

Scriptures." But neither is it a friendship founded on goodness, since friendship of this kind obtains only between the virtuous, as the philosopher says in 8 *Ethics* 4, whereas by charity we love even sinners. It follows that charity is not friendship.

On the other hand: it is said in John 15:15: "Henceforth I call you not servants . . . but I have called you friends." Now this was said to them by reason of charity, and not otherwise. Charity is therefore friendship.

I answer: as the philosopher says in 8 *Ethics* 2 and 3, it is not every love that has the character of friendship, but only the love which includes benevolence, by which we love someone so as to will some good for him. When we do not will good for the things we love, but seek their good for ourselves, as we do when we love wine, or a horse, or something of the kind, this is not the love of friendship, but a kind of concupiscence. It would indeed be ridiculous to say that one had friendship with wine, or with a horse. But benevolence is not enough for friendship. Friendship requires mutual love, because a friend is the friend of a friend, and such mutual goodwill is founded on communion.[1] Now man has communion with God, since God communicates his beatitude to us, and this communion is bound to be the foundation of a certain friendship. Of this communion I Cor. 1:9 says: "God is faithful, by whom ye were called unto the fellowship[2] of his Son." The love which is founded on this communion is charity. It is apparent, then, that charity is a friendship of man with God.

On the first point: the life of man is twofold. We have no communication or conversation with God or the angels through the outward life, which we live according to our sensible and corporeal nature. But we converse both with God and with the angels through the spiritual life of the mind, even in our present imperfect state. Thus Phil. 3:20 says that "our conversation is in heaven," and Rev. 22:3–4 says that this conversation will be made perfect in heaven, when "his servants shall serve him: and they shall see his face." Charity is imperfect in this life, but will be made perfect in heaven.

On the second point: there are two ways in which friendship is extended to another. To one's friend only, it is extended to another for his own sake. But it is also extended to another for the sake of a different person. For his friend's sake a man may love all who belong to his friend, whether they be sons or slaves, or connected with him in any way. Love for a friend may indeed

1 *communicatio.*   2 *societas.*

be so great that we love those who belong to him even though they should offend us or hate us. It is in this way that the friendship of charity extends even to enemies. The friendship of charity is first of all towards God, and we love them out of charity towards God.

On the third point: only one who is virtuous can be the principal friend to whom friendship based on goodness is extended. But those who belong to him are looked upon with love, even when they are not virtuous. Charity extends in this way to sinners, although it is especially a friendship founded on goodness. Through charity we love sinners for God's sake.

Article Two

WHETHER CHARITY IS SOMETHING CREATED IN THE SOUL

We proceed to the second article thus:

1. It seems that charity is not something created in the soul. Augustine says (8 *De Trin.* 8): "he who loves his neighbour loves love itself in consequence." Now God is love. It is therefore God whom such a one principally loves in consequence. He says also (15 *De Trin.* 17): "we say 'God is love' in the same way as we say 'God is a Spirit.' It follows that charity is God himself, not anything created in the soul."

2. Again, according to Deut. 30:20: "He is thy life," God is spiritually the life of the soul, just as the soul is the life of the body. Now the soul enlivens the body through itself. Therefore God enlivens the soul through himself. But he enlivens the soul through charity, according to I John 3:14: "We know that we have passed from death unto life, because we love the brethren." Hence God is charity itself.

3. Again, nothing created has infinite power. Rather is every created thing vanity. Now charity is not vanity, but repels vanity. Charity, also, has infinite power, since it leads a man's soul to infinite good. Hence it is not anything created in the soul.

On the other hand: Augustine says (3 *De Doctr. Christ.* 10): "What I call charity is the movement of the soul towards the enjoyment of God for his own sake." This movement is something created in the soul. Charity is therefore something created in the soul.

I answer: the Master examines this question thoroughly in 1 *Sent., Dist.* 17, and decides that charity is not something created in the soul, but the Holy Spirit dwelling in the mind. He does not mean that the movement of love by which we love

God is itself the Holy Spirit. He means to say that the Holy Spirit causes this movement of love without any habit serving as a medium, as do the habits of faith and of hope, for example, or the habit of some other virtue, when it moves us to other virtuous actions. He said this because of the excellence of charity.

If we consider the matter aright, however, this is detrimental to charity rather than the reverse. For the movement of charity does not arise from the mind being moved by the Holy Spirit merely as a body is moved by an external mover, without being in any way the principle of its movement. This would be contrary to the nature of voluntary action, which must have its beginning within oneself, as we said in 12ae, Q. 6, Art. 1. It would mean that love is not voluntary, which is a contradiction, since the very nature of love implies that it is an action of the will. Nor can we say that the Holy Spirit moves the will to the act of love as one moves an instrument. An instrument may be a principle of action, but it does not decide to act or not to act. This, again, would take away the nature of voluntary action. It would also exclude merit, and we have already said that it is especially by the love of charity that merit is acquired (12ae, Q. 114, Art. 4). If the will is moved to love by the Holy Spirit, it must itself perform the act of love.

Now no action is perfectly produced by an active power, unless it is made connatural to that power by means of some form which is the principle of action. For this reason God, who moves all things to their proper end, has provided individual things with forms which incline them to the ends which he has assigned to them. In this way he "disposes all things sweetly," as Wisdom 8:1 says. Now it is obvious that charity, as an action, exceeds the nature of the power of the will. Hence unless the will were inclined to charity by some form added to our natural power, this action would be more imperfect than its natural actions, and more imperfect than the actions of the other powers of the soul. Nor would it be performed easily and joyfully. But this is false, since no power inclines so readily to its proper action, nor performs it so joyfully, as charity. It is especially necessary for charity, therefore, that there should be in us some habitual form superadded to our natural power, inclining it to act with charity, and causing it to do so readily and joyfully.

On the first point: the divine essence itself is charity, just as it is also wisdom and goodness. The charity by which formally we love our neighbours is then a certain participation in the divine charity, in the same sense in which we are said to be good with the goodness which is God, or wise with the wisdom which is God (the goodness by which formally we are good being a kind of participation in divine goodness, and the wisdom by which formally we are wise being a kind of participation in divine wisdom). This manner of speaking is common among the Platonists with whose teaching Augustine was imbued, and his words have been a source of error to those who did not know this.

On the second point: God is the efficient cause both of life in the soul through charity and of life in the body through the soul. But charity is formally the life of the soul, just as the soul is formally the life of the body. We may therefore conclude that charity is directly united with the soul, just as the soul is directly united with the body.

On the third point: formally, charity is efficacious. But the efficacy of a form reflects the power of the agent who provides it. It is obvious that charity is not vanity. What it reveals, by its infinite effect of justifying the soul and thereby uniting it with God, is the infinite divine power which is its source.

Article Three

WHETHER CHARITY IS A VIRTUE

We proceed to the third article thus:

1. It seems that charity is not a virtue. For charity is a kind of friendship, and it is plain from 8 *Ethics* 1 that the philosophers do not regard friendship as a virtue, since they include it neither in the moral virtues nor in the intellectual virtues. Hence charity is not a virtue.

2. Again, it is said in 1 *De Coelo et Mundi* 116 that a virtue is what is ultimate in respect of a power. But charity does not come last. Rather do joy and peace come last. Hence it seems that charity is not a virtue, but that joy and peace are virtues, rather than charity.

3. Again, every virtue is possessed as a habit which is an accident. But charity is not possessed as an accident, since it is nobler than the soul, whereas no accident is nobler than its subject. Hence charity is not a virtue.

On the other hand: Augustine says (*De Mor. Eccles.* 11): "Charity is the virtue by which we love God, and which unites us to God when our attitude is faultless."

I answer: human actions are good in so far as they are regulated by their proper rule and measure. Human virtue therefore consists in the attainment of the rule of human actions, since it is the principle of all good human actions. Now we said in Q. 17, Art. 1, that the rule of human action is twofold, namely, human reason, and God himself. Accordingly, while "that which accords with right reason" serves as a definition of moral virtue (6 *Ethics* 2), the attainment of God constitutes the nature of this virtue of charity, just as we said that it constitutes the nature of faith and of hope (Q. 4, Art. 5; Q. 17, Art. I). Charity is therefore a virtue, since it attains God through uniting us to God, as the quotation from Augustine affirms.

On the first point: in 8 *Ethics* 1 the philosopher does not deny that friendship is a virtue. He affirms that it either is a virtue or implies virtue. It may indeed be described as a virtue concerned with action toward another, although it is not the same as justice. Justice is concerned with what is legally due in action toward another. Friendship is concerned with what is morally due as between friends, or better, with what free beneficence requires, as the philosopher explains in 8 *Ethics* 13. But we may say that friendship is not in itself a virtue distinct from other virtues. Its praiseworthy and honourable character depends on its object, that is, on the goodness of the virtues upon which it is founded. This is clear from the fact that every friendship is not praiseworthy and honourable. Friendship founded on the pleasant or the useful is obviously not so. Virtuous friendship is therefore the consequence of virtue, rather than itself a virtue. With charity, however, it is otherwise. For charity is founded on the goodness [1] of God, not on human virtue.

On the second point: it is the same virtue which loves something and also rejoices in it. As we said when dealing with the passions in 12ae, Q. 25, Art. 2, joy follows love, wherefore love is accounted a virtue rather than joy, which is the effect of love. That a virtue is ultimate in respect of a power implies not that it comes last in the order of effects, but rather that it comes last in a certain order of excess, as a hundred pounds exceeds forty.

On the third point: every attribute is inferior to its substance in respect of existence, since a substance exists in its own right, while an accident exists only in something else. In respect of its specific nature, however, although an accident which is caused

[1] *Cod. Tarrac.*: "on divine virtue."

by principles which lie within its subject is less noble than its subject, an accident which is caused by participation in a higher nature is more noble than its subject, in so far as it is a likeness of this higher nature. Light, for example, is nobler than a diaphanous body. In this way charity is nobler than the soul, since it is a certain participation in the Holy Spirit.

Article Four

WHETHER CHARITY IS A SPECIFIC VIRTUE

We proceed to the fourth article thus:

1. It seems that charity is not a specific virtue. For Hieronymus says (reference unknown, but Augustine says the same thing in *Epist.* 167): "I summarize all definitions of virtue thus—virtue is charity, by which we love God and our neighbour." Augustine also implies in *De Mor. Eccles.* 15, and says expressly in 15 *De Civ. Dei.* 22, that "virtue is the rule of love." But the definition of virtue in general makes no mention of any specific virtue. Hence charity is not a specific virtue.

2. Again, what extends to the operations of all virtues cannot itself be a specific virtue. Now charity extends to the operations of all virtues, according to I Cor. 13:4: "Charity suffereth long, and is kind," etc. It extends even to a man's every deed, according to I Cor. 16:14: "Let all your things be done with charity." Hence charity is not a specific virtue.

3. Again, the precepts of the law correspond to the acts of the virtues. Now Augustine says (*De Perf. Just.* 5): "The general commandment is 'Thou shalt love,' and the general prohibition is 'Thou shalt not covet.'" Charity is thus a general virtue.

On the other hand: the general is never numbered together with the specific. But charity is numbered together with the specific virtues of hope and faith, as in I Cor. 13:13: "And now abideth faith, hope, and charity, these three." Charity is therefore a specific virtue.

I answer: we have already explained (12ae, Q. 18, Art. 2, and Q. 54, Art. 2) that an act and a habit both derive their species from their object, and that the proper object of love is the good (12ae, Q. 17, Art. 1). There is therefore a specific kind of love where there is a specific kind of good. Now in its aspect as the object of happiness, divine good is a specific kind of good. The love of charity is consequently a specific kind of love, since it is the love of this specific good. Charity is therefore a specific virtue.

On the first point: charity is mentioned in the definition of virtue in general not because its nature is that which is common to every virtue, but because every virtue depends on it, as we shall show in Arts. 7 and 8. Prudence is mentioned in the definition of the moral virtues for a similar reason in 2 *Ethics* 6 and 6 *Ethics* 13, because they depend on prudence.

On the second point: a virtue or an art which is concerned with an ultimate end has authority over such virtues as are concerned only with other subordinate ends. Thus the art of the soldier commands the art of horsemanship, as is said in 1 *Ethics* 1. Now the object of charity is the final end of human life, which is eternal blessedness. Hence charity extends to the whole activity of human life by way of authority, not by directly determining every virtuous action.

On the third point: the precept of love is said to be the general commandment because all other precepts are subordinate to it as their end, according to I Tim. 1:5: "the end of the commandment is charity."

Article Five

WHETHER CHARITY IS A SINGLE VIRTUE

We proceed to the fifth article thus:

1. It seems that charity is not a single virtue. For habits are different if their objects are different, and charity has two objects which are infinitely apart, namely, God and one's neighbour. It follows that charity is not a single virtue.

2. Again, it was shown in Q. 17, Art. 6, and in 12ae, Q. 54, Art. 2, that a habit is diverse if its object has several aspects, even though its object is fundamentally one. Now there are many aspects of love to God, since we ought to love God in return for each benefit received. It follows that charity is not a single virtue.

3. Again, charity includes friendship towards one's neighbour, and there are several kinds of friendship named by the philosopher in 8 *Ethics* 11 and 12. It follows that charity is not a single virtue, but a virtue of several different kinds.

On the other hand: as God is the object of faith, so is he the object of charity. Now according to Eph. 4:5: "One faith," faith is a single virtue because of the unity of divine truth. Charity is therefore a single virtue because of the unity of divine goodness.

I answer: charity is friendship of man with God. Now

we may distinguish between friendships according to their different ends, and say that there are three kinds of friendship, founded on the useful, on the pleasant, and on the good. We may also distinguish between them as does the philosopher in 8 *Ethics* 11 and 12, according to the different types of communion on which they are founded, and say there are friendships between relatives, between fellow-citizens, and between travellers, founded on natural relationship, on civil community, and on the companionship of the road. But we cannot divide charity in either of these ways. For the end of charity is one, since it is the divine goodness, and the communion of eternal beatitude on which its friendship is based is likewise one. It remains that charity is simply a single virtue, and not a virtue of several kinds.

On the first point: this reasoning would be valid if God and one's neighbour were objects of charity equally. But they are not so. God is the principal object of charity, whereas one's neighbour is loved for God's sake.

On the second point: by charity we love God for his own sake. The love of charity is therefore of one single kind. According to Ps. 106:1 it is love for God's goodness, which is his substance: "O give thanks unto the Lord; for he is good." Other reasons for which we love God, or ought to love him, are secondary and consequential.

On the third point: the philosopher is speaking of human friendship, in which there are diverse ends and diverse kinds of communion. But there is no such diversity in charity, as we have said, so that the two are not the same.

Article Six

WHETHER CHARITY IS THE MOST EXCELLENT OF THE VIRTUES

We proceed to the sixth article thus:

1. It seems that charity is not the most excellent of the virtues. For the virtue of a higher power is the higher, just as its operation is the higher, and the intellect is a higher power than the will. It follows that faith, which is in the intellect, is more excellent than charity, which is in the will.

2. Again, that by means of which another thing works would seem to be inferior to it. A servant through whom his master acts, for example, is inferior to his master. Now Gal. 5:6 says that "faith worketh by love." It follows that faith is more excellent than charity.

3. Again, what is additional to something would seem to be more perfect. Now hope seems to be additional to charity, since the object of charity is the good, while the object of hope is arduous good. It follows that hope is more excellent than charity.

On the other hand: I Cor. 13:13 says: "the greatest of these is charity."

I answer: human actions are good in so far as they are regulated by their proper rule. Human virtue therefore consists in the attainment of the rule of human actions, since it is the principle of good actions. We have already said in Art. 3 that the rule of human actions is twofold—human reason and God. But God is the first rule of human actions, and human reason must be ruled by him. The theological virtues consist in the attainment of the first rule, since their object is God. It follows that they are more excellent than the moral and intellectual virtues, which consist in the attainment of human reason. The most excellent of the theological virtues, further, must be that which attains God the most perfectly.

Now what exists through itself is always greater than what exists only through something else. Faith and hope attain God through learning the truth from him, and through receiving some good from him. But charity attains God so as to rest in God, not through receiving something from him. Charity is therefore more excellent than faith and hope, and consequently more excellent also than all other virtues. Prudence is similarly more excellent than the other moral virtues, since it attains reason through itself, whereas the others attain reason only through reason itself determining the mean in actions and passions.

On the first point: the operation of the intellect is completed when the thing understood is in him who understands. The excellence of its operation is therefore measured by the intellect itself. But the operation of the will, and also of any appetitive power, is completed when the subject is inclined to something as an end. The excellence of its operation is therefore measured by the object sought. Now as the *Book on Causes* maintains (props. 12, 20), when one thing exists in another thing, it does so according to the mode of the thing in which it exists. Hence anything which is lower than the soul must exist in the soul in a mode higher than that in which it exists by itself. But anything which is higher than the soul must exist by itself in a mode higher than that in which it exists in the soul. It follows that knowledge of things beneath us is more excellent than love of them. This is the reason why the philosopher places the intellectual virtues above the moral virtues in 6 *Ethics* 7 and 12. But love of things higher than ourselves is more excellent than knowledge of them. This is especially true of love to God. Charity is therefore more excellent than faith.

On the second point: faith does not use charity as an instrument, which is the way in which a master uses his servant, but as its own form. The reasoning is therefore false.

On the third point: it is the same good which is the object of charity and of hope. But charity implies union with its object, whereas hope implies distance from it. This is the reason why charity does not look upon the good as arduous, as does hope. The good is not arduous for charity, since charity is already one with it. It is thus clear that charity is more excellent than hope.

Article Seven

WHETHER THERE CAN BE ANY TRUE VIRTUE WITHOUT CHARITY

We proceed to the seventh article thus:

1. It seems that there can be true virtue without charity. For it is a property of virtue to produce a good action, and those who lack charity nevertheless perform some good actions. They sometimes clothe the naked, feed the hungry, and do other similar things. There can therefore be true virtue without charity.

2. Again, there cannot be charity where there is no faith, since charity proceeds "out of faith unfeigned" (I Tim. 1:5). But those who lack faith can still have true chastity while they inhibit their desires, and true justice while they judge aright. There can therefore be true virtue without charity.

3. Again, it is evident from 6 *Ethics* 3 and 4 that science and art are virtues. But these are found in sinners who have no charity. There can therefore be true virtue without charity.

On the other hand: the apostle says in I Cor. 13:3: "And though I bestow all my goods to feed the poor, and though I give my body to be burned, and have not charity, it profiteth me nothing." But virtue is very profitable. According to Wisdom 8:7: "It teaches temperance, justice, prudence, and virtue, than which there is nothing in life more profitable to men." There is therefore no true virtue without charity.

I answer: virtue is directed to the good, as we said in 12ae, Q. 55, Art. 3, and the good is fundamentally the end, since means to an end are said to be good only because they relate to an end. Now there are two kinds of end, one ultimate and the other proximate. There are therefore two kinds of good also, one ultimate and universal, the other proximate and particular. According to Ps. 73:28: "It is good for me to draw near to God," the ultimate and principal good of man is the enjoyment of God. Man is directed to this by charity. The secondary and as it were particular good of man may be of two kinds. One of these is genuinely good, capable in itself of leading to the principal good which is his ultimate end. The other is only apparently good, not genuinely good, since it leads him away from his ultimate end. It is plain, then, that absolutely true virtue is virtue which directs a man to his principal good. As the philosopher says in 7 *Physics*, text 17, "virtue is the disposition of the perfect towards the best."

It follows that there cannot be any true virtue without charity. If, however, we are to call that a virtue which directs one only to some particular end, then any virtue may be said to be true without charity, in so far as it directs one to some particular good. If this particular good is not a genuine good, but only an apparent good, the virtue which directs one to it will not be a true virtue, but only the false imitation of a virtue. As Augustine says (4 *Cont. Julian.* 3), "the prudence with which misers devise diverse means of gain is not true virtue; neither is the justice by which they leave another's goods alone for fear of dire penalties; nor the temperance by which they curb their appetite for costly luxuries; nor the courage by which 'they flee from poverty across sea, rock, and fire,' as Horatius has it (1 *Epistol.* 1)." But if this particular good is a genuine good, such as the preservation of the state, or something of the kind, the virtue which directs one to it will be a true virtue. It will nevertheless be imperfect, if it is not brought into relation to the ultimate and perfect good. Absolutely true virtue, therefore, is impossible without charity.

On the first point: when a man lacks charity, his action may be of two kinds. When it is the expression of the very thing on account of which he lacks charity, it is always evil. What an unfaithful man does because he is unfaithful is always a sin, as Augustine says, even though he should clothe the naked for the sake of his infidelity, or do something similar (4 *Cont. Julian.* 3). His action, however, may not be the expression of his lack of charity, but the expression of some different gift which he has received from God, such as faith, or hope, or even of the natural good which sin does not entirely destroy, as we said in Q. 10, Art. 4, and in 12ae, Q. 85, Arts. 1 and 2. Any such action may be good in its own way, without charity. But it cannot be perfectly good, since it is not directed to the ultimate end as it should be.

On the second point: an end has the same significance in practical matters as a first principle in speculative matters. Now there cannot be genuinely true science if an indemonstrable first principle is not properly understood. Neither can there be absolutely true justice or chastity without their due relation to the end, which relation depends on charity, however correct one may be in other respects.

On the third point: science and art, by their very nature, imply a relation to some particular good. But they do not relate to the ultimate end of human life as do the moral virtues, which make one good in an absolute sense, as we said in 12ae, Q. 56, Art. 3.

Article Eight

WHETHER CHARITY IS THE FORM OF THE VIRTUES

We proceed to the eighth article thus:

1. It seems that charity is not the form of the virtues. The form of a thing is either its exemplary form or its essential form. But charity is not the exemplary form of the other virtues. If it were so, the other virtues would necessarily belong to the same species as charity. Neither is it their essential form. If it were so, it could not be distinguished from them. Hence charity is in no wise the form of the virtues.

2. Again, in Eph. 3:17 charity is compared to the root and the ground of the other virtues, "being rooted and grounded in love." Now a root or a ground has the nature of a material element, rather than of a form, since it is the first part to be made. Hence charity is not the form of the virtues.

3. Again, 2 *Physics*, text 70, makes it plain that form, end, and efficient cause[1] are not numerically identical. Now charity is said to be the mother of the virtues. We should not then say that it is their form.

On the other hand: Ambrose implies that charity is the form of the virtues (*Commentary on Corinthians*).

[1] See Q. 27, Art. 3, *infra*.

354

I answer: in moral matters, the form of an action depends principally on the end. The reason for this is that the principle of moral actions is the will, whose object, and as it were whose form, is the end. But the form of an action always depends on the form of the agent. In moral matters, therefore, what gives an action its form is the agency which directs it to its end. Now the preceding article made it clear that charity directs the actions of all other virtues to the ultimate end. It is therefore charity that gives their form to the actions of all other virtues. In this same sense it is said to "be the form of the virtues" since we speak of the virtues in relation to their actions as formed.

On the first point: charity is said to be the form of the other virtues neither as their exemplary form nor as their essential form, but rather as their efficient cause, in as much as it gives a form to each of them, as we have explained.

On the second point: charity is compared to a ground and a root because all other virtues are sustained and nourished by it, not because a ground and a root have the nature of a material cause.

On the third point: charity is said to be the end of the other virtues because all other virtues serve the end of charity. It is said to be the mother of the other virtues because it conceives the actions which it commands in them out of desire for the ultimate end, as a mother conceives in herself by another.

Question Twenty-Seven

OF THE PRINCIPAL ACT OF CHARITY, WHICH IS TO LOVE

There are eight questions concerning the principal act of charity. 1. Whether it is more proper to charity to love, or to be loved. 2. Whether the love of charity is the same as benevolence. 3. Whether God is to be loved for his own sake. 4. Whether God can be loved immediately in this life. 5. Whether God can be loved wholly. 6. Whether love to God has a mode. 7. Whether love to a friend or love to an enemy is the better. 8. Whether love to God or love to one's neighbour is the better.

Article One

WHETHER TO BE LOVED IS MORE PROPER TO CHARITY THAN TO LOVE

We proceed to the first article thus:

1. It seems that to be loved is more proper to charity than to love. For better persons have better charity, and they ought also to be loved more. To be loved is therefore more proper to charity.

2. Again, what is found in the greater number would seem to be the more in accordance with nature, and consequently the better. Now as the philosopher says in 8 *Ethics* 8, "there are many who wish to be loved rather than to love, and those who love flattery are always many." To be loved is therefore better than to love, and consequently more in accordance with charity.

3. Again, the philosopher says (1 *Post. An.*, text 5): "that on account of which anything is of a certain kind is itself more so." [1] Now men love on account of being loved, since "nothing evokes love so much as loving another first," as Augustine says (*De Catech. Rud.*, cap. 4). Charity therefore consists in being loved, more properly than in loving.

On the other hand: the philosopher says (8 *Ethics* 8): "friendship consists in loving rather than in being loved." Now charity is a kind of friendship. It therefore consists in loving rather than in being loved.

I answer: to love belongs to charity as charity. For charity is a virtue, and therefore inclines to its proper act by its very essence. But to be loved is not the act of the charity of the loved one. The act of his charity is to love. He happens to be loved because another is moved by charity to seek his good, as one instance of the universal nature of good. This makes it clear that to love belongs to charity more properly than to be loved. For what belongs to a thing essentially and substantially belongs to it more properly than what belongs to it on account of something else. There are two signs of this. One is that friends are praised because they love, rather than because they are loved. If they are loved and do not love, they are indeed blamed. The other is that mothers, who love supremely, seek to love rather than to be loved. Some of them, as the philosopher says in

---

[1] Aristotle meant simply that an essence is more truly itself than are the particulars wherein it is exhibited.

8 *Ethics* 8, "give their sons to a nurse, and love them without expecting any affection in return, if this is impossible."

On the first point: better persons are more lovable because they are better. But it is their own love that is greater because their charity is more perfect—although their love is proportionate to what they love. A better man does not love what is beneath him less than it deserves, whereas one who is not so good does not love a better man as he deserves to be loved.

On the second point: the philosopher says in the same passage that "men wish to be loved in so far as they wish to be honoured." For just as honour is shown to a man as a testimony of the good that is in him, so the fact that he is loved shows that there is some good in him, since only what is good can be loved. Thus men wish to be honoured for the sake of something else. But those who have charity wish to love for the sake of love itself, since love itself is the good of charity, just as the act of any virtue is the good of that virtue. The wish to love therefore belongs to charity more properly than the wish to be loved.

On the third point: some men do love on account of being loved. But this does not mean that they love for the sake of being loved. It means that love is one way of inducing a man to love.

Article Two

WHETHER THE LOVE WHICH IS AN ACT OF CHARITY IS THE SAME AS BENEVOLENCE

We proceed to the second article thus:

1. It seems that the love which is an act of charity is nothing other than benevolence. For the philosopher says that "to love is to will good for someone," and this is benevolence. The act of charity is therefore nothing other than benevolence.

2. Again, an act belongs to the same power as its habit, and it was said in Q. 24, Art. 1, that the habit of charity belongs to the will. It follows that charity is an act of the will. But it is not an act of charity unless it intends good, and this is benevolence. The act of charity is therefore nothing other than benevolence.

3. Again, in 9 *Ethics* 4 the philosopher mentions five characteristics of friendship—that a man should will good for his friend, that he should wish him to be and to live, that he should enjoy his company, that he should choose the same things, and that he should grieve and rejoice together with him. Now the

first two of these apply to benevolence. Hence the first act of charity is benevolence.

On the other hand: the philosopher says that "benevolence is neither friendship nor love, but the beginning of friendship" (9 *Ethics* 5). Now we said in Q. 23, Art. 1, that charity is friendship. It follows that benevolence is not the same as the love which is an act of charity.

I answer: benevolence is correctly said to be an act of the will whereby we will good for someone. But it differs from love, whether love be actualized in the sensitive appetite or in the intellectual appetite, which is the will. In the sensitive appetite, love is a kind of passion. Now every passion inclines to its object by impulse. Yet the passion of love is not aroused suddenly, but results from unremitting contemplation of its object. The philosopher accordingly explains the difference between benevolence and passionate love by saying that benevolence "has neither emotion nor appetition," meaning that it does not incline to its object by impulse, but wills good to another solely by the judgment of reason. Moreover, passionate love is the result of continual acquaintance, whereas benevolence sometimes arises suddenly, as it does when we want one of two pugilists to win. In the intellectual appetite also, love differs from benevolence. For love implies a union of affection between the lover and the loved. One who loves looks upon the loved one as in a manner one with himself, or as belonging to himself, and is thus united with him. Benevolence, on the other hand, is a simple act of the will whereby one wills good for someone, without the presupposition of any such union of affection. The love which is an act of charity includes benevolence. But as love, or dilection, it adds this union of affection. This is the reason why the philosopher says that "benevolence is the beginning of friendship."

On the first point: the philosopher is giving a definition of love, indicating the character by which the act of love is most clearly revealed. He is not describing the whole nature of love.

On the second point: love is an act of the will which intends good. But it includes a union of affection with the loved one, which is not implied in benevolence.

On the third point: as the philosopher says in the same passage, these are characteristic of friendship because they spring from the love with which a man loves himself. That is to say, a man does all these things for his friend as if for himself, by reason of the union of affection of which we have spoken.

Article Three

WHETHER BY CHARITY GOD IS TO BE LOVED ON ACCOUNT OF HIMSELF

We proceed to the third article thus:

1. It seems that by charity God is to be loved not on account of himself, but on account of what is other than himself. For Gregory says in a homily (*Hom. in Evang.* 11): "the soul learns to love the unknown from the things which it knows." Now by the unknown he means intelligible and divine things, and by the known he means the things of sense. Hence God is to be loved on account of things other than himself.

2. Again, according to Rom. 1:20: "the invisible things of him . . . are clearly seen, being understood by the things that are made," love to God is consequential. Hence God is loved on account of what is other than himself, not on account of himself.

3. Again, the gloss (on Matt. 1:2: "Abraham begat Isaac") says that "hope begets charity," and Augustine (*Tract. 9 in Joan.*) says that "fear begets charity." Now hope expects to receive something from God, and fear shrinks from something that God might inflict. It seems, then, that God is to be loved either on account of some good for which we hope, or on account of some evil which we fear. It follows that God is not to be loved on account of himself.

On the other hand: Augustine says (1 *De Doctr. Christ.* 4) that "to enjoy someone is to cling to him on account of himself," and he also says that "God is to be enjoyed." It follows that God is to be loved on account of himself.

I answer: "on account of" denotes a causal relation. But there are four kinds of cause—final cause, formal cause, efficient cause, and material cause.[1] A material disposition is reducible to a material cause, since it is a cause conditionally only, not absolutely. We can thus affirm that one thing is to be loved "on account of" another according to each of these four kinds of cause. We love medicine, for example, on account of health as a final cause. We love a man on account of virtue as a formal

---

[1] Cf. Aristotle's *Physics*, bk. 2, ch. 3 (194b); ch. 7 (198a); *Metaphysics A*, ch. 3 (983a); *D*, ch. 2 (1013a–b). The final cause is the end for the sake of which a thing is. The formal cause is the formula for the essence of a thing. The efficient cause is the source of the change through which a thing comes to be what it is. The material cause is the material element out of which a thing is made.

cause, since by reason of virtue he is formally good, and consequently lovable. We love some persons on account of their
being the sons of a certain father, which circumstance is the
efficient cause of our love. We are also said to love a person on
account of something which disposes us to love him, such as
benefits received from him, this being a material disposition
reducible to a material cause. Once we have begun to love a
friend, however, we love him not on account of such benefits,
but on account of virtue.

Now in each of the first three of these senses we love God on
account of himself, not on account of what is other than himself. For God does not serve anything other than himself as a
final end, but is himself the final end of all things. Neither is God
formally good by reason of anything other than himself. For his
own substance is his goodness, and his goodness is the exemplary form by which all things are good. Nor, again, is goodness in God through another, but in all things through God.
In the fourth sense, however, God can be loved on account of
what is other than himself. For we are disposed to love God the
more on account of other things, such as benefits received, or
rewards for which we hope, or even the punishments which we
hope to avoid through him.

On the first point: this quotation, "the soul learns to love the
unknown from the things which it knows," does not mean that
the known is the formal, final, or efficient cause of love for the
unknown. It means that one is disposed by what one knows to
love the unknown.

On the second point: knowledge of God is acquired through
other things. But once God is known, he is known not through
other things, but through himself, in accordance with John 4:42:
"Now we believe, not because of thy saying; for we have heard
him ourselves, and know that this is indeed . . . the Saviour of
the world."

On the third point: hope and fear lead to charity by way of a
certain disposition.

Article Four

WHETHER GOD CAN BE LOVED IMMEDIATELY IN THIS LIFE

We proceed to the fourth article thus:

1. It seems that God cannot be loved immediately in this life.
Augustine says (10 *De Trin.* 1, 2): "what is unknown cannot
be loved." In this life we do not know God immediately,

since "now we see through a glass, darkly" (I Cor. 13:12). Neither then do we love him immediately.

2. Again, if we cannot do what is less, we cannot do what is more. Now to love God is more than to know him, since I Cor. 6:17 says: "he who is joined unto the Lord [that is, by love] is one spirit" with him. But we cannot know God immediately. Much less, then, can we love God immediately.

3. Again, according to Isa. 59:2: "your iniquities have separated between you and your God," we are separated from God through sin. But sin is greater in the will than in the intellect. We are therefore less able to love God immediately than we are to know him immediately.

On the other hand: our knowledge of God is said to be dark because it is mediate, and it is evident from I Cor. 13 that it will vanish away in heaven. But the same passage says that the charity of the way does not fail. Hence the charity of the way adheres immediately to God.

I answer: we said in Pt. I, Q. 82, Art. 2, and Q. 84, Art. 7 that the act of the cognitive power is complete when the thing known is in him who knows, and that the act of an appetitive power is complete when the appetite is inclined to the thing itself. The movement by which an appetitive power inclines to things is therefore in accordance with the order of things themselves, whereas the action of the cognitive power is in accordance with the manner of the knower. The order of things themselves is such that God can be both known and loved in and through himself. For God is essentially existent truth and goodness, by which other things are known and loved. But since our knowledge begins from sense, things which are nearer to sense are known first, and the term of knowledge is in that which is furthest removed from sense.

Now love is the act of an appetitive power. We must therefore say that even in this life it tends first of all to God, and is thence turned towards other things. Hence charity loves God immediately, and loves other things through God as medium. With knowledge, however, this order is reversed. For we know God through other things, as we know a cause through its effect, whether we know him by the way of eminence or by the way of negation, as Dionysius says (4 *Div. Nom.*, lects. 2, 3).

On the first point: the unknown cannot be loved. But the order of knowing and the order of love need not be the same. Love is the terminus of knowledge, and may therefore begin at the very point where knowledge comes to an end, that is, in the thing itself which is known through other things.

On the second point: love of God is more than knowledge of him, especially in this life, and therefore presupposes knowledge of him. But while knowledge seeks higher things through the medium of created things in which it cannot rest, love begins with higher things, and turns from them to other things by a kind of rotation. Knowledge begins with creatures and tends towards God. Love begins with God as its final end, and turns towards creatures.

On the third point: turning away from God is cured by charity, not by knowledge alone, and charity joins the soul to God immediately in a bond of spiritual union.

Article Five

WHETHER GOD CAN BE LOVED WHOLLY

We proceed to the fifth article thus:

1. It seems that God cannot be loved wholly. Love follows knowledge, and God cannot be known wholly by us, since this would be to comprehend him. He cannot then be loved wholly by us.

2. Again, love is a kind of union, as Dionysius explains (4 *Div. Nom.*, lect. 9). But the heart of man cannot be united wholly with God, since "God is greater than our heart" (I John 3:20). God cannot then be loved wholly.

3. Again, God loves himself wholly. Hence if he were loved wholly by any other, another would love God as much as God loves himself. But this is impossible. It follows that God cannot be loved wholly by any creature.

On the other hand: it is said in Deut. 6:5: "thou shalt love the Lord thy God with all thine heart."

I answer: when love is understood as a medium between the lover and the loved, the question whether God can be loved wholly may be understood in three ways. If the character of wholeness refers to what is loved, God ought to be loved wholly, since one ought to love everything that pertains to God. If it refers to him who loves, again God ought to be loved wholly, since a man ought to love God with all his might, and to devote his all to the love of God in accordance with Deut. 6:5: "thou shalt love the Lord thy God with all thine heart." But the character of wholeness may be understood as referring to the comparison between the lover and what is loved, and as meaning that the manner of his love should be adequate to what is loved. This is impossible. God is infinitely lovable, since each thing is lovable in proportion as it is good, and since God's goodness is infinite. But no creature can love God infinitely, since every power that any creature possesses is finite, whether it be natural or infused.

The reply to the objections is then obvious. The three objections argue from this third meaning of the question. The contrary assumes the second meaning.

Article Six

WHETHER LOVE TO GOD OUGHT TO HAVE A MODE

We proceed to the sixth article thus:

1. It seems that love to God ought to have a mode. For Augustine makes it clear that the very nature of good consists in mode, species, and order (*De Nat. Boni* 3, 4), and love to God is the best thing in man, according to Col. 3:14: "above all things put on charity." Love to God ought therefore to have a mode.

2. Again, Augustine says (*De Mor. Eccles.* 8): "Tell me, I pray, the mode of love. For I fear lest I be kindled with desire and love toward God more than I ought." Now he would be asking in vain, if there were no mode of love to God. There must therefore be some mode of love to God.

3. Again, Augustine says (4 *Gen. ad Litt.* 3): "a mode is what its proper measure prescribes for each thing." Now reason is the measure of man's will as well as of his outward actions. Inward love to God ought therefore to have a mode which reason prescribes, just as the outward act of charity has a mode which reason prescribes, in accordance with Rom. 12:1: "your reasonable service."

On the other hand: Bernard says (*De Diligendo Deum* 1): "The cause of love to God is God. Its mode is to love him without mode."

I answer: the passage from Augustine quoted in the third point makes it clear that mode means a determination of measure. Now this determination is found both in a measure and in a thing which is measured, but in different ways. It belongs to a measure essentially, since a measure is itself determinative of other things, and gives them their form; whereas its presence in things measured is due to something other than themselves, that is, to their conformity with a measure. Hence a measure can contain nothing that is without mode. But a thing measured has no mode if it does not conform to its measure, but either falls short of it or exceeds it.

As the philosopher explains in 2 *Physics*, text 89, the proper reason for what we desire or do must be sought in the end. The end is thus the measure of anything that we may desire or do, and consequently has a mode on its own account. Things done for the sake of an end, on the other hand, have a mode because they are related to an end. Hence the philosopher says also, in 1 *Politics* 6, that "in every art, the desire for the end has neither end nor limit." But what is done for the sake of an end does have a limit. A doctor does not prescribe any limit for health, which he makes as perfect as he can. But he does prescribe a limit for medicine. He does not give as much medicine as possible, but as much as health requires, and medicine would be without mode if it exceeded or fell short of this amount.

Now love to God is the end of every human action and affection, wherein especially we attain our ultimate end, as we said in Q. 23, Art. 6. Love to God cannot then have a mode such as applies to things which are measured, and which may be either too much or too little. But it does have a mode such as applies to a measure, of which there is no excess, but the greater the conformity to rule the better. Hence love to God is the better, the more God is loved.

On the first point: to have a quality essentially is more significant than to have it on account of something else. Thus a measure, which has a mode essentially, is better than a thing measured, which has a mode on account of something other than itself. Hence also charity, which has a mode as a measure, is more eminent than the other virtues, which have a mode as things which are measured.

On the second point: as Augustine adds in the same passage, "the mode of love to God is to love him with all our heart," which means that God ought to be loved as much as he can be loved. So it is with any mode which applies to a measure.

On the third point: an affection is to be measured by reason if its object is subject to the judgment of reason. But the object of love to God is God, who transcends the judgment of reason. Hence love to God also transcends the judgment of reason, and is not to be measured by reason. Neither can we compare the inward act of charity with its outward acts. The inward act of charity has the nature of an end, since man's ultimate good consists in the adherence of his soul to God, in accordance with

Ps. 73:28: "It is good for me to draw near to God." Its outward acts, on the other hand, are the means to this end.

Article Seven

WHETHER IT IS MORE MERITORIOUS TO LOVE AN ENEMY THAN TO LOVE A FRIEND

We proceed to the seventh article thus:

1. It seems that it is more meritorious to love an enemy than to love a friend. For it is said in Matt. 5:46: "if ye love them which love you, what reward have ye?" Thus love to a friend does not merit a reward. But love to an enemy does merit a reward, as the same passage shows. It is therefore more meritorious to love enemies than to love friends.

2. Again, an action is the more meritorious the greater is the charity from which it springs. Now Augustine says that it is the perfect sons of God who love their enemies (*Enchirid.* 73), whereas even those whose charity is imperfect love their friends. It is therefore more meritorious to love enemies than to love friends.

3. Again, there would seem to be greater merit where there is greater effort for good, since it is said in I Cor. 3:8: "every man shall receive his own reward, according to his labour." Now it takes a greater effort to love an enemy than to love a friend, since it is more difficult. It seems, then, that it is more meritorious to love an enemy than to love a friend.

4. On the other hand: the better love is the more meritorious. Now to love a friend is the better, since it is better to love the better person, and a friend who loves one is better than an enemy who hates one. Hence it is more meritorious to love a friend than to love an enemy.

I answer: as we said in Q. 25, Art. 1, God is the reason why we love our neighbour in charity. Hence when it is asked whether it is better or more meritorious to love a friend or to love an enemy, we may compare the two either in respect of the neighbour who is loved, or in respect of the reason why he is loved. In respect of the neighbour who is loved, love to a friend is more eminent than love to an enemy. A friend is better than an enemy, and more closely united with oneself. He is thus the more fitting material for love, and the act of love which passes out to such material is consequently the better. The contrary act is also worse for the same reason. It is worse to hate a friend than to hate an enemy.

365

But love to an enemy is the more eminent in respect of the reason for it, on two grounds. First, we may love a friend for some reason other than God, whereas God is the sole reason for love to an enemy. Secondly, supposing that each of them is loved for God's sake, a man's love to God is shown to be the stronger if it extends his soul to what is farther removed from himself, that is, to the love of enemies; just as the power of a fire is shown to be greater if it extends its heat to objects more remote. For our love to God is shown to be so much the greater when we achieve harder things for the sake of it, just as the power of a fire is shown to be so much the stronger when it is able to consume less combustible material.

But charity nevertheless loves acquaintances more fervently than those who are distant, just as the same fire acts more strongly on nearer objects than on those which are more remote. Considered in itself, love to friends is in this respect more fervent, and better, than love to enemies.

On the first point: the word of our Lord must be understood through itself. Love to friends does not merit a reward in God's sight when they are loved only because they are friends, as would seem to be the case when we love them in a way in which we do not love our enemies. But love to friends is meritorious when they are loved for God's sake, and not merely because they are friends.

The replies to the other points are plain from what we have said. The second and third argue from the reason for love. The fourth argues from the person who is loved.

Article Eight

WHETHER IT IS MORE MERITORIOUS TO LOVE ONE'S
NEIGHBOUR THAN TO LOVE GOD

We proceed to the eighth article thus:

1. It seems that it is more meritorious to love one's neighbour than to love God. For the apostle presumably prefers the more meritorious, and according to Rom. 9:3: he would choose to love his neighbour rather than to love God: "For I could wish that myself were accursed from Christ for my brethren." It is therefore more meritorious to love one's neighbour than to love God.

2. Again, it was said in the preceding article that to love a friend is in one sense less meritorious. Now God is very much a

friend, since "he first loved us," as I John 4:19 says. Hence it seems that to love God is less meritorious.

3. Again, what is more difficult would seem to be more virtuous and more meritorious, since "virtue is concerned with the difficult and the good" (2 *Ethics* 3). Now it is easier to love God than to love one's neighbour. All things love God naturally. Moreover, there is nothing unlovable in God, which is not the case with one's neighbour. Love to one's neighbour is therefore more meritorious than love to God.

On the other hand: "that on account of which anything is of a certain kind is itself more so." Now love to one's neighbour is meritorious only on account of love to God, for whose sake he is loved. Hence love to God is more meritorious than love to one's neighbour.

I answer: this comparison may be understood in two ways. If, in the first place, each love is considered in isolation, love to God is undoubtedly the more meritorious. For love to God merits a reward on its own account, since its ultimate reward is the enjoyment of God, to whom its own movement tends. A reward is therefore promised to such as love God, in John 14:21: "he that loveth me shall be loved of my Father, and I . . . will manifest myself to him." But the comparison may also be understood to be between love to God alone and love to one's neighbour for God's sake. If so, love to one's neighbour includes love to God, whereas love to God does not include love to one's neighbour. The comparison is then between perfect love to God which extends to one's neighbour, and love to God which is insufficient and imperfect. For it is written in I John 4:21: "And this commandment have we from him, That he who loveth God love his brother also." In this latter sense, love to one's neighbour is the better.

On the first point: according to the exposition of one gloss (Lyrani), the apostle did not wish to be separated from Christ when in the state of grace, but had so desired when in the state of unbelief, and consequently is not to be imitated in this regard. Or we may say with Chrysostom (1 *De Compunct.* 8; *Hom. 16 in Epist. ad Rom.*) that this does not prove that the apostle loved his neighbour more than he loved God, but that he loved God more than he loved himself. For he was willing to be deprived for a time of the enjoyment of God, which he would have sought out of love for himself, to the end that God should be honoured among his neighbours, which he desired out of love to God.

On the second point: love to a friend is sometimes the less meritorious because the friend is loved for his own sake. Such love lacks the true ground of the friendship of charity, which is God. That God should be loved for his own sake does not therefore diminish merit, but constitutes the whole ground of merit.

On the third point: It is the good rather than the difficult that provides the ground of merit and of virtue. Hence all that is more difficult is not bound to be more meritorious, but only what is more difficult and also better.

BIBLIOGRAPHY

A. *Main Collected Editions* of the works of Thomas Aquinas.
Opera Omnia. Editio Piana, or *Vaticana* (First Roman edition. Ed.
Vincentius Justinianus et Thomas Manriques), *iussu S. Pii v*,
Rome 1570.
Opera Omnia, . . . *apud Dominicum Nicolinum et Socios*, Venice 1593–
1594.
Opera Omnia, . . . *apud Joannem Keerbergium*, Antwerp 1610 and
1624.
*Opera Omnia, apud Societatem Bibliopolarum. Partim a Joanne Nicolai ex
ordine Patribus Praedicatorum, partim ab aliis Patribus eiusdem ordine
emendata*, Paris 1660–1664.
Opera. Editio altera Veneta, Venice 1745–1760, 1765–1788.
Opera Omnia. Parma, 1852–1873.
Opera Omnia (Ed. E. Frette et P. Mare), Paris 1872–1880.
Opera Omnia (The Leonine Edition), *Iussu impensaque Leonis xiii*,
1882–1948.

B. *Editions of separate works.*
Summa Theologica (Ed. R. P. F. Joannes Nicolaius), Paris 1663.
*Summa Theologica, & Quaestiones Quadlibetales, cum commentariis
Thomae de Vio, Card. Cajetani, et elicidationibus literalibus P. Seraphini
Capponi a Pomecta*, Rome 1773.
*Summa Theologica. Accurante et denuo recognescente J. P. Migne editorem,
et Garnier Fratres editores et J. P. Migne successores*, Paris 1858,
1872–1877.
*Summa Theologica, diligenter emendata Hiedai Sylvii, Billuart, et C. J.
Drioux. Edit. nona*, London 1874.
Summa Theologica (Ed. Foucher), Paris (Lethiellieux) 3rd ed. 1924.
Summa Theologica, cura et studio Collegii Prov. Tolosanae Paris (Blot)
1926–1935.
*Summa Theologica, diligenter emendata, De Rubeis, Billuart et aliorum
notis selectis ornata*, Turin (Marietti) 1932.

St. Thomae de Aquino Ordinis Praedicatorum Summa Theologiae cura et studio Instituti Studiorum Mediaevalum Ottaviensis, ad textum S. Pii v, Ottawa 1941–1945.
Summa Theologica, cura et studio P. Caramello, cum textu ex recensione leonina, Turin 1948–1950.
Summa Contra Gentiles, Paris 1878.
Summa Contra Gentiles, Rome (Forzani) 1927.
Summa Contra Gentiles. Editio Leonina manualis, Rome (Desclee-Herder) 1934.
Opuscula omnia genuina . . . (Ed. P. Mandonnet), Paris (Lethellieux) 1927.
Quaestiones Disputatae (Ed. P. Mandonnet), Paris (Lethellieux) 1925.
Questiones Quadlibetales (Ed. P. Mandonnet cum Introd.), Paris (Lethellieux) 1927.
Quaestiones Disputatae et Questiones Quadlibetales, Turin (Marietti) 1927.

C. *Translations* of the *Summa Theologica.*
The Summa Theologica of St. Thomas Aquinas. Literally translated by Fathers of the English Dominican Province (second and revised edition), London (Burns, Oates & Benziger) 1912–1936; (Burns, Oates & Washbourne) 1923.
S. Thomas D'Aquin. Somme Theologique. Texte latin et traduction française (Direct. M. Gillet), Paris (Ed. Rev des Jeunes) 1925.
S. Thomae Aquin. Die deutsche Thomas Ausgabe. Vollständige ungekurzte deutschlateinische Gesamtausgabe der Summa Theologica des hl. Thomas von Aquin. Uebersetzt von den Dominikanern und Benedictinern Deutschlands und Oesterreichs; herausgegeben vom Katholischen Akademikerverband, Salzburg–Leipzig (Pustet) 1933.
Thomas von Aquin. Summe der Theologie. Herausgegeben von J. Bernhart. Bd. 1, Leipzig (Kroner) 1934; Bd. 3 Stuttgart (Kroner) 1938.
Theologische Summa van den H. Thomas van Aquin. Latijnische en Nederlandsche Tekst uitgegeven door een groep Dominicanen, Antwerp 1927. Incomplete.
S. Tommaso d'Aquin. Somma Teologica. Antologia. Introd. trad. e note di N. Petruzzellis, Bari (Laterza) 1936.
S. Thomae Aquin. Summa Theologica (Tr. (partial) P. Hortynski), Krakow 1927–1933.
S. Thomas de Aquin. Suma teologica. Primeira tradução portuguesa (Accompanhado do texto latino), São Paulo (Odeon). Incomplete.
Tch'ao Sing Shue Yao. Zi-ka-wei, Shanghai. 1930. A revision by Shanghai Jesuits of Father Buglio's seventeenth-century partial Chinese version of the *Summa Theologica.*

D. *Other translations* in English.
Aquinas Ethicus, or, the Moral Teaching of St. Thomas. A translation of the principal portions of the second part of the *Summa Theologica,* by J. Rickaby, London (Burns Oates) 1896.

Basic Writings of St. Thomas. Selected works in English (Ed. A. C. Pegis), New York (Random House) 1945.
Concerning Being and Essence. Tr. G. G. Leckie. New York (Appleton) 1937.
Of God and His Creatures. An abridged translation of *S. Contra Gentiles.* by J. Rickaby, London (Longmans) 1924.
On Being and Essence (Tr. C. C. Reidl), Toronto (St. Michael's College) 1934.
On the Governance of Rulers (Tr. G. B. Phelan), Toronto (St. Michael's College) 1935.
On the Power of God (Tr. L. Shapcote), London (Burns Oates); New York (Benziger) 1932–1934.
On the Ways of God (Tr. B. Delaney), London (Burns Oates) 1926; New York (Benziger) 1927.
St. Thomas Aquinas: Philosophical Texts (Selected and translated by T. Gilby), London 1951.
The Disputed Questions on Truth, Quest 1 (Tr. R. McKeon in *Selections from Mediaeval Philosophers*), New York (Scribners) 1930.
Thomas Aquinas: God and His Works (Selections from Pt. I of *Summa Theologica*, Ed. A. G. Hebert), S.P.C.K. 1927.
Thomas Aquinas: Selected Writings (Ed. M. C. D'Arcy), Everyman's Library; New York (Dutton) 1939.

E. *Works on Aquinas.*
V. J. Bourke: *Thomistic Bibliography 1920–1940*, St. Louis, Missouri 1945.
R. E. Brennan (Ed.): *Essays in Thomism*, New York (Sheed & Ward) 1942.
G. K. Chesterton: *St. Thomas Aquinas*, London (Sheed & Ward) 1933 (a life of St. Thomas).
  S. Thomas d'Aquin (Tr. M. Vox), Paris (Plon) 1935.
  De heilige Thomas van Aquin (Tr. H. Reijnen), Amsterdam (Voorhout) 1934.
  Der hl. Thomas von Aquin (Tr. E. Kaufmann), Salzburg (Pustet) 1935.
  San Tommaso d'Aquin (Tr. A. R. Ripamonti e G. Datta), Milan (Agnelli) 1938.
  Sto. Thomas de Aquin (Tr. H. Munoz), Madrid (Espasa-Calpe) 1935.
F. Copleston: *A History of Philosophy*, Vol. II (Augustine to Scotus), London (Burns, Oates & Washbourne) 1950.
N. C. D'Arcy: *Thomas Aquinas*, Boston (Little, Brown & Co.); London (Benn) 1930.
R. J. Deferrari and Barry: *A Lexicon of St. Thomas Aquinas, based on the Summa Theologica and selected passages of his other works* (with the technical collaboration of I. McGuiness), Washington 1948–1949.

M. De Wulf: *Histoire de la philosophie mediaeval*, Vol. II, Louvain-Paris (Vrin), 6th ed. 1936.
History of Mediaeval Philosophy, Vol. II (Tr. E. C. Messenger from 6th ed.), London and New York (Longman's) 1938.
Initiation à la philosophie thomiste, Louvain (Inst. Sup. de Philos.) 1932.
Manuale di storia della filosofia (Tr. P. I. Brunetta), Turin (Marietti) 1933.
Mediaeval Philosophy illustrated from the System of Thomas Aquinas, Cambridge, U.S. (Harvard Univ. Press), 2nd ed. 1929.
W. Farrell: *A Companion to the Summa*. 4 Vols., Sheed & Ward, New York., 1945–1949.
R. Garrigou-Lagrange: *The One God. A Commentary on the First Part of St. Thomas' Theological Summa*, St. Louis, Mo. 1944.
E. Gilson: *La Philosophie au moyen âge*, Paris (Payot) 1930; 2nd ed., revised and enlarged, 1947.
Le Thomisme. Introd. au système de S. Thomas d'Aquin, Paris (Vrin), 5th ed., revised and enlarged, with bibliographical notes, 1944.
The Philosophy of St. Thomas Aquinas (Tr. E. Bullough), St. Louis (Herder) 1929; Cambridge (Heffer) 1930.
L'Esprit de la philosophie mediaevale. Gifford Lectures 1931–1932, Paris (Vrin), 2nd ed., revised, 1944.
The Spirit of Mediaeval Philosophy (Tr. A. H. C. Downes), London (Sheed & Ward) 1936; New York (Scribners) 1940.
Christianisme et philosophie, Paris (Vrin) 1936; 1949.
Pourquoi S. Thomas a critiqué S. Augustine. (Archives d'histoire doctrinale et littéraire du moyen âge, I.), 1926–1927.
Reason and Revelation in the Middle Ages, New York and London (Scribners) 1939.
Realisme Thomiste et critique de la connaissance, Paris 1947.
S. Thomas d'Aquin. (Les Moralistes chrétiens) Paris (Gobalda) 1924; 4th ed., 1925; tr. L. Ward in *Moral Values and the Moral Life*, St. Louis and London (Herder) 1931.
Santo Tomas de Aquino (Tr. N. Gonzalea Ruiz), Madrid (Aguilar) 1930.
St. Thomas Aquinas. Lecture on a Master Mind, London (Oxford Press) 1935.
M. Grabmann: *Einfuhrung in die Summa Theologiae des hl. Thomas von Aquin*, Freiburg (Herder), 2nd ed., 1928.
Introduction to the Theological Summa of St. Thomas (Tr. J. S. Zybura), St. Louis (Herder) 1930.
La Somme théologique de S. Thomas d'Aquin. Introd. historique et critique (Tr. E. Vansteenberghe), Paris (Desclee) 1930.
Thomas von Aquin. Eine Einführung in seine Persönlichkeit und Gedankenwelt. Aufl. 6, München (Kosel & Pustet) 1935.
Thomas Aquinas. His Personality and Thought (Tr. V. Michel), New York and London (Longman's) 1929.

S. Thomas d'Aquin (Tr. E. Vansteenberghe), Paris (Bloud & Gay) 1936.
Santo Tomas de Aquino. Tr. de la 5a ed. alemana y anotodo per S. Minguijon, Barcelona, 2nd ed., 1945.
Filosofia medieval (Tr. S. Minguijon), Barcelona 1949.

A. G. Hebert: *Grace and Nature*, London (Church Lit. Assoc.) 1937.

E. G. Jay: *A Commentary on St. Thomas Aquinas' Five Ways of demonstrating the Existence of God.* London 1946.

R. Klibanski, and Paton: *Philosophy and History. Essays presented to E. Cassirer*, Oxford (Clarendon) 1936.

A. Lovejoy: *The Great Chain of Being.* Cambridge, Mass. (Harvard Univ. Press) 1936.

P. Mandonnet and J. Destrez: *Bibliographie Thomiste*, Le Saulchoir, Kain, Belgique, 1921.

J. Maritain: *Distinguer pour unir, ou les Degres du savoir*, Paris (Desclee de Brouwer) 1932.
The Degrees of Knowledge (Tr. B. Wall and M. Adamson), London (Bles) 1937; New York (Scribner) 1938.
Le Docteur Angelique, Paris (Desclee de Brouwer) 1930.
The Angelic Doctor. The Life and Thought of St. Thomas Aquinas (Tr. J. F. Scanlan), London (Sheed & Ward); New York (Dial); Toronto (Longman's) 1931.
Il Dottore Angelico (Tr. C. Bo), Siena (Ed. Cristiana) 1936.
St. Thomas and the Problem of Evil, Milwaukee (Marquette U. Press) 1942.
Science et Sagasse, Paris (Labergerie) 1935.
Science and Wisdom, New York (Sheed & Ward) 1939.

E. L. Mascall: *He Who Is. A Study in Traditional Theism*, London Longmans, Green & Co.) 1943.

H. Meyer: *Die Wissenschaftslehre des Thomas von Aquin*, Fulda 1934.
Thomas von Aquin. Sein System und seine geistesgeschichtliche Stellung, Bonn (Hanstein) 1938.
The Philosophy of Thomas Aquinas (Tr. F. Eckoff), St. Louis (Herder) 1944.

W. B. Monahan: *The Moral Theology of St. Thomas* (From the *Summa Theologica*), Worcester 1948.

F. Olgiati: *L'anima di S. Tommaso. Saggio filosofico intorno alla concezione tomistica*, Milano (*Vita e Pensiero*) 1923.
Key to the Study of St. Thomas (Tr. J. S. Zybura), St. Louis and London (Herder), 2nd ed., 1929.

M. T. L. Penido: *La Rôle de l'analogie en théologie dogmatique*, Paris (Vrin) 1931.

G. B. Phelan: *St. Thomas and Analogy*, Milwaukee 1943.

P. Rousselot: *L'Intellectualisme de S. Thomas*, Paris (Beauchesne) 1924.
The Intellectualism of St. Thomas (Tr. J. O'Mahony), London (Sheed & Ward) 1935.

A. D. Sertillanges: *La Philosophie moral de St. Thomas d'Aquin*, Paris (Alcan) 1946.
Les grandes thèses de la philosophie thomiste (Bibl. Cath. de Sc. Rel. 15), Paris (Bloud & Gay) 1928.
Foundations of Thomistic Philosophy (Tr. G. Anstruther) (Cath. Lib. of Relig. Kn. 20). London (Sands) and St. Louis (Herder) 1931.
S. Thomas d'Aquin, Paris (Flammarion) 1931 (A Life of St. Thomas).
St. Thomas Aquinas and his Work (Tr. G. Anstruther), London (Burns Oates) 1933.
Der Hl. Thomas von Aquin. Uebersetz. und Nachwort von R. Grosche, Hellerau bei Dresden (J. Hegner) 1929.
San Tommaso d'Aquin. Trad. Introd. di G. Bronzini, Brescia (Morcelliana) 1932.
A. E. Taylor: *St. Thomas as a Philosopher*, Oxford (Blackwell) 1924; also in *Philosophical Studies*, London (Macmillan) 1934.
P. H. Wicksteed: *Reactions between Dogma and Philosophy*, London (Williams & Norgate) 1920.
Dante and Aquinas, Jowett Lectures, London 1911.

(b) Biblical References

Genesis

1:26	I, Q. 3, Art. 1; Q. 4, Art. 3.
	22ae, Q. 1, Art. 8.
2:24	22ae, Q. 2, Art. 7.
4:13	22ae, Q. 20, Art. 2
8:21	12ae, Q. 85, Art. 3.
19	12ae, Q. 114. Art. 10.
22:12	12ae, Q. 112, Art. 5.
25:21	I, Q. 23, Art. 8.
39:21	12ae, Q. 110, Art. 1.

Exodus

1:21	12ae, Q. 114, Art. 10.
3:14	I, Q. 2, Art. 3.
6:2–3	22ae, Q. 1, Art. 7.

Numbers

12:6	12ae, Q. 113, Art. 3.

Deuteronomy

1:11	I, Q. 23, Art. 7.
4:2	22ae, Q. 1, Art. 9.
4:6	I, Q. 1, Art. 6.
6:5	22ae, Q. 27, Art. 5.
28	12ae, Q. 114, Art. 10.
30:20	22ae, Q. 23, Art. 2.
32:2	12ae, Q. 110, Art. 1.
32:4	22ae, Q. 6, Art. 2.
32:7	22ae, Q. 1, Art. 7.

I Samuel

7:3	12ae, Q. 112, Art. 2.
15:29	I, Q. 23, Art. 8.

I Kings

3	12ae, Q. 113, Art. 3.

Job

1:14	22ae, Q. 22, Art. 6.
3:11	22ae, Q. 19, Art. 4.
9:11	12ae, Q. 112, Art. 5.
11:8–9	I, Q. 3, Art. 1.
12:11	22ae, Q. 2, Art. 3.
15:22	22ae, Q. 18, Art. 3.
19:25	22ae, Q. 2, Art. 7.
22:14	I, Q. 22, Art. 2.
26:11	22ae, Q. 19, Art. 11.
28:28	22ae, Q. 19, Art. 7.
33-15–16	12ae, Q. 113, Art. 3.
34:13	I, Q. 22, Art. 3.
34:24	I, Q. 29, Art. 6.
35:7	12ae, Q. 114, Art. 1.
35:11	22ae, Q. 2, Art. 7.
36:26	12ae, Q. 112, Art. 5.
40:9	I, Q. 3, Art. 1.
40:23	22ae, Q. 18, Art. 3.
41:9	22ae, Q. 18, Art. 3.

Psalms

5:5	I, Q. 20, Art. 2.
6:2	12ae, Q. 85, Art. 4.
8:5	I, Q. 20, Art. 4.
11:7	I, Q. 21, Art. 1.
19:12–13	12ae, Q. 112, Art. 5.
19:9	22ae, Q. 19, Art. 11.
20:8	22ae, Q. 20, Art. 2.
23:6	12ae, Q. 111, Art. 3.
24:8	22ae, Q. 2, Art. 7.
25:10	I, Q. 21, Art. 4.
31:1	22ae, Q. 18, Art. 2.
32:2	12ae, Q. 110, Art. 1; Q. 113, Art. 2.
32:5	12ae, Q. 113, Art. 5.
34:5	I, Q. 3, Art. 1.
34:10	12ae, Q. 114, Art. 10.
34:14	12ae, Q. 113, Art. 8.

379

INDEX OF REFERENCES TO OTHER AUTHORS AND SOURCES

MAGISTER
Libri Sententiarum
1, *Dist.* 17	22ae, Q. 23, Art. 2.
2, *Dist.* 22	22ae, Q. 21, Art. 1.
Dist. 26	12ae, Q. 110, Art. 3.
3, *Dist.* 23	22ae, Q. 23, Art. 8.
Dist. 26	22ae, Q. 17, Art. 1, 8.
	Q. 18, Art. 4.
Dist. 34	22ae, Q. 19, Art. 2.

NICENE CREED
22ae, Q. I, Arts. 2, 8, 9.

NOVATIANS
22ae, Q. 20, Art. 2.

PELAGIANS
I, Q. 23, Art. 5.
12ae, Q. 109, Art. 5.
22ae, Q. 6, Art. 1.
12ae, Q. 109, Art. 4.

[PROCLUS] *Liber de Causis*
I, Q. 3, Art. 8.
22ae, Q. 23, Art. 6.

TULLIUS
Rhetoric 4	22ae, Q. 1, Art. 6.
De Invent 2	I, Q. 22, Art. 1.